The Lumbee Indians

For Dean Williams —
with love and appreciation

The Lumbee Indians

*An Annotated Bibliography,
with Chronology and Index*

by GLENN ELLEN STARR

Foreword by ADOLPH L. DIAL

McFarland & Company, Inc., Publishers
Jefferson, North Carolina, and London

Acknowledgments: I wish to thank Dean Williams, whose card file at Mary Livermore Library formed the nucleus for this bibliography. Several librarians provided valuable assistance during the book's four years of preparation, including: Michael Shoop (Robeson County Public Library), Dianna Moody and Sara Nixon (Interlibrary Loan, Belk Library, Appalachian State University), Barbara Brayboy-Locklear (formerly Indian Education Resource Center); Normie Bullard, John Shields, and Tela Brooks (Mary Livermore Library, Pembroke State University). Many individuals answered questions, made suggestions, and offered continual encouragement and interest, especially Wes Taukchiray, Stanley Knick, Bruce Barton, Adolph Dial, Robert Reising, Gerald Sider, Al Corum, and Belk Library's Research Interest Group. Others provided or suggested materials that I would not otherwise have found: Pat Baker, Elisha Locklear, Sandra Wurth-Hough, Ben Chavin, W. McKee Evans, Dexter Brooks, Ruth Wetmore, Charles R. Hackenberry, Robert Gustafson, Kate Rinzler, David Henige, Jimmy Hunt, Stoney Locklear, Morris F. Britt, Political Research Inc., Martha Girard, David Eliades, and Jennifer Mickles. Thanks also to Nisus Software for providing the tools I needed for the book's layout.

British Library Cataloguing-in-Publication data available

Library of Congress Cataloguing-in-Publication Data

Starr, Glenn Ellen, 1954–
    The Lumbee Indians : an annotated bibliography, with chronology and index / Glenn Ellen Starr.
      p. cm.
    ISBN 0-89950-511-2 (lib. bdg. : 50# alk. paper) ∞
    1. Lumbee Indians—Bibliography. 2. Carolina Indian Voice—Indexes. 3. Lumbee Indians—Newspapers—Indexes. I. Title.
Z1210. L8S73 1994
[E99.C91]
016.973'04975—dc20   89-43629
                                               CIP

Manufactured in the United States of America

McFarland & Company, Inc., Publishers
 Box 611, Jefferson, North Carolina 28640

TABLE OF CONTENTS

FOREWORD

Some librarians spend their lives working with books and never develop a taste for research and writing. Others become interested in certain topics, and go forward to do important research in that field. The latter is the case with Glenn Ellen Starr.

Ms. Starr lived from 1980 until 1984 in the Lumbee community, working as a reference librarian in the Mary Livermore Library of Pembroke State University, the institution which was founded as an Indian Normal School. She was, and remains, a friend of the Lumbee Indian people.

The Lumbee have not always been well known. With few exceptions it has only been when specific events arise (such as the routing of the Ku Klux Klan in 1958 or the question put by young Adrian Andrade to President Clinton on national television in 1993) that the Lumbee gain widespread attention.

Presently the Lumbee are involved in a more-than-100-year struggle for federal recognition, and I believe that this bibliography will be extremely important for research as the Lumbee continue this fight.

Ms. Starr has compiled what is without a doubt the most extensive bibliography on the Indians of Robeson County, North Carolina. This work will be useful for anyone doing research on this comprehensive subject, whether at the undergraduate, graduate, or professional level. With more than 1,400 entries, it demonstrates the extent of writing about the Indians of this area.

This work is more than a bibliography. Because of its organization into topics, and further into chronological sequence, it is also an important step forward in the study of the Lumbee. Its excellent organization will facilitate the work of all future researchers in this field. In addition to covering a wide range of topics, it also includes an index of the *Carolina Indian Voice,* a newspaper published in the Lumbee community by Lumbee people.

As a Lumbee historian, I recognize this work as an outstanding contribution to North Carolina history, and especially to Lumbee history. I highly recommend this bibliography to both Indian and non–Indian people. Anyone interested in the Lumbee will find this bibliography to be the most useful item in print. Congratulations to Glenn Ellen Starr on her endeavor.

Adolph L. Dial
Professor Emeritus
Pembroke State University

INTRODUCTION

The Lumbee are commendable in the pride they exhibit, in their struggles against continual problems and prejudices, and in their efforts to clarify and assert their identity. They have gone from achieving basic civil rights to striving for recognition as a unique group. Throughout this process, the Lumbees have attracted considerable popular and scholarly attention.

For some years, the Lumbees suffered prejudice because their history was not well documented. In 1975, Adolph Dial said their origins were "clouded in mystery" (see bibliographic entry 54 and p. xiv of that work). Progress has been made recently, however. The *Robeson Trails Archaeological Survey* (1988) found that Robeson County has been inhabited for at least 14,000 years; more intensive testing of its major sites has been conducted (see entry 1071). In 1989, several scholars (Jack Campisi, Raymond Fogelson, William Sturtevant, and James Merrell) asserted that, considering the scarcity of existing records on Carolina Indians, there is sufficient evidence to support Lumbee descent from the Cheraws. Gerald Sider (see entry 59 p. xii) concurs; he states, "None of the reasons that are usually given for the contestability of Lumbee identity can withstand even a few hours of close investigation; each of these 'reasons' refers to social and cultural conditions that are in fact widespread among Native Americans." The BIA's Branch of Acknowledgment Research, having examined the relevant data in the *Petition,* disagrees (see entry 1383).

Lumbees have been criticized for having no strong remnants or memory of what many people feel Indians should have—a "different" culture. Steadfastly, they have proclaimed, "We know who we are" and "We are what we say we are." Jeannette Henry, at the First Convocation of American Indian Scholars (1970), noted their lack of treaties, a separate language, and a tribal society. She added, "the Lumbee may be what everybody else [i.e., other Indians] is going to be in twenty or thirty years."

While their origins and culture may not conform to persistent stereotypes of Indians, their distinctiveness as a group is undeniable. They exhibit several strong and consistent values and characteristics: love of family and children; strong religious beliefs; several common surnames that occur in Robeson County only among Lumbees (see entry 48 and p. 8 of that work); characteristic speech patterns; a "decentralized, informal, kin-based leadership system" (see entry 1380 and p. 17 of that work); adherence to Robeson County as "home," wherever they settle; preference for rural living and the outdoors; resentment of authority; tendency to settle differences or react to insults by fighting or violence; and others, all noted in the literature. Indeed, William Sturtevant stated, in a 1988 Congressional hearing,

"Anthropologists over the last 100 years have agreed, everyone that has looked at the Lumbee case, that they are an Indian tribe ... I think one could say that anthropologists, as a profession, view the Lumbees as an Indian tribe" (see entry 1380 and p. 22 of that work). Karen Blu concluded *The Lumbee Problem* (1980) by stating, "Their identity has done more than allow the Lumbee to survive; it has been an active, motivating force enabling them to flourish" (p.235). Other tribes in North Carolina and California have emulated the Lumbees' political strategies because of their success, particularly in education and state recognition.

Because of this long-standing interest in the Lumbees — from all quarters of the popular and scholarly literature — and because their achievements have won attention that is likely to continue, an extensive guide to the literature was needed. When I worked as a reference librarian at Pembroke State University's Mary Livermore Library, our library staff observed the increase in "mainstream" publications on the Lumbees. Dean Williams, then assistant director for Public Services, had the foresight to begin a card file of Lumbee materials which is the nucleus of this bibliography.

Information on a topic related to Lumbee Indians might be found in several different sections of this book. Users should check the pertinent category in the annotated bibliography and also look under relevant terms in the subject index and in the *Carolina Indian Voice* index. Congressional hearings and reports, listed in the "Federal Bills, etc." section of the annotated bibliography, are rich sources of information.

Annotated Bibliography

In compiling this bibliography, I used many forms of research. I scanned the existing Lumbee bibliographies, consulted the notes and bibliographies of all items except those marked "Not seen" or "Forthcoming"; used bibliographies on Native Americans, North Carolina, Southern history, and other relevant topics; searched several online and CD-ROM databases (including ABC-CLIO's *Bibliography of Native North Americans*); contacted people who have written about the Lumbees or have a strong interest in them; searched printed periodical indexes, reference books, library card and online catalogs, OCLC and RLIN, and resource center holdings; scanned books on North Carolina, Southeastern, and American Indians; checked several libraries' vertical files; and taken advantage of serendipity.

The cutoff date for inclusion of new items was October 1993. The bibliography emphasizes materials available in collections open to the general public — libraries, museums, archives, and resource centers. There are undoubtedly other materials, not listed here, in individuals' private collections or in the offices of agencies that do not have a library function. Generally, I have not sought such items and have included few of them. I have not excluded any materials because of format. Given the volume of information, however, I have been comprehensive (rather than exhaustive) in including correspondence of government agencies with the Lumbees and manuscripts. Annotations in the pertinent sections note ways in which the researcher can obtain fuller lists of manuscripts, archival materials, and government correspondence found in the *Lumbee Petition*; some of the primary sources and most of the contemporary newspaper articles on Henry Berry Lowry cited in *To Die Game;* and the archaeological reports listed in the *Robeson Trails Archaeological Survey.*

Many brief mentions of the Lumbees, especially those which tend to duplicate information given in other sources, have been excluded. As an aid to reference librarians and to users outside Robeson County, I have noted a number of articles in reference books, sections in readily available books on North Carolina or on Southeastern Indians, and articles in widely available magazines and newspapers. To help researchers who visit or live in Robeson County, I have given Robeson County library locations for many items. I have not listed every Robeson County library location for a particular item, and have not given holdings for every item that may be in Robeson County libraries. Occasionally, I have given North Carolina research library locations.

My annotations are generally descriptive, rather than evaluative. Items I have not seen (including forthcoming works), or have seen only a portion of, are so marked. If the title is self-explanatory, or if the item duplicates information found in other items in the same section of the bibliography, I have left it briefly described or unannotated.

The categories in the bibliography reflect the patterns taken on by the literature itself. I have tried to "cluster" references, since people often look for information in the way they have heard or read about it. Conversely, I have tried to avoid too many subcategories. In nearly all cases, each item is listed only once. The cross-references in annotations and the subject index should provide users with several points of access. Within categories, citations are in chronological order. When the item provides no publication date, I have placed it according to my best estimate of the date. The entry numbers allow cross-referencing from one item to another within the bibliography, and from the chronology to the bibliography.

The annotated bibliography and the *Carolina Indian Voice* index include a few topics that are somewhat peripheral to research on the Lumbees (for instance, early articles on canoe trips down the Lumbee River; and items concerning "Britt's Blitz"). They are included as aids to research on Robeson County.

I have included newspaper articles found in the clippings files of various libraries. If the newspaper has been microfilmed, I checked the microfilm to verify the date and page number written in on the clipping. If I was unable to verify the clipping in the microfilmed version of the newspaper, or if the newspaper has not been microfilmed, I usually provided the bibliographic data that was pencilled in on the clipping and have also listed the location of the clippings file. For newspaper articles, section and page numbers are sometimes abbreviated: *Charlotte Observer* 22 April 1934: 3-2 refers to section 3, page 2.

Within annotations for newspaper articles, if only a date and page number are given for a related article, the article is from the same newspaper as the one in the main citation.

I have interchangeably used the terms Croatan, County Indians, Robeson County Indians, and Lumbees throughout this book. I have not always used the tribal name that corresponds to the historical period of the item being cited or annotated. The same is true for Pembroke State University and its earlier names.

Library Location Codes Used in the Annotated Bibliography

ASU-APP   Appalachian Collection, Appalachian State University, Boone, NC

ASU-BLK   Belk Library, Appalachian State University, Boone, NC

ECU   East Carolina University Library, Greenville, NC

ECU-ML	Music Library, East Carolina University, Greenville, NC
ELC	Elisha Locklear Collection, Pembroke, NC
EPFL	Enoch Pratt Free Library, Baltimore, MD
GPL	Greensboro Public Library, Greensboro, NC
IERC	Indian Education Resource Center, Lumberton, NC
IMC	Indian Museum of the Carolinas, Laurinburg, NC
IRM	Indian Religion Museum, Burnt Swamp Baptist Association, Pembroke, NC
NCS	North Carolina State University Library, Raleigh, NC
NCSL	North Carolina State Library, Raleigh, NC
PSU-MLL	Mary Livermore Library, Pembroke State University, Pembroke, NC
PSU-NARC	Native American Resource Center, Pembroke State University, Pembroke, NC
RCPL	Robeson County Public Library, Lumberton, NC
UGa	University of Georgia Library, Athens, GA
UNC-DL	Davis Library, University of North Carolina at Chapel Hill, Chapel Hill, NC
UNC-G	University of North Carolina at Greensboro Library, Greensboro, NC
UNC-UL	Undergraduate Library, University of North Carolina at Chapel Hill, Chapel Hill, NC
UNC-WL	Wilson Library, University of North Carolina at Chapel Hill, Chapel Hill, NC
WFU	Wake Forest University Library, Winston-Salem, NC
WFU-BHC	Baptist Historical Collection, Reynolds Library, Wake Forest University, Winston-Salem, NC

Note: Some of these collections are described in the "Resource Centers" section of the annotated bibliography.

Other Abbreviations Used in the Annotated Bibliography

AIM	American Indian Movement
BAE	Smithsonian Institute's Bureau of American Ethnology
BIA	United States Bureau of Indian Affairs
CIS	*Congressional Information Service*
CIV	*Carolina Indian Voice*
Comm.	Commission, Committee
LRDA	Lumbee Regional Development Association
LRLS	Lumbee River Legal Services
NCAI	National Congress of American Indians
PSC	Pembroke State College
•Rpt.	Reprinted
SATW	*Strike at the Wind!*
UNC	University of North Carolina

• OVERVIEWS OF EDUCATION; PUBLIC SCHOOLS. Newspaper articles on double-voting were excluded, since the topic received extensive coverage in the *Carolina Indian Voice.*

- LUMBEE CULTURE. For literary works, I have used the same selection criteria as Robert Reising in entry 326: belletristic works by and or about Lumbee Indians. I have omitted many of the works he lists, selecting only major works and works written or discovered since the publication of his bibliography. Only a few items on *Strike at the Wind!* are listed here, since there are many references in the *Carolina Indian Voice* index. Literary and dramatic depictions of Henry Berry Lowry are included here, rather than in Section IV.P. Only a few of the albums recorded by Lumbee gospel groups are included.

- ORIGINS OF THE TRIBE. Most works of the early travel writers who are frequently cited in support of the Lost Colony theory are not included, with the exception of John Lawson. References to these writings, as well as quotations from them, are easily obtained from the many discussions of the Lost Colony theory listed in this section.

- THE TUSCARORA INDIANS OF ROBESON COUNTY. This section is selective. Users needing more materials should consult the *Tuscarora Petition for Federal Recognition* (entry 755).

- COMMUNITY SERVICE; SPORTS AND ATHLETICS. Few items on Gene Locklear are included here, because there are numerous references in the *Carolina Indian Voice* index.

- BALTIMORE. Newspaper articles without page numbers were found in the clippings files of Enoch Pratt Free Library (Baltimore) or the Maryland Historical Society Library (Baltimore).

- BIOGRAPHICAL SOURCES. This section includes collective biographies. Items dealing with one person are found in the section(s) corresponding to that person's main achievements or contributions. Sketches on Joseph Oxendine, for example, are under Higher Education and Pembroke State University; Willie French Lowery, Lumbee Culture; and Dexter Brooks, Crime and Criminal Justice.

- GENEALOGICAL MATERIALS; PHOTOGRAPHY. This section lists a few basic tools for Robeson County genealogy and concentrates on materials related to Lumbees. Robeson County Public Library houses other useful items not listed here.

- ARCHAEOLOGY OF THE ROBESON COUNTY AREA. This section is selective, since the ROBESON TRAILS ARCHAEOLOGICAL SURVEY (entry 1071) lists all previous archaeological investigations of the area.

- THE HENRY BERRY LOWRY PERIOD. Many of the primary sources used by McKee Evans in *To Die Game* and cited in his footnotes and "Essay on Sources" are not included. I have listed the major works; a selection of newspaper articles, from the Lowry Gang era to the present; and items that have appeared since Evans' book.

- ACTIVISM SINCE THE LATE 1980s. Since coverage of the *Robesonian* hostage-taking and Julian Pierce's murder was voluminous, I have included only a selection of items, documenting the major developments.

- FEDERAL BILLS; STATE AND FEDERAL LAWS; FEDERAL HEARINGS AND REPORTS, ETC. This section includes government reports dealing directly with the Lumbees. Other government reports which mention or deal indirectly with the Lumbees are included in the pertinent section for the overall topic of the report.

Chronology of Significant Events in the History of Robeson County Indians

Emphasis is on laws, institutions, political events, major individual achievements, and contributions to research and scholarship on Lumbee Indians. The dates were verified in sources as close to the time of the event, or as reliable, as possible. Bracketed numbers refer to entries in the annotated bibliography. For other published chronologies, see the heading "Chronologies" in the subject index.

Index to the "Carolina Indian Voice," Jan. 18, 1973–Feb. 4, 1993

In terms of newspaper issues covered, this index is *complete* only through May 16, 1991, because of issues missing from my subscription. From that date through Feb. 4, 1993, I have indexed the issues I received. A few major articles from Feb. 11 through Oct. 28, 1993, were included. Because of space constraints and the time such indexing consumes, the index is selective. It includes major articles dealing with Lumbees or Tuscaroras which were judged potentially useful to researchers. These types of articles were excluded: weddings; wedding anniversaries; most family reunions; engagement announcements; birthday parties; beauty pageants; most retirements; most club and service organization news; notes on individuals in the military; most church and fire department news; high school homecomings; social columns; most obituaries; minor awards and achievements; and news on Indian tribes outside North Carolina (except for articles on Lumbees in other states). Regular columns are noted under their broad topic; for instance, "Baltimore (MD)." Except for installments with special research value, regular columns were not indexed. Articles on one particular political campaign, or articles listing results of one election, were indexed under that office (for example, "Robeson County— Board of Education—Elections"). If an article discusses several campaigns, or if an issue of the *Carolina Indian Voice* contains several separate articles on elections, only one entry appears, under "Elections." Articles on meetings of the county commissioners, county Board of Education, and Pembroke Town Council were indexed under the name of the organization. Only major articles on LRDA and the Title IV Compensatory Indian Education program were included.

Announcements of new businesses in Pembroke; biographical sketches on elderly Lumbees and on Lumbees who have made outstanding accomplishments; and PSU or high school class reunions were indexed. The following topics were indexed extensively: *Strike at the Wind!*; Lumbee Homecoming; Gene Locklear and other athletes and artists; any articles related to research, publications, or historical information on Lumbees or Tuscaroras; and controversial topics (double-voting, the school system merger, PSU chancellor selection, the PSU/UNC-P issue, and the *Robesonian* hostage-taking). Editorials and letters to the editor were indexed selectively.

If two or more articles on the same topic appear in the same issue, the references were combined. For instance:

Strike at the Wind!
L Jl 19 79: 1, 2.

indicates an article on page 1 and letters to the editor on page 2. Assume "Lumbee" as a modifier for general headings. For instance, "Art and Artists" refers to Lumbee people who practice art or are professional artists. An asterisk indicates an especially important article. Personal names, in most cases, were not standardized; they are listed exactly as given in the articles. Search under any variations of a person's name that you might be aware of. Articles on two different individuals with the same name may be listed together. Index headings and subheadings were not always applied consistently, so check under any possible headings for a topic. Follow up on all cross-references.

Abbreviations Used in the *Carolina Indian Voice* Index

A	Award, honor, political or organizational office or position, scholarship, or professional degree
Ad	Advertisement
Ag	August
Ap	April
B	Biographical sketch or article containing biographical information
C	Column
Dc	December
E	Editorial
Fe	February
Ja	January
Jl	July
Ju	June
L	Letter to the editor
M	Meeting
Mr	March
My	May
Nv	November
O	Obituary
Oc	October
P	Article includes a photograph
Rpt	Reprint
Se	September
Spec. Iss.	Special issue

For some issues of the *Carolina Indian Voice,* nothing was indexed because there were no articles meeting the criteria. Other issues were missing from the microfilmed edition of the *Carolina Indian Voice* held by libraries in Robeson County. Some issues were filmed out of focus; others were filmed with page 1 missing. Following is a list of issues I was unable to index, or issues out of sequence on microfilm.

Nov. 29, 1973	Page 1 missing from microfilm
July 11, 1974	Page 1 missing from microfilm
Feb. 13, 1975	Page 1 missing from microfilm
June 12, 1975	Entire issue missing from microfilm
Jan. 1, 1976	Entire issue missing from microfilm
Dec. 2, 1976	Entire issue missing from microfilm
Dec. 9, 1976	Entire issue missing from microfilm

Sept. 1, 1977	Indexed, but out of sequence on microfilm. Follows Aug. 26, 1976
Nov. 17, 1977	Entire issue missing from microfilm
March 30, 1978	Entire issue missing from microfilm
January, 1979	All issues missing from microfilm
Feb. 1, 1979	Entire issue missing from microfilm
Feb. 22, 1979	Entire issue missing from microfilm
May 3, 1979	Entire issue missing from microfilm
May 10, 1979	Entire issue missing from microfilm
May 17, 1979	Entire issue missing from microfilm
Aug. 9, 1979	Entire issue missing from microfilm
Aug. 16, 1979	Entire issue missing from microfilm
Aug. 23, 1979	Entire issue missing from microfilm
Nov. 15, 1979	Entire issue missing from microfilm
Nov. 29, 1979	Entire issue missing from microfilm
Jan. 1, 1981	Indexed, but out of sequence on microfilm. Follows Dec. 24, 1974
Jan. 21, 1982	Entire issue missing from microfilm
Jan. 28, 1982	Entire issue missing from microfilm
Dec. 2, 1982	Issue filmed out of focus; most pages illegible
Dec. 9, 1982	Issue filmed out of focus; most pages illegible
Dec. 16, 1982	Issue filmed out of focus; most pages illegible
Dec. 23, 1982	Issue filmed out of focus; most pages illegible
Dec. 30, 1982	Issue filmed out of focus; most pages illegible
Apr. 18, 1985	Issue filmed out of focus; most pages illegible
March 5, 1987	Entire issue missing from microfilm
Apr. 2, 1987	Entire issue missing from microfilm

Users interested in the missing issues since May 24, 1979, could consult the microfilm at the State Historical Society of Wisconsin, which is a different edition.

Author Index

The author index includes up to two authors for each item. It also includes editors, illustrators, composers, directors, and "implied" authors.

Subject Index

The subject index includes topics that are discussed in an item *in addition to* the main topic, which is represented by the section of the bibliography in which the item was placed. This index helps compensate for the fact that each item is placed under only one section in the bibliography. The subject index also includes, for convenience, some titles of major works in the bibliography.

The subject index provides access to the smaller, more specific topics and events in Lumbee history that are hard to find information on, or may not have been afforded separate chapters in books or entire periodical articles. For this reason, a fair amount of "value-added" indexing has been done. *The Lumbee Petition* (entry 57) received 94 entries; *Lumbee Indian Histories* (entry 59), 57 entries;

and *The Lumbee Methodists* (entry 422), 38 entries. The index may refer to a certain item in the bibliography, but the topic may not be mentioned in that item's title or annotation. This is probably *not* a mistake in the index. Somewhere in the item, the topic is discussed.

Biographical information has been emphasized in the index. For instance, all Lumbee individuals who were interviewed for the Doris Duke Indian Oral History Program (entry 1044) are indexed, as are all biographical sketches in *Historical and Contemporary Indian Leaders of Robeson County* (entry 1010).

Some of the topics in the index have their own section in the annotated bibliography; for instance, the Ku Klux Klan routing. The subject index, therefore, will alert users to discussions of that topic in items not listed in the topic's main section. Users should look under any possible headings—both broad and narrow—for a topic of interest and should investigate all cross-references.

ANNOTATED BIBLIOGRAPHY

OTHER BIBLIOGRAPHIES

1. Eliades, David K., and Adolph L. Dial, comps. "Bibliography: Lumbee Indians." Unpublished typescript, [1973]. [PSU-MLL] [Unannotated list of 39 items.]

2. Locklear, Janie Maynor, and Drenna J. Oxendine. "The Lumbee Indians: A Bibliography." *Indian Historian* 7.1 (Winter 1974): 52-54.
Unannotated list, alphabetical by author, of 81 items, including books, magazine and journal articles, theses, dissertations, government documents, newspaper articles, and newspaper special editions.

3. Feehan, Paul G., comp. *A Bibliography of Representative Materials on the Lumbee Indians of Robeson County, North Carolina*. ERIC, April 1978. ED 153 660. 10 p. [IERC]
Unannotated citations, grouped by material type, for 33 books and monographs; 57 pamphlets, magazine articles, and journal articles; and 16 theses, dissertations, and other unpublished items.

4. White, Wes. "Local History References and Lumbee Indian References in the Lumberton, NC *Robesonian*, 1897, 1900-1939." Unpublished manuscript. N.D. [PSU-MLL] [RCPL]
Microfilmed list of handwritten citations, in chronological order, with astute annotations. Topics include: World War I service, the Claxton, Georgia settlement, politics, deaths, weddings, court proceedings, violent crimes, letters to the editor, Henry Berry Lowry, schools, PSU, and community meetings and organizations.

BRIEF OVERVIEWS

5. Bellamy, John D[illard]. "Remarks of the Hon. John D. Bellamy, of North Carolina, in the House of Representatives." 56th Cong. 1st Session. *Congressional Record* 33 part 1 (2 Feb. 1900): 1457-58.
Historical overview occasioned by a bill requesting funding of a school for Croatan children (entry 1315). Croatans number "about 5,000." Some have migrated to Georgia, Mississippi, and Florida. Notes their War of 1812 service and propensity to

violence. Microfilmed by the Library of Congress.

6. [Purcell, J. E., Jr.] " The Croatan Indians." *Davidson College Magazine* 21.6
   (April 1905): [263]-65. [PSU-MLL]
In a supercilious tone, describes Croatans as suspicious, cowardly, "not caring much
for education," "incapable of taking a higher education," wicked, vicious, and morally
lacking.

7. M[ooney], J[ames]. "C roatan Indians." *Handbook of American Indians North of
   Mexico.* (Smithsonian Institution. Bureau of American Ethnology. Bulletin 30,
   part 1.) Washington: Government Printing Office, 1907. P. 365. Rpt. in McPherson (entry 49), Exhibit M, pp. 251-252.
Brief mention. The Lost Colony theory "m ay be regarded as baseless." Croatans
descend from "wasted native tribes, the early colonists or forest rovers, the runaway
slaves or other negroes, and probably also ... stray seamen of the Latin races from
coasting vessels in the West Indian or Brazilian trade."

8. Olds, F. A. "A Visit to the Croatan Indians." *Charlotte Observer* 21 June 1908:
   Sec. 2 pp. 2-3, 8. Rpt. in *Robesonian* 25 June 1908: 1; 29 June 1908: 1; 2 July
   1908: 1; 6 July 1908: 4.
Olds attended a Croatan Normal School commencement, then visited several Indian
homes (including Rhoda Lowry's). Photographs show Preston Locklear, Rosette
Brooks, Wash Lowry, a Croatan Normal School class, Harriet Graham's cabin, and
Wash Lowry's home. An iron tomahawk and an English-style cross-bow and
hand-mill had recently been found in the Croatan settlement. Mentions the Croatan
tradition of having taken Mattamuskeets as prisoners of war and kept them as slaves.
For background information on Olds, see *Dictionary of North Carolina Biography* vol.
4 (UNC Press, 1991) pp. 392-3.

9. McLean, A. W. "Historical Sketch of Indians of Robeson County." *Robesonian* 3
   April 1913: 2; 7 April 1913: 2. Rpt. in McPherson (entry 49), Exhibit F.
First appeared in a hearing (see entry 1326) on a 1911 bill requesting funds to construct
an industrial school for Robeson County Indians .

10. Olds, Fred A. " Croatan Indians of North Carolina." *Raleigh Times* 8 Nov. 1913.
Discusses log homes, hunting and fishing, Harper's Ferry, cross-bows, and the
Croatans' 1900 application for admission to the Indian Territory. Also notes that the
"proper name" of the Lumber River is "Lumbee." Notes Croatans' problems and
progress. Asserts that "they retain fully as many of their old characteristics as do the
Cherokees."

11. Henderson, James E. *The Croatan Indians of Robeson County.* Report to the
   Commissioner of Indian Affairs, Washington, D.C. from James E. Henderson,
   Supt., Cherokee Agency, U.S. Indian Service, Dept. of Interior. Cherokee, N.C.,
   11 Dec. 1923. 8 p. [National Archives and Records Service, Washington, D.C.
   RG 75, Entry 121, Central Classified Files, 1907-1939, 93807-1923-Cherokee
   School-150 (James Henderson's Report)].
Comments on the Croatans' education problems after the Civil War, dislike of the

name "Croatan," claims to be Cherokee, population, land holdings, homes, agriculture, use of alcohol, problems getting fair treatment in court, opposition to Black children attending their schools, and school enrollment.

12. MacNeill, Ben Dixon. "Riddle of the Lumbee Indians." *News and Observer:* 1926 Sec. 2 p. 1, in issues for 31 Jan., 7 Feb., 14 Feb., and 21 Feb.
The Lumbee Petition calls this the first known reference to "Lumbee" Indians.

13. Smithey, Sherman Bryan. "Robeson Indians Classed by State as Negroes 48 Years." *Charlotte Observer* 22 Nov. 1931: Sec. 3 p. 3.
Sympathetic historical overview. Smithey taught Lumbee children for 3 1/2 years.

14. Sharpe, Bill. "The Lost Tribes of Carolina." *The State* 16.47 (23 April 1949): 3-4, 21, 23.

15. [Johnson, Guy Benton]. "An Institutional Sketch of the Robeson County Indian Community." 1951? 22p. [Included in entry 468.]
The Lost Colony theory and Lowry Gang incidents "have played great part in the creation of the psychosocial Indian community." Discusses Indian townships; Whites and Blacks within them; transportation in the county; Indian surnames, and masculine first names. Indian social values are patterned after the White middle class, centering on industriousness, accumulating money, getting an education, and being honest and respectable. Explains physical traits and the class distinctions they generate. Discusses five major institutions: the family, economy, religion, education, and government.

16. Robeson County Historical Edition. *Robesonian* Feb. 1951: Sec. G. [RCPL]
Includes articles on the growth of PSU, history of the town of Pembroke, Odum Home, surnames, origin theories, Henry Berry Lowry, Col. Frank Wishart, and A. W. McLean's study of the Lumbees.

17. "The Indians of Robeson County." *The State* 18.47 (21 April 1951): 3, 22.
A delegation of county Indians testified before the state legislature on a bill (see entry 1359) to change their tribal name to Lumbee.

18. Pleasants, Paul. "Our Mysterious Indians." *The State* 20.26 (29 Nov. 1952): 9-11.

19. Rights, Douglas L. *The American Indian in North Carolina.* 2nd ed. Winston-Salem: John F. Blair, 1957. Pp. 144-49. [PSU-MLL]
Challenges the Lost Colony theory. Uncovering the Lumbees' ancient language would help settle the origin debate.

20. MRH. "Who Are the 'Lumbee' Indians?" *The Masterkey for Indian Lore and History* [Los Angeles: Southwest Museum] 32 (May-June 1958): 92. [PSU-MLL]
Brief mention prompted by the Ku Klux Klan routing. Author "could find nothing in the literature" about the Lumbees, so he wrote to the Bureau of American Ethnology.

21. Sharpe, Bill. "Down East Indians." *The State* 33.5 (1 Aug.1965): 13-14.

22. *Robesonian* 100th Anniversary Edition. *Robesonian* 12 July 1970: Sec. C.
Includes articles on the Ku Klux Klan routing, tribal origin, surnames, history of PSU
(by Dial and Eliades), Simeon Oxendine's World War II service, and PSU's building
program under English Jones.

23. Bledsoe, Jerry. "A Story of Indian Progress: 'We've Made It On Our Own'."
Greensboro Daily News 17 Jan. 1971: A1. [PSU-MLL]

24. Gaillard, Frye. "Lumbee Indians." *South Today* [Atlanta, GA] 3.2 (Sept. 1971):
4-5.
Explains the Lumbee economic situation, opposition to a 1970 school desegregation
plan, Indianness, and love of the land.

25. Chavers, Dean. "The Lumbee Story, Part I—Origin of the Tribe." *Indian Voice*
[Santa Clara, CA: Native American Pub. Co.] 1.10 (1971-72): 11-12, 24.
Summarizes the Lost Colony theory and the theory of descent from Cherokees who
fought with Col. John Barnwell. These two theories "can be regarded as no better than
circumstantial evidence." Suggests "a more eclectic approach."

26. [Chavers, Dean.] "The Lumbee Story—Part II: A Short History of the Lumbees
Since 1800." *Indian Voice* 1.11 (1971-72): 13-14, 26.
On the N.C. Constitution of 1835, White attempts to conscript Lumbees during the
Civil War, Henry Berry Lowry, education 1835-1868, remnants of Indian tribal culture
evident in contemporary Lumbees, Lumbee political processes, and tribal origins.

27. Burt, Jesse, and Robert B. Ferguson. *Indians of the Southeast, Then and Now*.
Nashville: Abingdon, 1973. Pp. 155-58, 221-23, 231-35. [PSU-MLL]
Credits Henry Berry Lowry with thwarting the Klan's terrorism against nonwhites.

28. Dial, Adolph L. "Lumbee Indians." 5th Gulf Coast History and Humanities
Conference, Pensacola, FL, Feb. 7-9, 1974. *Indians of the Lower South: Past and
Present*. Ed. John K. Mahon. Pensacola: The Conference, 1975. Pp. 77-92.
[PSU-MLL]
Covers the Lost Colony theory; Henry Berry Lowry; Hamilton McMillan's contribu-
tions; tribal name changes; education; military service; migrations to Georgia,
Baltimore, and Detroit; the Ku Klux Klan routing; Robeson County race relations;
double voting; the Tuscarora movement; the burning of Old Main; the Eastern Carolina
Indian Organization; the Lumbee Bank; and political and professional achievements.

29. Wetmore, Ruth Y. *First on the Land: The North Carolina Indians*. Winston-
Salem: F. Blair, 1975. Pp. 164-68. [PSU-MLL]
Discusses the period of disfranchisement, Henry Berry Lowry, Hamilton McMillan, the
Ku Klux Klan routing, and PSU.

30. Hudson, Charles. *The Southeastern Indians*. Knoxville: U of Tennessee P, 1976.
Pp. 493-96. [PSU-MLL]

31. *Good to Be an Indian: Proud and Free*. Videotape. Prod. Billy E. Barnes. Title

IV, Part A Indian Education Project, Robeson County Board of Education, 1980. 20 min.
Documentary-style program, narrated by Hope Sheppard and shown often at PSU's Native American Resource Center. Presents the salient points of Lumbee history, culture, education, and accomplishments. Mentions LRDA, *Strike at the Wind!*, Lumbee Homecoming, river pocosins, and the Miss Lumbee Pageant.

32. Spicer, Edward H. "Lumbees." *Harvard Encyclopedia of American Ethnic Groups*. Ed. Stephen Thornstrom. Cambridge: Belknap—Harvard UP, 1980. Pp. 70-71.

33. Kehoe, Alice B. *North American Indians: A Comprehensive Account*. Englewood Cliffs, NJ: Prentice-Hall, 1981. Pp. 201-203. [PSU-MLL]
Mentions recent pan-Indian activism and the influence of Lumbee success in gaining Indian status on other North Carolina tri-racial isolates.

34. *Public Policy and Native Americans in North Carolina: Issues for the '80's*. Ed. Susan M. Presti. Raleigh: North Carolina Center for Public Policy Research, 1981. [PSU-MLL]
Several Lumbees were panelists, and Lumbees are discussed frequently in these proceedings. Broad divisions are education, health, recognition, and economic status. Includes Adolph Dial's keynote address and concluding remarks.

35. Dial, Adolph L. "The Lumbee Indians: Still a Lost Colony?" *New World Outlook* 32 (May 1982): 19-22. [PSU-MLL]

36. Parramore, Thomas C. *North Carolina: The History of an American State*. Englewood Cliffs, NJ: Prentice-Hall, 1983. Pp. 55-56, 292-94.

37. *North Carolina Native American Resources*. Pembroke: North Carolina State Consortium on Indian Education, 1985. [IERC]
Lumbees are discussed in several sections. Gives 1980 Indian population by county and provides lists of the following: school systems with Indian Education programs; Title IV, Part A projects; Indian agencies and organizations; and Indian festivals.

38. Perdue, Theda. *Native Carolinians: The Indians of North Carolina*. Raleigh: Div. of Archives and History, North Carolina Dept. of Cultural Resources, 1985. Pp. 45-52. [PSU-MLL]

39. Dial, Adolph L. "The Lumbees: From Adversity to Progress." *Carolina Indian Voice* 1985: 24 Jan., p. 6; 31 Jan., p. 6; 7 Feb., p. 7; 14 Feb., p.9; 21 Feb., p. 6; 28 Feb., p. 6.
Reprints Dial's address (excerpted in entry 40) at Greensboro College upon receipt of an honorary doctorate. This version gives more detail on the Lost Colony theory, military service, Henry Berry Lowry, history of PSU, migrations, public schools, the Ku Klux Klan routing, and recent successes.

40. Dial, Adolph L. "From Adversity to Progress." *Southern Exposure* 13.6

(Nov.-Dec. 1985): 85-89.
Excerpts from a speech by Dial, followed by two interviews by Geoff Mangum.
Interviewees are Leon Locklear, chief of the Drowning Creek Tuscarora, who
participated in the Klan routing; and Lawrence Maynor, who successfully sued the BIA
in 1973-74 (see entry 1372) and was built a frame house.

41. Allen, James Paul, and Eugene James Turner. *We the People: An Atlas of
America's Ethnic Diversity*. New York: Macmillan, 1988.
See pp. 29 and 32. Maps and charts on pp. 26, 30, 31, and Appendix 2 give 1980
census data reflecting Lumbees.

42. Waldman, Carl. "Lumbee." *Encyclopedia of Native American Tribes*. New
York: Facts on File, 1988. Pp. 118-19. [PSU-MLL]

43. Dial, Adolph L. "Lumbee Indians." *Encyclopedia of Southern Culture*. Ed.
Charles Reagan Wilson. Chapel Hill: U of North Carolina P, 1989. Pp. 436-37.

44. Eliades, David K. "The Lumbee Indians: Searching for Justice, Searching for
Identity." *Tar Heel Junior Historian* 28.2 (Spring 1989): 47-49.

45. "Lumbee." *Encyclopedia of World Cultures*. Vol. 1, *North America*. Ed.
Timothy J. O'Leary. Boston: G. K. Hall, 1991. Pp. 208-209.

46. Lerch, Patricia Barker. "State -Recognized Indians of North Carolina, Including
a History of the Waccamaw Sioux." *Indians of the Southeastern United States in
the Late Twentieth Century*. Tuscaloosa: U of Alabama P, 1992. Pp. 44-71.
Lumbees are mentioned throughout. Discusses surnames, religion, Lumbee Regional
Development Association, and the North Carolina Commission of Indian Affairs. In
another chapter, Wes Taukchiray mentions the Smilings (pp. 75-76). For more on the
Smilings, see microfiche 24-27A of Taukchiray's papers, available at Emory University Library (Atlanta, GA) and Winthrop College Library (Rock Hill, S.C.).

47. Zak, Susannah K. "A Story of Survival: The Lumbee Indians." Thesis. U of
North Carolina at Chapel Hill, 1992. 53 p.
This three-part series of journalistic articles provides a good introduction to Lumbee
history, themes, and problems. The articles, derived from background reading and
interviews, cover the struggle for federal recognition; "A Portrait of Lumbee Country"
(themes and characteristics, such as home, family, traditional medicine, Henry Berry
Lowry, the Klan routing, and education); and Lumbee successes.

48. Blu, Karen I. "Lumbee." *Handbook of North American Indians*. Vol. 13, *The
Southeast*. Ed. William G. Sturtevant. Washington: Smithsonian P. Forthcoming. 25 p. [Draft at IERC] [Noted in S.Hrg. 100-881 (entry 1380), pp. 22-24.]

COMPREHENSIVE OVERVIEWS

49. McPherson, O. M. *Indians of North Carolina: Letter from the Secretary of the
Interior, Transmitting, in Response to a Senate Resolution of June 30, 1914 ...*

Caption Title: *Report on Condition and Tribal Rights of the Indians of Robeson and Adjoining Counties of North Carolina*. US. 63rd Congress, 3rd Session. S. Doc. 677. Dated 5 Jan. 1915. *Serial Set* 6772. 252 p. [IERC]

A Senate resolution in response to the Indians' interest in federal recognition as Cherokees (the North Carolina legislature had just changed their name to "Cherokee Indians of Robeson County"; see also entry 586) directed Special Indian Agent McPherson to make an investigation. His efforts were quite thorough, encompassing reading of history and ethnology, fieldwork in Robeson County, and extensive correspondence. He addresses statements from A. W. McLean that the Indians were originally part of the Cherokee tribe, but he rejects these claims (pp. 18, 19). He notes that "the 'Lumbee' River is a branch of the Pedee and the similarity of the names would suggest the same origin" (p. 23). Earlier than Swanton (entry 535), he mentions Cheraws in connection with Robeson County Indians. He finds it "not improbable ... that there was some degree of amalgamation between the Indians residing on the Lumber River and the Cheraws, who were their nearest neighbors" (p. 23). The 25-page report concludes that Robeson's Indians are descended from Hatteras Indians and the Lost Colony, further mixed with Scotch and Scotch-Irish settlers and with other races (p. 17). It recommends financial assistance, land, and an agricultural/mechanical school. The remaining pages are exhibits, reprinting legislation, correspondence, essays, and excerpts from histories documenting the conclusions. Microfilmed by the Library of Congress.

50. Oxendine, Clifton. "A Social and Economic History of the Indians of Robeson County, North Carolina." Thesis. George Peabody College for Teachers, 1934.
This frequently cited work covers much ground in Lumbee history. Chapter 1 reviews the Cherokee and Lost Colony origin theories. Chapter 2 is on Henry Berry Lowry. Chapter 3 discusses problems faced after suffrage was restored in 1868. Chapter 4, "Present-Day Progress," discusses land ownership, education, and religion.

51. Lowrey, Clarence E. *The Lumbee Indians of North Carolina*. Lumberton: Clarence E. Lowrey, 1960. 64p. [RCPL]
Discussion of, and agreement with, the Lost Colony theory. Reviews the Henry Berry Lowry story and mentions disfranchisement and name changes. Many photographs.

52. "Lumbee Indian History Soon to Be Released; New Book 18 Years in Making." *The Lumbee* 2 Dec. 1965: 1.
On entry 53; lists major writings on Lumbees to date.

53. Barton, Lew. *The Most Ironic Story in American History: An Authoritative, Documented History of the Lumbee Indians of North Carolina*. Charlotte: Associated Printing Corp., 1967. [PSU-MLL] [UNC-G]
Includes extensive quotations and excerpts from writings on the Lumbees. Explores major topics and includes some of Barton's poetry. A "Lumbee album" contains photographs and biographical sketches. Bibliography on the Klan routing, pp. 99-101.

54. Dial, Adolph L., and David K. Eliades. *The Only Land I Know: A History of the Lumbee Indians*. San Francisco: Indian Historian P, 1975. [PSU-MLL]
This readable work has become the standard overview and the first source consulted

for most topics. It discusses origin theories, the Siouan movement, Henry Berry Lowry, public schools, PSU, Old Main, Red Banks, migration to Baltimore and Georgia, the Tuscarora movement, religion, folklore, economics, politics, military service, the Klan routing, and the *Carolina Indian Voice*. Many illustrations. Appendices list the Lost Colonists and reprint major Lumbee legislation. Bibliography.

55. Blu, Karen I. *The Lumbee Problem: The Making of an American Indian People.* Cambridge: Cambridge UP, 1980. [PSU-MLL]
Blu did extensive fieldwork in Robeson County; excerpts from her notes are included as direct quotations. Her thorough research in both published and unpublished literature is reflected in the book's bibliography. Provides accurate, precise treatments of the major topics and events. Analyzes Lumbees' perception of themselves and the meaning of Indianness to them. Discusses how each race in the county perceives itself and the other two races. Covers political participation; the attempted coalition with Blacks; their tactics for improving conditions after 1865; and relations with other mixed-blood groups, such as the Smilings. The final chapter analyzes ways of looking at Lumbee identity.

56. Barton, Bruce. *An Indian Manifesto: Bruce Barton's The Best Of—As I See It: The Sometimes Irreverent but Always Honest Columns As They Appeared in The "Carolina Indian Voice" Newspaper Over the Last Ten Years by Bruce Barton, Editor; With Some "Musings" by Ol' Reasonable Locklear. A Special Ten Year Anniversary Edition, 1973-1983.* Pembroke: The Carolina Indian Voice, 1983. [PSU-MLL]
Reprints 132 installments of "As I See It," 19 of "Musings." Topics range widely, but many entries deal with double voting, Old Main, county schools, politics, Indians in the criminal justice system, and PSU/Pembroke relations. Entries on individuals include Henry Berry Lowry, Adolph Dial, D. F. Lowry, English Jones, Dexter Brooks, Janie Maynor Locklear, Bob Mangum, Joy Johnson, Jim Chavis, Carnell Locklear, and Glenn Maynor.

57. Lumbee River Legal Services. *The Lumbee Petition.* Prepared in cooperation with the Lumbee Tribal Enrollment Office. Julian T. Pierce and Cynthia Hunt-Locklear, authors. Jack Campisi and Wesley White, consultants. Pembroke: Lumbee River Legal Services, 1987. 3 vols. [PSU-MLL]
Copiously documented and admirably researched, the *Petition* is organized to address each requirement of the *Code of Federal Regulations* for "establishing that an American Indian group exists as an Indian tribe." Volume One is an extensive historical narrative, from European contact through the contemporary Lumbee community. There are separate sections on topics such as kinship, churches, schools, Lumbee Homecoming, the *Carolina Indian Voice*, values, LRDA, tribal recognition, and the Lumbee political process. There are tables, genealogical charts, maps, and photographs. Volume Two is primarily bibliographical, including many annotated references for early Robeson County newspaper articles. Some of these papers were short-lived, and only clippings exist. Volume Three summarizes arguments that the Lumbees descend primarily from the Cheraws. Most of the correspondence with government agencies and the archival materials cited are not listed in this bibliography; many of the unpublished legal documents, and many of the newspaper articles, are

likewise not included. Few researchers would fail to benefit from the *Petition*. Many of the topics discussed therein are listed in the Subject Index of this bibliography.

58. Dial, Adolph L. *The Lumbee.* Indians of North America. New York: Chelsea House, 1993. 112 p. [UNC]
This lucidly written, copiously illustrated work, meant for ages 12-16, also serves well as an up-to-date introduction for college students and general readers. Topics covered include tribal name and origin (emphasizing the Lost Colony theory), efforts to gain true federal recognition, history of their relations with Whites in Robeson County, Henry Berry Lowry, their struggle for education (especially the history of PSU), religion, agriculture, art, politics and civil rights, and recent accomplishments.

59. Sider, Gerald M. *Lumbee Indian Histories: Race, Ethnicity and Indian Identity in the Southern United States.* New York: Cambridge UP, 1993. [PSU-MLL][UNC]
Sider calls this work " both an anthropology and a history of histories," exploring "how people have lived and still live within and against the histories they have chosen and the histories that have been imposed upon them." He brings considerable knowledge and feeling to this work, based on scholarly research, work with the Lumbee as an activist and a *Petition* researcher, and numerous friendships among the tribe. He treats topics such as the various tribal names and claims of historical origin; agriculture, land ownership, and the politics of work; education; voter registration drives, and attempts to get Indian candidates elected; the Tuscarora movement; Pembroke Farms; the Henry Berry Lowry period; and Lumbee and Tuscarora attempts at federal recognition. He emphasizes events and conditions in Robeson County between 1968 and 1973 but also deals with the Colonial period and discusses developments as recent as 1991. One of many strengths of this work is that, while providing detailed descriptions of key events and periods in Lumbee history (including information not given elsewhere), Sider also places Lumbee history into a broader anthropological context (see the Preface).

60. Chavis, Ben. [Untitled book-length study.] Forthcoming.
Chavis and the late Robert K. Thomas had begun work on this study, which Chavis will complete. Topics to be covered include: Lumbee culture as of 1950, and changes since then; symbols of Lumbee peoplehood (Henry Berry Lowry, the Klan routing, the public schools, Lumbee English, and the importance of land); Lumbees as an American community; Lumbees as viewed by Blacks, Whites, and Cherokees; Lumbee history; and Lumbee relations with neighboring tribes. [From correspondence.]

TOPICS, EVENTS, AND PERIODS
EDUCATION
Overviews of Education; Public Schools

61. "School Board Hearings: Decisions of School Committeemen Debarring Children from School Reversed...." *Robesonian* 23 Jan. 1913: 1.
The School Committee had excluded certain children on grounds of Negro blood.

62. Pierce, Charles F. "The Croatan Indians of North Carolina." *Indian School Journal* [US Indian School, Chilocco, Oklahoma] 13.7 (March 1913): [303]-306.

Condensed version in *The Indian's Friend* 26.1 (Oct. 1913): 10-12. [PSU-MLL]

63. Edens, H. L. "Indian Race Problems: True Cause of Frequent Contentions
    Among Indians of Robeson Over Indian School Matters." *Robesonian* 16 April
    1914: 2.
Outsiders "of African origin have no legal or moral right to the privileges of the
Indians' schools; their ultimate design is amalgamation by marriage."

64. "A Puzzling Problem." *Robesonian* 4 Feb. 1915: 4.
Croatans have spread beyond Robeson, Scotland, and Hoke counties, where they have
separate schools. Superintendents want a state law forbidding Croatan children to
attend White schools. Responses by D. F. Lowry and others, 18 Feb. 1915: 7.

65. Hardin, N. B. "In Regard to Admitting Alleged Mulattoes into Indian Schools."
    Robesonian 8 March 1915: 2.
Letter. Indians should present a united front to their school committees in opposing
attendance of mulatto children from other counties. Responses, 15 March 1915: 3; 22
March 1915: 6; 15 April 1915: 7.

66. Chavis, Abner. "Cherokee Indians of Robeson—They Need More and Better
    Schools—No Provision for Care of Insane of the Race." *Robesonian* 15 Oct.
    1917: 6.
Indians have sent 75 men to World War I training camps, but the men are incapable of
writing home.

67. "First Indian County Commencement at Pembroke So Big It is Day to Reckon
    From." *Robesonian* 31 March 1924: 1.
All 31 Indian schools participated. Indian school attendance has tripled in the past 15
years and now totals 3,400 students.

68. "Robeson Builds Indian Schools: Large Program Is Going Forward in Several
    Localities." *Charlotte Observer* 6 Nov. 1925: 9.
The state will fund buildings at Indian Normal, Pembroke Graded, Union Chapel,
Green Grove, Barker Ten Mile, and Rowland.

69. "Indian School Case Results in Mistrial." *Robesonian* 20 May 1926: 1.
Lawyers argued that admission of two Smiling children to Hopewell Indian School
would lead to "a great influx of Negroes and undesirables from the county of Sumter to
Robeson County."

70. "Smilings Debarred from Indian Schools by Court Action." *Robesonian* 13 Dec.
    1926: 1.
Robeson Superior Court affirmed the action of a legislative committee.

71. "Supreme Court Upholds Midyette in Robeson Indians School Case." *Robesonian* 31 March 1927: 1.
Upholds Superior Court decision that children of David Smiling cannot attend schools
for Indians of Robeson County.

72. "Smilings Apply for a Separate School District." *Robesonian* 8 Sept. 1927: 1.
A special committee was formed to investigate a district for a fourth race (30 Smiling children).

73. "Smilings Denied Special School by Education Board." *Robesonian* 8 Dec. 1927:
1. [Would be "inadvisable on economic and other grounds."]

74. "Indian School Is Ending Big Year." *Brevard News* 2 May 1929: 3. [ASU-BLK]
Prospect Indian School had 10 students in its first graduating class. Sixteen students completed 7th grade. The school was the first to "raise the standard ... to the point where it could be recognized as second only to the Indian Normal at Pembroke."

75. Barnes, Bahnson N. "A History of the Robeson County School System." Thesis.
U of North Carolina, 1931.
Traces educational development through the Civil War; rapid growth up to 1927; and present conditions, noting changes needed. Quotes extensively from primary and secondary materials. Cites "a need for further consolidation in order to provide standard schools throughout the county at a minimum of expense" (p. 107).

76. "Separate School Set-Up Granted Robeson Indians." *Robesonian* 27 July 1933: 1.
The N.C. School Commission placed Indian schools under six Indian administrative units. County schools for all three races had been under fourteen administrative units.

77. "State Commission Grants Request of Pembroke School." *Robesonian* 22 Oct.
1934: 1.
Pembroke White school. A second teacher, formerly paid out of pocket by White parents, would be paid with state funds.

78. Lowry, M. L. "Education Among Indians Growing at a Rapid Pace." *Robesonian*
Nov. 1937: Sec. 6 p. 3. (Industrial—Historical—Agricultural Progress Edition.)
Describes the history of Pembroke Normal School and growth of Indian public schools.

79. "Patrons Protest Consolidation of Indian Schools." *Robesonian* 77 June 1939: 1.
Indian parents from Harper's Ferry protested construction of a school in the Pembroke Farms area to consolidate the Hillymead, White Hill, and Harper's Ferry schools.

80. Morgan, Ernest West. "A Racial Comparison of Education in Robeson County
(North Carolina)." Thesis. U of North Carolina, 1940.
Compares schools for each race during county control (1923-33) vs. the fifth year of state control (1937-38). In 1932-33, schools were equal only in that they used the same basic textbooks. By 1937-38, gains had been made; but disparities were still apparent.

81. Stone, Jake Ward. "A Comparative Study of Three Types of High School
Teachers in Robeson County, North Carolina." Thesis. Duke U, 1941.
Surveyed teachers from Indian, White, and Black schools on income, training, teaching experience, and other factors. Found few differences among the races.

82. "Indian Schools." *State School Facts* [Raleigh: N.C. Dept. of Public Instruction]

17 (Sept. 1944). 1 p.
Describes state laws providing for separate schools for Croatans in Robeson, Sampson,
and Richmond counties. Lists state Supreme Court decisions and Attorney General's
rulings related to the law. Gives 1943-44 enrollment statistics for state Indian schools.

83. "Over 125 Teachers in Indian Schools." [Newspaper article, 1947?]. [PSU-MLL.
PSU Clippings File]
Robeson's eight Indian schools have 127 Indian teachers. Names listed, by school.

84. "Condition Reported Poor at Pembroke Grade School." *Pembroke Progress* 20
Nov. 1947? [PSU-MLL. PSU Clippings File]
Overcrowding, low ceilings, poor lighting and heating.

85. "School Report Lists Educational Needs in Detail." *Robesonian* 14 June 1948: 3.
For each school, lists facilities needed, staff needed, and estimated cost for improvements.

86. Kennedy, Harold W. "Suggests Changes in School Survey Recommendations."
Pembroke Progress 24 June 1948: 6B.
Letter. In the 1947-48 school year, "less than 12% as many pupils attend the Indian
high schools as attend the elementary schools that feed these high schools." Figures
were slightly higher for the White and Black schools.

87. Beckwith, Evelina Gilbert. "A Study of the Physical Equipment and Teaching
Personnel of the Indian Schools of Robeson County, North Carolina." Thesis. U
of North Carolina, 1950.
Surveys the 17 Indian schools on equipment and personnel standards. Finds that
buildings need repairs and additional space, property needs better upkeep, and teachers
are inadequately or too narrowly prepared. Microfilmed by the UNC Library Photo-
graphic Service in 1961.

88. Thompson, Vernon Ray. "A Study of the Indian Schools of Robeson County,
North Carolina." Thesis. Ohio State U, 1951. [UNC-G]
Surveys the teaching personnel and physical facilities of the county's 18 Indian
schools, then gives 13 recommendations for improvements. Chapter II is a "Brief
History of the Robeson County Indians." Includes photographs of some school
buildings.

89. *Robesonian* Progress Edition: Robeson County Schools. *Robesonian* Sept. 1951:
Sec. A. [RCPL]
Twelve-page section following the Sept. 24 issue on the *Robesonian* microfilm. Gives
statistics on enrollment, busing, and number of teachers by race. Discusses construction and inprovements, budgets, capital outlays, and tax rates. Includes photographs of
schools.

90. "School Bond Approval Follows Indians' Suit." *News and Observer* 10 Jan.
1952: 14.
Scotland County voters approved a $550,000 bond referendum including funds to

enlarge the Oak Grove Elementary School, the county's only Indian school. This
followed a lawsuit against the county by several Indian parents.

91. Walls, Frances. "Johnston Children To Enter White Schools If Parents Prove
They're Indian." *News and Observer* 11 Sept. 1955: 12.
GS 115-2 (*North Carolina General Statutes*), which allowed Croatan children to attend
only Croatan schools, was changed to meet desegregation requirements imposed by the
Supreme Court.

92. "Indians Ask School Entry at Sanford." *Greensboro Daily News* 20 Dec. 1955.
Belton Bullard applied to the city school board for admission of his children to Sanford
schools. The family had moved there from Robeson County because of reduced
tobacco allotments.

93. Hunter, Marjorie. "Robeson County's FOUR School Systems." *Winston-Salem
Journal and Sentinel* 5 Feb. 1956: C3. [On the Smiling Independent School.]

94. "Improved School Facilities Granted Smilings Community." *Robesonian* 18 Oct.
1957: 1.
The six to ten high school students will move to the old building, and the thirty
younger students will occupy the new, four-room school when it is completed.

95. "Indian School Case Gets Full Hearing." *New York Times* 23 Oct. 1960: 88.
Indian students were given permission to attend all-White Dunn High School, but a
federal judge dissolved the order.

96. Maynor, Lacy W. "A Lumbee Speaks." *Indian Affairs* [Newsletter of the
Association of American Indian Affairs, Inc.] 39 (Dec. 1960): 2. [IERC]
Deplores the actions of school offficials in Dunn, N.C. (Harnett County) who barred
three Lumbees from the community's only high school.

97. "N.C. Continues Desegregation: Indian Children Get Transfers." *AFSC Bulletin*
[American Friends Service Committee] No. 74 (Fall 1961): 1, 3. [UNC-WL
Clippings File]
Lumbee children in Harnett County will be allowed to attend the White high school in
Dunn, following a year-long struggle including a student sit-in and a lawsuit filed by
parents.

98. American Friends Service Committee, High Point, N.C. "School Desegregation
Report—Staff Work with Lumbee Indians." 30 June 1962. Unpublished
typescript. 7 p. [IERC] [Included in entry 468.]
The 32,000 Lumbees in a seven-county area suffer three-way segregation in schools
and numerous other facilities. Discusses the 1960 Dunn school sit-ins; AFSC's
assistance to Sampson County Indians in fighting inadequate facilities in their
300-student school; and a 1960 lawsuit by Indians in Lumberton over a city annexation. Notes that "there has been little or no organized activity among the Lumbees
for civil rights." Concludes that an intensive community relations program to deal with
school desegregation and other problems involving the three races is "vitally needed."

99. "County Education Board to Have Indian Representation." *Robesonian* 26 March 1963: 1.
Harry West Locklear will be the first Lumbee to serve on the Robeson County Board of Education.

100. "Indian Group Will Protest Policies of School Board." *Robesonian* 17 April 1964. [PSU-MLL. PSU Clippings File]
A group of Indian citizens, chaired by Curt Locklear, was expected to meet with the Robeson County Board of Education to request improvements in the county school system. A similar group met with county commissioners on March 2, filing a protest. The group wanted equal school facilities for Indians (in particular, facilities that would meet Southern Association of Secondary Schools and Colleges standards) and wanted Indians in top administrative positions in the school system. A delegration, led by Dr. Martin Brooks, also met with the state board of education in Raleigh (see *Robesonian* 4 Sept. 1964; PSU-MLL. PSU Clippings File).

101. "Indian Pupils Admitted to W. Lumberton School." *Robesonian* 1 Sept. 1964: 1.
Six students were admitted, based on a new Pupil Assignment Act; names given.

102. Egerton, John. "Six Districts, Three Races and More Things." *Southern Education Report* 4 (Dec. 1968): 4-10. [PSU-MLL]
Notes unusual busing and attendance patterns and teacher salary discrepancies among the districts. The county district was 60% Indian; none of the township districts had more than 5% Indian enrollment. Desegregation plans are discussed.

103. Peck, John Gregory. "Community Background Reports: Robeson County, North Carolina: Lumbee Indians." *The National Study of American Indian Education.* Series I, No. 1. *Final Report.* Washington: Office of Education, Bureau of Research, Aug. 1969. 12 p. ERIC ED 039 077
Brief overview of Lumbee origins and physical appearance. Describes Robeson County towns, income sources, geography, schools, housing, and organizations. The appendix gives a statistical analysis of the county.

104. Maynor, Waltz. "Academic Performance and School Integration: A Multi-Ethnic Analysis." Diss. Duke U, 1970. ERIC ED 052 863
Measures academic performance of Black, White, and Indian students in a newly integrated school system in Hoke County. Black children's performance improved after integration. White and Indian children experienced no negative effects. Both groups increased their their language achievement scores when teachers were of their own race.

105. Williamson, Hadley. "Lumbees Hold Meet on School Action." *Robesonian* 25 Aug. 1970: 1.
Two hundred Lumbees, members of Independent Americans, vowed to retain separate schools and reject busing.

106. "Lumbee Complaints Aired for State, Federal Officials." *Robesonian* 26 Aug. 1970: 1.

L. H. Moore, representing Prospect School, met with Dewey Dodd, of the Office of Civil Rights.

107. Jones, J. Marshall. "Lumbee Boycott 'Undetermined' at Red Springs." *Robesonian* 28 Aug. 1970: 1.
Total number of absences can't be estimated. School operations were orderly.

108. "Lumbee Indian Exemption from HEW Order Sought." *Robesonian* 2 Sept. 1970: 1.
Reprints a letter from Helen Scheirbeck to the director of the National Council of Indian Opportunity, asking him to "seek direct intervention by the White House and Department of Justice."

109. "School Officials, Lumbees Remain in Disagreement." *Robesonian* 6 Sept. 1970: 1.
About 500 of the county's 9,000 Indian children are still sitting in at their old schools. Indian parents were warned by the school superintendent and a DHEW official that time is running out.

110. "Lumbee School Protest Aired for Commission." *Robesonian* 9 Sept. 1970: 1.
Robeson County Board of Education officials met with County Commissioners on sit-ins. Reprints the Board's statement.

111. "Schools to Bar Defiant Lumbees." *News and Observer* 10 Sept. 1970: 3.
County Commissioners ordered principals not to admit Indian children trying to sit in.

112. Watts, Carroll. "Lumbee Fund-Raising Drive Nets $2,200 for Legal Battle." *Robesonian* 10 Sept. 1970: 1.
Parents of children sitting in will take their battle to federal court.

113. Andrews, Al. "Indians File Suit in School Dispute." *News and Observer* 11 Sept. 1970: 3.
Indian students ended their sit-in yesterday. Their parents filed suit asking that school boards be restrained from enforcing a pupil assignment plan. They also want to keep the previously all-Indian schools.

114. "Lumbee School Suit Lists 46 Officials." *Robesonian* 13 Sept. 1970: 2A.
Bostic Locklear and others filed the "Prospect Suit" in Fayetteville District Court. They want pupils reassigned so that Indian children can attend Indian schools. On dismissal of the suit, see *CIV* 28 Sept. 1978: 1; rpt. *CIV* 20 Jan. 1983: 10A.

115. Deese, James W. "Believes It to Be 'Will of God' to Protect the Indian Heritage." *Robesonian* 13 Sept. 1970: 8A.
Letter. Deese, 65, recalls Lumbee struggles to establish schools for their children. Useful articulation of the Lumbee position on school desegregation.

116. Franklin, Ben A. "Indians Resist Integration Plan in Triracial County in Carolina." *New York Times* 13 Sept. 1970: 78. Rpt. in *Akwesasne Notes* 2.6

(Oct. 1970): 40.
Some say sit-ins are caused by resistance to integration with Blacks; others cite unfair district boundaries. Quotes Lew Barton on reasons for lawsuit filed by Lumbee parents.

117. "Schools Demand, Indians Comply." *News and Observer* 25 Sept. 1970: 3.
The Robeson County Board of Education asked a judge to force Lumbee parents to comply with HEW's desegregation plan.

118. Coit, John. "The Gentle Warrior for Lumbee Indians." *News and Observer* 18
      Oct. 1970: Sec. 4 p. 3.
Lew Barton is Tar Heel of the Week. Discusses his writings, leadership in the school desegregation controversy, and educational background.

119. Bledsoe, Jerry. "'Our Schools Are Close to Us': Will Loss of Indian Schools
      Mean Loss of Identity?" *Greensboro Daily News* 19 Jan. 1971: A9.
Discusses the desegregation plan and double voting. A third of all Indian college students are Lumbee, and half of all Indian public school teachers.

120. "Lumbee Sit-ins May Get Unofficial Study Credit." *Robesonian* 8 June 1971: 6.
The "longest sit-in in US history" has ended. The Concerned Indian Parents Association may form an accrediting body to give certificates for work completed by sit-ins.

121. Gaillard, Frye. "Desegregation Denies Justice to Lumbee Indians." *Indian
      Historian* 4.3 (Fall 1971): 17-22, 43. [PSU-MLL]
The HEW desegregation plan frequently grouped Indian and Black children (resegregation), did not merge the six school systems, bused large numbers of Indian children, and displaced many Indian teachers. Lumbees also feared desegregated schools would ignore their unique educational needs.

122. Dennis, Henry. *The American Indian, 1492-1974: A Chronology and Fact
      Book*. 2nd ed. Oceana, 1972. P. 62.
Brief mention. In 1960, Eugene and James Chance were fined for defying a court order. They persisted in sending their children to Dunn High School rather than the nearest Indian school, which would require a 73-mile round trip daily.

123. *To Live On This Earth: American Indian Education*. Estelle Fuchs and Robert J.
      Havighurst. Garden City, NY: Doubleday, 1972. Pp. 97-106.
Separate education, though problematic, provided steady non-agricultural jobs for Lumbees. Describes the Pembroke and Baltimore schools most often attended by Lumbee children.

124. "Integration Went Smoothly." *Scottish Chief* 10 Sept. 1972. [PSU-MLL. PSU
      Clippings File].
Seven Indian children residing in Lumberton began attending Lumberton schools.

125. "Indians Square Off with Deputies." *News and Observer* 31 Oct. 1972.
Two hundred Tuscaroras crowded county school offices, protesting desegregation and

misuse of federal funds earmarked for Indians. [See also Section IV-F of bibliography.]

126. Thompson, Vernon Ray. "A History of the Education of the Lumbee Indians of Robeson County, North Carolina, 1885-1970." Diss. U of Miami, 1973.
[ECU] [UNC-WL] [UNC-G]
Explains the "half-century Dark Ages" (1835-1885), during which Lumbees lost their civil rights and could not attend public schools. Describes Lumbee efforts after 1868 to establish separate schools for their children rather than send them to Black schools. Discusses each of the six school districts; lack of Indian representation on the county board of education; and the 1970-71 upheavals when a desegregation plan was implemented. Recommends merging school districts and abolishing double-voting.

127. Coit, John. "Robeson Indians Arrested." *News and Observer* 25 March 1973: Sec. 1 p. 1.
After a 7-hour standoff in front of Prospect School, Tuscarora Chief Howard Brooks, AIM's Vernon Bellecourt, and 63 other demonstrating Tuscaroras were arrested. They had been denied use of the school auditorium for a tribal meeting. [See also the "Tuscarora Indians of Robeson County" section of this bibliography.]

128. Burchette, Bob. "1st Indian on School Board Not a 'Token'." *Greensboro News* 9 April 1973: B1.
Earl Hughes Oxendine is the first Indian on the NC Board of Education. For his obituary, see *Robesonian* 9 Aug. 1991: 2A.

129. Flair, Kim. "Red, White, and Black: Aliens in Our Own Land." *California Council for the Social Studies Review* 12.3 (1973): 19-20, 22.
Ninth-grade English students in Chapel Hill created a unit on the American Indian. They became pen-pals with Lumbee students and had the Lumbee students spend a weekend in Chapel Hill.

130. Maynor, Gerald D. "The Effects of Socio-Economic Status and Race on Parental Attitudes toward Public Education in a Tri-Racial School District." Thesis. Coral Gables, FL: U of Miami, 1974.
Parents in the county district completed the "Your School" scale. Maynor found that parents' socioeconomic status had no bearing on responses. Black parents were more positive toward educators and desegregated schools than were Indian or White parents.

131. Maynor, Waltz, and W. G. Katzenmeyer. "Academic Performance and School Integration: A Multi-Ethnic Analysis." *Journal of Negro Education* 43.1 (1974): 30-38.
Looks for differences in measured ability and achievement among Black, White, and Indian children in Hoke County's recently integrated school system. No appreciable differences were seen, except in language and mathematics scores of Black students.

132. Maynor, Waltz, and Vernon R. Thompson. *Indian Education Elementary and Secondary School Assistance Program, Robeson County, N.C., 1973-74.* Lumberton: Robeson County Board of Education, 1974. ERIC ED 147 064

This evaluation of a program serving 25 schools was based on questionnaires to parents, students and teachers, along with principals' descriptions of its operation in their schools.

133. Brooks, Dalton Peter. "Student Perception of Teacher Behavior in a Tri-Racial School District." Thesis. Coral Gables, FL: U of Miami, 1975.
Lumbee students perceived Indian and Black teachers similarly but rated White teachers very differently. The student's sex and socioeconomic status, the teacher's race, and the subject matter of the class affected ratings.

134. Vela, Karen. "Racial Discrimination Found in L'ton Schools." *Robesonian* 5 June 1975: 11.
The U.S. Justice Department found "substantial evidence" that discrimination prompted the Lumberton District's annexation of Clyburn Pines/Country Club, Lakewood Estates, and Barker Ten Mile.

135. Maynor, Waltz. *An Evaluation of Education for Indians, Robeson County, North Carolina 1975-1976.* Lumberton: Robeson County Board of Education, 1976. 24 p. ERIC ED 147 065
Analyzed the scores of all 3rd and 10th grade students in the county school system on the Comprehensive Test of Basic Skills. Scores were higher in 1976, after three years of the Indian Education Program, than in 1973, when it began.

136. "Lumbee: A Position Paper Presented to the American Indian Policy Review Commission Task Force No. 5. Additionally: Statistical Data Reflecting Educational Issues To Be Addressed by Panel." Unpublished typescript. 17 April 1976. [IERC]
Gives statistics on adult education; a statement on higher education problems; a description of Indian Education in Maxton city schools; and a report on LRDA's Indian Education project.

137. Brooks, Dexter. "Desegregation in Robeson: Old Misrepresentations and New Directions." Revised. Unpublished typescript. 22 April 1976. 31 p.
Thorough analysis of student and faculty desegregation. Examines the HEW plan implemented in 1970/71; the impact of *Locklare v. Culbreth*; and the desires of each race regarding desegregation. Statistical appendices.

138. Woods, Ruth Dial. *Robeson County Indian Education Needs Assessment, FY-79.* Lumberton: Robeson County Compensatory Indian Education Project, Jan. 1978. 30 p. ERIC ED 161 606
A needs assessment survey was filled out by 9,524 persons. It asked respondents to rank, in order of importance, ten needs. Tables summarize the results.

139. Tafoya, Dennis W., and Boyd G. Combs. *Robeson County Compensatory Indian Education Project.* Evaluation and Final Report. U of North Carolina. Center for Human Communication Research, July 1978. ERIC ED 161 605
Participants ranked classes in Indian arts, crafts, and music as the most successful; counseling programs, least. The project reached over 43,000 people in 9 months.

140. Scheirbeck, Helen Maynor. "Education: Public Policy and the American Indian." Diss. Virginia Polytechnic Institute, 1980.

This detailed, well-researched study discusses, among other things, the effects of federal, state and local government actions on Lumbee education. Scheirbeck concludes that "state sponsored education of Indians as illustrated by ... the Lumbees ... indicates a failure to achieve assimilation or cultural adjustment of the Indians into the dominant culture of that state." Appendix A is a bibliography. Appendix E is a comprehensive "List of North Carolina Laws Affecting Public Education of Indians Not Living on Reservations." Appendix F is a very thorough "List of Significant Actions Regarding Lumbee Indians of North Carolina."

141. Brown, Joye. "Indians Lose Appeal of School Convictions." *News and Observer* 5 March 1980: 34.

The N.C. Court of Appeals upheld the conviction of Indian parents who allowed their children to "sit in" at Prospect School, rather than attend the school to which they were reassigned under a desegregation plan. See also entries 1210 and 1211.

142. "Suit Claims Robeson Schools Segregated." *News and Observer* 29 May 1980: 58.

Twelve parents filed suit against the county's five schools systems. They allege manipulation of school district boundaries to achieve segregation, and duplication of costs by maintaining five systems. See also 20 Oct. 1980: 21.

143. U.S. Cong. House. Comm. on Education and Labor. Subcomm. on Elementary, Secondary and Vocational Education. *Oversight Hearings on Indian Education.* 96th Congress, 2nd Sess. Sept. 3, 5, 1980. ERIC ED 204 065

Includes statements from Charlie Rose (pp. 2-3), Agnes Chavis (pp. 46-69), and Ruth Dial Woods (pp. 38-46).

144. Bishop, Lynette. "Two School Suits Claim Violations." *Robesonian* 4 Jan. 1981: 1D.

Suits filed in May and December, 1980, claim that the five school systems "perpetuate segregation" and that the Lumberton district's three recent annexations dilute minority voting strength.

145. "Helen Scheirbeck Named by Save the Children to Indian Position." *Wassaja* Nov.-Dec. 1982: 13.

Will supervise Save the Children projects for 50 reservations. Earlier she was project advisor for Indian Education programs in Washington, D.C. and chaired the Indian Education Task Force for the American Indian Policy Review Commission.

146. "Ruth Dial Woods." *Wassaja* Nov./Dec. 1982: 13.

Woods, who supervised the county's $3.5 million in Title IV Indian Education funds, became the county's first female assistant superintendent.

147. Cox, Stephanie Ann. *Minority Political Participation in North Carolina.* Raleigh: North Carolina Human Relations Council, North Carolina Dept. of Administration, 1983.

Brief mention. The Lumberton school district's annexation of three areas provoked an attorney general's objection. Also discusses county voter registration and minority elected officials.

148. U.S. Cong. House. Committeee on Education and Labor. Subcommittee on Elementary, Secondary and Vocational Education. *Indian Education Act—Title IV.* Hearing. 98th Cong., First Session. 22 Feb. 1983. ERIC ED 239 817
See testimony by Purnell Swett, pp. 68-77. In five years, county Indian absenteeism dropped from 5.10% to 4.82%. The dropout rate decreased to 9.5%. More students were identified as gifted and talented, standardized test scores increased, and students going directly from school into the workforce decreased.

149. Herring, Roger Dale. "A Study of the Relationships of Ethnicity, Sex, and School to Competency Level Achieved by High School Juniors on the North Carolina Minimum Competency Test for the Robeson County School System Between 1978-1983." Thesis. Appalachian State U, 1984. [ASU-BLK]
Studied scores of 2,681 students in six county high schools on nine factors. Found significant differences when comparing ethnicity to mathematics scores, reading scores, and pass-fail rates.

150. Snider, Margie. "The Value of Title IX: It Goes Beyond Athletics." *Charlotte Observer* 9 Sept. 1984: 3B.
Discusses an $82,000 Women's Educational Equity Act grant, awarded by the North Carolina Commission of Indian Affairs, to hold career equity conferences for 300 Indian high school girls in a 10-county area. Twelve of the students also completed a summer internship working with Indian professional women.

151. *Educational Alternatives: Robeson County, Fairmont City, Lumberton City, Red Springs City, and St. Pauls City 1983-84*. [Raleigh]: Division of School Planning, N.C. Dept. of Public Instruction, 30 Nov. 1984. 246 p.
Used data from federal, state, and local records and from school visitations. Describes each community and school system, making recommendations. Urges that "immediate steps be taken to dissolve the five units ... and form a new administrative unit to serve the entire county" (p. 234).

152. "Woods, Ruth Dial." *Who's Who of American Women*. 15th ed., 1987-1988. Wilmette, IL: Marquis Who's Who, 1986. P. 887. [IERC]
Woods, an educational administrator, won the Henry Berry Lowry Award in 1980. She was involved in the International Women's Year, Girl Scouts USA, and more.

153. Indian Education Project. *"Making a Difference": A Pictorial Profile of the 1984-1985 Title IV, Part A Indian Education Project*. Lumberton: Robeson County Board of Education, 1986. 34 p. [IERC]
This program, which began in 1974, had reached over 49,000 Indian students by 1986. The booklet profiles the wide range of Title IV services. Numerous photographs.

154. Munger, Guy. "Promoting an Awareness of Indian Culture in the State." *News and Observer* 2 Feb. 1986: 3D.

Betty Oxendine Mangum, Tar Heel of the Week, heads the North Carolina Department of Public Instruction's Indian Education office.

155. Davis, E. Dale. "The Lumbee Indians of Robeson County, North Carolina, and Their Schools." Paper presented at the National Conference of Christians and Jews (Pembroke, 19 Dec. 1986). ERIC ED 280 666 [PSU-MLL]
Brief history of Lumbee education, beginning with the 1835 disfranchisement. Gives statistics on Indian students, schools, and teachers during various periods.

156. "4 School Boards in Robeson Sued." *Charlotte Observer* 24 Dec. 1987: 3B.
Protests the at-large election of board members in Lumberton, Red Springs, Fairmont, and Saint Pauls, which resulted in 3/4 of board members White, while 1/3 of students were White.

157. "Robeson Accomplishment." *Fayetteville Times* 10 March 1988: 4A.
Editorial. The merger of the county's school systems was a tremendous feat in spite of the closeness of the vote.

158. Talbert, Malissa. "Superintendent Selected for Merged System." *Robesonian* 21 Dec. 1988: 1A. [William Johnson of Lee County.]

159. Talbert, Malissa. "Board OKs District Lines for 6 High School Plan." *Robesonian* 22 Feb. 1989: 1A.
Explains student transfers and includes a map of boundaries.

160. Talbert, Malissa. "John Bridgeman Instrumental in Developing New Cooperation. *Robesonian* 26 Feb. 1989: 10.
Education consultant to the Interim Board since Aug. 1, 1988.

161. Talbert, Malissa. "Barker Chairs Interim [School] Board, Selects Committees Carefully." *Robesonian* 26 Feb. 1989: 11.
Discusses public perception of the merger and John Barker's personal reflections.

162. North Carolina Division of School Planning. [NC Dept. of Public Instruction.] *Robeson County Schools, A Special Report, 1988-89*. Raleigh: The Division, 6 March 1989. 31 p. NC Documents Depository Microfiche G11 9: R653
Recommendations to the merged system on how to organize the superintendent's central office staff.

163. Guyton, Nanette. "School Board Hirings Spark Controversy." *Robesonian* 17 May 1989: 1A.
The merged system will have six assistant superintendents: 4 White, 1 Black, 1 Indian.

164. "School Merger Is Taking a Bad Rap." *Robesonian* 18 June 1989: 4A.
Editorial discusses the race of new administrators and a 33.6-cent property tax increase.

165. "County Tax Hike Sometimes a Victim of Misconceptions." *Robesonian* 21 June 1989: 4A.

Editorial on the proposed 50% property tax increase to fund the school system merger.

166. Kelly, Deborah. "High School Renamed for Purnell Swett." *Robesonian* 25
   June 1989: 1A.
West Robeson High School was renamed for the retiring superintendent of the county
school system. For reactions to the change, see the *Carolina Indian Voice* Index.

167. Herring, Roger D. "Minimum Competency Testing: Implications for Ethnicity."
   Journal of Multicultural Counseling and Development 17.3 (July 1989): 98-104.
Compares scores of juniors from Robeson County's six high schools on the state
minimum competency test. The three races differed on mathematics and reading
scores. Male and female students differed on pass/fail rates on both parts of the test.

168. Culbreth, John. "Officials Defend Funding Methods." *Robesonian* 30 Aug.
   1989: 1A.
Points of contention in the funding formula for the merged school system are discussed
by the county manager and others.

169. Culbreth, John. "County Files Action to Void Funding Mandate." *Robesonian*
   29 Sept. 1989: 1A.
County commissioners asked that the funding portion of the school merger law be
voided, claiming its vagueness is unconstitutional.

170. Kelly, Deborah. "Robeson Officials Agree to Put Tap on School Funding."
   Robesonian 15 April 1990: 1.
Will ask legislators to allow funding at 70% of state average, rather than the 75%
required by the merger law. Related article, 11 Jan. 1991: 1A.

171. Verkuilen, Kathy. "Lowry Ready to Face Challenges as NCAE's New
   President-Elect." *Robesonian* 10 June 1990: 1A.
Rose Marie Lowry is the first Indian head of the N.C. Association of Educators.

172. Locklear, Donald. "Native American Accountability for Academic Learning
   and its Relationship to Standardized Test Achievement." Diss. South Carolina
   State College, 1991. 130 p. [Not seen.]
A large percentage of students in this study were Lumbee [from correspondence].

173. Bigelow, Scott. "Race, School Choice Not Only Achievement Factors."
   Robesonian 24 July 1991: C1.
Analysis of detailed information released by the Public Schools of Robeson County on
students' California Achievement Test scores. Graphs compare scores by race, sex,
and parents' education. Charts show results, by school, for 3rd, 6th, and 8th grades and
compare 1989-90 scores to 1990-91.

174. Toole, Judith. "Dropout Rate Increasing at Slower Pace." *Robesonian* 26 Aug.
   1991: 1A.
About 85 fewer students in county schools dropped out during the 1990-1991 school
year than in 1989-1990. Over half the dropouts in those two school years were Indian.

175.   Toole, Judith. "New School District Lines to Be Checked by Board." *Robeso-nian* 27 Sept. 1991: 1A.

A redistricting plan drawn up by the Native American Political Action Committee was voted on by the present school board. A new state law requires that the board change from 15 members (eleven appointed) to eleven members (all elected). Related article, 1 Oct. 1991: 1A.

176.   Toole, Judith. "Johnson's Promise to Resign Fails to Satisfy Caucus." *Robeso-nian* 17 June 1992: 1A.

County school superintendent William Johnson had promised to resign when his contract ends in June, 1993; but Robeson County Black Caucus spokesperson Joy Johnson requested, for the sixth time, that Johnson's contract be terminated immediate-ly. The Caucus presented the school board with statistics on racial inequities in hiring and salaries in the school system. Several other recommendations are listed. See also letter in support of Joy Johnson's stance, 19 July 1992: 1A.

177.   Bigelow, Scott. "Top School Post Is Offered to Purnell Swett." *Robesonian* 2 Dec. 1992: 1A, 10A.

The Robeson County school board voted, 9-2, to offer the superintendent's position to Purnell Swett. The county will still have to pay $97,000 to William Johnson, former superintendent, who was forced out of the position in July with one year left in his contract. A major task for Swett will be getting the county school system removed from the state's takeover list. The manner in which the school board voted to offer Swett the position, and differing viewpoints on Swett's prior record as superintendent, prompted much discussion. See *Robesonian* 15 Nov. 1992: 4A (editorial and cartoon); 30 Nov. 1992: 4A (letter); 4 Dec. 1992: 4A (column); 6 Dec. 1992: 5A (letter); 11 Dec. 1992: 4A (column); 16 Dec. 1992: 1A (more details on Swett's contract); and 13 Jan. 1993: 1A (on Swett's plans for addressing the school system's problems).

178.   Bigelow, Scott. "Rev. McLean: Early Presbyterian Leader." *Robesonian* 13 Dec. 1992: 4A.

The Rev. Hector McLean's diary (with a transcription) was presented to Robeson County Public Library. McLean was a Presbyterian minister in the county from 1832-1879. He also organized schools for both White and Indian children.

HIGHER EDUCATION AND PEMBROKE
STATE UNIVERSITY

179.   "School for Indians." *Robesonian* 18 April 1912: 1.

An Indian appropriations bill amendment would grant $25,000 for a school for county Indians. It would be built at Pembroke and maintained by the federal government.

180.   Brown, L. A. "Indian Training School: Robeson County Indians and A. W. McLean Before House of Congress Committee—Ask for Appropriation of $50,000." *Robesonian* 17 Feb. 1913: 1.

Senator Simmons asked for money because county Indians cannot attend North Carolina colleges open to other races and have no industrial education facility. For an earlier comment on the bill from H. L. Edens, principal of the Indian Normal School, see 18 Sept. 1911: 4.

181. "Death of Preston Locklear: One of the Leaders Among Indians of Robeson." *Robesonian* 24 Jan. 1916: 1.
Locklear made the first move for separate schools for Indians and Blacks. He helped with McMillan's legislation (entry 1308) and was an Indian Normal School trustee.

182. "Bills Introduced for New Cherokee Indian School; Would Provide $50,000 for School at Pembroke for Indians of Robeson and Adjoining Counties—Introduced by Simmons and Godwin." *Robesonian* 14 Feb. 1916: 1.
Federal bill; text included.

183. "Contract Let for Constructing New Pembroke Normal Building." *Pembroke Herald* 1.3 (April 1922): 1. [PSU-MLL. Special Collection]
Includes architect J. M. Kennedy's drawing of the proposed administration building (Old Main). Construction price will be $51,710.

184. "Indians of Robeson Demand Right to Attend Federal Indian Schools." *Robesonian* 17 March 1924: 1.
Senator Varser will redraft a bill to include ideas from a delegation of Robeson Indians.

185. "Oscar R. Sampson: A Faithful Tribute." *Robesonian* 16 Jan. 1928: 8.
Letter. Sampson was a long-time member of the Indian Normal School's Board of Trustees.

186. "Indian Normal at Pembroke Will Open Oct. 1." *Robesonian* 27 Sept. 1928: 1.
For the first time the school will actually train teachers, and no elementary grades will be taught.

187. "Life of Rev. W. L. Moore, Prominent Indian and Leader of His Race." *Robesonian* 9 Feb. 1931: 3.
Describes Moore's funeral and reviews his accomplishments. Moore urged the introduction of the bill which established the Indian Normal School, helped fund the school's construction, and was its first teacher and headmaster. He was also a long-time pastor of Prospect Church and aided Indian public schools.

188. "Bill to Change Supervision of Indian Normal." *Robesonian* 5 March 1931: 4.
A bill was introduced to remove the school from the Negro School Supervisor in the state department of education and place it under the White School Supervisor.

189. Lawrence, R. C. "Pembroke Indian School." *The State* 10.42 (20 March 1943): 5, 37. [PSU-MLL]
History of the college, from the initial appropriation championed by Hamilton McMillan in 1887 to state accreditation as a four-year college in 1940.

190. Oxendine, Clifton. "Pembroke State College for Indians: Historical Sketch." *North Carolina Historical Review* 22.1 (Jan. 1945): 22-33. [PSU-MLL]

Emphasizes state appropriations, enrollment, facilities, changes in curriculum, and progress under various heads.

191. Wellons, R. D. "State Faces Problem of Providing Graduate Education for Indians; PSC Degree Ends Opportunity for Schooling in N.C." [Newspaper article, Feb. 1947?] [PSU-MLL. PSU Clippings File.]

192. "Official PSC Name Declared Taboo by Pembroke Students." *Pembroke Progress* 19 June 1947? [PSU-MLL. PSU Clippings File]
Students dislike having to explain "for Indians" in the name.

193. "Indians and U.N.C." *Charlotte Observer* 3 March 1948: 8A.
Editorial on Pembroke State College Chancellor Wellons' call for admission of Indians to UNC and other North Carolina graduate programs.

194. "Indians Want Law Revised." *News and Observer* 5 March 1948: 20.
PSC Chancellor Wellons wants an amendment to the 1885 state law (see entry 1306) which specifies a separate education system for North Carolina Indians.

195. "Floyd To Work To Prevent PSC Bill from Being Passed." *Robesonian* 16 Feb. 1949: 1.
The bill would send PSC funds to an out-of-state facility to teach the county's deaf, dumb, or blind Indian children.

196. Oxendine, Clifton, and Mrs. J. T. Sampson. "O. R. Sampson and Anderson Locklear Memorialized at Pembroke College." *Robesonian* 22 March 1949: 4.
Sketches of teachers for whom PSU's Sampson and Locklear Halls were named.

197. Wellons, R. D. "Last 10-Years Growth of College 60 Years Old Reported to Trustees." *Pembroke Progress* 9 June 1949: 8.
Discusses students, alumni, buildings, campus, and equipment.

198. "State University Should be Opened to Pembroke Grads." *Pembroke Progress* 28 Sept. 1950. [PSU-MLL. PSU Clippings File.]
Plea from Chancellor Wellons as he submits PSC's budget request.

199. "Pembroke Board Still Would Have Control over College Admissions." *Robesonian* 28 Jan. 1953: 1.
The bill, called "a new twist in segregation" by reporters, would allow "others approved by the Board of Trustees" to attend PSC—but not Blacks.

200. "Pembroke College Bill Is Given Committee Approval." *Robesonian* 6 Feb. 1953: 1.
Will admit non-Indians, with approval of the Board of Trustees (see entry 1358). The present enrollment of 125 could increase to 300 without additional staff or facilities.

201. "School Racial Bars May Go." [Newspaper article.] 6 Feb. 1953. [PSU-MLL]
A bill introduced in the General Assembly would allow non-Indians to attend PSC. Its

sponsor notes that "Indians are now being allowed to attend other state-supported schools."

202. "Rags to Riches Story of a Tar Heel Indian." *News and Observer* 9 June 1953: 5. [Herbert G. Oxendine, the first Lumbee to earn a doctorate.]

203. "Most of PSC Grads Enter Teaching Profession Here." *Pembroke Progress* 17 Nov. 1955? [PSU-MLL. PSU Clippings File.]
Of 314 graduates with 4-year degrees since 1940, 75% are teachers.

204. "Dr. W. J. Gale Named Pembroke College Head." *Pembroke Progress* 24 May 1956? [PSU-MLL. PSU Clippings File]
To begin July 1, 1956; qualifications listed.

205. Brown, Dick. "Pembroke State College Answers Indians' Desire for Higher Education." *Greensboro Daily News* 1 June 1958: 1.
Enrollment has almost tripled in the past 2 years; details on president Walter Gale.

206. Simkins, Virginia. "Indians Hail Whites on PSC Board." *Robesonian* 2 Sept. 1959: 1.
Four White men were appointed to the previously all-Indian Board of Trustees. Three were members of the North Carolina General Assembly. John L. Carter, who resigned and was one of the members replaced, favored the idea.

207. Womble, Bill. "Pembroke: A College Degree for Less." *News and Observer* 4 Feb. 1962: Sec. 3 p. 1.
Discusses current costs, progress under Walter Gale, and degree programs.

208. Warren, Gene. "Pembroke Seeks Regional University Status." *Greensboro Daily News* 23 March 1969: A9.
English Jones comments on the implications of a bill in the General Assembly (see entry 1366).

209. Thompson, Norma J. "An Analysis of Factors Relating to Job Satisfaction and Training of American Indian Graduates of Pembroke State University with Emphasis on Business Education Graduates." Diss. Georgia State U, 1971.
PSU Indian graduates tend to remain near PSU, work as teachers, not seek higher degrees, be active in professional organizations, and rate PSU as satisfactory in teacher preparation.

210. Bledsoe, Jerry. "A Symbol of Accomplishment." *Greensboro Daily News* 19 Jan. 1971: A9.
Brief history of PSU; mentions recent changes and percentage of Indian employment.

211. Dial, Adolph, and David K. Eliades. "Lumbee Indians of North Carolina and Pembroke State University." *Indian Historian* 4.4 (Winter 1971): 20-24. [PSU-MLL] Rpt. in *The American Indian Reader: Education*. Ed. Jeannette Henry. San Francisco: Indian Historian P, 1972. Pp. 51-60.

Concise, thorough, readable account. Highlights individuals who helped PSU develop from the 15-student Croatan Normal School in 1887 (the first state-supported school for Robeson Indians) to university status in 1969.

212. Barton, Lew. " 'De-Indianization' Trend Observed at Pembroke U." *Robesonian* 18 Nov. 1971: 27.
Barton heard the phrase on campus. Lists several points supporting the opinion. See letters of reaction from Gene Warren (21 Nov. 1971), Randall Ackley (23 Nov. 1971, 8 Dec. 1971), James M. Locklear (2 Dec. 1971, 12 Dec. 1971), and Wm. R. Ashurst Jr. (9 Dec. 1971). See editorial, 12 Dec. 1971.

213. Wooten, Sylvester Wendell. "A Comparison Between Lumbee Indian Commuting Students, Non-Indian Dormitory Students, and Non-Indian Commuting Students in Terms of Their Perceptions of the College Environment." Diss. U of Virginia, 1972.
Lumbee commuters saw a balance of vocational and collegiate emphases; orderly supervision; and a structured environment. Non-Indian commuters felt "a need for increased personal status, practical benefits, procedures, and organization."

214. "Indians Protest Razing Landmark." *News and Observer* 16 Jan. 1972: 1.
Picketing by the Eastern Carolina Indian Organization. PSU President English Jones wants an arts center and auditorium on the Old Main site.

215. Blue, Brantley. "Wants To Preserve 'Old Main' and Get New Auditorium Too." *Robesonian* 25 Jan. 1972: 6.
Thoughtful, reasoned letter considers Old Main's significance to Lumbees as well as English Jones' position.

216. "Pembroke State University Plans American Indian Studies Department." *Red Springs Citizen* 26 Jan. 1972: 6. [PSU-MLL. PSU Clippings File]
A committee of ten, and consultant Roger Buffalohead from U. of Minnesota, are planning.

217. Coit, John. "Indians Rally Against Democrats on Razing Plan." *News and Observer* 6 Feb. 1972: Sec. 1 p. 5.
Indians threaten to switch to the Republican Party because Democrats favor razing Old Main. They are also critical of university publicist Gene Warren.

218. "Indian Leader Protests Action." *Greensboro Daily News* 11 Feb. 1972: B20.
Leo Vocu of the NCAI protests the planned razing of Old Main.

219. Bledsoe, Jerry. "There Could Be Trouble, Indians Say." *Greensboro Daily News* 13 Feb. 1972: A1. [Many Lumbees fear violence if Old Main is razed.]

220. Bledsoe, Jerry. "Battle of Emotion Over a Building They Love." *Greensboro Daily News* 13 Feb. 1972: A1.
Good explanation of Old Main's significance to Lumbees. Their recent emphasis on Indianness has influenced the situation.

221. "Governor Acknowledges Save Old Main Pleas." *National Congress of American Indians Bulletin* [Washington, DC] 28.1 (March 1972): 1.
Leo Vocu, NCAI director, received a letter from the North Carolina governor, stating that Old Main is "receiving the full attention of my office." This letter was the first official acknowledgement of the three-month-old Save Old Main movement.

222. "Indians to Stage Rally in Save-Old-Main Drive." *Greensboro Daily News* 18 March 1972: B7. [Leo Vocu of NCAI will speak; over 1,000 are expected.]

223. Scism, Jack. "Old Main Rally Fails to Draw Big Candidates." *Greensboro Daily News* 19 March 1972: C1.
Major state candidates did not attend. Lumbees' legal counsel says the Council of State failed to have an environmental impact statement prepared before deciding to raze the building.

224. Edwards, Tom. "Old Main: A Commentary." *National Congress of American Indians Bulletin* 28.2 (April 1972): 1, 3. Rpt. in: *Contemporary Newspapers of the North American Indian* (microfilm). [PSU-MLL]
Condemns the Governor's Office, state senators, and PSU Chancellor English Jones for their positions on the planned destruction of Old Main. Quotes Leo Vocu, who gave the keynote address at the Save Old Main rally.

225. Ackley, Randall. "Discussion: Pembroke State University." *Indian Historian* ns 5.2 (Summer 1972): 43-45.
Contends that PSU has "always been White dominated." Cites refusal to sponsor an Upward Bound program; White preponderance in faculty, administration, and students; lack of curriculum and services aimed at Indian students; low faculty salaries; and insensitivity in planning the Indian Studies program.

226. Bledsoe, Jerry. "Lew Barton Seeks the Middle of Indian-Centered Controversy." *Greensboro Daily News* 12 March 1973: B1. [Old Main controversy.]

227. "Indians Waiting for Word." *Greensboro Record* 19 March 1973: A1.
Old Main was gutted by fire. Tuscaroras held a vigil outside the remains, waiting to hear the governor's statement.

228. "Two Persons Hurt in Fights After Blaze Guts Old Main." *Greensboro Daily News* 19 March 1973: A1.
The cause of the fire was not yet determined. The governor offered $5,000 for information leading to the perpetrator.

229. McLaurin, C. E. "Old Main, Grocery Destroyed as Robeson Fire Continues." *Robesonian* 19 March 1973: 1.
Detailed account, with comments from Howard Brooks.

230. "The Gutting of Old Main." *Greensboro Daily News* 27 March 1973: A6.
Editorial. Arson "poisons the political dialogue, and divides people who ought to be united."

231.   Cline, Ed. "Old Main Likely to Cost Taxpayers a Million-Plus." *Greensboro Daily News* 10 June 1973: A1.
A federally-funded study commission will give a reconstruction estimate and decide how the building should be used.

232.   North Carolina State University. School of Design. Community Development Group. *Old Main Study*. August, 1974. 111 p. [IERC] [NCS] [NCSL]
On the feasibility of renovating Old Main. Sections include: Historical overview of the controversy; economic impact of Old Main on the community; sociological impact; educational programming; and suggested design concepts.

233.   "Grant Announced for Restoration." *Greensboro Daily News* 8 March 1975: B6.
$30,000 was authorized to begin restoration. The Old Main Commission has requested $1.3 million.

234.   "Red Man 'Rubbed Wrong' by Pembroke Aid Status." *Greensboro Daily News* 28 Aug. 1975: A4.
Chancellor English Jones states that Lumbees are eligible for minority student aid at any North Carolina college except PSU.

235.   Warren, Gene. "Pembroke Campus Has Indian Relics on Display." *Greensboro Daily News* 18 July 1976: C2.
The Native American Resource Center has been open for two years.

236.   Allen, Robert Craig. "Beliefs Held by Selected Robeson County Leaders Regarding Robeson Technical Institute." Diss. North Carolina State U, 1977.
Allen interviewed 122 Robeson County leaders. He found significant relations between ethnic origin and beliefs about RTI's policies, financing, and purpose/objectives. Includes detailed background information on the school.

237.   Warren, Gene. "Dr. English E. Jones: A Great American Indian." *Pembroke Magazine* no. 11 (1979): 274-77. [PSU-MLL]
Brief sketch highlighting the adversities Jones overcame, his accomplishments, and his support of *Pembroke Magazine*.

238.   Warren, Gene. "Dedication of Indian Teacher Inspired Escape from Poverty." *Robesonian* 25 March 1979: 6C. "Shrapnel Bit is Momento [sic] of Duty in World War II." *Robesonian* 1 April 1979: 8A. "Administrative Talent Seen Early in Career." *Robesonian* 8 April 1979: 8A. "'Right Man at Right Time' Propelled PSU Expansion." *Robesonian* 15 April 1979: 1C.
Biographical series, "The English Jones Story," occasioned by the statewide English Jones Day, 20 April 1979.

239.   Lynn, Lynette B. "Jones Says His Farewell to PSU." *Robesonian* 22 April 1979: 7B.
Describes an appreciation dinner. During Jones's 17 years as chancellor, PSU grew from 35 to 95 acres, 9 to 25 buildings, and 570 to 2,000 enrollment.

240. O'Connor, Paul. "PSU Chancellor Selection Process Hit." *Robesonian* 1 May
      1979: 1.
The faculty is demoralized by delays and by the addition of a name to the list of
candidates sent to the UNC Board of Governors.

241. O'Connor, Paul. "Friday Expected to Name Givens as PSU Chancellor."
      Robesonian 11 May 1979: 1.
Givens has been announced to PSU faculty and will be recommended to the Board of
Governors. UNC System President William Friday received numerous letters and a
petition in support of two Indian candidates.

242. "Pembroke Appointment Angers Legislator." *News and Observer* 12 May 1979:
      25.
Horace Locklear wants the resignation of UNC System President William Friday for
his appointment of Paul Givens over two Indian candidates.

243. O'Connor, Paul. "Dr. Givens Asks for Chance: 'To Show What I Can Do'."
      Robesonian 13 May 1979: 7B.
Will work with the Indian community to "develop as strong an institution as we can."
Discusses his plans for PSU and his views of its problems.

244. O'Connor, Paul. "Turner Rebuts Locklear's Criticism." *Robesonian* 15 May
      1979: 1.
E. B. Turner, Secretary of the UNC System Board of Governors, wanted to support an
Indian candidate; but "divisions in the Indian community made it impossible" for one
of the two Indian candidates to be elected.

245. Lowry, Shirley. "Sees New PSU Chancellor as Serving 'Long, Vital Need'."
      Robesonian 28 May 1979: 6.
Lowry, a PSU alumna, believes Givens wants to do what's best for the university.

246. Lynn, Lynette B. "Anti-Givens Rally Fails to Materialize." *Robesonian* 4 June
      1979: 1.
The speakers listed on an anonymous rally announcement were never invited to speak.

247. Lynn, Lynette B. "Givens Opposed by Indian Commission." *Robesonian* 8
      June 1979: 1-2.
The North Carolina Commission of Indian Affairs adopted a list of actions to take in
voicing its opposition.

248. Swofford, Stan. "Job Choice Racist, Lumbees Maintain." *Greensboro Daily
      News* 23 June 1979: A1.
Account of UNC System president William Friday's meeting with Lumbee leaders
about the appointment of Givens.

249. O'Connor, Paul. "Indians Appeal for Unity at Protest Rally." *Robesonian* 24
      June 1979: 1A.
Two hundred gather to protest the appointment of Givens as PSU chancellor.

250. O'Connor, Paul. "Lumbee-HEW Meeting: 'Limited Success'." *Robesonian* 1
   July 1979: 1.
Attendees discussed changes in minority scholarship programs, rumors about down-grading of PSU's university status, appointment of Givens, and definition of Indian for
Title IV Indian Education funds.

251. Marks, Eddie. "Pembroke Candidate Files Discrimination Complaint."
   Greensboro Daily News 24 July 1979: A1.
Joseph Oxendine filed a complaint with the Equal Employment Opportunity Commis-sion. He was the top candidate submitted by PSU's selection committee and felt the
Board of Governors' decision was strictly racial.

252. Middleton, Lorenzo. "N.C. Indians Oppose Selection of a White to Head
   College Originally Built for Them." *Chronicle of Higher Education* 18.22 (6
   Aug. 1979): 1, 10.
Indians feared Paul Givens' appointment would cause a dissociation of PSU from its
Indian heritage and community. The selection of Givens over two Lumbee semifinal-ists was labelled racist. Other fears and complaints are discussed.

253. Warren, Gene. "Givens Seeks Greater Cooperation." *Robesonian* 2 Oct. 1979:
   11.
Givens addressed the Pembroke Lions Club, urging PSU-community interaction to
solve local problems.

254. Henshaw, Diana M. "An Analysis of Barriers to Post-Secondary Educational
   Participation by Mature Women." Diss. North Carolina State U, 1980.
A preliminary questionnaire was administered to a self-selected sample of women 25
or older enrolled at Pembroke State University or Robeson Technical Institute in the
spring of 1978. [The actual research study was conducted in Texas.] The 27-item
questionnaire was completed by 311 women. More minority than White women felt
less than well prepared for college work and preferred group discussion or student
reports over lectures. Reprints the questionnaire and total responses.

255. Lynn, Lynette. "Old Main Rededicated Saturday." *Robesonian* 17 Feb. 1980: 1.
The ceremony was attended by 400. Speakers included Janie Maynor Locklear and
North Carolina Governor Holshouser. Locklear was a major figure in the "Save Old
Main" movement. See also obituary listing her accomplishments: 2 Dec. 1992: 1, 10.

256. Pate, J. L. "PSU Cheers Rededication of Old Main." *Fayetteville Observer* 17
   Feb. 1980: 1A.
Old Main is the "only structure in the U.S. formerly used for an all-Indian college."

257. Sharpe, John. "Old Main History Series Is Planned." *Robesonian* 17 Feb. 1980:
   1D.
A radio program and county-wide lecture series will serve as a follow-up to the
rededication ceremony. The idea came from John Rimberg's sociology class at PSU.

258. Wright, Bill. "Givens Believes 'He's Accepted'." *Fayetteville Observer* 9 May

1980: 1B.
Lists Givens' first-year efforts to improve communication with the community and plans for PSU's future.

259. "Dr. English Jones Dies After Extended Illness." *Carolina Indian Voice* 21 May 1981: 1-2, 8. Rpt. in *Carolina Indian Voice* 20 Jan. 1983: 13A.
Jones, PSU's first Indian president, died on May 18 (see entry 264, p. 82). The article reviews PSU's growth during his 17-year administration; his work with the public schools and extension service before coming to PSU; his involvement with Harper's Ferry Baptist Church; and the many honors he received. Note: A tribute to Jones, reprinted from the *Robesonian*, appeared in *Congressional Record*, 90th Cong., 1st Sess., 9 June 1981, pp. 11919-11920.

260. Oxendine, Reginald Lee. "A Study of Participation in Adult Education Programs of American Indians in a North Carolina Correctional Institution." Diss. North Carolina State U, 1982. [ECU]
Investigates Indian inmates' participation in the Robeson County Prison's education programs. Only 40% participated in 1981. They preferred social education and vocational programs over adult basic education.

261. Lowry, Jason B. "Letter to Gene Warren, PSU, Director of Public Information." Unpublished typescript. Jan. 1984. 37 p. [IERC]
Voices concerns about extremes in Warren's coverage of some Lumbees and gives opinions on the advancement of Lumbees and PSU. A table of contents lists the many individuals mentioned.

262. Church, Leon H. "Riddle of History Solved in Lebanon." *The Lebanon Advertiser* [Lebanon, IL] 6 June 1984: 5. Rpt. in *Carolina Indian Voice* 12 July 1984: 1, 7.
Gives information sent to Church by Clifton Oxendine and Earl C. Lowry. Includes photographs of ten Lumbees who attended McKendree College (Lebanon, IL) between 1924 and 1935. Shows Lowry's genealogy (back to James Lowry, judge of Virginia in 1666) and the movement of White's Lost Colony, 1587-1711.

263. Evans, R. L. "Opposition to Proposed Name Change of Pembroke State University Surfaces." *Fayetteville Observer* 4 Dec. 1984: 1B.
A group of Lumbees opposes a proposal to change the school's name to University of North Carolina at Pembroke. The final decision rests with the N.C. General Assembly.

264. Eliades, David K., and Linda Ellen Oxendine. *Pembroke State University: A Centennial History.* Columbus, GA: Brentwood UP, 1986. 110 p. [PSU-MLL]
This thorough, readable account covers: founders, administrators, buildings, curricular changes, distinguished faculty, campus publications, and impact on the county. Campus- and community-wide issues discussed include Old Main, de-Indianization, and the UNC-P movement. Photographs, appendices, and selective bibliography.

265. Ohles, John F., and Shirley M. Ohles. *Public Colleges and Universities.* New York: Greenwood, 1986. Pp. 565-66.

Brief historical overview of PSU, covering growth to 1940 (when the first bachelor's degrees were offered); racial composition; name changes; chancellors; names and construction dates of buildings; programs offered; student organizations; and more.

266. Warren, Gene, ed. *Centennial Report, 1887-1987*. Pembroke: The University, 1986? 30 p. [PSU-MLL]
Covers PSU's history, recent accomplishments, and facilities, with many photographs. Includes Chancellor's Scholars, *Pembroke Magazine*, Native American Resource Center, Performing Arts Center, graduate programs, athletics, and enrollment statistics.

267. Seessel, Adam. "Pembroke State Remembers Its Indian Heritage." *News and Observer* 31 Aug. 1986: 41A.
Brief overview, occasioned by the centennial celebration.

268. Pullen, Lisa. "Pembroke to Mark Centennial." *Charlotte Observer* 5 March 1987: 5D.
List of events commemorating the centennial of the passage of a state law, introduced by Hamilton McMillan, founding the school.

269. Wilson, Bonnie. "Squabble Resurfaces Over PSU Name-Change Proposal." *Fayetteville Times* 29 June 1987: B1.
Reviews the UNC System Board of Governors' 1985 endorsement of changing PSU's name to University of North Carolina at Pembroke. Mentions a 1984 opinion survey.

270. Seessel, Adam. "Lumbee Historian Dedicated to the Only Land He Knows." *News and Observer* 15 March 1988: 3D.
Adolph Dial, Tar Heel of the Week, has a national reputation as a spokesperson for his people. He taught for 30 years at PSU, coauthored *The Only Land I Know*, built two shopping centers, served on the American Indian Policy Review Commission, helped start the Lumbee Bank, and more.

271. Witten, Scott. "Discussion at PSU Forum Centers on Race of School's Next Chancellor." *Robesonian* 15 Nov. 1988: 1A.
Open forum held by the Chancellor Selection Committee.

272. "Indian Wanted as Head of PSU." *Winston-Salem Journal* 26 Dec. 1988: 34.
Comments from Jack Morgan, Horace Locklear, and Ken Maynor. Joseph Oxendine has local support.

273. Talbert, Malissa. "County Group Supports Oxendine for PSU Post." *Robesonian* 6 April 1989: B1.
A triracial group of thirty county residents favors Joseph Oxendine.

274. Warren, Gene. "PSU's 'Givens Era' Keyed to Personal Diplomacy." *Robesonian* 30 April 1989: C1. [Reviews accomplishments of retiring chancellor.]

275. Warren, Gene. "New PSU Chancellor Wants 'To Impact on the Community'." *Robesonian* 29 June 1989: 14A.

PSU should aid the public schools and the social climate, cultural level, and economics of Robeson County.

276. Rives, Julie Powers. "A Native Son Returns as Cool Healer, 40 Years Later." *News and Observer* 30 July 1989: 3D. Rpt. in *CIV* 3 Aug. 1989: 2.
Joseph B. Oxendine, new PSU chancellor, is Tar Heel of the Week. He plans to "use the strength of this office to heal and to act as a unifying influence in the community." Gives biographical data and comments from family and former colleagues.

277. Culbreth, John. "Oxendine Installed as Chancellor, Pledges PSU to Community Service." *Robesonian* 29 Oct. 1989: 1A, 10A.
Describes the installation service and summarizes Oxendine's remarks. He is the college's second Native American president.

278. Warren, Gene. "PSU's Chancellor Happy with His First Year in Office." *Robesonian* 1 July 1990: 1C.
Gives Joseph Oxendine's views on his accomplishments during the year and explains his plans for the future of PSU.

279. Warren, Gene. "Prine Retiring After 48 Years at PSU." *Robesonian* 10 Jan. 1991: 6A.
Berteen Prine has been secretary or administrative assistant to every PSU president or chancellor since 1943.

280. "Class of '35's Howard Oxendine Remembers Indian Normal's Song." *Robesonian* 8 Feb. 1991: 8B.
Gives the lyrics to "Indian Normal School," written in the early 1930's by A. F. Corbin, the school's first agricultural teacher and shop foreman.

281. "Getting Heads Together to Educate in Robeson." *Robesonian* 14 Feb. 1991: 4A.
This editorial commends the recent involvement of both PSU faculty and Robeson Community College in several programs for Robeson County children.

282. Bridges, Elinor. "PSU Library's History Linked to Progress." *Robesonian* 26 April 1992: C1.
Discusses changes in the library's facilities; collection growth; and introduction of information technology. Recounts the individuals who have served as head librarian.

283. "Oxendine Attends Indian Conference." *Robesonian* 18 Nov. 1992: 6A.
Linda Oxendine attended the National Indian Education Association conference and distributed brochures on PSU's opportunities for American Indian students. PSU hopes to increase its 23% American Indian enrollment.

LUMBEE CULTURE

284. Chesnutt, Charles Waddell. *Mandy Oxendine: A Novel*. [1897?] Ed. Charles Hackenberry. Urbana: U of Illinois P, 1994? [Annot. based on dissertation.]

Mandy Oxendine is the earliest and, according to Hackenberry, probably the most significant of Chesnutt's six unpublished novels (*DAI* 43-01, July 1982, p. 168-A). It is "the story of two fair-skinned lovers of mixed race ancestry who have chosen to live on opposite sides of the color line" ("Introduction," p. 1). The novel, begun sometime between 1889 and 1894 and probably finished in 1897 ("Introduction"), was set 75 miles from Sampson County, the former home of the two lovers, Mandy Oxendine and Tom Lowrey. The prejudices suffered by people of mixed race, and their lack of opportunity, are major themes in the novel. Mandy Oxendine moves from her home and decides to pass for White. Tom Lowrey also leaves home, to improve his opportunities by getting a college degree and teaching; but he never gives up his love for Mandy. Mandy is courted by a wealthy White man, Robert Utley, who she hopes will marry her. Utley is murdered, and both Mandy and Tom confess to the crime—bringing several situations to a head. Numerous clues permit interpretation of the two lovers as Lumbee (known then as Croatan). Chesnutt had attended, taught at, and been principal of what became Fayetteville State University, so he undoubtedly encountered Lumbee people. Both Mandy and Tom grew up in Sampson County; Tom remarks that "there are a good many Oxendines" there. Besides the two lovers, other characters have Lumbee or Robeson County surnames (Revels, Brewington, Pate, McMillan, Murchison). There are mentions of the Lumberton Plank Road and "Rosinville." Mandy sings an old song brought over by "the Scotch exiles who with Flora McDonald had settled the Cape Fear." Most importantly, Chesnutt provides a lengthy description of North Carolina's "free colored people" (from whom Tom and Mandy descended) and the inequities they suffered. He explains how the "blood of three races commingled" formed Mandy's temperament. Her time period and her environment made her feel, "A person has got to be white or black in this worl', an' I ain't goin' to be black." [Note: I am preparing a journal article exploring *Mandy Oxendine* as a novel of the Lumbees. GES]

285. Baily, Waldron. *The Homeward Trail*. New York: W. J. Watt, 1916. 313 p.
This novel, by a North Carolina businessman and outdoorsman (see *Dictionary of North Carolina Biography* v. 1 (1979) p. 86), is set near the end of the Civil War. The main character is David, a young mountain boy. Henry Berry Lowry is depicted as the fifty-year-old chief of a Croatan settlement 75 miles south of Salem. David falls in love with Lowry's daughter, princess of the tribe.

286. Parsons, Elsie Clews. "Folk-lore of the Cherokee of Robeson County, North Carolina." *Journal of American Folklore* 32.125 (July-Sept. 1919): 384-93. [PSU-MLL]
Notes Black and White (probably Scotch) sources in Indian tales, riddles, and beliefs. Describes Indian quilting, reprints 25 riddles, and discusses tales (especially about witches), superstitions, and folk remedies.

287. Green, Paul. *The Last of the Lowries: A Play of the Croatan Outlaws of Robeson County, North Carolina*. New York: Samuel French, 1922.
—Reprints and Anthologies: Samuel French 1925, 1950. In *Carolina Folk-Plays*. Ed. Frederick H. Koch. New York: Henry Holt, 1922. Pp. [113]-48. In *The Lord's Will and Other Carolina Plays*. By Paul Green. New York: Samuel French, 1928. Pp. [228]-64. In *More One-Act Plays by Modern Authors*. Ed. Helen Louise Cohen.

New York: Harcourt, Brace, 1927. Pp. 37-64. In *Plays as Experience: One-Act Plays for the Secondary School*. Ed. Irwin J. Zachar. New York: Odyssey, 1944. Pp. 79-99. In British and American Drama series, no. 4043. Microfiche. Cambridge: General Microfilm Co., 19??
—Set in Scuffletown in the winter of 1864. Features Henry Berry Lowry and other family members. This was the first play produced by the Carolina Playmakers.

288.   "Playmakers Delight Large Audience at Red Springs." Robesonian 20 Nov. 1924: 1.
Carolina Playmakers perform William Norment Cox's *The Scuffletown Outlaws*. Cox grew up in the Robeson County town of Rowland.

289.   Cox, William Norment. "The Scuffletown Outlaws: A Carolina Folk-Play." *Southwest Review* 11.3 (April 1926): [179]-204. [PSU-MLL]
—Reprints and Anthologies: In *The Carolina Folk-Plays. Third Series*. Ed. Frederick H. Koch. New York: Henry Holt, 1928. Pp. [1]-42. In *North Carolina Drama*. Ed. Richard Walser. Richmond, VA: Garrett & Massie, 1956. Pp. [35]-56. In *The Scholastic* [Pittsburgh: Scholastic Pub. Co.] 14 (11 May 1929): 6-7, 30-32; 14 (25 May 1929): 8-9, 28.
—Two-scene play featuring Henry Berry Lowry and other family members. Frederick H. Koch's introduction discusses the writing, performance, and reception of the play and notes another version of Henry Berry Lowry's death. *The Carolina Folk-Plays, Third Series* adds a page on "The Croatan Dialect."

290.   Buffalo Child Long Lance [Sylvester Clark Long]. *Long Lance: The Autobiography of a Blackfoot Chief*. New York: Cosmopolitan, 1928.
A. LaVonne Ruoff (*American Indian Literatures*, 1990) states that this is "actually a fictional account of growing up on the far western Plains, beginning in the 1890's" (p. 70). Simply and engagingly written, it describes Blackfeet battles with enemy tribes, the brutal indoctrination of male children, war dances, strength contests, the derivation of Indian names, medical practices, the Sun Dance, hunting, Chief Carry-the-Kettle, warrior Almighty Voice, and more. Smith (entry 356) discusses at length this book by a Croatan who gained acclaim and acceptance by claiming to be a Blackfoot. Microfilmed by the Library of Congress.

291.   Johnson, Gerald W. *By Reason of Strength*. New York: Milton, Balch & Co., 1930.
Brief mention. Catharine Whyte, the main character in this novel set before and during the Civil War, leaves Scotland with her husband to set up a farm and a ministerial practice in the Robeson County area. Later in life, she goes to Scuffletown for three weeks and uses medicinal herbs to treat a smallpox outbreak among the Croatans (pp. 111-127). The novel is "based on [Johnson's] family's migration from Scotland to America" (*Dictonary of North Carolina Biography*, vol. 3 [UNC Press, 1988], p. 290). The Whytes are mentioned in entries 1054 and 1057.

292.   Jackson, George Pullen. *White Spirituals of the Southern Upland*. 1933. New York: Dover, 1965. Pp. 417-18.
Brief mention. Describes singing conventions among Robeson County Indians and

includes a letter from John R. Oxendine, Lumbee singing teacher, on shape-note music.

293. Buffalo Child Long Lance [Sylvester Clark Long]. *Redman Echoes: Comprising the Writings of Chief Buffalo Child Long Lance and Biographical Sketches by his Friends.* Los Angeles: Frank Wiggins Trade School, Dept. of Printing, 1933.
Includes Long's writings on Canadian Indians, the Carlisle Indian School, and West Point; some speeches and correspondence; his military service record; and newspaper articles, letters of commendation, essays, and poems about him. Many photographs.

294. Snider, Evelyn, and Hubbard Fulton Page. *Beyond Revenge.* [Unpublished play.] 1936. [Not seen.]
Play written by two Campbell College faculty members and performed on May Day in 1936. Based on Paul Green's *Last of the Lowries.* Note: Snider does not have a script, nor is there a copy in the Campbell College Archives. Both Page and his wife are deceased (from correspondence).

295. "Story of Robeson Indians Is May Day Play at Campbell." *Robesonian* 30 April 1936: 5. [*Beyond Revenge.*]

296. "May Day Play at Campbell Based on Lowry Outlaw Gang of Robeson." *Robesonian* 7 May 1936: 6.
Three descendants of Henry Berry Lowry attended, as did Paul Green.

297. "Singing Convention at Normal Biggest in History of Event." *Robesonian* 8 April 1938: 2. (*Odako* vol. 1 no. 12—special supplement)
Nineteen localities were represented; delegations listed.

298. "'Swamp Outlaw,' Play with Setting in Robeson County, Is Well Received." *Robesonian* 26 July 1939: 5.
The Carolina Playmakers presented Clare Johnson Marley's play about the Lowry Gang at the Playmakers Theater in Chapel Hill. Dr. Frederick Koch announced that this play completes a trilogy on the Lowry Gang.

299. "Clare Marley Reads 'Swamp Outlaw' to Lumbee Study Club." *Robesonian* 10 Nov. 1939: 5.
Mentions club members in attendance and summarizes the play.

300. "'Swamp Outlaw' to Be Presented in Missouri Festival." *Robesonian* 13 Nov. 1939: 2.
Permission was requested to produce the play in the state's folk play festival. Marley is working on another play set in Robeson County.

301. Deloria, Ella. *Life Story of a People.* [Pageant.] Pembroke: Pembroke State College for Indians, 1940. [Not seen.]
This community pageant was performed in Pembroke in 1940 and 1941. No extant script has been located. Sources queried include the library of the University of South Dakota; that university's Institute of Indian Studies, where Deloria's papers are

housed; and Robeson County libraries. Vine Deloria, Jr. reports that the family does
not have a copy (from correspondence).

302. Lucas, John Paul, Jr., and Bailey T[roy] Groome. *The King of Scuffletoun: A
    Croatan Romance*. Richmond, VA: Garrett and Massie, 1940. [PSU-MLL]
Five-part novel on Henry Berry Lowry and Rhoda, "based for the most part on the
story told to the late Bailey T. Groome by Sinclair Lowrie, a brother of the outlaw" (p.
vii). Lucas invented characters; he notes that only the Lowries and their cousins
actually existed.

303. Marley, Clare Johnson. "Swamp Outlaw: A Drama of the Croatan Rebellion."
    Carolina Play Book. Chapel Hill: The Carolina Playmakers, May 1940-Dec.
    1941. Pp. 10-21. [PSU-MLL]
Brief one-act play featuring Henry Berry Lowry, Rhoda, Steve Lowrie, Shoemaker
John, Owen Wright, and Brant Harris. Contains numerous allusions to Henry Berry's
family history, the Lost Colony theory, and Lumbee history. A photograph of a
production of the play appears in *Players Magazine* 19.8 (May 1943): 24.

304. Thompson, Marshall. "Ethnologist Links Robeson Indians with 'Lost Colony'."
    Greensboro Daily News 1 Dec. 1940: A9.
Presents Deloria's professional background and her opinions on the Lost Colony
theory. Note: A brief article on Deloria and *Life Story of a People* from the *Sioux
Falls* [South Dakota] *Daily Argus Leader* is reprinted in *Congressional Record*, 77th
Cong., First Sess. (1941), Appendix, p. A5715.

305. "Pageant Has Large Cast to Show Phases of Indian Life." *Robesonian* 3 Dec.
    1940: 1, 6.
Lists cast members for principal parts in *Life Story of a People*. Outline of the
pageant, p. 7. The three-part pageant portrays aboriginal life; life along the "Old
Lumbee" River (including church, education, and the Lowry Gang); progress since
1885 (including the American Legion, a children's clinic, and scouting); and Indian
loyalty to home, family, country, and God.

306. "Students Take Leading Roles; Scenes Will Depict Life from Primitive Stage to
    Present Day Progress." *Charlotte Observer* 5 Dec. 1940: 8.
Mentions a scene in which "the post commander reads the honor roll of [13] Robeson
Indians who made the supreme sacrifice in the World War" and points out that there
were also 13 leading members of the Lowry Gang.

307. "Capacity Audience Sees First Performance of Pageant at Pembroke School."
    News and Observer 6 Dec. 1940: 2.
Describes the plot, staging, and community participation in *Life Story of a People*.
About 150 people (mostly students from the Normal School and other area schools)
participated in the two-hour pageant, "told for the most part in pantomime, and with
disarming candor and good will." The play "suggested" the Indians' kinship with the
Lost Colony. The presentation of the Henry Berry Lowry period was "almost
gingerly" in its scripting, but the participants were enthusiastic. Polly Lowery
Oxendine, last surviving daughter of Henry Berry Lowry, appeared, as did a great-

nephew of the outlaw. Lowry's Winchester rifle was used as a prop.

308. Speck, Frank G. *Gourds of the Southeastern Indians: A Prolegomenon on the Lagenaria Gourd Culture of the Southeastern Indians*. Boston: New England Gourd Society, 1941. Pp. 72-75. [PSU-MLL]
Information from Hayes Lochalear, Chesley Lockee, and Lochey Oxendine on the use of gourds for water pails and dippers, soup ladles, birdnests, lifebelts for children learning to swim, and vivarium for fish bait.

309. "Indian in National Defense to Be New Feature of Pembroke Pageant." *Robesonian* 29 Oct. 1941: 3.
Mentions changes for the 1941 season of *Life Story of a People*. Ella Deloria was employed by the Indians themselves this year.

310. "Robeson Indians Open Pageant Tonight." *News and Observer* 5 Dec. 1941: 16.
Second annual production of *Life Story of a People*. Lists members of committees for production, finance, and publicity.

311. Lowry, Ira Pate. "The Instrumental Music of the Indians of Robeson County, North Carolina." Thesis. Ohio State U, 1942. [PSU-MLL]
Lowry visited Indian schools to record their music needs and accomplishments. This history, based partly on interviews, notes the first band (Clint Burns, 1905); early concerts; instrumental music in the schools; music at PSC; and Ella Deloria's pageant. Lowry was long-time chairperson of PSU's Music Department and a major benefactor of the school; for his obituary, see *Robesonian* 24 Aug. 1992: 1A. See also a related article, *Robesonian* 27 Nov. 1992: 4A.

312. Ater, Elma Louise. "A Historical Study of the Singing Conventions of the Indians of Robeson County, North Carolina." Thesis. Ohio State U, 1943.
Singing conventions were "gatherings of groups of singers from the churches of one denomination ... at a central meeting place for ... singing religious music." Ater used interviews, questionnaires and observation to compile this history.

313. Dunlap, A. R. "The Speech of the Croatans." *American Speech* 21.3 (Oct. 1946): 231-32.
Says Stephen B. Weeks' observations on Croatan speech (in entry 508) may interest readers of this journal, but they "should make allowance for the fact that Professor Weeks was a historian and not a linguist." Reprints the pertinent paragraph.

314. "Book 'Croatan' by Pembroke Man Will Probably Be Made into Movie." *Pembroke Progress* 22 Jan. 1948. [PSU-MLL. PSU Clippings File.]
A book by Bill Paul, son of A. Y. Paul, has the Lost Colony theory as a backdrop but centers on Henry Berry Lowry. *Croatan* is not the book's original title. Paul dropped the movie project due to insufficient funding; see *CIV* 11 Nov. 1976: 4.

315. Burnt Swamp Singing Convention. Records, 1949-1961. [IERC]
Ledger book maintained by Lacy Maynor, secretary. Lists songs performed, meeting places, and singing groups in attendance.

316. Wellman, Manly Wade. *The Haunts of Drowning Creek*. New York: Holiday, 1951. 205 p.

This juvenile novel involves two boys who set out on a canoe trip on Drowning Creek. Lumbees play minor roles in the boys' search along the river for Chimney Pot House and Confederate gold. For background information on Wellman, see "Manly Wade Wellman: A Tribute," *North Carolina Literary Review* 1.2 (Spring 1993): 54-108.

317. "Construction of National Park Begins: Historical Play to Be Presented in Large Outdoor Amphitheatre." *Scottish Chief* 20 May 1955: 1. [PSU-MLL. PSU Clippings File]

Lumbee Village National Park is being constructed at Red Banks. "On the Banks of the Lumbee," James N. Lowery's pageant featuring Henry Berry Lowry and Virginia Dare, will be presented.

318. "Lumbee Park Is Lowry's Brain Child." *Scottish Chief* 21 July 1955. [PSU-MLL. PSU Clippings File]

James Norman Lowery is chief executive of the Lumbee Park at Red Banks. He hopes his play, "On the Banks of the Lumbee," will be performed there by the Carolina Playmakers in its first year of production. He aspires for the play to eventually be performed by an all-Indian cast. He emphasizes that "Lumbee Park" "has no connection with the name 'Lumbee' as given by the Legislature in 1953" and that he is only chief executive of the park, not chief of the tribe.

319. Barton, Lew. *Rhythm a Little Lumbee*. An Amerind Good Will Publication. N.p: n.p., 1961. 24p. [PSU-MLL]

Several poems by this Lumbee author have Indian themes, including "The Lumbee Trail," "The American Indian," and "Some Popular Misconceptions of the American Indian."

320. Cole, Willard G. "Robeson Indian Drama Proposed." *News and Observer* 8 Dec. 1963.

English Jones suggests a drama based on the Lost Colony theory. The idea came after a Lumbee beauty queen posed as an Indian princess in the legend of Lake Waccamaw.

321. Kimball, Gwen [pseud. of Robert Edward Gard]. *The Puzzle of Roanoke, the Lost Colony*. New York: Duell, Sloan & Pearce, 1964. 136 p.

Juvenile novel about an adolescent library assistant in Wisconsin who helps a wealthy townsperson establish a link between his great-grandmother and John Cheven of the Lost Colony. Her search takes her to a performance of *The Lost Colony*, then to the Robeson County farm of a Lumbee actor in the play.

322. *Lumbee Homecoming Festival*. [Program] Pembroke: N.p., 1970- . [PSU-MLL]

Each program for the annual festival (sponsored by LRDA) includes a calendar of events, sketches of award winners, photographs of Miss Lumbee contestants, and sketches of the master of ceremonies and judges.

323. Owen, Guy. *Journey for Joedel*. New York: Crown, 1970. [PSU-MLL]

Set after World War I, the novel centers on a teenaged Lumbee and his first trip to the tobacco auction. Many incidents in the plot illustrate prejudices against Lumbees. See *Pembroke Magazine* 13 (1981), p. 105 for brief comments by Owen on the novel's Lumbee theme. See *North Carolina Folklore Journal* 24.3 (Nov. 1976): 111-14 for an analysis of the novel's folk motifs.

324. Coit, John. "Indians Organize; Celebrate Holiday." *News and Observer* 5 July 1970: 1.
First Lumbee Homecoming. Independent Americans for Progress elects officers.

325. "'Lost Colony' Sequel on Lumbees Is Planned." *The Pilot* [Southern Pines, N.C.] 5 Aug. 1970. [UNC-WL Clippings File]
Robeson Historical Drama is selling memberships to support the play. Paul Green and Randolph Umberger are writing the script.

326. Bledsoe, Jerry. "The Culture: Not Distinctly Indian: They Have Chosen to Follow the White Man's Ways." *Greensboro Daily News* 17 Jan. 1971: A-14.

327. Haas, Joel. "Celebrating a 'Oneness'." *News and Observer* 11 July 1971: Sec. 4 p. 1. [Lumbee Homecoming reflects the Pan-Indian Movement.]

328. Barton, Lew. "Me-Told Tales Along the Lumbee." *North Carolina Folklore* 19.4 (Nov. 1971): 173-76. [PSU-MLL] Rpt. in *CIV* 21 April 1977: 3.
Recounts stories based on these Lumbee beliefs: tokens; being struck by a spirit as foreshadowing of death; being quiet while digging for buried money so as not to disturb the treasure's guardian; and rootworkers.

329. Warren, Gene. "Gene Locklear: Lumbee Indian Artist Who Made It to Big Leagues." *Robesonian* 29 April 1972.
On Locklear's baseball successes as well as his artistic style. Numerous photographs.

330. Hoover, Daniel C. "Lumbee Fete Draws Crowd." *News and Observer* 2 July 1972: Sec. 1 p. 5.
Third annual Lumbee Homecoming. Notes political accomplishments, two "Save Old Main" floats, and Lew Barton's receipt of the Henry Berry Lowry Award.

331. Oxendine, Lloyd E. "23 Contemporary Indian Artists." *Art in America* 60.4 (July-August 1972): 58-60+.
Brief mention. See p. 60, a photograph of a mixed-media work by Lumbee artist Lloyd Oxendine. The latter founded American Art (the country's first gallery dedicated to contemporary Indian artists) and directed Native North American Artists, the first national association for them. Some of his works are reproduced in Dial (entry 58).

332. "Indian Outdoor Drama Scheduled in Robeson." *The Pilot* [Southern Pines, NC] 6 Sept. 1972. [UNC-WL Clippings File]
Strike at the Wind! begins production next summer; Thad Mull is business manager.

333. Ronnie, Art. *Locklear: The Man Who Walked on Wings.* South Brunswick: A. S. Barnes, 1973.

Ronnie conducted extensive research to document the sixteen-month professional career of stunt pilot and movie star Ormer Leslie Locklear. Locklear was born in 1891 in Greenville, Texas. No mention is made of his having Native American heritage.

334. Fields, Jeff. *A Cry of Angels*. New York: Atheneum, 1974.
Em Jojohn, Lumbee (p. 34), is given to lengthy, rambling trips followed by drunken binges when he returns to Quarrytown, Georgia. He earns money by killing rats and by construction work. He befriends Earl, the fourteen-year-old main character, teaching him to climb trees, swim, and overcome his fear of the dark. He "lives for the moment he's in, and lets the rest slide by" (p. 191), a characteristic that has been noted among Lumbees (see entry 944). Em experiences some problems with racial identity (see pp. 197-200, 312, and 321-22). In chapter 31, Quarrytown's historical society undertakes a search for the grave of Easter Robinson, a historical figure somewhat reminiscent of Henry Berry Lowry. Jojohn is more like Henry Berry Lowry (as Reising also notes in entry 385), particularly at the end of the novel. He uses his prodigious fighting abilities to resolve a political situation in Quarrytown and benefit oppressed residents of all races. Ironically, the resolution probably ended Jojohn's life.

335. Murray, Janette K. "Ella Deloria: A Biographical Sketch and Literary Analysis." Diss. U of North Dakota, 1974. Pp. 136-38.
Brief mention. Deloria, a Dakota Indian linguist, was sent to Pembroke by the Farm Security Administration to write a community pageant on the Lumbees. Murray quotes from two letters Deloria wrote to her advisor, Franz Boas, giving her impressions of them. She mentions their dislike of the name Croatan; physical appearance; disputes between Cherokee and Siouan factions; discrimination by Whites; and attendance of colleges outside North Carolina because of exclusion by all N.C. colleges except PSU.

336. D & L Gospel Singers. *The Holy Hills*. Temple Records. Nashville, TN, LST 394, n.d. [UNC-WL]
A family group of Lumbee gospel singers performs hymns, with guitar accompaniment, which illustrate "that hardships and disappointments are often tests of faith."

337. Evans, William, and Jerome Van Camp. "*To Die Game*." [Unpublished screenplay.] Registered: WGAW. [Los Angeles, CA: Barbara's Place Script Specialists, N.d.] 75 p.
Based on Evans' *To Die Game* (entry 1118). Carefully chosen, colorfully drawn scenes highlight the political background of the Lowry Gang incidents, the role of the Ku Klux Klan, support given the Gang by lower-class Countians of all races, and disparities in living conditions between the upper-class Whites and others in the county. Scenes include: Henry Berry and Rhoda's wedding; the Battle of Wire Grass Landing; Henry Berry's breaking into Col. McQueen's home (John McNair's home in entry 1118), demanding to be served breakfast, and then insisting that McQueen arrange the release of four gang members' wives from the Lumberton Jail; and ambiguity over whether Henry Berry was killed or simply disappeared.

338. Lowery, Willie French. *"Proud to Be a Lumbee."* With Miriam Oxendine and Lumbee Children. 33 1/2 rpm sound disc. Lowery Pub. Co., 812011B-2077, [197?] [IERC]

Songs written, produced, and performed by Lowery, with vocal and instrumental accompaniment by others. Titles include "Proud to Be a Lumbee Indian," "Old Main," "Lumbee Homecoming," "Rowing Down the Lumbee River," "Lumbee Leaders," "Henry and Rhoda's Love Song," and "Henry Berry Lowery Is My Hero."

339. *Lumbees & Friends.* 33 1/2 rpm sound disc. Pembroke: Lumbee Regional Development Associates, [197?]. [IERC] [ECU-ML]
Twenty-six singers (both Lumbee and White) perform 25 Indian songs. The group was founded by Joe Liles, a White. The album is mentioned in *Old Glory: A Pictorial Report on the Grass Roots History Movement* (Warner, 1973), p. 127

340. Umberger, Randolph. [*Strike at the Wind!* Script.] Pembroke: N.p., 197?. [PSU-MLL] [The Henry Berry Lowry story.]

341. Hudson, William Lane, Jr. "Public Relations: Defined and Applied Specifically for Outdoor Drama." Paper for CMA 499. Pembroke State U, Spring 1976. [PSU-MLL]
On Hudson's public relations work as an intern with *Strike at the Wind!* Includes his public service announcements, photographs, and newspaper articles.

342. Jurgensen, Paquita. "Lumbee Indians: Lost Colony Descendants?" *Chapel Hill Newspaper* 18 June 1976. [UNC-WL Clippings File]
Strike at the Wind!, a triracial outdoor drama, will premier on July 1.

343. McNeill, John Charles. *Possums and Persimmons: Newly Collected Poems.* Wendell, NC: Broadfoot's Bookmark, 1977. [PSU-MLL]
Dialect poems from *Wake Forest Student, Century Magazine,* and *Charlotte Observer.* Includes "Quatrain," "Croatan Philosophy," and "In Robeson County."

344. Wallace, Charles. *CARRADINE: An Original Screenplay.* First draft. Unpublished typescript, [1977?] 126 p. [PSU-NARC]
Carradine Lumbee, a Marine who served in Vietnam, inherits a mansion, the surrounding farmland, and a $100,000-a-year salary at the death of his uncle, Auburn Locklear. All locations in the play are "within 50 miles of Fayetteville."

345. Barton, Lew. "List of Common Lumbee Terms." Unpublished typescript. N.d. 9 p. [IERC] [Gives definitions and examples of usage.]

346. Dempsey, Hugh A. "Sylvester Long, Buffalo Child Long Lance." *American Indian Intellectuals.* 1976 Proceedings of the American Ethnological Society. St. Paul: West, 1978. Pp. 197-203. [PSU-MLL]
A difficult question is whether to view Long Lance as "a charlatan and a fraud, or ... a man who desperately wanted to break out of the chains that society had cast upon him." Acknowledges Long's skills as a writer and field worker among native peoples but rues the editorial license he often took, telling events as if they happened to him.

347. Snow, Claude H. "An Annotated Transcription of Eight Lumbee Indian Sermons in Upper Robeson County, North Carolina." Thesis. U of North

Carolina at Chapel Hill, 1978.
Snow, a White Robeson County native, worked with a Lumbee respondent to study
phonological, nonverbal, lexical, and grammatical items indigenous to Lumbees.
Notes that Weeks (entry 508) devoted one paragraph to Lumbee speech, comparing it
to Elizabethan English without explaining the methodology used.

348. Lucas, Sarah. "Outdoor Drama Production Crews, Actors Get Ready." *Robeso-*
          nian 19 June 1979: 15.
Strike at the Wind! enters its fourth season. Article focuses on Julian Ransom.

349. Munger, Guy. "An Indian Whose Heart Is Filled with Music." *News and*
          Observer 11 Nov. 1979: Sec. 4 p. 3.
Willie French Lowery, Tar Heel of the Week, wrote the score for *Strike at the Wind!*
He received an award from the North Carolina Federation of Music Clubs for his
album, *Proud to Be a Lumbee* (entry 338). He is distantly related to Henry Berry
Lowry. See *Robesonian* 14 Oct. 1992: C1 and 2 Sept. 1993: 3B on Lowery's recording
studio, Soundsation, focusing on local gospel music.

350. Schmalleger, Frank. "Criminal Justice-Related Magical Practices Among the
          Lumbee Indians of North Carolina." Paper presented at the Conference of the
          Academy of Criminal Justice Sciences, May 1980. 11 p. [PSU-MLL]
Schmalleger and his students interviewed ten Lumbee rootworkers, focusing on the
origins, transmission, and powers of rootworking. Some 25 rootworkers practice in the
county, with clients of all races. Their methods include courtroom dusting, spells,
roots, the evil eye, and dirt from someone's tracks.

351. Jennings, Jan. "Ex-Padre Outfielder Hopes to Make Big Hit as Artist." [San
          Diego, CA] *Tribune* 29 Sept. 1980. Rpt. in *NewsBank: Fine Arts and Architec-*
          ture vol. 7 (July 1980-June 1981) card 6: G9-10.
Gene Locklear retired from baseball in 1978. He now paints and sketches "Indian
scenes, sports figures and basic Americana," but 75% of his work has Indian themes.

352. Reising, Robert W. "The Literature of the Lumbee Indians: An Introduction."
          Pembroke Magazine 13 (1981): 48-54. [PSU-MLL]
Includes a 56-item "Selected Bibliography of Belletristic Literature By and/or About
the Lumbee Indians," grouped into seven categories and noting Lumbee authors. The
introduction explains selection criteria, discusses the categories, and identifies areas
needing further research. Forty-five items are by Lumbees.

353. Schmalleger, Frank. "The Root Doctors and the Courtroom." *North Carolina*
          Folklore Journal 29.2 (Fall-Winter 1981): 102-05.
Schmalleger and his students interviewed ten Lumbee conjurers in 1980. Conjurers try
to influence witnesses and the judge. They attribute any failure of their methods to the
client's lack of faith or faulty followthrough on instructions.

354. Wilbur Smith and Associates. *A Feasibility Study and Concept Plan for the*
          North Carolina Indian Cultural Tourist Center. Prepared for the North Carolina
          Commission of Indian Affairs. Columbia, SC: Wilbur Smith and Associates,

November, 1981. [ECU]
This six-month study tried to identify viewpoints of the constituent Indian population; assess the need for cultural resources; evaluate the economic feasibility; identify a possible site; and develop a concept plan. Discusses groups that would attend, estimates costs for the early years of operation, and estimates space needs.

355. Brewer, Jeutonne, and Robert W. Reising. "Tokens in the Pocosin: Lumbee English in North Carolina." *Essays in Native American Speech.* San Antonio: Trinity U, 1982. Also in *American Speech* 57.2 (1982): 108-20.
Lumbee use of certain words, meanings, and pronunciations is part of their ethnic identity. Analyzes writing samples, LRDA oral history tapes, and conversations for use of the words "token," "budges," and "juvimber." Also discusses the Tidewater diphthong, a "linguistic marker" which identifies community of origin.

356. Smith, Donald B. *Long Lance: The True Story of an Impostor.* Toronto: Macmillan, 1982; Lincoln: U of Nebraska P, 1983. [PSU-MLL]
Biography of Sylvester Clark Long, born in Winston, North Carolina, who claimed to be a Blackfoot warrior named Long Lance. His mother was White and Croatan; his father, probably White and Robeson County Cherokee. Sympathetic, engagingly written, and copiously researched, the book shows the wide range of Long's achievements: Canadian military service; New York society; magazine, newspaper, and book writing; a starring role in *The Silent Enemy*; presidential appointment to West Point; boxing; stunt flying; running shoe spokesperson; and the lecture circuit. Smith traces and dissects Long's lies and deceptions but balances these with an understanding of the racial situation, during Long's lifetime, in North Carolina and in the country as a whole. Long's deceptions enabled him to be a spokesperson for Indians and to realize his own ambitions but brought about his suicide at age 42. An award-winning 55-minute color documentary [available at UNC-WL] based on this book was released by the National Film Board of Canada in January, 1987.

357. Bayes, Ronald H., ed. *North Carolina's 400 Years: Signs Along the Way. An Anthology of Poems by North Carolina Poets to Celebrate America's 400th Anniversary.* Durham: Acorn P, 1986. [PSU-MLL]
Includes photographs of twelve artworks by Lumbee Indian Art Guild members Sheila G. Godwin, Derek Lowry, Butch Chavis, DeLora Cummings, and James Locklear.

358. Rinzler, Kate. "The Miracle of Maxton Field." Unpublished typescript. 1988. [IERC]
Two-act documentary drama based on first-hand accounts of the 1958 Klan routing. Covers the 19th-century Klan as well as conditions and events prior to, during, and immediately after the routing. Includes Rinzler's "Ballad of Henry Berry Lowry."

359. Witten, Scott. "Cultural Center Will Bring Boost to Entire County." *Robesonian* 24 July 1988: B1.
The North Carolina Indian Cultural Center could eventually employ 500 people and attract half a million tourists annually. It should be completed by 1995.

360. The Pierces. *Thinkin' Bout Home.* Produced by Milton Smith. Living Waters

Records [Hope Mills, NC], 8823, [1989?]
Nine gospel songs "in memory of Julian." The back of the album cover has a photograph of family member Julian Pierce and a note on his accomplishments.

361. Rollins, Brenda Whitehurst. *"Bane and Blessing."* [Original novel.] Thesis. U
    of South Alabama, 1989. [UNC-WL]
Lelia, a young Lumbee, leaves her abusive White husband Luther but allows her son,
Gordon, to stay with Luther's mother. Gordon devises an ingenious scheme to get his
mother to come home. Gordon also becomes friends with his maternal grandfather,
who once led demonstrations for equal rights for Lumbees. Gordon's identity
problems, due to his mixed-race background, are a major theme.

362. Smith, Donald B. "From Sylvester Long to Chief Buffalo Child Long Lance."
    Being and Becoming Indian: Biographical Studies of North American Frontiers.
    Ed. James A. Clifton. Chicago: Dorsey, 1989. Pp. 183-203. [PSU-MLL]
Sympathetic overview of Long's accomplishments and deceptions, emphasizing the
racial barriers which necessitated the subterfuge and highlighting the sensitivity of
Long's writings about Indians. Editor James A. Clifton notes, "Had this talented man
been born a generation later, he might have marched pridefully with Martin Luther
King, or served the resurgent Lumbee Indians ... in a leadership capacity" (p. 184).

363. Quillin, Martha. "Plans Unveiled for Robeson Indian Center." *News and
    Observer* 1 March 1989: Sec. C p. 1.
Developers announced the first specific plans for the $50 million North Carolina Indian
Cultural Center, to be completed by 2000.

364. Gingrich, Stephanie. "Area Native Promotes Indian Center's Benefits."
    Robesonian 28 March 1989: 5A.
Helen Scheirbeck, development director of the North Carolina Indian Cultural Center.

365. Godfrey, R. L. "Homecoming Renews a Sense of Tradition." *Robesonian* 1
    July 1989. Lumbee Homecoming Supplement, p. 3.
History and purpose of the 20-year-old celebration.

366. Guyton, Nanette. "Lumbee Homecoming Helps Lumbees Keep in Touch with
    Heritage." *Robesonian* 1 July 1989. Lumbee Homecoming Supplement, p. 9.
The annual event helps Lumbees in urban areas maintain the tribal affiliation required
by tribal membership guidelines.

367. Payne, Alton W. "'A Fool's Errand': The Discovery of a Proto-Lumbee
    Language. The True Origin of the Lumbee Indians." Unpublished typescript.
    Sept. 1989. 34 p. [IERC]
Relates place names in Lumbee country to the Maskohegan or Algonquian Indians.
Extensive discussion of the place names Shoe Heel and Ashpole as well as the
surnames Oxendine, Brooks, Braveboy, Dial, Lowrie, O'Berry, Revel, and Locklear.

368. Guyton, Nanette. "The Pierce Family ... Gospel Music Is Their Ministry."
    Robesonian 10 Sept. 1989: C1.

Nine-member group, "compelled to sing," has produced two albums.

369. Rinzler, Kate, and Wanda Locklear. "Going Seining: A Play in Three Acts." Unpublished typescript. 1989.
Based on oral history from Johnny Bullard and others, this children's play, set in the 1920's, involves seining for subsistence, which was outlawed to protect game fishermen. Illustrates sex roles, beliefs about ghosts and tokens, and Lumbee speech.

370. Williams, Bronwyn [pseud. for Dixie Browning and Mary Williams]. *Stormwalker*. Harlequin Historical, vol. 47. Toronto: Harlequin Books, 1990. [UNC-WL]
Stormwalker, a mixed blood who lives among the Hatorask Indians, is the son of a Hatorask chief and a White woman. He was educated in White schools. His aspires to quelch the hostility between Whites and Indians and teach his people to live in the changing, White-influenced world. He dresses as a White, John Walker, when trading in White towns; yet feels shame and confusion over his mixed breeding. Born on the island of Croatoan, he has Indian features except for his blue eyes. He protects, befriends, and falls in love with Laura Gray, a White girl who was raped–and whose parents were killed–by Three Turtle, a Mattamuskeet and formerly his friend.

371. Culbreth, John. "Cultural Center in Jeopardy Due to Land Dispute." *Robesonian* 1 May 1990: 1A.
The North Carolina Commission on Indian Affairs will not lease a 495-acre site to the Center because some want a 100-acre golf course in the middle of the site to be sold to private developers. Related letters and articles which track the progress of the dispute: *News and Observer* 2 April 1990: 1B; *Robesonian* 20 May 1990: 5A; 1 June 1990: 1A; 6 June 1990: 1A; 11 Oct. 1990: 11A; 25 Oct. 1990: 1A; cartoon, 28 Oct. 1990: 4A; Ed. 20 May 1991: 4A; 18 Dec. 1991: 1A; 30 Jan. 1992: 1A; 4 Feb. 1992: 1A; 23 Feb. 1992: "Potpourri" p. 5; 5 April 1992: 1A; 28 May 1992: 4A; 9 June 1992: 4A; 9 July 1992: 1A; 22 Sept. 1992: 4A; 24 Sept. 1992: 1A; 6 Oct. 1992: 4A; *13 Oct. 1992: 1A; 15 Oct. 1992: 1A, 20 Dec. 1992: 1A, and 26 Feb. 1993: 1A.

372. Hamilton, Lee. "Pembroke Artist's Work To Be Sold at SATW Auction." *Robesonian* 25 June 1990: 5A. [DeLora Cummings; see also 27 June 1990: 1A.]

373. Warren, Gene. "[Mike] Wilkins to Exhibit Carving Skills During Heritage Celebration." *Robesonian* 14 Sept. 1990: 1A.

374. McLaurin, Tim. "An Early Planting." *Southern Exposure* 18.4 (Winter 1990): 30-34.
Brief mention. Short story about Buck Calahan, a farmer and former basketball star who is dying of cancer. Dexter Oxendine, his farm hand and friend since high school, helps him fulfill his wish to plant a last field of wheat and see it sprout.

375. Scipio, Sylvester. "D & L Gospel Singers Mark 25th Year Saturday." *Robesonian* 23 Nov. 1990: 6A.
Based in Pembroke, the group performs about 150 concerts a year throughout the Southeast. Initially all members were Dials or Locklears; thus the name "D & L."

376. Guyton, Nanette. "Successful Pembroke Native Encourages Students."
         Robesonian 16 Dec. 1990: 1A.
On Gene Locklear's baseball and art careers. He played outfield for the Cincinnati
Reds, San Diego Padres, and New York Yankees. His paintings hang in the White
House, a Las Vegas casino, Duke University, and PSU. He produced the 1988 Super
Bowl print.

377. Ferbel, Peter Jordan. "Reading Objects, Positioning Selves: Narratives of
         Material Culture and Social Identity at the Museum of the Native American
         Resource Center, Pembroke, North Carolina." Thesis. U of South Carolina,
         1991. [PSU-NARC]
Looks at "how a material expression of Lumbee history and culture can be read as
narratives concerning Lumbee social identity" (p. xiii). Uses the Museum "as a case
study to address academic topics of material culture, museums, and the constitution of
social identity" (p. xiii). [From partial photocopy.]

378. Scipio, Sylvester. "Local Gospel Group Goes National." *Robesonian* 11 Jan.
         1991: 6A.
The Bullards, who have been singing 17 years, have signed a two-year recording
contract with Living Waters Records.

379. Chamberlain, Knight. "Lela Brooks: An Example of the Power of Folk Art."
         Robesonian 3 May 1991: 6A.
Lela Hammonds Brooks, of Saddletree, won a North Carolina Folk Heritage Award for
her tobacco twine crochet needlework.

380. Bigelow, Scott. "SATW Move to I-95 Pondered." *Robesonian* 22 May 1991:
         1A.
The *Strike at the Wind!* Board of Directors will hold public hearings on moving the
drama to the Interstate 95 corridor to attract tourists and boost failing finances. Related
articles, 24 May 1991: 1A; Editorial. 29 May 1991: 4A; Editorial. 26 June 1991: 4A;
18 July 1991: 1A; Letter. 15 March 1993: 4A.

381. Locklear, Barbara Brayboy. "Playwright Lets Native Americans Tell Own
         Story." *Robesonian* 29 Sept. 1991: 1C.
Scott Meltsner is coordinating the Robeson County Indian Play Project, jointly
sponsored by LRDA, Title V Compensatory Indian Education, the North Carolina
Indian Cultural Center, and the Tuscarora Tribe of North Carolina. A writing group of
20 people will produce a pageant on the history and culture of Robeson County
Indians; it will go on tour around the county. Related articles, *Robesonian* 13 May
1992: 7A and 23 April 1993: 7A. IERC has a copy of the script of the pageant.

382. Reising, R. W. "Lumbee Literature and Hero, 'Henry Bear'." *Agora: The
         Magazine for Gifted Students* [Raleigh, NC: AG Publications, Inc.] 6.2 (Jan.
         1992): 7-8.
For this teachers' supplement on Native American literature, Reising gives a terse but
detailed review of literature inspired by the Lumbees. Mentions all genres, with
special attention to works treating Henry Berry Lowry.

383. Guyton, Nanette. "Pembroke Town Council Gives Support to Drama Study."
    Robesonian 3 March 1992: 1A.
The study will help decide whether to move *Strike at the Wind!* to Lumberton. The
play's artistic director supports moving the drama to I-95, making it more accessible to
its primary audience, tourists (see his letter, 4 July 1993: 7A). Lumberton City Council
approved a recommendation by David Carter, chairperson of Robeson Historical
Drama Association, to move the play to Lumberton (27 July 1993: 1A). Randolph
Umberger might revoke the rights to the play if changes aren't made within a year (19
Aug. 1993: 1A).

384. Reising, R. W. "Literary Depictions of Henry Berry Lowry: Mythic, Romantic,
    and Tragic." *MELUS* 17.1 (Spring 1991-1992): 87-103.
Wide-ranging and perceptive, this essay analyzes seven published literary works
depicting Lowry, including *The Last of the Lowries, Swamp Outlaw, The Scuffletown
Outlaws, The King of Scuffletoun*, and *Strike at the Wind!* Reising compares these
works to each other and notes literary parallels and influences on them, including Sir
Walter Scott, John Rollin Ridge, Gladys A. Reichard, and the Trickster.

385. LRDA Public Relations. "Lumbee Fall Festival, Pow-Wow Celebrates Ancient
    Indian Heritage." *Robesonian* 1 Nov. 1992: C1.
Over 25 tribes will participate. The event will "debunk the theory that Lumbee culture
has vanished" and "offer Indian alternative programming in this 500th year of
Columbus' voyage to America." See also 8 Nov. 1992: 1A.

386. N.C. General Assembly. Legislative Research Commission. "North Carolina
    Indian Cultural Center." Report to the 1993 General Assembly of North
    Carolina. [Raleigh]: The Commission, [15 Jan. 1993]. N.C. Docs Microfiche
    Y4/2 2:I39 1993 [PSU-MLL]
The committee held several meetings as well as an open hearing. Recommends that
the state purchase land for a new golf course, open to the public but operated by PSU.
The Cultural Center should be given a long-term lease to its present site. Appendix D
lists accomplishments of the Center as well as funds raised or received as allocations.

387. Owen, Howard. *Littlejohn*. 1992. New York: Villard Books, 1993.
This account of the life of Littlejohn McCain, 82-year-old farmer, includes Lumbees as
minor characters. Kenny Locklear, who teaches high-school agriculture, farms some of
Littlejohn's land; an additional relationship between them is revealed late in the novel.
Littlejohn has an affair with Rose Lockamy, youngest daughter of neighboring Lumbee
tenant farmers, at age 27.

RELIGION

388. Burnt Swamp Baptist Association. Minutes of the Annual Session. 1881-1983.
    [IERC] [UNC]
IERC has photocopies of minutes published by Edwards and Broughton (1881-1901)
and later by Robesonian Printing House (1904-), as well as minutes printed annually in
subsequent years as brochures. Minutes for 1881-1911 (scattered) and 1914-1987 are
also in WFU-BHC. UNC has minutes since 1904.

389. Deep Branch Baptist Church. Manuscripts, 1882-1984. [Not seen.] [WFU]
Photocopies of conference minutes (1882-1897), including membership rolls and rules
of conduct. Contains a church cemetery inventory, ca. 1984. [From OCLC record.]

390. "Notice to Citizens of the Indian Race." *The Argus* 25 Sept. 1902: 2.
"Piously inclined" Indians from Robeson and 11 other counties are invited to a meeting
to organize "a Union Methodist Conference of the Indian Race."

391. "First Baptist Church—Training Indian Preachers." *Robesonian* 11 Feb. 1915:
5. [Minister is training Indian preachers at their church at Deep Branch.]

392. Locklear, A. S. "The Catawba Indians: Reservation of 600 Acres Near Rock
Hill, S.C.—Missionary Work Among Them." *Robesonian* 15 Oct. 1917: 3.
Letter. Locklear, also known as Arren Spencer Lockee, was asked to preach at a new
church built by the Baptist State Convention. Photograph of Lockee at PSU-NARC.

393. Lowry, D. F. "Robeson's Indians Taking Interest in Religious Affairs."
Robesonian Nov. 1937: Sec. 3 p. 6.
Discusses Methodist and Baptist Conferences; gives number of churches, ministers.

394. "Vigorous Church Life." 1940; rpt. *Robesonian* 21 July 1954: 7.
This article by Mary Livermore surveys Indian churches and ministers.

395. "Well Known Religious Leader Lost in Passing of Rev. Maynor." *Pembroke
Progress* 1 Jan. 1948: 1.
The Rev. Arthur Maynor served as a Holiness moderator and an evangelist for the
Mount Olive, Evergreen, and Shiloh churches.

396. Carter, J. L. "Burnt Swamp Association History Traced." *The Biblical
Recorder* 5 Jan. 1949. [Newspaper reprint in PSU-MLL. PSU Clippings File.]

397. Lowry, Reba. "He Carried the Mail for Thirty Years." *Pembroke Progress* 10
Nov. 1949: 1. [The Rev. D. F. Lowry had the Pembroke route.]

398. [Johnson, Guy B.?] "A Survey of the Churches of Robeson County, North
Carolina, 1948-1949." Tentative compilation: 3 Oct. 1948. Revised introductory remarks: 20 Jan. 1950. 12 p. [Included in entry 468].
Churches were visited mainly during the summer of 1948. The survey found 216
churches (three townships were omitted). Estimates the Indian population at over
15,000. Of the Indian churches, 10.8% were Baptist and 6.4% Methodist. Notes a
strong influence by Free Will Baptists, Pentecostal Holiness, and Church of God.
Found that revivalism was important among the Indians, as was righteous living.
Provides a checklist of churches, arranged by township, which gives name, denomination, and race of each church.

399. Robbins, Cecil W. "Meet the Methodists of Pembroke Parish." *North Carolina
Christian Advocate* 23 Aug. 1951: 4-5.
Discusses the Rev. D. F. Lowry; Lumbee denominations and the number of churches in

each; and individual churches in the Pembroke Parish (two in South Carolina).

400. "Burnt Swamp Association Observes 75th Anniversary." [article]. 20 Oct. 1952. [PSU-MLL. PSU Clippings File] [From lecture by John L. Carter.]

401. Thompson, Betty. "A 'Lost Colony' of Methodists?" *World Outlook* [New York: Board of Missions, United Methodist Church] 24 (Aug. 1954): 16-18.
Discusses the Pembroke Parish; D. F. Lowry's role in persuading the state legislature to change the tribe's name to Lumbee; and the tribe's history.

402. Free Will Baptist Historical Collection. Moye Library. Mount Olive College. Mount Olive, NC 28365 (919-658-2502) [Not seen.]
Minutes of the 1957 St. Annah Conference, which included churches in Sampson, Bladen, Robeson, Columbus, and possibly some S.C. counties [from correspondence].

403. Lowry, D. F. "Recalls Lumbee Conference Formed Around Union Chapel." *Robesonian* 9 Jan. 1958.
Letter mentions an upcoming trial on a land dispute between Union Chapel Holiness Methodist Church and the Lumbee Conference and gives background data on the dispute. Lowry states, "It has been discovered that a local group can never amount to anything. The Lumbee Conference is now 57 years old and smaller than it was 50 years ago. No race of people can survive in a local church group." See also Lumbee River Conference of H.M.C. v. Locklear, 98 S.E.2d 453 (7 June 1957).

404. Lowry, D. F. "Calls for Unification of Indian Methodists." *Robesonian* 13 Feb. 1958: [4].
Gives history of the rift; urges merger of Methodist and Holiness Methodist churches.

405. Lowry, D. F. "Stresses Unity for Advance in Indian Church." *Robesonian* 6 March 1958.
After the Klan routing, a *New York Herald Tribune* article asked "how these oldest of all Americans have got themselves into an 'inferior' category." Lowry believes Indians' clannishness caused this misconception. He deplores separate Indian church conferences, stating that "it is impossible to get along without the white man from any angle .... Since we are a local group we must work with another race that is universal."

406. Barton, Lew. "Lumbee Leader Has Lived a Full and Fruitful Life." *Robesonian* 5 Feb. 1959: 16. [On D. F. Lowry.]

407. Barton, Lew. "Day Starts Early, Ends Late for This Friend of Mankind." *Robesonian* 23 March 1959: 5. [Venus Brooks.]

408. "Pleasant Grove Church Organized in 1900." *The Lumbee* 11 Nov. 1965: 1.
Daniel Edwin Lowry, the only living charter member, recounts the formation of the Lumbee Conference of Methodists and the construction of Pleasant Grove.

409. "Rev. D. F. Lowry Day Observed at Pembroke First Methodist Church." *North Carolina Christian Advocate* 111.1 (6 Jan. 1966): 1, 5.

Reviews the church's growth since its founding in 1922, emphasizing Lowry's role.

410.   Barton, Lew. "Most Influential Man Among the Lumbee Dies." *The Lumbee* 1
Feb. 1968: 1.
The Rev. L. W. Jacobs had been a Baptist minister, teacher, principal, PSU trustee,
Pembroke postmaster, and moderator of the Burnt Swamp Baptist Association.

411.   " 'Miracle' on Branch Street." *The Methodist Story* [Evanston, IL] Feb.
1968: 1. Rpt. in *The Lumbee* 15 Feb. 1968: 1.
Describes the local hard work, conference loans, and gifts which enabled Branch Street
Church in Lumberton to be built. First published in *The Lumbee* 23 March 1967: 1.

412.   *Indian Pentecostal Service. Eastern North Carolina, 12 Aug. 1980.* Videotape.
No dir., no prod. 60 min. [UNC-UL]
Black-and-white tape of an unidentified Lumbee Pentecostal Sunday School and
worship service, showing the emotionalism and demonstrativeness of preacher and
congregation. The informal, unstructured service is dominated by singing and
piano-playing. Includes faith-healing. Good example of a "hacking preacher."

413.   Lowry, Jason B. "An Evaluation of the Eighty-First Annual Session of the
Lumber River Conference of the Holiness Methodist Church Held at Union
Chapel Church, Nov. 6-8, 1981." Unpublished typescript. [1982]. [PSU-MLL]
Lowry, a Hopewell Methodist Church delegate, charges the Rev. Ward Clark, Jr.,
conference bishop from 1974-1981, with gross neglect of duty. Explains the history,
doctrine, organization, and activities of the conference.

414.   Reaves, Malik. "How Strong a Foundation." *The Interpreter* [Dayton, OH:
United Methodist Communications] 27.8 (Nov.-Dec. 1983): 10-13.
On Prospect Church, the country's largest Native American church. Discusses
Robeson County's Methodist leadership in the 1972-1975 voter registration drive, as
well as efforts to obtain a Native American district superintendent.

415.   Barton, Bruce. *Religious Experience an Important Part of Lumbee Heritage.*
Pembroke: Lumbee Regional Development Association, June 1984. 197 p.
[IERC]
Extensively researched, this work includes historical sketches of the Burnt Swamp
Baptist Association, Lumber River Holiness Methodist Association, North Carolina
Conference of the United Methodist Church, and Prospect Methodist Church, with
leader profiles for each. The appendix covers 104 Lumbee churches, listing conference
journals, church histories, minutes, membership rolls, biographical sketches, land
records, newspaper articles, and Indian cemeteries.

416.   Oliver, James Ralph. "Development of a Campus Ministry Program by First
United Methodist Church, Pembroke, North Carolina." Professional Project for
Doctorate of Ministry. Drew U, 1987.
Oliver, pastor of First Methodist, discusses these aspects of his campus ministry
program: what PSU students expected from it; planning and implementation; and the
church administrative board's evaluation.

417. Lowry, Jerry. "A Brief History of Native American Methodist Missions."
   Unpub. typescript. Durham: Duke U Divinity School, [20 Mar. 1987]. 59 p.
Covers Lumbee Methodism from the earliest written references (1787) through early
1987. Discusses conference structure; ministers and spiritual leaders; and individual
churches. Good overview of Prospect Church.

418. Tyson, Ruel W., Jr. "The Testimony of Sister Annie Mae." *Diversities of Gifts:
   Field Studies in Southern Religion*. Ed. Ruel W. Tyson, Jr. Urbana: U of
   Illinois P, 1988. Pp. 105-25. [PSU-MLL]
A 50-year-old Lumbee woman delivered a lengthy testimony during a revival service at
a Robeson County Holiness church on July 6, 1979. Tyson provides a transcription
and analyzes the gestures, rhetoric, and theology.

419. Norton, Bill, Jr. "A Tearful William Foster Jacobs–Lay Person of Year." *North
   Carolina Christian Advocate* 28 June 1988: 2.
Jacobs, a retired Pembroke farmer and member of Sandy Plains Church, was the first
Lumbee to receive the award.

420. Rouse, Jeanne. "Native American Church Has First Worship Service." *North
   Carolina Christian Advocate* 44 (15 Nov. 1988): 5.
Opening of the Fayetteville United Methodist Native American Church. Related
article, p. 7.

421. Bumgarner, George William. *The Methodist Episcopal Church in North
   Carolina, 1865-1939: Among the White Population, the Lumbee Native
   Americans, and, to a Limited Extent, the Black Population*. [Charlotte]:
   Committee on Archives and History, Western North Carolina Conference of the
   United Methodist Church, 1990. Pp. 223-35. [ECU]
Discusses Lumbee Methodism in North and South Carolina, with sections on W. L.
Moore, D. F. Lowry, French R. Lowry, P. M. Locklear, and the Prospect, Ashpole
Center, Pleasant Grove, Sandy Plains, Pembroke, and Thessalonica churches. Dis-
agrees with Dial and Eliades (entry 54) on 1880 as the date of the Lumbees' first
formal religious organization (Baptist). Notes that there were Indian names on the
membership rolls of the Methodist Episcopal Church, South, Robeson Circuit, for
1870-1877. See also entry 1040.

422. Smith, Joseph Michael, and Lula Jane Smith. *The Lumbee Methodists: Getting
   to Know Them. A Folk History*. Raleigh: Commission of Archives and History,
   North Carolina Methodist Conference, 1990. [PSU-MLL] [ECU] [UNC-G]
This popular history presents information from individuals and from local church
committees, with many photographs. Chapters cover tribal origins and history;
Methodist impact on Lumbees; sketches on individual churches; the impact of specific
events and individual Lumbee Methodists; Lumbees and social justice, with sketches
on leaders; and a look at the future for Lumbees and their Methodist churches.

423. Rhodes, Barbara. "First Native American Woman Is Pastor." *Robesonian* 22
   June 1990: 7A.
Carolyn C. Woriax, appointed to the New Philadelphus United Methodist Church (Red

Springs), is North Carolina's first female Native American Methodist pastor.

424. Gustafson, Robert K. "The Religion of the Lumbee Indians." Paper presented at
the American Academy of Religion conference, New Orleans, 14 Nov. 1990.
Traces Christianity among the Lumbees since the earliest recorded church deed (1792),
noting conferences, associations, and the prevalence of Protestantism. Gustafson
analyzes two videotaped interviews with Lumbee religious leaders; writings about
Vernon Cooper; and a conversation with a Tuscarora tribal leader, who provided
information on conjuring, herbal remedies, root workers, totens, and blowing out fire.
Notes descriptions of similar practices in writings of Gregg, Lawson, and McMillan.

425. Scipio, Sylvester. "From Tents to TV, Locklear's Ministry Grows."
Robesonian 3 May 1991: 8A.
The Rev. Gerald Locklear conducts tent revivals, has two radio shows, and has signed
a contract with Channel America for a weekly television show.

426. Wilcox, Ed. "Robeson Preacher Opens His Own TV Station." *Robesonian* 8
March 1992: C1.
Billy Locklear has a church on Oak Grove Church Road and a gospel television station
which broadcasts from 6 p.m. until midnight, six nights a week.

427. "Native American Pastors Seek Degrees at Campbell." *Robesonian* 24 April
1992: 8A.
Six Baptist pastors, who have served from 12 to 20 years, are working on BA degrees
in Christian ministry. One remarked that "it used to be considered unethical for
ministers in our area to get an education."

428. Locklear, Barbara Braveboy-. "Friendship Missionary Baptist Church Building
on Dedication and Devotion." *Robesonian* 4 Sept. 1992: 6A.
The church began in December, 1985, with 33 friends meeting in a private home. The
new church building, made of logs, was erected on a site three miles west of Pembroke.

429. Borchert, John L. "WNCC Organizes New Native American Church." *North
Carolina Christian Advocate* 26 Jan. 1993 No. 2 WNCC: 1, 10.
A new United Methodist Native American church, pastored by the Rev. Kenneth
Locklear, will begin in Greensboro with Bible study sessions at the Greensboro Native
American Association day care center. It is only the second Native American church
in the Western North Carolina Conference.

430. Garfield, Ken. "United Methodists to Launch Mecklenburg Church for Indians."
Charlotte Observer 9 June 1993: 1C.
Mecklenburg has 3,000 Indians, mostly Lumbee. About 90% of them do not attend
church regularly because they are uncomfortable in non-Indian churches.

431. Pembroke State University. American Indian Studies Dept. "Early Lumbee
Religion." Oral history audiotapes. [Not seen.]
Linda Oxendine and Robert Gustafson received a grant to produce 12-15 taped
interviews with Lumbee elders. Transcripts will be made. [From correspondence].

SOCIAL SCIENCES, HEALTH, AND MEDICINE
Physical Health, Conventional Medicine, and Folk Medicine

432. "Pembroke Man Honored in Va. as 'Good Citizen'." *Robesonian* 19 Dec. 1955: 11. [John A. B. Lowry, physician in Crewe, Virginia, since 1919.]

433. "Native Son Plans Return as Physician in Pembroke." *Robesonian* 18 Oct. 1957: 1. [Martin Luther Brooks, second Lumbee to practice among his people.]

434. Manning, Charles. "Col. Lowry Could Have Helped." *Greensboro Daily News* 26 Jan. 1958: A9.
Col. Earl C. Lowry, with the Surgeon General's office. He is the son of D. F. Lowry.

435. Collins, Doris Emmelyn. "The Effect of Improved Medical Facilities and Personnel for Prenatal Care on Perinatal Mortality." Thesis. Duke U, 1963.
Compares perinatal deaths in Robeson County in 1956, when there were separate prenatal clinics, to 1960, when a centrally located clinic was in place. Found only a 5% decline in perinatal deaths.

436. Brayboy, Bobby D. "A Study of the AAHPER Fitness Test Scores of Indian High School Boys Compared to the National Norms." Thesis. West Chester State College, 1965. [PSU-NARC]
Compares scores of 120 boys in Pembroke and Prospect high schools to AAHPER norms on seven test items. On all items, scores were higher than national norms.

437. Alston, Cecile S. "Indian Vital Statistics: Robeson County, North Carolina, 1971." No. SRS-5503-04-06-73. Raleigh: Public Health Statistics Section, North Carolina State Board of Health, Dept. of Human Resources, 1973. 13 p.
Tables show Indian natural increase rate, live births by sex, premature births, fetal deaths, perinatal deaths, neonatal deaths, postneonatal deaths, and selected causes of death, by age. See *News and Observer* 22 April 1973: Sec. 1 p. 4 for reactions from the director of the Robeson County Health Department.

438. Vestal, Paul K., Jr. "Herb Workers in Scotland and Robeson Counties." *North Carolina Folklore Journal* 21.4 (Nov. 1973): 166-70.
Will D. and his mother, both Lumbee, describe remedies using these plants: boneset, popular bark, goldenrod, rabbit tobacco, stargrass, red oak bark, catnip, sage, calmus root, tansy, sassafras, pine splinter, and rat's vein.

439. *Indian Voices: Native Americans Today. The Second Convocation of American Indian Scholars*. San Francisco: Indian Historian P, 1974. [PSU-MLL]
Lumbee participants included Adolph Dial, Brantley Blue, Samuel Kerns, and Bobby Dean Brayboy. Dial commented on Lumbee physicians and on the Soil Bank. Brayboy was a discussant on the panel for health professionals.

440. Jacobs, Bobby E. "A Comparative Study of the Physical Abilities of the Lumbee Indians of North Carolina Who Have Specific Learning Disabilities with City Dwelling Caucasian and Minority Groups Having the Same Disabilities as Related to the Norms of the AAHPER Physical Fitness Test." Thesis. Trinity College [Washington, DC], 1978. [IERC]
Learning-disabled Lumbee children's best performance on AAHPER youth fitness tests was lower than the poorest performance of learning-disabled children in the other two groups. Physical fitness programs for Lumbees are inadequate for improvement of strength and endurance in legs and upper arms.

441. Steedly, Mary Margaret. " 'The Evidence of Things Not Seen': Faith and Tradition in a Lumbee Healing Practice." Thesis. U of North Carolina, 1979. [UNC-WL]
Describes Vernon Cooper's use of prayer, annointment, and herbal medicines. Deeply religious, he opposes magic and conjuring. Quotes Cooper at length and includes patients' descriptions of their treatment. The appendix lists 40 herbs Cooper uses. Cooper is remembered in "Along the Robeson Trail" (column), *Robesonian* 20 Aug. 1992: 4A.

442. "Perspective ... Health Status of American Indians in North Carolina." PHISB Studies, no. 15. Raleigh: Dept. of Human Resources, Div. of Health Services, Public Health Statistics Branch, June 1979. 6 p.
Tables include live births by race; birth outcomes; race-specific number and percentage of deaths by underlying cause; and selected case-specific death rates for county Indians, for the entire county, and for the state, 1973-1977.

443. Lassiter, Tom. "Folk Medicine: Probing Lumbee Plant 'Cures'." *Fayetteville Observer/Times* 21 Oct. 1979: 1G. [PSU-MLL]
Interview with Edward Mortimer Croom, who spent two years studying Lumbee folk medicine (see entry 446). Describes five plants and their uses; mentions others.

444. Grier, J. O., R. J. Ruderman, et al. "HLA Profile in the Lumbee Indians of North Carolina." *Transplantation Proceedings* 11.4 (Dec. 1979): 1767-69.
Lumbees were blood typed for HLA-A, B, and C locus specificities and found to be heterogeneous. The study "aided in the definition of new B-cell specificities and ... contributed information regarding the multi-locus constitution of the DR region."

445. "Update on Health Status of American Indians in North Carolina." Prepared for North Carolina Commission of Indian Affairs. State Center for Health Statistics, Aug. 1982. 41 p.
Statistics on birth, death, and disease rates. Violence causes an inordinate number of Indian deaths; other major causes are atherosclerosis and diabetes. See also entry 447.

446. Croom, Edward Mortimer, Jr. "Medicinal Plants of the Lumbee Indians." Diss. North Carolina State U, 1982. [ECU] [UNC] [WFU]
Croom gathered remedies from 25 Lumbees, most over 60. Describes the plants used; their harvesting, preparation, and administration as remedies; comparisons with uses by other cultures; and published literature on the plants.

447. Surles, Kathryn B. "Update on the Health Status of American Indians in North Carolina." Prepared for North Carolina Commission of Indian Affairs. NC Dept. of Human Resources, Div. of Health Services, State Center for Health Statistics, June 1985. 6p. NC Documents J2 409: # 35
Most tables show totals for Whites, Blacks, reservation Indians, and nonreservation Indians. Many also show totals (by race) for the 20 counties with an Indian population. Factors affecting health include economics, education, family structure, fertility, housing, labor force participation, and marital status. Health statistics presented include natality; birth weight; prenatal care; fetal, neonatal, and infant death rate; SIDS death rate; abortions; causes of death (by age); median age at death (by race); and communicable disease rates (by race).

448. Constans, J., et al. "Population Distribution of the Human Vitamin D Binding Protein: Anthropological Considerations." *American Journal of Physical Anthropology* 68.1 (Sept. 1985): 107-22.
Sampled 242 Lumbees (along with 53 other populations worldwide); found a high frequency of Gc^2 (a common allele) in Lumbees. Also found Gc^{1C10}, a rare mutant allele. Notes in general that the "distribution [of the alleles] coincides with historic and prehistoric isolation and human migration patterns" (p. 112).

449. Knick, Stanley G. "Growing Up Down Home: Health and Growth in the Lumbee Nation." Diss. Indiana U, 1986. [PSU-MLL] [ECU] [UNC-WL] [UNC-G]
Knick surveyed 2,048 Lumbee children and their parents, and took four growth measures on the children. Discusses differences in health, how the differences affected child growth, other factors coexisting with level of health or growth, and Lumbee views of their health needs.

450. Wofford, David. "Jim Jones: Doctor Who Blossomed from a Farm in Pembroke Leads the National Fight on Behalf of Family Medicine." *Winston-Salem Journal* 16 April 1989: A11.
Jones was elected president of American Academy of Family Physicians.

451. "Lucie Mae Hammonds Locklear, Lumbee Herbologist: An Informal Conversation." Videotape. Lumberton: Title IV Compensatory Indian Education Program, Public Schools of Robeson County, 7 Dec. 1989. 50 min. [IERC]
Mrs. Locklear is interviewed by her grand-nephew, Ernie Hammonds. She explains uses of wooly mullein, sage, wormwood, mint, garlic, and huckleberry. She makes a broom and discusses quilts made from tobacco twine and guano sacks or workpants.

452. Croom, Edward M., Jr. "Herbal Medicine Among the Lumbee Indians." *Herbal and Magical Medicine: Traditional Healing Today*. Ed. James Kirkland. Durham: Duke UP, 1992. [137]-69.
Based on Croom's doctoral research in 1977-78, which involved 25 Lumbee informants over age 60. Croom documents 87 species, 75% of which are common or abundant in the wild. He states that present use of herbal remedies among the Lumbee "is difficult to estimate but does occur on a regular basis." Includes tables and

appendices listing disorders treated and plant uses unique to the Lumbee. Provides detailed descriptions of uses for five plants.

453. "Pembroke Man Conducting Study of Lumbee Women's Diet." *Robesonian* 6 May 1992: C1.
Ronny Bell is interviewing Lumbee women aged 21-60 and having them keep a 3-day food diary. He will perform a computer analysis of their diet, as part of his doctoral research at UNC-Greensboro and for a project funded by the National Cancer Institute.

454. Witten, Scott. "Brooks to Serve on State's Vet Board." *Robesonian* 23 Aug. 1992: 8A.
David E. Brooks, the first Native American from North Carolina to earn the Doctor of Veterinary Medicine degree, was also the first Native American appointed to the North Carolina Veterinary Medical Board. Brooks opened the Pembroke Veterinary Hospital (Robeson County's first minority veterinary practice) in 1978.

455. Cohen, Marla. "Child Fights for Transplant." *News and Observer* 3 March 1993: 1A.
Rachel Ward, a 6-year-old Lumbee, suffers from leukemia and needs a bone transplant. Because Lumbee ancestry includes several Indian tribes as well as Blacks and Whites, and because few Indians are in the American Red Cross bone marrow registry, finding a suitable match is difficult. See also *Robesonian* 5 March 1993: 1A.

Social Science Studies

456. Hancock, Earnest D. "A Sociological Study of the Tri-Racial Community in Robeson County." Thesis. U of North Carolina at Chapel Hill, 1935.
Discusses population, economics, health, housing, education, religion, community life, crime, and social disorganization. Mentions problems caused by tribal name changes.

457. Harper, Roland M. "A Statistical Study of the Croatans." *Rural Sociology* 2.4 (Dec. 1937): [444]-56. [PSU-MLL] [ECU]
Analyzes data from 1790 through 1930 on literacy, fertility, rural-farm population, and percentage of population by age. Croatans are "intermediate between their White and Negro neighbors in some respects."

458. Harper, Roland M. "The Most Prolific People in the United States." *Eugenical News* 23.2 (March-April 1938): 29-31. [PSU-MLL]
Used 1930 census figures and other data to calculate a Croatan birth rate of almost 40 per thousand. Noted a 4.00 ratio of births to deaths, a large number of males aged 10-15, and 10% of maternal deaths between the age of 10 and 15.

459. "Dr. Lowry Gives Annual Address." *Robesonian* 1 April 1938: 2. (Odako v. 1 no. 11).
Dr. Earl C. Lowry spoke on "Inhibitory Factors in the Development of the Indians of Robeson County." His experimental measures, including 200 Binet tests, showed that Robeson Indians have a potential as high as the general population but have "suffered a social and economic retardation." Note: Dr. Lowry has done extensive research on his

people, compiling files from 1913-1950. His main interests have been Lumbee origins and Henry Berry Lowry (from correspondence).

460. Johnson, Guy B. "Personality in a White-Indian-Negro Community." *American Sociological Review* 4.4 (Aug. 1939): 516-23. [PSU-MLL] Excerpted in: *When Peoples Meet*. New York: Hinds, Hayden, and Eldredge, 1946. Pp. 576-82.
Analyzes adjustment problems of Lumbees, who form a middle class in the county's triracial society. Discusses White political dominance, "cleavages" in the Indian community, and discriminations Lumbees faced during this period. The copy in Johnson's papers (entry 468) notes a printer's error.

461. U.S. Bureau of the Census. *Census of the Population: 1960.* Volume 1: *Characteristics of the Population.* Part 35: *North Carolina.*
See Table 28, "Characteristics of the Population, for Counties, 1960," p. 35-129. In this census, Robeson County's racial breakdown includes Indians. The *Census of Population: 1950* (see Volume II: *Characteristics of the Population.* Part 33: *North Carolina.* Table 42, "General Characteristics of the Population, for Counties: 1950," p. 33-111) offered only the designations of native White, foreign-born White, Negro, and other races. Calvin Beale's 1957 article (entry 708) explains the Census Bureau's instructions to Census of 1950 enumerators regarding triracial isolates. Table 1 of his article shows 1950 totals for triracial isolates by state, county, and name of isolate.

462. Franklin, John Hope. *The Free Negro in North Carolina, 1790-1860.* 1943.
New York: Russell & Russell, 1969. Pp. 79-80.
Robeson Countians attempted, in 1850-1857, to persuade the General Assembly to pass a law forbidding free Negroes or mulattoes to buy or use alcoholic beverages.

463. [Johnson, Guy B.] "Dr. and Mrs. Johnson Plan Study of Indian Community."
Pembroke Progress 12 Aug. 1948: Sec. 2 p. 1B.
The Johnsons, who had visited the county earlier, were gathering material for a book. They wished to examine letters, land grants, deeds, oral tradition, words, riddles, and remedies. Note: The book was never published (from correspondence).

464. North Carolina Fund. *A Profile of Community Problems: Richmond, Scotland, and Robeson Counties.* Compiled for Tri-County Community Action, Inc. by the Fund. 2 v. N.p., 1965? [UNC-WL]
Health data covers tuberculosis, venereal disease, and infant mortality. Crime data includes murder, rape, assault, robbery, burglary, larceny, and juvenile delinquency. Also documents school dropouts. Maps in Vol. 2 show areas of the problems.

465. North Carolina Fund. *Characteristics of Households in Areas Served by the Tri-County Community Action Program.* (Survey of Low-Income Families in North Carolina. Report No. 2K.) Durham, NC, June 1967. 53 p. [UNC-WL]
Gives survey data on housing, facilities, utilities, household composition, employment, income source, and health care. Provides different data gathered on a sample of adults.

466. North Carolina Fund. *Characteristics of Individuals in Areas Served by the Tri-County Community Action Program.* (Survey of Low Income Families in

North Carolina. Report no. 3K.) Durham, Aug. 1967. 63 p. [UNC-WL]
Sampled 400 households in each county, reporting on race, sex, family income,
education, religion, marital status, residential mobility, occupations, periods of
unemployment, and more. See especially pp. 52-54.

467. Briley, Mollye Hughes. "A Study of the Interpersonal Value Orientations of
    Extension Homemakers in Robeson County, NC." Thesis. North Carolina State
    U, 1968. ERIC ED 032 499
Compared extension homemakers' interpersonal values to their age, educational level,
family size, ethnic group, income level, and years in club work. Lumbees ranked the
values in slightly different order from Whites and Blacks.

468. Guy Benton Johnson Papers (3826). Southern Historical Collection. Wilson
    Library, University of North Carolina at Chapel Hill.
See Subseries 11.4, Lumbee Indians of Robeson County, N.C., Boxes 87-90. Contains
materials collected for an article and a speech, as well as copious data for a book he
planned to write (see entry 463). Dates range from 1937 to 1970. Johnson analyzed
farm family schedules, migration schedules, census data, criminal cases involving
county Indians, and papers contemporary with the Lowry Gang. Includes extensive
field notes and transcripts from interviews of Robeson County residents of all ages and
races in 1937 and 1948-49. Topics discussed include: the Lowry Gang, surnames,
movie theaters, white/Indian intermarriage, race relations, language, farming, swamps,
bootlegging, history/origins, social characteristics/differentiation, physical types, dress,
handicrafts, remedies, migration, schools, voice characteristics, family size, and jury
service. [Note: I am writing a journal article describing this collection. GES]

469. Levensky, Kay. *The Performance of American Indian Children on the Draw-A-
    Man Test*. (National Study of American Indian Education, Series III, Assorted
    Papers, No. 2.) Washington: Office of Education, 1971. ERIC ED 039 081
The Goodenough Draw-A-Man test was intended as a "culture-free" measure of
general intelligence. See brief comments on Lumbee children from Magnolia and
Pembroke. Their age, sex, and IQ are shown in tables.

470. Temple, Dennis Michael. "Comparative Approach to the Study of a White-
    Indian-Negro Caste System in Robeson County, North Carolina." Thesis. North
    Carolina State U, 1971. ERIC ED 079 006
Lumbees resemble Blacks or Whites in family adjustment but fare much worse
economically than Whites. Tables compare the races on factors including education,
income, residence type, family size, anomia, and level of adjustment.

471. Borowsky, Christina Marie. "Behavioral Characteristics of Lumbee Children
    According to Sibling Position." Thesis. U of Maryland at Baltimore, 1973.
Studied 49 middle-grade children in southeast Baltimore. Rated siblings on initiating
tasks at home, setting self-standards for achievement, behaving negatively, seeking
companionship from family members, and more. Four of 19 scales were significant.

472. Magdol, Edward. "Against the Gentry: An Inquiry into a Southern Lower-Class
    Community and Culture, 1865-1870." *Journal of Social History* 6.3 (1973):

259-83. [PSU-MLL]
Lumbees and Blacks in Robeson County during the Henry Berry Lowry period exemplifed a lower-class subculture's Reconstruction response to the gentry. Uses census records to describe the social stratification of Settlement (Scuffletown) residents. The Lowry Band revitalized Lumbees to strive for better conditions.

473. Davis, Adam Clarke, et al. *Fertility Behavior in a Tri-Racial, Low Income Rural County.* Project report. Raleigh: North Carolina State U, Dept. of Sociology and Anthropology, 1974. [PSU-MLL has paper copy.] ERIC ED 096 076
Findings include: 73% of wives approved of family planning, more Whites approved than Blacks, and more Blacks approved than Indians.

474. Tobin, Patricia L., et al. "Value of Children and Fertility Behavior in a Tri-Racial, Rural County." *Journal of Comparative Family Studies* 6.1 (Spring 1975): 46-55.
Indians showed the strongest correlation between value of children and desired and actual family size. For Indian males, value of children is strongly related to desired family size.

475. Clifford, William B., et al. "Modern and Traditional Value Orientations and Fertility Behavior in a Rural County." *International Journal of Contemporary Sociology* 12.3-4 (July & Oct. 1975): 232-43.
Survey data showed (1) an inverse relationship between socioeconomic status and fertility behavior, and (2) a correlation between modern value orientations and a smaller ideal, desired, and expected family size.

476. Kupferer, Harriet J., and John A. Humphrey. "Fatal Indian Violence in North Carolina." *Anthropological Quarterly* 48.4 (Oct. 1975): 236-44. [PSU-MLL]
Lumbees have a higher homicide rate than Cherokees because they value courage and its expression, when necessary, through fighting. Lumbees do not have "a culture of violence," but the latter themes "predispose them to violence."

477. Beltrame, Thomas F. "Urban and Rural Lumbee Indian Drinking Patterns. Diss. Johns Hopkins U, 1976.
Surveyed 230 Lumbee males in Baltimore and Pembroke and found more heavy drinkers in Baltimore and among males holding low-prestige jobs. High scores on achievement, social status, or occupational prestige correlated with abstinence; low scores, with heavy drinking.

478. Bull, Rex Warren. "A Tri-Racial MMPI Study." Thesis. U of North Carolina at Chapel Hill, 1976. [UNC-WL]
Gave the Minnesota Multiphasic Personality Inventory to 178 Robeson Technical Institute students of both sexes and all races "to provide a local comparison group for clinical use." Responses among the races were surprisingly similar in both the multivariate and the item level analysis, with few sex-by-race differences. Indians scored between Blacks and Whites on most scales. Mean profiles were elevated for all six groups. Sc, Pt, and Pd were above a t-score of 70; and for all groups except White females, Ma was above 70. For Indian and White males, Hs was elevated. Concludes

that the Minnesota norms are not accurate for Robeson County and that "in this study, racial differences are not very important, but subcultural differences are."

479. Johnson, Meighan George. "Social-Demographic and Role Performance
   Differences in Fertility in a Rural, Low-Income, Tri-Racial County." Diss.
   North Carolina State U, 1976.
Found that socioeconomic status and fertility were inversely related, and race and fertility were statistically related. White and Indian fertility patterns were similar.

480. Sporn, Leslie K. "Alcoholism and Individual Social Disorganization Among the
   Lumbi [sic] Indians." Thesis. U of Maryland at Baltimore, 1977.
Studied 100 alcoholic males who sought counseling from Baltimore's American Indian Study Center. Alcoholic Lumbees showed general dissatisfaction with life, little interest in church, feelings of alienation, and frequent unemployment.

481. Wicker, Leslie Cleveland. "Racial Awareness and Racial Identification Among
   American Indian Children as Influenced by Native-American Power Ideology
   and Self-Concept." Diss. U of North Carolina at Greensboro, 1977.
Compared Indian children from Pembroke Elementary, who were exposed to a strong Indian movement, to children from Sampson, Richmond, and Guilford counties, who were not. Found more Native American power ideology among the former.

482. Locklear, Herbert H. "American Indian Alcoholism: Program for Treatment."
   Social Work 22.3 (May 1977): 202-07.
Gauges the extent of alcoholism among Indians in Baltimore. Describes a rehabilitation and treatment program administered by the American Indian Study Center.

483. Beasley, Cherry Maynor. "A Descriptive Study of the Denver Developmental
   Screening Test Scores of Lumbee Children in Robeson County, North Carolina."
   Thesis. U of North Carolina, 1978. [UNC-WL]
Tested first-born male and female Lumbee children, aged 34-38 months. All earned normal scores. Because they differ from the population on which the test was developed, however, Lumbee children differed in age on some developmental items.

484. Southeastern Mental Health Center. *Pembroke Indian Alcohol Project.* John E.
   Harrison, Coordinator. ID# PH 23-5878. 8/1/78. [PSU-MLL]
Grant application for a Pembroke treatment, education, and outreach project. Of the 30,000 Indians in the county, an estimated 1,140-2,550 are heavy drinkers. Attachments give extensive statistical data.

485. Dixon, Laura Beth. "Minority Group Status and Fertility in a Tri-Racial, Rural
   Population." Thesis. North Carolina State U, 1979.
In Robeson County, Whites had fewer children, expected fewer, and planned fertility more successfully than Indians or Blacks. Orientation toward work had little effect on fertility. For Indians, the highest level of education increased fertility.

486. Beltrame, Thomas, and David V. McQueen. "Urban and Rural Drinking
   Patterns: The Special Case of the Lumbee." *International Journal of the*

Addictions 14.4 (1979): 533-48. [PSU-MLL]
Compared drinking patterns of Baltimore and Pembroke Lumbees, considering age, education, occupational satisfaction, church attendance, and commitment to work. More Baltimore than Pembroke Lumbees were heavy drinkers, and the latter were more often abstainers. Presented at the 32nd Int'l. Congress on Alcoholism and Drug Dependence, Warsaw, Poland, Sept. 3-8, 1978. See proceedings, vol. 3, pp. 165-77.

487. Sampson, Nancy Morgan. "A Study of the Self-Concepts of Black, White, and Indian Students, Grades Three through Twelve, Living in an Urban and a Rural Setting." Diss. New York U, 1980.
Compared the self-concept of Lumbee children in Robeson County and Baltimore with White and Black classmates. Found no significant differences among races or between urban and rural residence. Female self-concept was more positive than male.

488. Baker, Nancy Roux-Teepen. "American Indian Women in an Urban Setting." Diss. Ohio State U, 1982.
Studied 50 Indian women (including seven Lumbees) in a five-county SMSA in a northern midwestern state. Asked how the urban setting affected their attitudes, achievements and lifestyles. Includes excerpts from several Lumbee responses.

489. Ross, Thomas E. *One Land, Three Peoples: An Atlas of Robeson County, North Carolina.* Lumberton: Thomas Ross, 1982. [PSU-MLL]
Maps, photographs, and text on education, Carolina Bays, climate, agriculture, population, government, politics, churches and more. See Map 26 (Distribution of Indian Inhabitants, 1980) and Map 28 (Predominant Race by Township, 1980).

490. White, Jack Chapman. "American Indian Youth Alcohol Abuse and Alcoholism Prevention Project." Diss. Union for Experimenting Colleges and Universities, 1982.
Pretests and posttests measured personal drinking habits, attitudes toward drinking, and relationship of drinking to religion and Indian identity. Includes details on the Lumbee community in Baltimore.

491. Humphrey, John A., and Harriet J. Kupferer. "Homicide and Suicide Among the Cherokee and Lubee [sic] Indians of North Carolina." *International Journal of Social Psychiatry* 28.2 (Summer 1982): 121-28. [PSU-MLL]
Studied homicide and suicide rates for the two tribes and their counties in 1974-1976, compared to 1972-1973. Lumbee homicide decreased 25%, while suicide rose 24%.

492. Coyle, Norman. "Adoption Problems Among Ethnic Groups: Lumbee Indian Children." *Residential Group Care and Treatment* 2.1-2 (Fall-Winter 1983): 149-60. Rpt. in: *Adoption for Troubled Children.* Haworth, 1984. Pp. 149-60.
Case study of an abused Lumbee girl who came to a residential program after brief stints in Black, White, and Indian foster homes. Enhancing her awareness of her Indian identity helped her meet treatment goals and prepared her for adoption.

493. Bertoli, Fernando, et al. "Infant Mortality by Socio-Economic Status for Blacks, Indians and Whites: A Longitudinal Analysis of North Carolina, 1968-1977."

Sociology and Social Research 68.3 (April 1984): 364-77.
An analysis of birth and infant death records showed the greatest infant mortality decline during the 10-year period among Indians (19.9%). Indians had a higher postneonatal mortality rate than Whites or Blacks. For overall infant mortality, Indians fell between Whites and Blacks. Statistics for Indians are not broken down by tribe.

494. Barkley, Key L. "Inter- and Intra-Group Levels of Esteem Among Three Ethnic Groups." *Journal of Negro Education* 54.1 (1985): 56-70.
A 1964 study of county high school students found that each race held people of their own race in high esteem. Each had an ordering of esteem for the three races. All were favorable except White males toward Blacks and Indian males toward Whites.

495. Locklear, Von Sevastion. "A Cross Cultural Study to Determine How Mental Health Is Defined in a Tri-Racial County in Southeastern North Carolina." Diss. Ohio State U, 1985. [UNC-WL] [ECU] [UNC-G]
Lumbees have a high tolerance for a wide range of behaviors; use natural support systems to resolve problems; do not distinguish between mental health and mental illness; and see alcohol, drugs, and evil spirits as significant causes of mental illness.

496. Shoieb, Farouk Tammam Ali. "Socioeconomic Influences on Initial and Subsequent Childbearing: A Hazard Model Analysis." Diss. North Carolina State U, 1985.
Data was collected in Robeson County in the summer of 1972. The sample included 526 couples, and 169 women not currently married, aged 18-49. Shoieb determined that Black and Indian women begin childbearing at a younger age and then have subsequent births at a faster pace than White women. As a result, Black and Indian women have more children and higher fertility than White women. Race and educational attainment also influence initial and subsequent childbearing.

497. Chavis, Ben. "The Teacher-Student Relationships as Perceived by Lumbee Indians." Diss. U of Arizona, 1986. [UNC-G]
Surveyed 44 adult Lumbees on their recollected relationships with their teachers. Half attended Indian schools; half, integrated. Concludes that integration has not been advantageous for Lumbee students. Gives abstracts from answers to each question.

498. Gade, Ole, and H. Daniel Stilwell. "Population Dynamics of the Coastal Plains Region. Robeson County." *North Carolina: People and Environments*. Boone, NC: Geo-App, 1986. Pp. 135-42. [PSU-MLL]
Robeson's fertility rate was 33% higher than the state average between 1970 and 1980. Lumbees had a lower life expectancy than Whites and the lowest female/male ratio of the races. Predicts, like Ross (entry 499), that by the end of the century Lumbees will be the county's largest racial group. Note: 1990 census data shows Indians as the county's largest race; see *Robesonian* 28 April 1991: C1 and 3 May 1991: 6A.

499. Ross, Thomas E. "The Lumbees: Population Growth of a Non-Reservation Indian Tribe." *A Cultural Geography of North American Indians*. Ed. Thomas E. Ross. Boulder: Westview, 1987. Pp. 297-309. [PSU-MLL]
Reasons for Lumbees' rapid population increase during the 20th century include high

birth rate, low death rate, and increased willingness to be identified as Indian. Better economic status has decreased out migration and increased returning home. Gives the number of Lumbees in each census since 1890.

500. Hitt, Greg. "Violence Among Indians Hangs as a Backdrop to Investigation." *Winston-Salem Journal* 13 March 1988: A9.
Indians are more likely to die violently than other races in the county. Many seek counseling due to abuse in the home.

501. Ransom, Ronald Gene. "The Tie That Binds: The Grandparent/Grandchild Relationship Among the Lumbee Indians of Robeson County, North Carolina." Thesis. U of Arizona, 1989. [PSU-MLL] [ECU]
Interviewed 50 Lumbees on their recollected grandparent/grandchild relations. Identified four values grandparents used to aid the development of their grandchildren. Concludes that the strength of this relationship has dissolved.

502. "Officials Report 10,000 Lumbees Among 5.3 Million Missed in Census." *Robesonian* 26 March 1990: 5A.
LRDA's James Hardin and North Carolina Commission on Indian Affairs' Lonnie Revels react to a report stating the 1980 census miscounted Indians by 480 percent.

503. U.S. Dept. of Commerce. Bureau of the Census. *1990 Census of Population. General Population Characteristics. North Carolina.* (1990 CP-1-35). Washington: GPO, June 1992. C3.223/6: 990 CP-1-35
Table 80 provides age and sex data for the Lumbee TDSA (Tribal Designated Statistical Area). Table 81 gives household and family data.

504. U.S. Dept. of Commerce. Bureau of the Census. *1990 Census of Population. General Housing Characteristics. North Carolina.* (1990 CH-1-35). Washington, DC: GPO, July 1992. C3.224/3: 990 CH-1-35
Table 74 gives occupancy, structural, and financial housing data for the Lumbee TDSA (Tribal Designated Statistical Area).

LUMBEE IDENTITY
Origins of the Tribe

505. Lawson, John. *A New Voyage to Carolina*. 1709. Ed. Hugh Talmage Lefler. Chapel Hill: U of North Carolina P, 1967. P. [69]. [PSU-MLL]
Often cited as evidence for the Lost Colony theory. Lawson began his journey in 1700 and spent eight years in North Carolina. He mentions the Hatteras Indians, "who either then lived on Roanoak-Island or much frequented it." The Hatteras claimed some White ancestors; they "could talk in a book [read]" and often had gray eyes.

506. McMillan, Hamilton. *Sir Walter Raleigh's Lost Colony: An Historical Sketch of the Attempts of Sir Walter Raleigh to Establish a Colony in Virginia, with the Traditions of an Indian Tribe in North Carolina. Indicating the Fate of the Colony of Englishmen Left on Roanoke Island in 1587.* Wilson, NC: Advance

Presses, 1888. 29 p. Rev. ed. Raleigh: Edwards and Broughton, 1907. 46 p.
Rpt. in McPherson (entry 49), Exhibit C. Microfilmed by the Library of
Congress.
An often-cited work. Quotes early travel writers on Indians who may have been
descendants of the Lost Colonists and Manteo's tribe. Relates several origin traditions.
Mentions their "Anglo-Saxon" language, Lost Colonists' surnames still found among
them, road-building, walking "Indian-file," and raising tobacco for their own use.

507. Johns Hopkins University Seminary of History and Politics. *Minutes.* April 18,
     April 25, and May 9, 1890. Vol. 3, pp. 701-707, 716. Manuscript. Ferdinand
     Hamburger, Jr. Archives. Johns Hopkins U, Baltimore, MD.
Describes a paper Stephen B. Weeks read before the Seminary as a doctoral student.
He stated that White's colonists' "descendants can be identified in a peculiar people
now living in Robeson County ... and officially recognized by that state as Croatan
Indians" (p. 704). The Seminary asked two students to study the arguments. At the
May 9, 1890, meeting, they said: "While his conclusions were exceeding plausible yet
it was a matter that could not with existing information be demonstrated" (p. 716).

508. Weeks, Stephen B. "The Lost Colony of Roanoke: Its Fate and Survival."
     Papers of the American Historical Association 5.4 (1891): 107-46. Summarized
     in *Annual Report of the American Historical Association 1890*: 97-98. Pub-
     lished as a separate; New York: Knickerbocker, 1891. Rpt. in McPherson (entry
     49), Exhibit CC.
One of the earliest and, due to Weeks' subsequent regard as a historian, most cited
arguments for the Lost Colony theory. The Croatans were "fixed in their present
homes as early as 1650." Cites the history, migrations, and accomplishments of the
tribe, then connects the Lost Colonists to the Croatans using maps and written
accounts. Other arguments are based on Croatan traditions, character, disposition,
spoken language, and family names.

509. Weeks, Stephen B. "Raleigh's Settlement on Roanoke Island: An Historical
     Survival." *Magazine of American History* 25 (Feb. 1891): 127-39.
Summary of entry 508.

510. Baxter, James Phinney. "Raleigh's Lost Colony." *New England Magazine* n.s.
     11 (1894-1895): 565-87. [See pp. 585-87.]

511. Wilson, E. Y. "The Lost Colony of Roanoke." *The Canadian Magazine* 4
     (April 1895): [500]-504. [PSU-MLL]

512. Melton, Frances Jones. "Croatans: The Lost Colony of America." *Mid-
     Contintinent Magazine* 6.3 (July 1895): [195]-202. [PSU-MLL]

513. McMillan, Hamilton. *The Lost Colony Found: An Historical Sketch of the
     Discovery of the Croatan Indians. With: Their Advance Movement: Condition
     Before and After the War, Progress in Civilization and Religion.* By the Rev. J.
     J. Blanks. Lumberton: Robesonian Job Print., [c1898?] 35 p. [UNC-WL]
Includes chapters from McMillan's pamphlet (entry 506). Discusses Croatan origins,

disfranchisement, lack of schools, common surnames, "almost pure Anglo-Saxon language," and more. States that C. Wilkins, licensed by the Raft Swamp Church, was the father of Croatan religion.

514. Stringfield, Mary Love. "The Lost Colony of Sir Walter Raleigh." *American Monthly Magazine* [National Society, Daughters of the American Revolution] 6 (June 1900): 1159-63.
Asserts that if their descent from the Lost Colony can be proved, Croatans should be "considered peculiarly the wards of the Nation."

515. Proctor, James D. "The Croatan Indian: An Interesting Account of the Lost Colony." *The Argus* 22 July 1904: 4.
Reprinted from *Wake Forest Student*. Croatans number about 1,500. All have prominent cheekbones, are fond of 'fire water,' and are dangerous when aroused. Most are farmers and vote Democratic. Their favorite colors are red and yellow.

516. Mangum, O. R. "The 'Lost Colony' Found." *Wake Forest Student* 25.7 (April 1906): 517-25.

517. Ford, Alexander Hume. "The Finding of Raleigh's Lost Colony." *Appleton's Magazine* 10 (July 1907): 22-31. [PSU-MLL] Rpt. in *Charlotte Daily Observer* 7 July 1907: Sec. 2 p. 4.
Claims to be the first article on Croatans in a general magazine. Croatans in Red Springs walked single file, made their own liquor, and grew scuppernong grapes. Ford talked with Hamilton McMillan.

518. Ashe, Samuel A'Court. *History of North Carolina*. Greensboro: Charles L. Van Noppen, 1908. Vol. 1, pp. 20-21, 286-87. [1971 reprint at PSU-MLL]
Ashe is skeptical of the Lost Colony theory. He doubts English names would have been "preserved among a tribe of savages beyond the second generation" and feels the names and customs should have caused more comment by explorers or historians.

519. Keokuk, Fanny. "The Croatan Indians." *Indian Craftsman* [US Indian School, Carlisle, PA] 2.3 (Nov. 1909): 22.
Croatans are "peculiar people who combine in themselves the blood of native tribes, of the early settlers, the Negro, and stray seamen of the Latin races" (from Mooney, entry 7). Smith (entry 356) mentions a connection between this article and Sylvester Long.

520. McMillan, Hamilton. "The Croatans." *North Carolina Booklet* 10.3 (Jan. 1911): 115-21. [PSU-MLL]
Discusses the Lowrie Road, the claim of Cherokee origin, Lost Colony surnames, Chaucerian language, education, farming, and churches.

521. Mooney, James. "[Comments recorded in] Proceedings of the Anthropological Society of Washington. Meeting of October 24, 1911." *American Anthropologist* ns 14 (1912): 563.
Brief description of the tribe, based on Mooney's summer work. They are descended from "original native tribes of the same region, largely mixed with alien blood."

522. McLean, Angus W. "Historical Sketch of the Indians of Robeson County."
    Statement Before the House Committee on Indian Affairs, 14 Feb. 1913.
    Hearings on S. 3258 (entry 1326), pp.19-25. Rpt. in McPherson (entry 49),
    Exhibit F.
Says Robeson County Indians "were originally a part of the great Cherokee Tribe ...."
He "can not reconcile" McMillan's position of Cherokee descent with his "main
contention" of Lost Colony descent. Also in Exhibit F of entry 49 is a later letter from
McLean (7 Sept. 1914) saying the Indians are descendants of Lost Colonists and are
also mixed with Cherokees. McLean interviewed Wash Lowrie (age 80) in 1914 and
sent McPherson a statement summarizing the interview (included in Exhibit F).

523. Dart, A. D. "Raleigh's Lost Colony." *The Southern Workman* [Hampton, VA:
    Hampton Normal and Agricultural Institute] 42 (August 1913): 445-46.
    [PSU-MLL] [Lost Colony theory is "now a well-established fact."]

524. Terry, G. Cunningham. "Sir Walter Raleigh's Lost Colony of Roanoke."
    Blackwood's Magazine [194 no. 1175 (Sept. 1913): 320-28. [PSU-MLL]
Romanticized description of a visit to Robeson County, in the "'backwynds' of North
Carolina's Blue Ridge." Describes John Cotsmuir, noting his Chaucerian speech,
Saxon cross-bow, flint-lock musket, and Indian tomahawks. Croatans recount for
Terry the traditions of their journey from Roanoke to Robeson County, the story of
Virginia Dare, and the "two-storeyed stone houses, forts, and water wheels" built by
their Indian ancestors with instruction from the English.

525. "A British View of the Croatans." *Robesonian* 25 Sept 1913: 3.
Reprinted from *Greensboro News*. Notes errors and misrepresentations in entry 524.

526. Fitch, William Edward. *The First Founders in America, with Facts to Prove
    that Sir Walter Raleigh's Lost Colony Was Not Lost*. New York Society of the
    Order of the Founders and Patriots of America, 29 Oct. 1913. 40 pp.
Borrows heavily from Weeks. Discusses Croatan traditions, history, education,
migrations, military service, language, and family names.

527a. "Report on Indians: Special Indian Agent McPherson, Who Spent Several
    Weeks in Robeson Studying History and Ways of These People, Makes Report."
    Robesonian 20 May 1915: 7. [On release of McPherson Report (entry 49).]

527b. "Hamilton McMillan Passes." *Robesonian* 2 March 1916: 3. [Obituary.]

528. "Monument to H. McMillan: Prominent Indian Suggests That Indians of Robeson
    Erect Monument to ... Their Late Friend and Benefactor." *Robesonian* 9 March
    1916: 1. [Angus Chavis calls for a meeting. See also letter, 20 March 1916: 3.]

529. National Anthropological Archives. Smithsonian Institution. Washington, DC.
    Manuscript 3775. Collector: J. N. B. Hewitt.
This undated, two-page pencil note mentions a "statement" attributed to Swanton and
notes that Mooney "did not hold the view that the Croatan were Siouan.". The writer
adds, "... I know of no data to make it probable that these mixed bloods should be

classed as Siouan. The name of their chief is clearly Algonquian and the toponymic designations are likewise from this stock."

530. Ashe, S. A. "Correct Names of Indians in Robeson County." [article, 192?] [UNC-WL Clippings File, "Indians of North Carolina," vol. 3, p. 39.]
The Indian blood in the tribe is from Congarees, locally known as Burghaws.

531. McFarland, A. J. "The Lost Colony." *Popular Educator* 40 (April 1923): 464-66.
McFarland, on a canoe trip in an eastern North Carolina swamp, meets an elderly Croatan who describes his descent from a beautiful young girl (a Lost Colonist) who was carried off and married by an Indian chief.

532. Lindquist, G. E. E. "The Lost Colony of Roanoke Today." *The Southern Workman* 57.10 (October 1928): [442]-44. [PSU-MLL]
Describes Lumbee population centers, occupations, population growth, schools, race relations, physical features, and religion.

533. Jenkins, Paul B. "American Indian Cross-Bow." *Wisconsin Archeologist* 8.4 (1928-29): 132-35.
On a crossbow made (according to Calvin Lowrey) 100-150 years earlier. Its manufacture and use support the Lost Colony theory. Jenkins adds, "It is indisputable that [it] must have been learned by [Lumbee] ancestors from European arrivals." See note, *Robesonian* 29 May 1916: 3, that Hamilton McMillan gave the cross-bow to Col. Fred Olds for the Hall of History (North Carolina Historical Commission).

534. Woods, Lenora W. "Tribe Known as Croatans Thought to be Remnant of Mysterious 'Lost Colony'." *Charlotte Observer* 27 Oct. 1929: Sec. 3 p. 9.
General overview. Reprints the Smithsonian Institution photograph of A. S. Lockee (see also *CIV* 8 Dec. 1988: 1).

535. Swanton, John R. "Probable Identity of the Croatan Indians." U.S. Dept. of Interior. Office of Indian Affairs. Washington, DC, 1933. 5p. [PSU-MLL]
Rpt. in Senate Report 73-204 (entry 1347) and House Report 73-1752 (entry 1348). Excerpted in *The Lumbee Petition* (entry 57), 83.7 HN pp. 68-70.
Croatans "are descended mainly from certain Siouan tribes of which the most prominent were Cheraw and Keyauwee." Probably the Eno, Shakori, Waccamaw, and Cape Fear also contributed. Disagrees with the Lost Colony and Cherokee origin theories. The National Anthropological Archives has notes and correspondence collected by Swanton (manuscript group 4126) while writing this paper. The materials include (1) a 5-page mimeographed draft of this report, with a handwritten note at the end: "A more accurate designation would be 'Siouan Indians of Lumber River,' or something similar"; (2) rough notes from Swanton's research on Lumbee surnames, census counts, and history; and (3) a 1934 letter written by Douglas Rights regarding Croatans in Alamance and Rockingham Counties, North Carolina.

536. McKay, Arnold A. "Nobody Knows Anything about the Croatans." *The State* 1.39 (24 Feb. 1934): 1-2. [PSU-MLL]

Discusses Hamilton McMillan's lack of proof for the Lost Colony theory and his
political reasons for propagating it. Considers other origin theories but concludes:
"They are still as much lost socially as Sir Walter Raleigh's colony is lost historically."

537. Rights, Douglas L. "The Lost Colony Legend." *Bulletin of the Archaeological
      Society of North Carolina* 1.2 (Sept. 1934): 3-7.
Reviews data on the Lost Colony theory, pronouncing it slight but "not yet disproved."
Advances other theories, noting that linguistic study would yield determining evidence.

538. Swanton, John R. "Geographical Record--North America--The Croatan
      Indians." *Geographical Review* 28 (1938): 323-24.
Croatans came from Siouan tribes in eastern N.C. The Lost Colony Theory is
"romantic but erroneous." Notes their fertility; deems them worthy of more study.

539. Pearce, Haywood J. "New Light on the Roanoke Colony: A Preliminary
      Examination of a Stone Found in Chowan County, North Carolina." *Journal of
      Southern History* 4.2 (May 1938): [148]-63.
On the Dare Stone, which was being examined at Emory University. Notes four early
writings that Weeks used to support the Lost Colony theory. The Dare Stone, if
authentic, would render Weeks' thesis "hardly tenable."

540. "Thinks Virginia Dare's Grave May Be in Robeson." *Greensboro Daily News* 8
      May 1938: Sec. 3 p. 1. [Under a hickory tree near Philadelphus Church.]

541. Lawrence, Robert C[arbelle]. *The State of Robeson: "As You Love Your State,
      Hold Robeson."* Lumberton: J. J. Little and Ives, 1939. Pp. 111-20.

542. Speck, Frank G. "The Catawba Nation and Its Neighbors." *North Carolina
      Historical Review* 16.4 (Oct. 1939): 404-17.
Native Catawba speakers discuss the Catawba name identity of tribes, including the
"so-called Croatan." Margaret Brown said the Croatans originated from Catawbas who
fled over a century earlier to avoid recognition by "the plague" (smallpox).

543. Sparks, Boyden. "Writ on Rocke: Has America's First Mystery Been Solved?"
      Saturday Evening Post 26 April 1941: 9.
Brief mention. Sparks finds the Croatans' claims of descent from the Lost Colonists
"more convincing to me than the [Dare] stones."

544. Mook, Maurice A. "Algonkian Ethnohistory of the Carolina Sound." *Journal of
      the Washington Academy of Sciences* 34.7 (15 July 1944): 213-28.
Brief mention, pp. 217-18. Since a connection between the Hatteras Indians and the
Croatans' ancestors cannot be proved, Mook deems the Lost Colony theory "baseless."
He asserts that the Croatans "are legally Indians, but not ethnically Algonkian."

545. Lawrence, R. C. "Background of the Croatans." *The State* 13 (20 Oct. 1945): 7.

546. Robinson, Melvin. *Riddle of the Lost Colony.* New Berlin, NC: Owen G. Dunn,
      1946. 64p. [PSU-MLL]

Contends that White's Lost Colony was established on Cedar Island in Carteret County. Quotes conversations with elderly Lumbees. See also Josiah W. Bailey II, "Was the Lost Colony Really Lost?" *The State* 58.9 (Feb. 1991): 12-14, and "Lost Colony Claims Disputed by Historian," *Morganton News-Herald* 16 May 1993: 1.

547. Swanton, John R. *The Indians of the Southeastern United States.* (Smithsonian Institution. Bureau of American Ethnology. Bulletin 137) Washington: GPO, 1946. Pp. 112, 145, 178, 183.
Brief mentions. The Keyauwee, Pedee, Saponi, and Shakori, in their migrations, could have contributed blood to the Croatans.

548. Stick, David. "The Lost Colony 'Mystery'." *The State* 17 (2 July 1949): 11, 20-21. [Summarizes early travel writers; supports the Lost Colony Theory.]

549. Lowry, D. F. "No Mystery." *The State* 20.29 (20 Dec. 1952): 24. [PSU-MLL] Lowry traces Lumbee origins from his own grandfather, Allen Lowry, back to the Henry Berry of the Roanoke Colony in 1587. Since Lumbees are descended from mixtures of several colonies and Indian tribes, they should take the geographical name rather than the name of a historical Indian tribe.

550. Brown, Dick. "This Carolina Mystery Still Unsolved." *News and Observer* 19 July 1953: Sec. 4 p. 1.

551. Crockett, Charles. "Warren 'Issues' Believe Croatans Their Ancestors; Clues Few." *News and Observer* 9 Aug. 1953: Sec. 4 p. 2.
Indians of Franklin, Nash and Halifax counties trace their origin to the Lost Colony.

552. Rutledge, Archibald. "The Lost Colony." *From the Hills to the Sea: Fact and Legend of the Carolinas.* Indianapolis: Bobbs-Merrill, 1958. Pp. 30-41.
Raleigh's Lost Colony was not really lost; it was absorbed by the friendly "Croatan" Indians. The "mysterious Croatan Indians" in Robeson County, who "have gifts that usually belong to the white race," might be "direct descendants of the famous Lost Colony." Croatans are "totally unlike any other Indians in North America ... They do not look at all like typical Indians; nor is their folklore Indian, but English."

553. Prpic, George J. "Early Croatian Contacts with America and the Mystery of the Croatans: Were Some Croats Present at the Discovery of America?" *Journal of Croatian Studies* 1 (1960): 6-24.
From Prpic's dissertation. Provides historical background on Dubrovnik's seafaring prowess and gives evidence that Croatian sailors may have been part of Columbus' crew at the discovery of America. Relates a Dalmatian legend that a fleet containing refugees fleeing the Turks left Dubrovnik around 1540 and wrecked off the coast of N.C. Also notes the claim by several Croatian historians that a Croat ship headed for the Indies wrecked off the coast of North Carolina around 1558. Discusses reports in Hakluyt's *Voyages* that Amadas and Barlow, in 1584, found among the friendly Indians in the area of Roanoke Island "children that had very fine auburn and chestnut hair" (p. 16). Hawks proves that the Indians called themselves Hatteras, not Croatan. Thus the name Croatan, and the traces of the White race among the Croatan (Hatteras)

Indians before the arrival of the first permanent English settlers, might have come from mixture of the Indians with Croatian sailors from wrecked Dubrovnikian ships. Prpic notes that after the Klan routing, "Croatian papers in America and in Croatia joined the American press in the discussion of the old and still unsolved question on the origin of the first Croatans" (p. 24).

554.   Dunbar, Gary S. "The Hatteras Indians of North Carolina." *Ethnohistory* 7.4
        (Fall 1960): 410-18.
Brief mentions of Hatteras Indians by 18th-century writers caused "erroneous impres-sions." Finds "too far-fetched to be considered ... the suggestion that the mixed-bloods of Robeson County ... are descendants of the Lost Colony via the Hatteras Indians."

555.   Spearman, Walter. "The Lost Colony of Roanoke Island." *American History
        Illustrated* 4.2 (1969): 22-30. [PSU-MLL]

556.   "Robeson Field May Hold Grave of Virginia Dare." *Robesonian* 16 Aug. 1970:
        12D. [The mound near Philadelphus Crossroads is a hoax.]

557.   Johnson, F. Roy. *The Algonquians*. Murfreesboro, NC: Johnson Pub. Co., 1972.
        Vol. 2, pp. 148-50.
Reviews the Lost Colony theory and the theories of Ashe and Mooney. Mentions Lumbee ancestors' involvement in the Tuscarora War. The warriors brought home Mattamuskeets as slaves and prisoners, then found they had common traditions.

558.   Shepard, Edith Vines. "Our Roanoke Island Heritage." *Carolina Indian Voice* 5
        July 1973: 1, 3; 12 July 1973: 1, 3.
Quotes McMillan, Weeks, Lawson, Ashe, and McPherson. Notes research by William S. Powell, Lew Barton, and Guy B. Johnson. Johnson's unpublished work holds the most promise for clarifying the Lost Colony connection.

559.   Arnett, Ethel Stephens. *The Saura and Keyauwee Indians in the Land That
        Became Guilford, Randolph, and Rockingham*. Greensboro: Media, Inc., 1975.
Brief mention, p. 85. Quotes Stanley South and John R. Swanton, who believe the Saura (Cheraw) and Keyauwee may or may not have joined with the Catawba but did migrate to Robeson County. Their descendants are the Lumbee.

560.   Bible, Jean Patterson. "Are They Kin to the 'Lost Colony'?" *Melungeons
        Yesterday and Today*. Rogersville, TN: East Tennessee Printing Co., 1975. Pp.
        88-92.
Reviews the history of attempts to link the Melungeons to the Lumbees through Lost Colony ancestry. Compares the Melungeons and the Lumbees on several points: surviving Lost Colony surnames; physical features; lack of tribal culture; migration; and tendency to longevity and large families. Rejects any "larger-scale relationship" other than possible intermarriage during Melungeon migrations from North Carolina.

561.   Sisevic, Ivo. "Kroatski Indijanci: Tragom historijskih Podataka i Nekih
        Jezicnih Tragova." Dubrovnik: Nase More, 1976. 28p. [Not seen.]
On the origin of Croatan Indians and Croatian presence at the discovery of America.

562. Lawing, Michelle F. "The Origin of the Robeson County Indians: A Preliminary
   Study." Unpublished ms. [N.C. Comm. of Indian Affairs, 1978.] [IERC]
Using primary sources, traces ten Lumbee surnames from 1790 back to their origins
with one or more Indian tribes. For each surname [Braveboy, Brooks, Chavis, Cumbo,
Kersey, Lockleer, Lowry, Oxendine, Ransom, and Revels], gives a list of references.

563. Nelson, Bryce. "Looking for a Little Anthropological Delight?" *Washington
   Post* 12 March 1978: G22. [Vine Deloria, Jr. comments on Lumbee progress.]

564. White, Wes. "A Report on the Origins of the Lumbee Indians: A Somewhat
   Revised and Proofread Version." Unpub. typescript. 1 April 1978. [IERC]
White used archival and published materials in North and South Carolina to determine
the Indian language(s) spoken by Lumbee ancestors. Note: He now disagrees with the
conclusions described in the Introduction (from correspondence).

565. Thomas, Robert K. *A Report of Research on Lumbee Origins.* Unpublished
   manuscript. 1977. 71 p. [Not seen.]

566. "How We Came to Be." Lumberton: Robeson County Board of Education, Title
   IV Compensatory Indian Education Program, n. d. 11 p. [IERC]
For each North Carolina region, lists the tribes present in 1700. Discusses common
Lumbee surnames, the aboriginal tribes from which they came, and "probable
descendancy of North Carolina Eastern tribes." The information is based on discus-
sions with the late Robert K. Thomas, an Oklahoma Cherokee anthropologist.

567. Durant, David N. *Raleigh's Lost Colony.* New York: Atheneum, 1981. P. 164.
Brief mention of "romantic attempts" in the late 19th century to show Lumbee descent
from Lost Colonists. Questions McMillan's reliance on surname similarities.

568. Roland, Donna. *Grandfather's Stories.* Illus. Gene Locklear. El Cajon, CA:
   Open My World, 1981. 28 p. [PSU-MLL]
Children's version of the Lost Colony theory. Lumbee children are, in most respects,
"just like you." They "don't always look like or talk like other Indians. Because they
became friends of the White man long ago."

569. Thomas, Maude. *Away Down Home: A History of Robeson County, North
   Carolina.* Lumberton: Historic Robeson, 1982. *Index.* By May Bell Lontz, et
   al. Lumberton: Historic Robeson, 1988. [RCPL]
Ch. 2 analyzes various origin theories. Ch. 11, pp. 149-61, covers Lumbee disfranchisement and the Henry Berry Lowry period. The book includes other brief mentions.

570. Hunter, Marvin N. "A Watery Fate for the Lost Colony." *The State* 50.4 (Sept.
   1982): 8-10.
Hunter, a National Weather Service meteorologist, believes the Lost Colonists were
killed in the fall of 1588 by a hurricane which caused a storm surge.

571. Johnson, F. Roy. *The Lost Colony in Fact and Legend.* Murfreesboro, NC:
   Johnson Publishing Co., 1983. Pp. 83-85.

Balanced summary of views of Mooney, McMillan, McPherson, and others.

572. Stick, David. *Roanoke Island: The Beginnings of English America*. Chapel Hill: U of North Carolina P, 1983. Pp. 231-33, 241-43, 245. [PSU-MLL]
Brief mention. Holds that the Lumbee/Lost Colonist surname similarity "has since been seriously challenged," and the Indians' "Anglo-Saxon" speech is a dialect found in many isolated areas of the eastern United States.

573. Oakley, Eve. "James Lowery: Seeking the Truth." *Fayetteville Observer* 12 July 1983: 10A. [PSU-MLL]
Lowery, great-grandson of Henry Berry Lowry, founded the Hattadare Indian Nation in 1968 to unite the state's mixed-race Indians under a common name.

574. Quinn, David Beers. *The Lost Colonists: Their Fortune and Probable Fate*. Raleigh: N.C. Div. of Archives and History, 1984. Pp. 49-50. [PSU-MLL]
Brief mention. The Lumbee/Lost Colony link "is not wholly without historical foundation, even though it is far from being fully established."

575. White, Wes. "Summary of a Restricted Report on Lumbee Origins Made by David Wilkins in 1983." Unpublished typescript. N.d. 6 p. [IERC]
Wilkins believed the Lumbees originated in South Carolina but found no supporting evidence. White provides tables summarizing Wilkins' data on the surnames Braveboy, Chavis, Cumbo, Lowrie, Locklear, and Oxendine.

576. Henige, David. "Origin Traditions of American Racial Isolates: A Case of Something Borrowed." *Appalachian Journal* 11.3 (Spring 1984): 201-13.
See pp. 204-207. Well-documented survey of the ebb and flow of support for the Lost Colony theory since McMillan's 1888 work. Finds "no good evidence at all" of the theory among Lumbees prior to McMillan. Through feedback, it became "subsumed into, and subsequently often ... indistinguishable from, pristine 'oral tradition'."

577. "'Lost Colony'–A Mystery Now Solved?" *U.S. News and World Report* 97.2 (9 July 1984): 61. Rpt. in *CIV* 5 July 1984: 7. [Interview with Adolph Dial.]

578a. White, Wesley. "The American Indian Population in Robeson County, N.C. from 1837-1854." Report for Lumbee River Legal Services. 15 Jan. 1986. [Not seen.]

578b. Barnett, Barbara. "Historian Claims Evidence for Theory on Lost Colony." *Charlotte Observer* 3 Feb. 1986: B1-2.
Views of Adolph Dial vs. William Powell on the Lost Colony theory.

579. Knick, Stan. "How Long Have the Lumbees Been Here?" *Robesonian* 16 Jan. 1992: 4A.
Historical references suggest that small numbers of Native Americans from the Siouan, Iroquoian, and Algonkian language families moved into the Robeson County area between the 1580's and 1860's. Archaeological research done in 1988 shows that Native Americans were here much earlier: 1200-1750 A.D. Further archaeological

research is needed to determine who these earliest Native Americans were. Local Indians' use of the word "Lumbee" as the river name by Indians as far back as the early 1800's fits the Eastern Siouan linguistic pattern, providing historical evidence that "Lumbee" is "an accurate, and worthy, ancestral name."

Tribal Name and Identity

580. "Croatan." *Robesonian* 24 Jan. 1910: 1.
Orren (Aren?) Locklear and others supporting Godwin's federal bill (entry 1320) have been led to believe that changing the tribal name to Cherokee could lead to "several millions of dollars at Washington." The author of this article "[can] not see why any Indian should object to being known as Croatan." Changing the name would lose the connection to the Lost Colony.

581. "Croatan to Cherokee: Croatan Indians Want Name Changed to Cherokee."
   Robesonian 3 Feb. 1910: 3.
Reprints the federal bill (entry 1320), which was introduced by Godwin. Aren S. Locklear, Daniel Locklear, and Aaron Brooks visited Godwin and prompted him to sponsor the bill. Quotes Aren S. Locklear's arguments.

582. Locklear, A. S. "A Protest. The Indians of Robeson Merely Want Their
   Original Name and Are Not 'Pursuing a Shadow'." *Robesonian* 7 (8?) Feb.
   1910: 8.
Lengthy letter. Croatans do not expect to get millions, as the *News and Observer* spoke of. They "are only trying to fix [their] prestige among the Indian tribes of the United States." McMillan and the BAE agree that Croatans are a branch of the Cherokees. Croatans fought with Whites against the Tuscaroras in 1713.

583. Hunt, James. "Seriously Objects to the Name 'Croatan'." *Robesonian* 11 Aug.
   1910: 3.
Letter. Croatans are White and Black and should not be called Indian or recognized as Indian. Robeson County Indians should be called either Cherokee Indians or just Indians. Notes a dinner held by the "Cherokee Indian Union" at Piney Grove. Similar letter, *Robesonian* 18 Aug. 1910: 8.

584. "Croatans Want Name Cherokees: The Rival Indian Forces Appeal to Legislature." *News and Observer* 4 Feb. 1911: P. 3 col. 1.
Gives arguments presented by both Croatans and western North Carolina Cherokees, and their supporters, in the Senate Judiciary Committee. A lively and lengthy hearing was held on a state bill to rename the Croatans "Cherokee Indians of Robeson County." Hamilton McMillan testified on problems caused by his bill, which had named the Indians Croatans. Since then, "indisputable evidence" had been presented–by investigators from the Smithsonian Institution, by examination of skulls, etc.–that Robeson County Indians are indeed Cherokee. The Cherokees stated that they did not want to impede the advancement of eastern North Carolina Indians, but "would not consent to giving them a name they were not entitled to." The committee asked representatives from the Croatans and the Cherokees to stand side by side, then asked Cherokee Chief John Goins (who spoke through an interpreter) what he thought of the

Croatan next to him. See also *Robesonian* 6 Feb. 1911: 1 and *Charlotte Observer* 4 Feb. 1911: 1.

585. "Cherokee Indians of Robeson: Rightful and Ancient Name of Indians of
   Robeson and Adjacent Counties Restored." *Robesonian* 13 March 1913: 4.
A bill was passed in the North Carolina General Assembly, changing "Indians of
Robeson County" to "Cherokee Indians of Robeson County" (see entry 1327).

586. "Investigation of Indians: Simmons and Godwin Want to Know Whether There
   Are Any Lands or Monies Due Indians of Robeson and Adjoining Counties from
   the Government." *Robesonian* 30 April 1914: 1.
Requests an investigation by the Interior Department in connection with an attempt to
change the tribal name to Cherokee. Related article, 30 July 1914: 1, quotes the *News
and Observer*, which speculates that the Croatans, if declared a branch of the Cherokees, would receive "quite a sum" of government funds.

587. "Uncle Sam Is Probing Identity of Croatans: To Ascertain If They Are Branch of
   Cherokees." *Wilmington Star* 2 Aug. 1914.
Investigation by McPherson. Mentions Col. Fred Olds' photographs of the Croatans,
"the first pictures ever made of them to illustrate their life," and the Croatans' 1887
visit to Indian Territory in Oklahoma to get admission into the Cherokee Nation.

588. McMillan, Hamilton. Letter to O. M. McPherson, Special Indian Agent. 2 Aug.
   1914. Rpt. in McPherson (entry 49), Exhibit M, pp. 242-3.
McMillan discusses Croatan history and traditions, based on his 30 years of study. He
states, "... I have interviewed hundreds of them, and the inquiry as to their origin was,
without exception, in favor of their being Cherokees." Washington Lowrie and other
Croatans have lived among the Cherokees in Indian Territory. The only Indian names
among the Croatans (Lowrie, Lochlayah, Oxendine) are Cherokee.

589. Butler, George E. *The Croatan Indians of Sampson County, North Carolina:
   Their Origin and Racial Status: A Plea for Separate Schools.* Durham, NC:
   Seeman Printery, 1916. [PSU-MLL] [NCS]
Butler is petitioning the Sampson County Board of Education. In 1910, 100 Indian
children were forbidden to attend White schools and would not attend Black schools.
Discusses their political and educational history, with brief sketches on 14 persons.
Microfilmed by the New York Public Library.

590. Josiah William Bailey Papers. Special Collections Department, Perkins Library,
   Duke University. [Not seen.]
Includes information on Robeson County Indians 1932-1936 and on the Wheeler-
Howard Indian Reorganization Act (1934). Bailey served as North Carolina's senator
from 1930-1946. [Description based on: Fischer, Kirsten. *Indians of North America:
A Guide to the Sources on Native Americans in the Special Collections Department of
Perkins Library.* Duke U, 1991. Item 34].

591. Ashe, S. A. "The Croatans." *News and Observer* 20 Oct. 1933: 4.
Letter. Croatans "probably were those pirates who escaped ... the pirate settlement ...

when Rhett, in 1719, captured the pirate ship and the crew on board. As the Charleston Court hung [sic] all the pirates who were captured, these who, being on land, escaped, would not have anything to do with the new settlers."

592. "Croatans Again Seek Recognition." *Charlotte Observer* 4 Feb. 1934: 3-1.
A delegation led by Joseph Brooks and B. Y. Graham appeared before a Senate hearing on legislation to change the tribal name to Siouan Indians of the Lumber River.

593. "Robeson Indians Would Be Called Siouans Under Senate Bill." *Robesonian* 12 Feb. 1934: 1.
The bill originally under consideration would designate them Cheraws. After the Secretary of the Interior read a letter stating that the Indians wanted to be called Siouans, a substitute bill was presented and accepted.

594. The Diamond Kid. "As the Wind Changeth—A New Name." [Poem.] Dated 14 Feb. 1934. Rpt. in Thomas (entry 569), p. 248.
Attributed to Carlee Hunt; occasioned by the Siouan Movement. Pokes fun at efforts of experts and the Indians themselves to find a suitable tribal name. Another poem by the Diamond Kid, "Lis'en Mr. Siouan 'n' Mr. Cherokee," is reprinted in the *Robesonian* Historical Edition, Feb. 1951, p. 4-G.

595. Sharpe, J. A., Jr. "Sentiment Among Indians Divided on Change of Name." *Robesonian* 15 Feb. 1934: 1.
Many were surprised by the Siouan Bill's quick passage in the Senate. Those for and against it both claim to have the support of most county Indians. Discusses the role of Joseph Brooks. Lists Indians lobbying in Washington for each name.

596. Sharpe, J. A., Jr. "Dispute of Robeson Indians Over New Name Based on Motives for Adoption." *Robesonian* 19 Feb. 1934: 1.
Discusses promotion of the bill by Joseph Brooks and James E. Chavis. Mentions the earlier Cheraw bill, the Siouan Council, and research supporting the Siouan name.

597. Godwin, W. H. "Proposed Change of Name to Siouan." *Robesonian* 26 Feb. 1934: 4.
Letter. Godwin opposes the bill if it will allow children from other counties to attend Robeson's Indian schools.

598. Hunt, L. B. "There's No History of a Tribe Named Croatan." *Robesonian* 26 Feb. 1934: 1.
Letter. "The name was not liked from the beginning as the older ones knew they was no such." Indians acquiesced to it because it led to better schools and churches.

599. McInnis, N. "Thoughts Regarding Indians of Robeson." *Robesonian* 5 March 1934: 4.
Former Pembroke mayor discusses two earlier letters from Indians on the tribal name.

600. "Indians Protest Strongly Against Name of 'Siouan'." *Robesonian* 19 April 1934: 1.

Remarks from a public meeting debating the Siouan Bill vs. a substitute Cherokee Bill. The Siouan name would eliminate connection with the Lost Colony. The Cherokee Bill would allow connection with Cherokees in western North Carolina and in other states. Mentions an 1806 treaty with the U.S. government signed by John Lowry on behalf of Cherokees of Robeson County.

601. "The Cherokees' Objection to the 'Siouan Bill'." *Robesonian* 23 April 1934: 4. Letter from the Cherokee Indians of Robeson and Adjacent Counties. The Siouan Bill sets aside the Lost Colony theory, claiming county Indians are descended from runaway slaves, stray seamen, forest rovers, and wasted native tribes. See D. F. Lowry's statement, same page.

602. "Indians at Big Mass Meeting Vote Unanimously to Adopt Name Siouan." *Robesonian* 23 April 1934: 1, 8.
The meeting was led by Joseph Brooks. The group also voted to join the National Council of American Indians.

603. "The Cherokee Indians' Objection to the 'Siouan Bill'" *Robesonian* 26 April 1934: 4.
Another letter from the Indian Committee of the Cherokee Indians of Robeson and Adjacent Counties, reflecting changes in the Siouan Bill since their April 23 letter. See also letter (same page), "Mrs. What-Nots Decides to Be a Siouan," which mentions the proposed Resettlement Administration project.

604. "Robeson Indians Farther Advanced, Speaker Asserts." *Robesonian* 26 April 1934: 6.
Mrs. Raymond T. Bonnin, a Sioux and president of the National Council of American Indians, praised the progress of the county's Indians and explained the purpose of the Council. The article also discusses the status of the Siouan bill.

605. Mrs. What-Nots. "Leaving the Siouans and Going to the Cherokees." *Robesonian* 3 May 1934: 4.
The letter-writer has changed her mind since her earlier letter (see entry 603), because "the Siouan Bill is dead as a door-nail." Several individuals who went to Washington "put it to sleep," and Joseph Brooks "asfixated [sic] or suffocated it" during the mass meeting at St. Anna when he ordered politicians and officers to leave (see entry 602). A letter from D. F. Lowry espousing the Lost Colony theory appears on the same page.

606. Cohen, Felix S. "Memorandum for the Commissioner of Indian Affairs." Washington: Office of the Solicitor, US Dept. of the Interior, 8 April 1935.
Robeson County Indians who are 1/2 or more Indian blood can organize under the Wheeler-Howard Indian Reorganization Act and receive educational, employment, or reservation benefits. In this two-page memo, Cohen outlines a plan whereby the Siouan Council could attain these benefits.

607. McNickle, D'Arcy. "Memorandum [for the Commissioner of Indian Affairs]. Re: Indians of Robeson County, North Carolina." Washington: Bureau of Indian Affairs, 7 April 1936. 7 p. [National Archives and Records Administration.

Record Group 75. File no. 64190. 1935. 066.]
Because county Indians requested educational assistance under the Indian Reorganization Act, McNickle spent a week in Robeson County. He states, "That they are Indians can not be doubted." He notes that it "speaks strongly of the racial identity which these Indians have never lost cognizance of that they refused to associate with the Negroes in church and in school." Quotes Swanton [entry 535]. McNickle is very sympathetic and in favor of recognition, noting that "they keep within themselves an unfailing recognition of their link with the past." Recommends, as proof of Indian blood, that a commission be appointed to "sit continuously and hear applicants and witnesses under oath."

608. McNickle, D'Arcy. "Memorandum [for the Commissioner of Indian Affairs]. Re: Indians of Robeson County, North Carolina." Washington: Bureau of Indian Affairs, 1 May 1936. 13 p. [IERC] [National Archives and Records Administration. Record Group 75. File no. 64190. 1935. 066.]
As background for the Commissioner's consideration of enrolling Robeson County Indians under the Indian Reorganization Act, McNickle provides a chronological account of their repeated requests, since 1888, for educational aid and federal recognition. He mentions that McPherson's report relied heavily for historical data on Hamilton McMillan, "whose findings at best are of doubtful value." If Swanton's conclusions on the origins of county Indians are accepted instead of the Lost Colony theory, then "the quantity of Indian blood is probably greater than we have been assuming heretofore." McNickle agrees with A. W. McLean that Indians have always been separated from others in the Robeson County area.

609. Sharpe, J. A., Jr. "Siouan Council's Main Objective Realized in Indian Resettlement Project, Biggest Federal Benefit." *Robesonian* 22 July 1938: 1.
James E. Chavis called it "the greatest federal government benefit received by the Indians of Robeson County since their first petition to the government ... in 1888." The Council believed they had received semi-official recognition from the Interior Dept. in a letter from John Collier, Commissioner of Indian Affairs. James E. Chavis noted a telegram from the Ellsworth field division of the 1935 farm census, stating that the census would list Indians in North Carolina separately as Indians, not as colored.

610. Zimmerman, William. Letter to Joseph Brooks. Washington: Office of Indian Affairs, US Dept. of the Interior, stamped 12 Dec. 1938. Correspondence no. Ind-Org. 71526-38. [3] p.
Reports that of the 209 Siouan applicants for benefits under the Indian Reorganization Act, 22 were 1/2 or more Indian blood. Lists the 22, with their age, number of children, and parents' names. IERC has a list of the 22.

611. "First Annual Robeson County Indian Fair to Close Saturday in Pembroke." *Robesonian* 31 Oct. 1947: 1.
Funded by Pembroke Chamber of Commerce and Agriculture; held at PSC. Describes a historical exhibit by the Robeson County Indian Historical Society.

612. "Pembroke Indians Organize to Obtain 'Special Rights'." *Robesonian* 22 April 1949: 1.

Indians in Pembroke Township, led by Chief Turkey Tayac from Washington, DC, met for four days at the Long House. Tayac formed a club for them, named them Lumbees, and made membership cards allowing them to enter any White institution and be served. Gives views of Indians opposed to the plan.

613. "Says Indians in Town of Pembroke and Educated Members of Race Have Not Taken Part in Recent Agitation." *Robesonian* 25 April 1949: 1.
Ira Pate Lowry, president of Pembroke's Chamber of Commerce, calls the Long House meetings "another outcropping of a kind of agitation ... carried on at different times over a period of years among uneducated Indians in some of the rural areas."

614. Maynor, Jesse. "Says Indians Have 'God-Given Rights'." *Robesonian* 9 May 1949: 4.
Letter about entry 612. Indians at Long House meetings want their God-given rights, not "special rights." The tribal name chosen at the meetings "and by which they have been known recently [is] better than [that] by which they have been called for so long, one which we'll never be made to accept."

615. "Robeson Indians to Decide Name ...." *News and Observer* 30 March 1951: 24.
A state bill to change the tribal name from Cherokee to Lumbee will be read and voted on at a mass meeting.

616. "Indians Approve Change in Name." *Robesonian* 2 April 1951: 1, 7.
A meeting was held at the request of county legislators to gauge Indians' sentiment toward a bill to change the tribe's name to Lumbee. Former Siouan proponents supported the bill. Reprints D. F. Lowry's statement at the meeting.

617. "'Lumbee Indians' Designated in Bill Introduced by Watts." *Robesonian* 5 April 1951: 1. [Text of bill reprinted.]

618. "Indians' Historic Heritage Retold as Petition Circulates." *Hamlet News-Messenger* 28 Aug. 1951. [UNC-WL Clippings File]
A petition calling for a referendum to change the tribal name to Lumbee will be presented to county commissioners. Reprints D. F. Lowry's statement on the tribe's origin and on problems caused by the name Cherokee.

619. "Robeson Indians Will Vote on Name ... Feb. 2." *Robesonian* 8 Jan. 1952: 1.
Options are Cherokees of Robeson County or Lumbee Indians of North Carolina.

620. Sharpe, Helen Seawell. "Indians Voice Name Change Opinions." *Robesonian* 23 Jan. 1952: 1.
Heaviest opposition to the name Lumbee is in the town of Pembroke, where Indians "prefer not to perpetuate the Indian tradition and heritage of their background." Opposition "is shown mainly by ignoring the issue entirely."

621. Gray, Penn. "30,000 North Carolinians Vote Themselves a Name." *The State* 19 (26 Jan. 1952): 6-7, 14. Rpt. in *CIV* 14 Dec. 1978: 9; 3 Nov. 1983: 10.
State legislators required an Indian-only referendum before changing the name to

Lumbee. Notes D. F. Lowry's role. Includes a composite photo of county Indians.

622. "Indians Vote Name Change." *News and Observer* 5 Feb. 1952: 1.
Referendum results were announced on Feb. 4. The vote was 2,109 in favor of
Lumbee, 35 opposed. Final action will be taken by the state legislature.

623. "Indians Plan to Fight Bill." *News and Observer* 21 Feb.1953: 7.
Some county Indians object to the state bill to change the tribal name to Lumbee. A
public hearing will be held. A similar bill, introduced in 1951, aroused opposition.

624. "Group Approves Name-Change for Robeson Indians." *News and Observer* 26
   Feb. 1953: 11.
Approval was granted by a committee of the state legislature. Discusses testimony in
favor by D. F. Lowry, against by L. R. Varser. D. F. Lowry's article, *Robesonian* 22
Feb. 1973: 3, reprints the law and gives background of the name-change movement.

625. Maynor, Lacy W. "The Trail of the 20th Century Brave." Address. National
   Congress of American Indians, 15th Annual Convention, Missoula, Montana, 15
   (?) Sept. 1958. [IERC]
Indians need political education. Their leaders "must guard against the following evils:
local and national disunity; illiteracy; misinformation and misrepresentation." Maynor
also addressed the 19th convention in Cherokee, NC (speech reprinted in
Congressional Record, 87th Cong., 2nd Sess., 21 Sept. 1962, pp. 20296-20297).

626. Gray, Penn. "'Indian Nations' Sends Envoys to Tell Lumbees About Unity."
   Robesonian 2 Sept. 1959? [clipping in MLL]
Mad Bear, a New York Tuscarora, visited Robeson County to get Lumbee support for
an effort to unite all U.S. reservation Indian nations in a United Nations of Indians.

627. "Pembroke Indian Conference Ends." *Scottish Chief* 24 April 1961. [PSU-
   MLL. PSU Clippings File]
Lumbees hosted, at PSC, the Southeastern Regional Preparatory Conference for the
American Indian Chicago Conference. This was the first time southeastern Indians met
to discuss common problems. Lacy W. Maynor was the organizing chairperson.
Called "the most inclusive meeting of Indians ever held in the U. S.," the Chicago
Conference was organized by Sol Tax and the University of Chicago (see *Christian
Century* 78.27 (July 5, 1961): 819-20). For discussion of the Lumbee role in planning
the Chicago Conference, see: Hauptman, Lawrence, and Jack Campisi. "The Voice of
Eastern Indians: The American Indian Chicago Conference of 1961." *Proceedings of
the American Philosophical Society* 132.4 (Dec. 1988): 316-29.

628. "Sampson's Indians Once Operated Own Schools." *The Sampsonian* [Clinton,
   NC] 31 Marcl 1966. [UNC-WL Clippings File]
Sampson Indians petitioned the Sampson County Board of Education in 1910 for an
Indian school, claiming to be from the same family as Robeson County Indians.
Includes Enoch Emanuel's historical sketch of his family.

629. *Indian Voices: The First Convocation of American Indian Scholars.* San

Francisco: Indian Historian P, 1970. Pp. 117-23.
Adolph Dial is a discussant and is questioned on Lumbee identity.

630. Johnson, Guy B. "What's in a Name: The Case of the Lumbee Indians." Paper delivered at the Annual Meeting of the Southern Anthropological Society, Athens, GA. 9 April 1970. 8 p. [Included in entry 468.]
Among mixed-race racial enclaves in the eastern U.S., Lumbees have been "the most conspicuously successful instance" of achieving a good name. Reviews the motivations behind various names, and results of the changes. The Lumbees' "power and progress contributed to the acquisition of a 'good name' at last; the name, in turn, has elevated their progress and sense of identity."

631. Bledsoe, Jerry. "Lumbee Pride and Politics: 'A Mighty Stirring' of People." *Greensboro Daily News* 19 Jan. 1971: A1.
Indian identity is manifested by joining NCAI, starting Lumbee Homecoming, making inroads in county politics, and forming the Independent Americans for Progress.

632. Olson, Delmar W. "The Lumbee Community: A Proposal to Restore, Reactivate, Recreate, Perpetuate, Promote the Lumbee Culture and to Establish a Lumbee Identity Expressible Within the Totality of the Lumbee Community." Written for Lumbee Regional Development Commission. Unpublished typescript. 5 April 1971. 5 p. [IERC]
Explains possible components of these facets of Lumbee identity: research, the Lumbee village, contemporary Lumbees, traditions, Lumbee museum, Lumbee community, the University, the school, the administration, the promotion, and the church.

633. Barton, Lew. "Evidence of Legal 'Indianness' Shown in Long-Lost Document." *Robesonian* 6 Dec. 1971: 11.
A 1938 letter confirms Indianness of 22 of the 209 tested by Carl Seltzer (entry 610).

634. Blu, Karen I. " 'We People': Understanding Lumbee Indian Identity in a Tri-Racial Situation." Diss. U of Chicago, 1972. [IERC] [UNC-WL]
Investigates Lumbee identity by (1) examining cultural content and (2) analyzing Lumbee social interaction. Discusses problems of historical documentation of origins and the search for an acceptably "historicized" name. Mentions racial implications of tobacco farming, land ownership, politics, teaching, and Indian fundamentalist Protestantism. Explains how Lumbees assign racial identity—including surnames, physical appearance, and "action characteristics."

635. "New Pembroke Facility [Henry Berry Lowry College] to Teach Indian Culture." *News and Observer* 14 Feb. 1972: 5.
The school will have an Indian newsletter and teach Indian history, culture, arts and crafts, largely to members of the Eastern Carolina Tuscarora Indian Organization.

636. "Indian Delegates Launch Drive Here." *News and Observer* 18 March 1972: 10.
The newly formed North Carolina Commission of Indian Affairs begins operation by hearing grievances of the state's four non-reservation tribes.

637. Nichols, Rick. "Indian Rights Is Smoldering Issue." *News and Observer* 11
    March 1973: Sec. 1 p. 5.
John Gregory Peck says recent demonstrations show that Robeson Indians are
beginning to identify with national Indian afffairs.

638. "Legal History Between Lumbee Indians and the United States Congress."
    Unpublished typescript. [1974?] [8] p. [IERC]
Lists petitions, bills, Congressional reports, and acts, 1888-1974.

639. Woods, Ruth Dial. "Testimony: Indian Definition Study." Pembroke: R. D.
    Woods, [1974?] 75 p. [UNC-WL]
Discusses "the social, economic, and political oppression" of Lumbees which resulted
from the federal government's inconsistent policies. Appendix A is a legal history of
Lumbee relations with the US Congress.

640. Betts, Jack. "Rose Seeks Aid for Lumbees." *Greensboro Daily News* 28 Aug.
    1974: B1.
The proposed amendment to the 1956 Lumbee Act would make Lumbees eligible for
federal programs now available to other nonreservation Indians and would also allow
dissident Indians to resign from the tribe.

641. McKellar, Brenda C. "A Name to Live By." Unpub. typescript. N.d. [IERC]
Astute essay on the four names by which Robeson County Indians have been known.
One source was an interview with Guy B. Johnson.

642. "Lumbee Bill Revision Dies in 93rd Congress; Senator Sam Ervin Disavowal
    Strikes Death Blow." *Carolina Indian Voice* 24 Dec. 1974: 1.
The bill was opposed by United Southeastern Tribes and by the NCAI.

643. "Senator Jesse Helms Reintroduces Amended Lumbee Bill." *Carolina Indian
    Voice* 23 Jan. 1975: 1.

644. "Adolph Dial Named to American Indian Policy Review Commission."
    Carolina Indian Voice 13 March 1975: 1.

645. U.S. Senate. Select Comm. on Indian Affairs. American Indian Policy Review
    Commission. Task Force Ten. *Report on Terminated and Non Federally
    Recognized Indians*. Washington: GPO, 1976. Pp. 160-73. [PSU-MLL]
Statement from LRDA reviews Lumbee legal history, LRDA, and racial disparities in
Robeson County. Also mentions the Jan. 22, 1974, Lumbee recognition bill.

646. American Indian Policy Review Commission. "Public Hearing." Pembroke,
    April 16 and 17, 1976. Fayetteville, NC: Worth Reporting Co., 1976. [IERC]
Testimony from terminated and nonfederally recognized tribes on their tribal history,
status, and current conditions. Recommends changes to federal programs, policies, and
laws. Several Robeson County Indians testified.

647. Woods, Ruth Dial. "A Position Paper Presented to the American Indian Policy

Review Commission–Task Force #10, Terminated and Nonfederally Recognized Indians, April 16, 1976." Unpublished typescript. 8 p. [IERC]
Recounts the forced assimilation of the Lumbees. Government definitions of Indian should be revised to consider historical records and state and federal legislation.

648. Blu, Karen I. "Varieties of Ethnic Identity: Anglo-Saxons, Blacks, Indians, and Jews in a Southern County." *Ethnicity* 4.3 (1977): 263-86.
Explains how Blacks, Lumbees, and Jews viewed their own ethnic group and how Anglo-Saxon Whites viewed each minority in the county during Blu's fieldwork, 1967-68. Whites had no widely held image of Lumbees. Lumbees used this disagreement to gain separate schools and legal recognition.

649. Deloria, Vine, Jr. *A Better Day for Indians*. New York: Field Foundation, 1977. Pp. 19-21.
The NCAI and some tribes oppose recognizing Lumbees, believing they have Black ancestors—a view Deloria calls "discriminatory, simplistic, and without precedent in Indian policy."

650. Warren, Harold. "Are They Indians? Congress Must Decide." *Charlotte Observer* 2 May 1977: 1.
Adolph Dial, an American Indian Policy Review Commission member, will submit a report to Congress requesting full federal recognition and benefits for all Indians.

651. Zucchino, David. "The Lumbees." *News and Observer* 18 Sept. 1977: 4-1.
Explains recent political successes, benefits to come from passage of the pending federal recognition bill, and a Tuscarora lawsuit.

652. 95th Cong. 2nd Sess. *Hearing ... on S. 2375, to Establish an Administrative Procedure and Guidelines to Be Followed by the Dept. of Interior in Its Decision to Acknowledge the Existence of Certain Indian Tribes*. Senate Select Comm. on Indian Affairs. Dated 18 April 1978. (*CIS* 1978, S961-16.)
Includes statements from Adolph Dial, Dexter Brooks, and Raymond Gibbs (attorney for the Robeson County Tuscaroras).

653. Vaden, Ted. "Indians Wage War of Names." *News and Observer* 7 Aug. 1978: 25.
A 1913 state law naming Robeson Indians "Cherokee Indians of Robeson County" was not repealed when they were redesignated Lumbees in 1953. Cherokees of Western North Carolina fear Lumbees will use it in their campaign for federal recognition.

654. "The Lumbees: Their Status Is a Knotty Problem." *Durham Morning Herald* 19 Aug. 1978. [UNC-WL Clippings File]
Editorial on Cherokee opposition to Lumbee federal recognition.

655. Blu, Karen I. "The Uses of History for Ethnic Identity: The Lumbee Case." *Currents in Anthropology: Essays in Honor of Sol Tax*. Ed. Robert Hinshaw. The Hague: Mouton, 1979. Pp. [271]-85. [PSU-MLL]
Discusses (1) Henry Berry Lowry's band, and (2) attempts to determine and document

tribal origins and select a suitable tribal name. Documentation contemporary with both events was written mainly by Whites, giving little insight into Indian views.

656. North Carolina Commission of Indian Affairs. "A Historical Perspective about the Indians of North Carolina and an Overview of the Commission of Indian Affairs." *North Carolina Historical Review* 56.2 (April 1979): 177-87.
Mentions the 1835 disfranchisement, the Lowry Gang, Hamilton McMillan, the Croatan Normal School, and the formation, purpose and programs of the Commission.

657. Maynor, Douglas W. "Claims Cherokee Name for Robeson Indians." *Robesonian* 4 July 1979.
Letter. Cherokee is still the proper name for Robeson Indians. Maynor is a member of the Cherokee Indians of Robeson and Adjoining Counties.

658. Rose, Hewitt. "Lumbee Indians and the Law." Memorandum to John Merritt and Andria Turner, 16 Aug. 1979. 30 p. [IERC]
Analyzes laws on the definition of Indian. Provides information for monitoring all Indian funding legislation affecting Lumbees.

659. "Lumbee Petition Demands Federal Recognition of Tribal Status." *Wassaja: The Indian Historian* 13.1 (March 1980): 60. Rpt. in *CIV* 19 June 1980: 8.
On Lumbee attempts to join the NCAI. Linzey Revels, of the Lumbee Brotherhood, inquired in 1955. Lacy Maynor received a reply suggesting individual memberships.

660. Fanning, Adrian. "On Certification Moving Slowly." *Fayetteville Observer-Times* 13 April 1980: 1B-2B.
LRDA's Certification Project is preparing a tribal roll for BIA recognition. Discusses records used for verification.

661. Lynn, Lynette B. "Indian Status Proved." *Robesonian* 1 May 1980: 17.
Parents of 8,000 students in the county's Indian Education Act program—the nation's second largest—have filed Indian Student Certification forms, which required researching birth records.

662. "NCAI Considers Lumbees for Tribal Membership." *Wassaja: The Indian Historian* 13.2 (June 1980): 50.
Lumbees have been trying for forty years. The tribe's size caused some NCAI members to fear the control Lumbees would be able to levy. Mentions the United Lumbee Nation of North Carolina and California. Adolph Dial has stated that the group is disclaimed by Robeson County Lumbees.

663. Costo, Rupert. "An Object Lesson: The Lumbee Observance of Indian Heritage Week." *Wassaja: The Indian Historian* 13.3 (Sept. 1980): 51-52.
Lumbees, victims of segregation and discrimination for many years and still not fully recognized by the BIA, have gained enough respect and recognition to carry out a highly successful statewide Indian Heritage Week.

664. *Words of Today's American Indian Women, Ohoyo Makachi: A First Collection* *of Oratory by American Indian/Alaska Native Women*. Washington: U.S. Dept. of Education; Wichita Falls, TX: Prepared and distributed by Ohoyo, Inc., 1981. Ruth Dial Woods spoke on "Cross-Cultural Networking," mentioning N.C.'s Title IV Indian Education projects. Helen Maynor Scheirbeck discussed the need to combat stereotypes of Indians and of Indian women, and to wipe out hatred of other minorities.

665. Berde, Stuart. *Coharie Reemergence: Attaining Religious and Educational Freedom in Eastern North Carolina, 1850c-Present*. Lumbee River Legal Services and Coharie Intra-Tribal Council, 1982. [UNC-WL]
Discusses Lumbee influence on formation of the Coharie Tribe, especially through the Burnt Swamp Association (a group of Indian Missionary Baptist churches), which sent preachers to their area. Lumbees–especially individuals–are mentioned throughout.

666. Wilkins, David Eugene. "An Analysis of Colonial, State, and Federal 'Definitions of Indian'." Thesis. U of Arizona, 1982. [IERC]
Useful background information on state definitions of "free persons of color"; mixed-blood Indians' relations with the federal government; the concept of measuring degree of Indian blood; and the Indian Reorganization Act. Brief mention, pp. 117-18, of Robeson County Indians' attempt at recognition as Siouans and Carl Seltzer's "highly questionable" analysis of physical characteristics.

667. Bizzell, Oscar M., ed. *The Heritage of Sampson County, North Carolina*. Newton Grove, NC: Sampson County Historical Society with Hunter Pub. Co., 1983. Pp. 83-84.
For nearly two centuries, the Coharie preferred to be called Croatan. Like Lumbees, they built roads, served in major wars, and were disfranchised in 1835. Robeson County's Burnt Swamp Association helped them organize to get school funding.

668. 98th Cong. 1st Session. *Oversight of the Federal Acknowledgement Process*. Hearing, Select Comm. on Indian Affairs. S.Hrg. 98-690. Y4.In2/11:S.hrg.98-690 (*CIS* 1984: S961-13) 164p. Dated 21 July 1983.
Julian Pierce's testimony (pp. 48-59; typescript at IERC) examines the special situation of Southern tribes, which find it difficult to meet the BIA criterion of documented autonomy throughout history. Discusses three other concerns of North Carolina tribes about the BIA's Federal Acknowledgement Project. Another Senate hearing on the federal acknowledgement process (May 26, 1988; Y4.In2/11:S.hrg.100-823) contains testimony by Adolph Dial (pp. 27-34 and 178-189) on the history of Lumbee efforts at Federal recognition; the burden that federal acknowledgement requirements place on Eastern tribes; and conflict of interest in the Branch of Acknowledgement Research's Indian-preference hiring policy.

669. Hazel, Forest. "Black, White & 'Other': The Struggle for Recognition." *Southern Exposure* 13.6 (Nov.-Dec. 1985): 34-37.
Historical overview of the difficulties faced by Lumbees and other nonfederally recognized tribes in North Carolina.

670. Clotfelter, Sallie. "Pembroke Has Special Place in the Hearts of Lumbee Indians." *Greensboro News and Record* 2 Nov. 1986: G1.

Quotes Ruth Revels, Herbert Locklear, Calvin Hunt, Arlinda Locklear, Adolph Dial, and others on the importance to Lumbees of Robeson County as home.

671. Henderson, Bruce. "Lumbees Fight for Recognition as Tribe." *Charlotte Observer* 15 Oct. 1987: 1A.
The petition nears completion. LRDA and Lumbee River Legal Services began it in 1980 and have enrolled about 32,000 Lumbees.

672. Price, Mark. "'Man with No Shoes' Lends Lumbees Hand—Wes White, Advocate of Native Americans." *Fayetteville Times* 8 Dec. 1987: 13A.
Wes White (now Wes Taukchiray) assisted Lumbee River Legal Services in preparing the *Lumbee Petition*.

673. Patterson, Dennis. "Lumbees Await Word from Congress on Recognition." *Charlotte Observer* 3 Aug. 1988: 3E.
Bills were filed by Charlie Rose and Terry Sanford. Congressional recognition would be much quicker than the BIA petition process, which could take ten years.

674. Gibbs, Jeralene. "Leaders Optimistic About Lumbee Recognition." *Robesonian* 15 Aug. 1988: 1A.
Arlinda Locklear discusses the views of Ross Swimmer, assistant secretary of Indian Affairs. Lumbees have been before Congress eight times since 1888.

675. "Updates: Senate Committee Favors Lumbee Recognition." *Daybreak* 2.4 (Autumn 1988): 27.
The Select Committee on Indian Affairs approved the bill, which will not go to the full Senate until a plan is devised to prevent conflicts with other tribes (about 110) seeking recognition.

676. "Cherokee Opposition Helped Kill Bill on Lumbees." *Charlotte Observer* 30 Sept. 1988: 5B.
Representative James Clarke, from the western North Carolina Cherokee district, urged that the bill be set aside. Other tribes were also opposed.

677. Talbert, Malissa. "National Indian Group Endorses Recognition for Lumbees." *Robesonian* 3 Nov. 1988: 1A.
NCAI passed a resolution at annual convention. Cherokees read a letter of opposition.

678. -----. "Lumbee Recognition Is Debated." *Robesonian* 4 Nov. 1988: 1A.
Views of LRDA, the Lumbee Tribal Enrollment Office, the BIA, and the Cherokees.

679. Locklear, Barbara Brayboy. "Land of the Lumbee." Unpublished typescript. 1989. 5p. [IERC] Rpt. in *Robesonian* 29 Sept. 1991: 4A.
Lumbee identity is inextricably linked to the physical environment. Home is: the land of Robeson County in all its seasons and aspects; the Lumbee River; and the swamps, woodlands, and tobacco fields.

680. Witten, Scott. "Pembroke Native Honored for Human Relations Work."

Robesonian 6 March 1989: 1A.
Lonnie Revels, chairperson of the NC Commission of Indian Affairs, received a
Community Involvement Award from the NC Human Relations Council.

681. "Indian Peace Talks Canceled." *Robesonian* 8 March 1989: B1.
Cherokee Band's chief cancelled a meeting to discuss differences over Lumbee federal
recognition. The talk was to smooth the way for introduction of another bill.

682. Witten, Scott. "Lumbees Use Cheraw Link in Effort for Recognition."
          Robesonian 2 April 1989: 1A.
The forthcoming bill for recognition as "Lumbee Tribe of Cheraw Indians" will solve
an inconsistency between the 1988 bill, which didn't pass, and the 1956 Lumbee Act.

683. Healey, Jon. "Sanford Introduces Bill to Give Lumbees Full Federal Recogni-
          tion, but No Aid." *Winston-Salem Journal* 4 May 1989: 36.
Similar to the 1988 bill blocked by the Cherokees. It would bypass the BIA petition
process, which could take ten years and cost $150,000.

684. Guyton, Nanette. "Helms Is at Odds with Lumbee Recognition Petitioners."
          Robesonian 31 May 1989: 1.
Helms refuses to back any departure from the BIA recognition process. Lumbee Bill
supporters accuse him of a flip-flop because he introduced a similar bill in 1975 (see
entry 1369). BIA officials note that the petition process did not exist then.

685. Lavell, William G. "Memorandum To: Deputy to the Assistant Secretary—Indi-
          an Affairs (Tribal Services). From: Associate Solicitor, Indian Affairs. Subject:
          Lumbee Recognition Legislation." Washington: Office of the Solicitor, US
          Dept. of Interior, 23 Oct. 1989. Correspondence no. BIA.IA.0929 5p. Rpt. in
          House Report 101-685 (entry 1384), House Report 102-215 (entry 1387), and
          Senate Report 102-251 (entry 1388).
Advises that the "nothing-in-this-act" portion of the 1956 Lumbee Act terminates or
forbids the Federal relationship. The BIA cannot consider the *Lumbee Petition* unless
Congress amends that portion of the act.

686. Perdue, Theda. "Native Southerners." *Southern Changes* [Atlanta: Southern
          Regional Council] 11.5 (Nov. 1989): 1, 4-8.
Briefly mentions Lumbee achievements, as well as discriminations suffered, in context
of other Southern tribes.

687. Allday, Martin L. "Memorandum ... Interpretation of the Lumbee Act."
          Washington: Office of the Solicitor, US Dept. of Interior, 20 Nov. 1989. 4 p.
Reviews this Office's interpretation of the Lumbee Act, from 1972 through *Maynor v.
Morton* (1975) to the Associate Solicitor's Oct. 23, 1989 opinion (entry 685).

688. Guyton, Nanette. "Tribal Lawyer: Ruling Will Help Chances for Lumbee Bill."
          Robesonian 19 Jan. 1990: 1A.
Arlinda Locklear's views on the ruling (entry 685) which prevents the BIA from
processing the *Lumbee Petition*.

689.   Guyton, Nanette. "House Panel to Vote Today on Lumbee Recognition."
           Robesonian 7 Feb. 1990: 1A.
The House Committee on Interior and Insular Affairs will vote on whether the bill
should be sent to the House floor. Lists tribes and organizations opposing the bill.

690.   Guyton, Nanette. "Lumbee Leaders Vow to Continue to Fight for Recognition."
           Robesonian 11 Feb. 1990: 1A.
Jamie Clarke's amendment to the pending bill (entry 1382) repealed the part of the
Lumbee Act forbidding the petition process. Related articles, *News and Observer* and
Robesonian 8 Feb. 1990: 1A.

691.   Henderson, Bruce. "Martin Names Charlotte Woman to Head NC Indian
           Commission." *Charlotte Observer* 9 Aug. 1990: 3D.
Patrick Clark, Lumbee, replaced Lonnie Revels, five-year chairman of the Commission
of Indian Affairs. Related articles, *Robesonian* 5 Aug. 1990: 4A; *Charlotte Observer* 9
Sept. 1990: 1B; and *Robesonian* 31 May 1991: 6A.

692.   "Lumbee Bill Reintroduced." *Robesonian* 14 March 1991: 1A.
Reintroduced by Charlie Rose on March 13. A field hearing of the House Committee
on Interior and Insular Affairs was scheduled for June 7, 1991, in Pembroke
(*Robesonian* 19 May 1991: 1A) but was cancelled. A joint House/Senate hearing was
held in Washington on August 1, 1991 (*Robesonian* 2 Aug. 1991: 1). On Sept. 11,
1991, the bill was approved by the House Commitee on Interior Affairs (*News and
Observer* 12 Sept. 1991: 5B). On Sept. 26, 1991, it was approved by the full House
(*Charlotte Observer* 27 Sept. 1991: 5C). The Eastern Band of Cherokee Indians asked
Sen. Jesse Helms to block the bill (*Robesonian* 4 Oct. 1991: 1A). The bill was
approved by the Senate Select Committee on Indian Affairs on Nov. 20, 1991
(*Robesonian* 20 Nov. 1991: 1A). A procedural vote that would have brought the bill to
full debate on the Senate floor failed by two votes (*Charlotte Observer* 28 Feb. 1992:
1A; *Robesonian* 2 March 1992: 1A, 4A). The bill never made it out of committee (see
Robesonian 28 June 1992: 1A and 25 Aug 1992: 1A). Charlie Rose reintroduced it as
H.R. 334 (see *Robesonian* 6 Jan. 1993: 1A). It cleared the House and was backed by
the White House but was opposed by at least one N.C. senator (see *Robesonian* 30
Sept. 1993: 1A and 2 Nov. 1993: 4A; *Charlotte Observer* 29 Oct. 1993: 1C).

693.   Siceloff, Bruce. "Identity and Honor: Lumbee Indians and the Quest for
           Recognition." *News and Observer* 20 Oct. 1991: 1J.
Reviews the current legislation, how Lumbees would use the BIA and Indian Health
Service funds, why some other tribes oppose Lumbee recognition, and why Lumbees
have persisted in their recognition efforts since 1889.

694.   Hunt, Cynthia L. "A Guide to Understanding Lumbee History." *Robesonian* 5
           Jan. 1993: 4A.
Hunt, a paralegal working for Lumbee River Legal Services, provides a lengthy
response to a letter to the editor (*Robesonian* 28 Dec. 1992: 4A) questioning the tribe's
name and culture. She addresses Lumbee origin from Cheraws; the large volume of
research available on Lumbees (including ten federally commissioned reports);
"Lumbee" as the tribal name; Lumbee culture and language; and "Indian money."

695. Lumberton Youth Stumps Clinton on TV." *Robesonian* 21 Feb. 1993: 1A.
Fifteen-year-old Adrienne Andrade, daughter of Ronald Andrade, was one of forty
children appearing on the ABC special, "President Clinton: Answering Children's
Questions." She asked Clinton if he planned to do anything about federal recognition
for Lumbee Indians. He admitted he did not realize there were tribes that were not
federally recognized but would have his staff research the question and reply to her.
See also *Robesonian* 23 Feb. 1993: 1A and *News and Observer* 23 Feb. 1993: 5B.

696. Shepard, John, Jr. "Recognition Process Needs Revision." *Robesonian* 21
March 1993: 45.
Comments from a former chief of BIA's Branch of Acknowledgement Research,
prompted by entry 695. Shepard feels Clinton will be told that the BIA's process exists
to handle requests such as the Lumbees', and that 133 groups totalling 80,000 people
have submitted petitions. With the BIA's present staff and rate of review, it could be
2059 before the 133 petitions are reviewed.

Literature on Tri-Racial Isolates or Mixed Bloods

697. Reuter, Edward Byron. *The Mulatto in the United States, Including a Study of
the Role of Mixed-Blood Races Throughout the World.* Boston: Richard G.
Badger, 1918. Pp. 81-85.
Croatans, who claimed special privileges with the "baseless" Lost Colony theory, are
"a mixture of wasted Indian tribes, forest rovers, runaway slaves and other Negroes."

698. Estabrook, Arthur H., and Ivan E. McDougle. *Mongrel Virginians: The WIN
Tribe.* Baltimore: Williams and Wilkins, 1926. Pp. 188-94.
All names (county, tribe, surname) are changed in this book. The section on "Robin
County, North Carolina" and its Indians called "Rivers" discusses, in a somewhat
belittling tone, the Indians' physical characteristics and attitudes toward Blacks.
Nicole Rafter notes that Estabrook was one of 250 field workers trained at a summer
school run by the Eugenics Records Office at Cold Spring Harbor, NY, from 1910-
1924 (*White Trash: The Eugenic Family Studies 1788-1919*, Northeastern UP, 1988, p.
20). She asserts that the eugenics movement had as "another, less insistent, theme ...
the inferiority of foreigners and dark-skinned people" (p. 7) and calls *Mongrel
Virginians* the "most racist of all" of family studies reflecting this theme (p. 8).

699. Porter, Kenneth W. "Relations Between Negroes and Indians Within the Present
Limits of the United States." *Journal of Negro History* 17.3 (July 1932):
287-367.
See p. 317. Lumbees, a superior type compared to Melungeons, were forbidden by
state law to intermarry with Blacks "that the blood of the Elizabethan settlers might be
no further contaminated."

700. Seltzer, Carl C. "Report on the Racial Status of Robeson County Indians." 30
June 1936. National Archives and Records Admin., Washington, DC. RG 76,
Entry 616, Applications and other records relating to registration under the
Indian Reorganization Act of 1934, North Carolina.
Gives results of Seltzer's June, 1936, blood quantum study of county Indians for

Wheeler-Howard Act enrollment. The report cannot be released by the National Archives and Records Administration because it contains confidential information on persons still living.

701. Gilbert, William Harlan, Jr. "Memorandum Concerning the Characteristics of the Larger Mixed-Blood Racial Islands of the Eastern United States." *Social Forces* 24.4 (May 1946): 438-47. [PSU-MLL]
Background information on triracial isolates and the problems they face or cause. Checklist of facts and bibliography on ten groups (Croatans, pp. 440-42). Calls for a government policy to assimilate these "Native American backward minorities."

702. Nielson, Alfred Melville. "A Study of Certain 'Racial Islands' in the Eastern United States." Thesis. Ohio State U, 1947.
Overview of 13 groups, based on library research and correspondence. Lumbees are mentioned often in excerpts from published sources. Includes annotated bibliography.

703. Gilbert, William Harlan, Jr. *Synoptic Survey of Data on the Survival of Indian and Part Indian Blood in the Eastern United States*. Washington: Library of Congress, Legislative Reference Service, March 1947. Pp. 25-28.
Gives Lumbee population, physical characteristics, counties, family names, legal status, and occupations.

704. Dunlap, A. R., and C. A. Weslager. "Trends in the Naming of Tri-Racial Mixed-Blood Groups in the Eastern United States." *American Speech* 22.2 (April 1947): [81]-87. [PSU-MLL]
Documents forty names for triracial groups. "Croatan" exemplifies names with geographical associations.

705. Price, Edward Thomas. "Mixed Blood Populations of the Eastern United States as to Origins, Localizations, and Persistence." Diss. U of California at Berkeley, 1950. Pp. 285-91.
See also tables 28 and 29, and the discussion which follows, on the frequency of certain surnames among mixed groups. "McMillan's name study appears to be valueless in any attempt to link the Croatans to the Lost Colony" (p. 290).

706. Price, Edward T. "The Melungeons: A Mixed-Blood Strain of the Southern Appalachians." *Geographical Review* 41 (1951): 256-71.
Sees no evidence for Croatans as the origin of the Melungeons. Goins is the only family name the two groups have in common.

707. Price, Edward T. "A Geographic Analysis of White-Negro-Indian Racial Mixtures in Eastern United States." *Annals of the Association of American Geographers* 43 (June 1953): 138-55.
The Lost Colony theory helped Lumbees gain status but was disproved by Swanton (entry 535). Sees no similarity between Lost Colony surnames and those in the 1790 census for Robeson County.

708. Beale, Calvin L. "American Tri-Racial Isolates: Their Status and Pertinence to

Genetic Research." *Eugenics Quarterly* 4.4 (Dec. 1957): 187-96.
Defines triracial isolates. Lumbees are living in these counties: Evans and Richmond (GA); St. Marys (MD); Dillon, Marion and Marlboro (SC); and Bladen, Columbus, Cumberland, Harnett, Hoke, Robeson, Sampson, Scotland and Wayne (NC).

709. Pollitzer, William S., et al. "Hemoglobin Patterns in American Indians." *Science* 129 (23 Jan. 1959): 216.
Brief mention. Of 1,332 Lumbees whose hemoglobin was tested by paper electrophoresis, 1.7% showed sickle cell trait and 1.75% showed hemoglobin C trait.

710. Berry, Brewton. "The Myth of the Vanishing Indian." *Phylon* 21.1 (1960): 51-57. [PSU-MLL]
The 1950 census "reports no Indians living in Robeson County." [For background data, see entry 461.] Lumbees "are but one of hundreds of 'quasi-Indians' (some would say 'pseudo') to be found living in the eastern United States."

711. Berry, Brewton. *Almost White*. New York: Macmillan, 1963. [IERC]
Covers several mixed-blood groups, with frequent mention of Lumbees. Explains how they perceive and identify themselves racially; how their communities perceive them; state laws; problems in military service and education; and etiquette (water fountains, church seating, movie theaters). Reprints (without title) Chapman Milling's poem, "Croatan" (originally published in his *Singing Arrows*, 1939).

712. Pollitzer, William S. "Analysis of a Tri-Racial Isolate." *Human Biology* 36 (1964): 362-73.
In 1958, Pollitzer collected 1,273 blood samples in Pembroke. Tables, figures, and formulas show blood factors, gene frequencies, distances between the parental populations and the hybrid, and percentages of blood each parental population contributed to the hybrid. UNC-WL's copy has a handwritten note by Pollitzer.

713. Roberts, D. F. "Methods of Analysis of the Genetic Composition of a Hybrid Population." *Human Biology* 37.1 (Feb. 1965): [38]-43.
Discusses the four statistical methods applied by Pollitzer in entry 712, remarking on problems inherent in all but the least squares method.

714. Pollitzer, W. S.; R. M. Menegaz-Bock, and J. C. Herion. "Factors in the Microevolution of a Triracial Isolate." *American Journal of Human Genetics* 18.1 (Jan. 1966): 26-38. [PSU-MLL]
Performed a gene frequency analysis on 423 Lumbees. One group was 18% White, 41% Black, and 41% Indian. The other was 35% White, 34% Black, and 31% Indian.

715. Dane, J. K., and B. E. Griessman. "The Collective Identity of Marginal Peoples: The North Carolina Experience." *American Anthropologist* 74.3 (June 1972): 694-704.
Discusses efforts of the Haliwa Indians of Halifax and Warren Counties, and the Sampson County Lumbees, to "maintain a recognized Indian status."

716. Beale, Calvin L. "An Overview of the Phenomenon of Mixed Racial Isolates in

the United States." *American Anthropologist* 74.3 (June 1972): 704-10.
Defines tri-racial isolates; notes their location in the U.S.; and discusses common
themes. Lumbees sparked anthropologists' interest by claiming Lost Colony descent.

717. Pollitzer, William S. "The Physical Anthropology and Genetics of Marginal
People of the Southeastern United States." *American Anthropologist* 74.3 (June
1972): 719-33.
Also treats the formation and the medical or dental conditions of triracial isolates.
Gives Lumbee allele frequencies and blood percentages from ancestral populations.

718. "Researchers Say Lumbee Bloodlines Diluted." *Greensboro Record* 16 May
1973: A9.
Interest has revived in Pollitzer and Chernoff's 1958 research (reported in entry 712).
Pollitzer cautions that there is no "fixed and rigid definition of race." Related article,
Winston-Salem Twin City Sentinel 17 May 1973: 1.

719. Monaghan, William Patrick. "Frequencies of Blood Group Antigens in the
Lumbee Indians of North Carolina." Thesis. Bowling Green State U, 1974.
Blood from 130 older, isolated, agricultural Lumbees did not show significant genetic
contributions from Cherokees, Blacks or Seminoles. Lumbees "could have undergone
admixture with early White settlers and Tuscarora Indians" (p. 37).

720. Gildemeister, Enrique Eugene. "Local Complexities of Race in the Rural South:
Racially Mixed People in South Carolina." Thesis. State U of New York
College at Purchase, 1977.
Explains how mixed-blood groups emerge and persist when society theoretically
doesn't recognize shades between Black and White. Review of the literature on mixed
bloods, noting questions left unanswered. Useful discussion of White-oriented vs.
Indian-oriented groups, such as the Lumbee. See brief mentions, pp. 7 and 29-30.

721. Sovine, Melanie Lou. "The Mysterious Melungeons: A Critique of the Mythical
Image." Diss. U of Kentucky, 1982. [ASU-APP]
Brief mention. Table 4, "Theories of Melungeon Origin," lists 35 publications linking
Melungeons to Lumbees through descent from the Lost Colony. Also discusses Will
Allen Dromgoole and the reception of her *Arena* articles on Melungeons.

722. Forbes, Jack D. "Mulattoes and People of Color in Anglo-North America:
Implications for Black-Indian Relations." *Journal of Ethnic Studies* 12.2
(Summer 1984): 17-61.
Brief mention. Robeson Indians were listed as "free persons of color" in the
1800–1830 censuses. North Carolina's definition of mulatto was one White and one
non-White parent. Lists dates and decrees for NC legislation on mixed-blood people.

723. Daniel, G. R. "Passers and Pluralists: Subverting the Racial Divide." *Racially
Mixed People in America*. Newbury Park, CA: Sage, 1992. Pp. 91-107.
Brief mention. See "Runaways and Refuseniks: Triracial Isolates," pp. 98-102. Most
triracial isolates deny African ancestry and venerate Native American descent. Groups
such as the Lumbee have successfully used flexibility in definitions of Native

American (i.e., differing definitions used by the Census Bureau and the BIA) to gain status as nontreaty Native Americans.

The Tuscarora Indians of Robeson County

724. "Lumbee Unit Forms Plan for State Organization." *News and Observer* 31 Dec. 1971: 5.
A group which met at the Hopewell Community Center on December 30 formed the Eastern Carolina Indian Organization. The officers are listed. Their purpose is to seek federal recognition through the Indian Reorganization Act of 1934. They are also concerned that Robeson County's current Indian leaders are insensitive to their needs.

725. Nichols, Rick. "Are They Indians? Are They Lumbees?" *News and Observer* 9 Jan. 1972: Sec. 4 p. [3].
Discusses Lumbee lack of political power, the Eastern Carolina Indian Organization, the Original 22, and ECIO members' frustration with the name Lumbee. Meetings to form the ECIO began last month. One observer commented, "If you could draw a parallel to the Black movement, they'd probably be the Huey Newtons."

726. "Attorney: Tuscaroras May Have Own Schools." *News and Observer* 15 Oct. 1972: Sec. 1 p. 5.
150 Tuscaroras met with an attorney for the National Coalition of Indian Controlled School Boards, which had organized 52 Indian school boards in the past 15 months. See related article, *News and Observer* 31 Oct. 1972, on Tuscarora desires to form a new, all-Indian school and on assistance from Dennis Banks and AIM.

727. Price, Bill. "Chief of Tuscaroras Calls for Unity in Support of Wounded Knee Indians." *Robesonian* 8 March 1973: 1.
In a news conference at the Pow-Wow Restaurant (Pembroke), Howard Brooks announced that he was elected, on December 15, chief of the Tuscarora Indians of Robeson and Adjacent Counties. The goals of the organization were to "present a unified voice when making demands," restore Indian schools to Robeson County, and support AIM activities at Wounded Knee. Also attending were Bob Garvey of AIM and Bill Sargent, executive director of the Eastern National AIM Office in Lumberton.

728. "Indians Continue Protest." *News and Observer* 9 March 1973: 27.
Tuscaroras, touring Robeson County in a 40-vehicle caravan, demonstrated to support Wounded Knee and protest double-voting. See also *Robesonian* 7 March 1973: 1.

729. Lang, Melvin. "Fire Razes Former School for Indians in Robeson County." *Greensboro Daily News* 11 March 1973: B1.
Hopewell School in Rowland burned shortly after a Tuscarora demonstration.

730. Poole, Bob. "Papers Reveal Cause of Indian Ire: Tuscaroras Didn't Get Federal Funds." *Winston-Salem Twin City Sentinel* 17 March 1973: 1.
Howard Brooks was interviewed regarding the FBI's recovery (March 16) of 75 pounds of documents which might have been stolen during the BIA Building takeover. The documents included a list of the 22 Robeson County Indians recognized by the

Secretary of Interior in 1938 as one-half or more Indian blood (names reprinted). Brooks claims descent from the Hatteras Tuscaroras. His Tuscarora Movement, now composed of 500 members, seeks federal recognition and has other aims.

731. Price, Bill. "Tuscarora Chief Offers Tribal History Account." *Robesonian* 18 March 1973: 2A.
Howard Brooks tours two places of significance to Tuscaroras. Similar article, *News and Observer* 18 March 1973: I-5.

732. Coit, John. "Robeson Indians Arrested." *News and Observer* 25 March 1973: Sec. 1 p. 1.
Sixty-five Tuscaroras, including chief Howard Brooks, were arrested in front of Prospect School. They had demonstrated for seven hours because the school's principal and its advisory committee would not allow Brooks and AIM organizers to meet in the school's auditorium. Also arrested was Vernon Bellecourt, national director of AIM.

733. Wright, Bill. "Tuscarora Indian Organization Files Suit Seeking Interior Department Assistance." *Carolina Indian Voice* 29 March 1973: 1.
Attorney Thomas N. Tureen filed the suit on behalf of the Eastern Carolina Tuscarora Indian Organization. The suit asked the court to declare that the Lumbee Act did not preclude Indians from receiving benefits under the Indian Reorganization Act of 1934. The article notes the division between the ECTIO and Howard Brooks' Tuscaroras.

734. Fazio, Thomas P. "Indian Group on Protest Trek." *News and Observer* 5 April 1973: 39.
Thirty Tuscaroras in Raleigh demand a return to Indian control of schools originally established by Indians for their children.

735. Hall, Doug. "100 Tuscaroras Rally in Raleigh." *News and Observer* 9 April 1973: 21.
Tuscaroras ally with the Southern Christian Leadership Conference to petition Gov. Holshouser to convene the North Carolina Commission of Indian Affairs. They want problems of welfare, culture and tribal recognition addressed. A related article (same page) notes that Carnell Locklear's Eastern Carolina Indian Organization "has been in direct conflict" with Howard Brooks' Tuscarora Movement.

736. Holtz, J. "Robeson Fire Charged to 3." *News and Observer* 9 April 1973: 21.
Joe's Cash Store was burned on March 18. There was a shooting at the home of Carnell Locklear, who was lobbying for state aid to restore Old Main. Another 2,000 pounds of BIA documents (see also entry 730) were found in an abandoned house.

737. "Frinks Is Becoming Leader of Black-Indian Coalition." *Winston-Salem Journal* 11 April 1973: 6.
Golden Frinks often assumes control of public gatherings of Tuscaroras. The article speculates that "Frinks has taken up the slack in leadership" left by Dennis Banks.

738. Coit, John. "Hunt, Indians Meet; Holshouser Spurned." *News and Observer* 11

April 1973: 25.
Howard Brooks refused to meet with the governor, who "put restrictions on the matters to be discussed," or with the state Commission of Indian Affairs.

739. "Indians Defy Ban, March in N.C." *Workers World* 13 April 1973: 12.
Howard Brooks' Tuscaroras, as part of their 100-mile, four-day caravan to Raleigh, tried to march through Smithfield, then known as headquarters for the Ku Klux Klan in southeastern North Carolina. On arriving, they were arrested, told they could not march without a permit, and harassed by the Klan. More Indians arrived to support them; the charges were dropped and a permit was issued.

740. Coit, John. "Authorities, Media Blamed for Poor Indian Showing." *News and Observer* 14 April 1973: 19.
Golden Frinks had claimed 15,000 would attend. Speakers at the Tuscarora rally blamed the governor, state troopers, and media for attendance of only 80.

741. Carroll, Ginny. "Indians' Suit Dismissed in Wake Court." *News and Observer* 20 April 1973: 31.
Howard Brooks and Golden Frinks filed against Gov. Holshouser and the N.C. Comm. of Indian Affairs. The Commission refused to meet on Tuscarora recognition if White attorneys or Black supporters accompanied the Indians. The suit was dismissed.

742. Doster, Woody. "Lumbees Must Organize to Get Slice of BIA Budget." *Greensboro Daily News* 17 May 1973: D9.
Tom Oxendine, BIA communications officer and a Lumbee, discusses Tuscarora recognition efforts and explains steps Lumbees must take to obtain full federal recognition. Similar article, *News and Observer* 17 May 1973.

743. Lang, Melvin. "Indian Life: Doubt Stemming from Ancestral Uncertainty Sparks Robeson Unease." *Durham Morning Herald* 27 May 1973. [UNC-WL Clippings File]
Background of the Tuscarora movement and reactions of several Robeson County Indians to the Lumbee vs. Tuscarora controversy.

744. Owens, Pamela. "Indians Rebel in Carolina." *Southern Patriot* [Southern Conference Educational Fund, Louisville, KY] 31.5 (31 May 1973): 1, 3. Rpt. in *CIV* 14 June 1973: 1, 3.
Robeson County Tuscaroras formed an alliance with the Black Liberation movement, participated in a takeover of the BIA building, and demonstrated in support of Wounded Knee. Explains their objections to the name "Lumbee."

745. "Deputy Tells of Finding Missing BIA Papers." *News and Observer* 14 Dec. 1973: 35.
Hubert Stone testified during a trial that he found 3,000-4,000 pounds of government papers in an old school bus near Maxton.

746. Baker, Donald P. "Lack of Education Is Factor in Acquittal of Indians." *Washington Post* 26 Dec. 1973: A2.

Lengthy, detailed article. Keever Locklear and cousin Dock Locklear were acquitted in federal district court on charges related to theft of documents from the BIA Building in Washington. Neither can read or write, and thus "had little reason to, as the indictment charged, 'receive, conceal or retain property of the Department of Interior (BIA)'." Related articles, *Washington Post* 20 Dec. 1973: A2; *News and Observer* 20 Dec. 1973: 39; and *Greensboro Daily News* 30 Dec. 1973: A9. See especially Jack Anderson, "False Testimony Used in Indian Trial," *Washington Post* 31 Dec. 1973: B7. The Justice Department, Anderson asserts, "staged a seven-day show trial" and tried to link him, his research assistant, and his column to the North Carolina case.

747. Adams, Jack. "Indians Want Tribe, Not Handout." *Durham Morning Herald* 10
      April 1974. [UNC-WL Clippings File]
Howard Brooks' Tuscaroras oppose a proposed amendment to the 1956 Lumbee Act because it would retain the Lumbee name and would not grant full BIA recognition.

748. McDonald, Laughlin. "'Undisciplined' Indians." *Civil Liberties* 303 (July
      1974): 3-4. Rpt. in *CIV* 18 July 1974: 4.
Forty Tuscaroras went to the Robeson County Board of Education to ask how Indian Education Act funds were being spent. The superintendent did not show up, and all were arrested. The children were convicted for failure to attend school. The case was reversed on appeal, with help from the ACLU.

749. "Indian Lawsuit Rules in Favor of Original 22's Rights under IRA." *Carolina
      Indian Voice* 17 April 1975: 1. [Reprints case report for *Maynor v. Morton*.]

750. Rainbolt, Harry A. "Memorandum To: Commissioner of Indian Affairs. From:
      Area Director, Eastern Office. Subject: Hatteras Tuscarora Indians of North
      Carolina." Washington: U.S. Dept. of Interior, Bureau of Indian Affairs, Eastern
      Office, 26 Sept. 1975. 10 p.
A BIA task force held a three-day meeting with 25-35 Tuscaroras on services available to them as a result of *Maynor v. Morton*.

751. *Trail of Broken Treaties: B.I.A., I'm Not Your Indian Anymore*. Rooseveltown,
      NY: Akwesasne Notes [Mohawk Nation], 1976. P. 7.
Brief mention. Describes participation by the Eastern Carolina Tuscarora Indian Organization. Reprints a news release on the acquittal of four Tuscaroras who stole documents from the BIA headquarters.

752. "Robeson Indians Seek Recognition So They Qualify for Federal Aid." *Durham
      Sun* 12 July 1977. [UNC-WL Clippings File]
The Tuscaroras filed suit asking that the Lumbee Act be declared unconstitutional and that they be able to choose their own name.

753. "N.C. Indian Tribes in Bout Over Official Recognition." *Durham Sun* 3 Aug.
      1977. [UNC-WL Clippings File]
The Tuscarora Tribal Council's suit asks for damages, but some feel they really want a reservation. Outlines differences between Lumbee and Tuscarora expectations from federal recognition.

754. Barton, Peggy, and Darlene Locklear. "BIA Building Homes for Recognized Indians in Robeson." *Carolina Indian Voice* 6 Oct. 1977: 7.
The BIA will build houses for eight survivors of the Original 22, as a result of *Maynor v. Morton*. Reprints the contract between the BIA and Lawrence M. Maynor.

755. The Tuscarora Tribe of North Carolina. *Petition for Federal Recognition*. Unpublished typescript. Approx. 180 p. Dec. 1989.
Gives accounts of the tribe's factual and political history, the present-day tribe, membership criteria and by-laws, affiliation with other tribes, and a list of sources. As of 1980, there were 11,000 Tuscaroras in Robeson County (see p. 13).

756. "Tuscarora Seek Help on Petition." *News and Observer* 16 Dec. 1989: 1B.
The Tuscarora Tribe of N.C., Inc. (formed in 1984 by the consolidation of four Maxton-based Tuscarora groups) submitted a petition to the BIA on Dec. 5. It includes a tribal roll of 213 members. Recognition would bring funds for education, job training, and substance abuse prevention and treatment.

757. Bolch, Judy. "Indian Mysteries for Sale." *News and Observer* 18 June 1990: 1A.
Chief Wise Owl of Maxton (Tuscarora Tribe, Drowning Creek Reservation) is being investigated on complaints from purchasers of blankets blessed by him. Similar article, *Robesonian* 1 July 1990: 1A. Obituary, *Robesonian* 3 June 1993: 1A.

758. "Tribal Officials Fired by Council." *Robesonian* 20 Oct. 1991: 1A.
Chief Brawleigh Graham and his wife were fired by the Tribal Council for withholding information about the tribe's financial records. Related articles which follow the progress of the incident: *Robesonian* 6 Oct. 1991: 1A; 10 Oct. 1991: 1A; 13 Oct. 1991: 1A; 3 Nov. 1991: 4A; 12 Nov. 1991: 1A; 31 Jan. 1992: 1A; 2 Feb. 1992: 1A, 4A; 19 Feb. 1992: 1A; 12 March 1992: 1A, 8A; 12 April 1992: 1A; 8 June 1992: 1A; 8 July 1992: 1A; Ed. 26 July 1992: 4A; 26 Aug. 1992: 1A; 31 Aug. 1992: 1A; 4 Sept. 1992: 1A; 9 Sept. 1992: 1A; 16 Oct. 1992: 1A.

CRIME AND CRIMINAL JUSTICE; LAW; BUSINESS, ECONOMICS, AND EMPLOYMENT; POLITICS AND GOVERNMENT; MEDIA; RACE RELATIONS AND SEGREGATION

759. Humphrey, W. H. "A Card." *Robesonian* 26 June 1900: 1.
This letter favors a proposed North Carolina constitutional amendment requiring people to read and write a section of the Constitution to qualify for voter registration. Reminds Croatans how much Democrats have done for them. Reprints the proposed amendment. See also 29 July 1900: 2.

760. "Strong Argument for the Amendment." *Robesonian* 17 July 1900: 2.
Croatan teachers should support the proposed amendment to the North Carolina Constitution. O. R. Sampson says it will "stimulate education to a higher degree" and "solve the race problem in the state."

761. "The Pembroke Petition." *The Argus* 12 Feb. 1903: 2.
A petition was given to committees in 14 townships. It asked the General Assembly to authorize a special election on moving the county seat from Lumberton to Pembroke. Similar article, *Robesonian* 13 Feb. 1903: 2.

762. Stancill, G. W. "A Lie Denounced: An Old Confederate Soldier and Preacher Denounces as a Lie the Report That He Is Preaching Social Equality." *Robesonian* 25 May 1908: 1.
Letter. Stancill had been pastor of two Croatan churches.

763. Locklear, A. W. "The 'Macs' of Robeson: Hon. Hamilton McMillan and What He and Other 'Macs' Have Done for the Croatan Indians." *Robesonian* 6 Aug. 1908: 1.
Letter. "Every bill that has been of great interest to [Indians], and printed in the statute laws of North Carolina, was presented by a Mac."

764. Wilkins, W. S. "State Should Provide for Indian Insane: White and Colored Insane Are Provided For But There Is No Place for the Indian Insane." *Robesonian* 6 Sept. 1915: 3.
Wilkins' wife was ruled insane. The county physician says she must go to jail or to a hospital. For an earlier, similar complaint, see A. S. Locklear's letter (entry 582).

765. "Robeson Indians." *Robesonian* 10 Jan. 1916: 4.
Indians were once present "in droves" in Superior Court but now are conspicuously absent. They have been intensely interested in education for the past ten years.

766. "Recorder's Court: White Woman and Indian in the Toils for Living Together." *Robesonian* 26 Feb. 1917: 4.
Duncan Locklear was sentenced to fourteen months' road work; Minnie Brockwell got six months in jail. Judge N. McInnis wrote a contract, signed by both, to allow the relationship (see below).

767. "Justice McInnis Replies: He Justifies His Act in Drawing Up Contract Between Indian and White Woman." *Robesonian* 5 March 1917: 3.
Minnie Brockwell would be paid to keep house and care for Duncan Locklear's children while he worked in South Carolina for a year.

768. "Superior Court: Dr. G. W. Locklear, Indian, of Pembroke, Must Leave the State to Live with the White Woman He Married in Georgia–Marriage Not Recognized in This State." *Robesonian* 26 Jan. 1920: 1.

769. Locklear, Patrick. "Some Questions." *Robesonian* 19 April 1928: 4.
Letter inquiring why the town officers of Pembroke are appointed by the governor of North Carolina (not elected) and why Indians no longer serve on juries. Twelve years ago, "almost every court in [the] County had from two to three" Indians on the jury.

770. McInnis, N. "Mayor McInnis Resents New Name for Pembroke." *Robesonian* 1 Jan. 1931: 4.

The mayor of Pembroke rebuts remarks of Solicitor T. A. McNeill, who called the section around Pembroke a "Hell hole" due to violent crime.

771. "Why the Distinction?" *Robesonian* 28 Sept. 1931: 4.
Letter. Veterans' and school children's day at the county fair applies to Whites only.

772. Wilkins, Cherry. "The Strange Case of Nick and Versha." *The State* 1.47 (21 April 1934): 18.
Misfortunes of a Croatan girl who married a mulatto boy in Virgilina, a hamlet between Virginia and North Carolina.

773. "Indian Files for F'mont Constable." *Robesonian* 30 April 1934: 1.
Debo Oxendine, the county's first Indian to run for public office.

774. "Indians and Negroes on Jury for First Time in Nearly 40 Years." *Robesonian* 18 Aug. 1937: 1.
The judge received a petition asking that Indians be chosen to serve. After investigation, he "found that names of Indians had been in the box but had not been drawn." Related articles, *Robesonian* 11 Aug. 1937: 1; *Greensboro Daily News* 18 Aug. 1937.

775. "Rowland Theatre to Open Monday." *Robesonian* 29 Oct. 1937: 8.
Whites use the main entrance under the marquee and sit on the lower floor; they are allotted 338 of the 478 seats. Indians use another main entrance but sit in their section of the balcony. Blacks use a side entrance and sit in another section of the balcony.

776. "Indians and Negroes to Be Segregated at Prison Camp." *Robesonian* 16 May 1938: 4.
Indians had complained to the Highway Chairman that Indians and Negroes were mixed in the camp. Related article, *Robesonian* 18 April 1932: 1.

777. "Revels Given Fifty Years for Assault on White Girl." *Robesonian* 14 Nov. 1938: 1.
A jury found Duckery Revels not guilty of rape but guilty of assault. The judge sentenced him to 50 years' hard labor. See also *News and Observer* 13 Nov. 1938, which includes the judge's remarks before passing sentence.

778. "White Man to Leave State to Live with Indian Wife He Loves." *Robesonian* 17 May 1939: 1.
Jim Baxley pleaded guilty to fornication and adultery and waived rights to N.C. citizenship. He and his wife will leave N.C., where interracial marriages are illegal.

779. "Robeson's First Indian Dies in Gas Chamber; Lumberton Negro Also Is Put to Death." *Robesonian* 7 July 1939: 1.
Bricey Hammonds, for killing a prison camp guard. 221 people had been executed since the chamber's installation in 1910. Alfred Caper was the 180th Negro executed.

780. "Pembroke Will Elect Officials: Senate Bill Provides for Election of Mayor and Commissioners Heretofore Appointed." *Robesonian* 22 Feb. 1945: 1.

On Senate Bill 247, introduced by Sen. Carson Brooks. The town's officials had been appointed since 1917.

781. "Pembroke to Hold Primary April 24; Town Will Elect Officials for First Time under New Charter." *Robesonian* 3 April 1945: 1.
The bill was ratified on March 7; see entry 1355.

782. Barton, Lew. "A Report on the Robeson County Indian." *Robesonian* 18 May 1949: 4.
On segregation practiced against and by Lumbees. This article may have been prompted by debate over the Long House meetings; see entries 612, 613, and 614.

783. "Indian Prison Camp to Be Moved Here: All-Indian Staff ... Headed by Harry West Locklear." *Robesonian* 10 Nov. 1949. [PSU-MLL. PSU Clippings File].
The Indian camp will be moved from Walnut Cove. Most Indian prisoners are from Robeson, Sampson, Bladen, and Columbus Counties.

784. "Woman Advised 'to Go North' after Two Court Appearances." *Robesonian* 22 Jan. 1954: 1.
A White woman from Baltimore, charged with vagrancy for being in the company of two Indian men, is admonished by the Recorder Judge that "whenever one race of people mix[es] with another, it's bad."

785. " ... Cover Limited Territory." *Robesonian* 25 Jan. 1954: [4].
Simeon Oxendine says Pembroke VFW Post members found the judge's remarks (entry 784) prejudicial and the story's front-page placement in bad taste. The editorialist deems the remarks reasonable in context of the case. See letters, 29 Jan. 1954.

786. "Judge Ivey Says He Followed Law and Practices of People." *Pembroke Progress* 28 Jan. 1954: [4].
Letter. Ivey states, "We will have much better people in all races by using pure bred stock in raising children."

787. "Indian Leader Announces for Seat in State Legislature." *Robesonian* 18 March 1954: 1. [D. F. Lowry, first county Indian to seek a legislative post.]

788. Barton, Lewis Randolph. "Contrasts." *Robesonian* 19 July 1954: 10.
On a White reporter's interview with Bricey Hammonds before his execution for killing a White prison guard. Notes the "sympathy of one human being for another."

789. "Classmate of Immortal Jim Thorpe Is Now Progressive Pembroke Mayor." *Scottish Chief* 6 Aug. 1954. [PSU-MLL. PSU Clippings File]
James C. Oxendine.

790. "First Indian Recorder in Robeson Begins His Work." *Robesonian* 9 Dec. 1955? [PSU-MLL. PSU Clippings File] [Early Bullard, district court.]

791. "Pembroke Indians Form Political Activity Group." *News and Observer* 28 Feb.

1958: 24.
The unnamed male-only organization will "increase political activity among Lumbees" and choose a slate of candidates for the upcoming Democratic primary. Notes that other, similar organizations exist in the county.

792. "First Indian Commissioner." *Robesonian* 2 June 1958: 1.
Tracy Woodward Sampson was elected county commissioner. For Sampson's obituary, see *Robesonian* 21 Oct. 1991: 1A.

793. Jones, English. "The Educational and Occupational Status of Former Students of Vocational Agriculture of Pembroke High School, Pembroke, North Carolina." Thesis. North Carolina State College, 1959. [Not seen.]

794. Waynick, Capus M., ed. *North Carolina and the Negro*. Raleigh: North Carolina Mayors' Co-Operating Committee, 1964. Pp. 127-28.
In 1963, Indians asked county commissioners for more job opportunities. Lumberton's mayor formed a Triracial Committee to help desegregate stores, restaurants, motels, and theaters.

795. Rollins, Ray. "Lumbees Grateful for Work in Piedmont." *Winston-Salem Journal and Sentinel* 20 March 1966.
The North Carolina Fund helped Johnnie Oxendine move to Thomasville to work in a furniture plant. In Robeson County, 32% of people worked less than 6 months/year.

796. "Non-White Registration ... Highest in County." *Robesonian* 30 April 1968: 1.
Over 7,000 new voters were registered during the year. For the first time, nonwhite registration outnumbered White [14,424 White, 6,634 Black, 7,896 Indian].

797. "Lumbees on the Warpath for Industry." *Greensboro Record* 23 March 1970: A13. [Pembroke should create more jobs to keep youth from migrating.]

798. Gruson, Kerry. "Lumbees Seeking Political Power." *News and Observer* 25 May 1970: 6.
Bill Brewington helped form Independent Americans for Progress, to build Indian unity on community and political issues.

799. "President of Indians Is Elected." *News and Observer* 6 July 1970: 22.
Ward Clark was elected president of Independent Americans for Progress, called the first Lumbee political organization.

800. Witherspoon, David. "At NCCU, Lumbees Pursue Careers in Law Field." *Durham Morning Herald* 26 Oct. 1970.
Horace Locklear, Arnold Locklear, Ertle Chavis, and Henry Oxendine are attending North Carolina Central University.

801. Sider, Gerald Marc. "Political History of the Lumbee Indians of Robeson County, North Carolina: A Case Study of Ethnic Political Affiliations." Diss. New School for Social Research, 1971. [ECU]

Sider provides a comprehensive period by period analysis of Lumbee political history, with special attention to the intense activity during his field research (May 1967-Aug. 1968). Topics include: local explanations for Henry Berry Lowry's deeds; the county's role in the 1875 referendum to revise the state constitution; The Movement, a 1960's Indian-Black coalition; social and political activities in various parts of the county; efforts to get "Indian money"; the political impact of landlord-tenant relations on county agriculture; and Indian locality leaders.

802. Bledsoe, Jerry. " ... Still Suffering and Hungry: Desperately Poor Lumbees Are There If You Look." *Greensboro Daily News* 18 Jan. 1971: A1.

803. "Lumbees Ask Red, Black Voting Unity." *Durham Morning Herald* 20 Oct. 1971.
Adolph Dial and Tom Dial discuss an LRDA program to increase Lumbee unity and identity, perhaps leading to a political coalition with Blacks.

804. "First Indian Lawyer in N.C. Honored by Saddletree Jaycees." *Robesonian* 3 Sept. 1972: 2A. [Horace Locklear.]

805. "Survey Discovers Robeson Job Bias." *News and Observer* 1 Oct. 1972: I-5.
A report by the U.S. Comm. on Civil Rights showed Blacks and Indians clustered in low-paying, non-skilled jobs. Of 320 firms in the county, only 88 returned surveys.

806. Briggs, Delores. "Control County School Board: Sociologist." *Robesonian* 1 Oct. 1972: 1.
John Gregory Peck, in hearings on Lumbee economic and political plight, advocated the abolition of double-voting and discussed low Indian political participation.

807. Briggs, Olin. "Further Hearings with Subpoena Powers Eyed as Civil Rights Advisory Panel Ends Sessions Here." *Robesonian* 1 Oct. 1972: 1
Hearings on Lumbee economic and political plight were led by a N.C. Advisory Committee to the U.S. Comm. on Civil Rights. Because it had no subpoena power, many invited officials did not attend. See also *News and Observer* 30 Sept. 1972: 5.

808. Tarleton, Larry. "Robeson County's Indians Bolting Democratic Ranks." *Charlotte Observer* 5 Nov. 1972: 3B.
Carnell Locklear and Dennis Banks urge Lumbees to support Republican Holshouser, who has often intervened for the tribe.

809. Coit, J. "Panel Cites Robeson Bias." *News and Observer* 31 March 1973: 17.
Comments from W. W. Finlator and Brenda Brooks, N.C. Civil Rights Advisory Comm. Findings are listed. Related articles: *CIV* 5 April 1973: 1; 12 April 1973: 1.

810. Schlosser, Jim. "Indians Represented." *Greensboro Record* 3 April 1973: B1.
Henry Ward Oxendine is the first Lumbee to serve in the General Assembly. Lonnie Revels almost won that honor the previous fall.

811. Gamble, Douglass R. *Pembroke Revitalization Program*. Raleigh: Community

Development Group, North Carolina State U, 1974. [UNC-WL]
Recommends a public park, preservation of the railroad depot, visual controls, signage, curbs and sidewalks, and parking.

812. Nichols, Rick. "Indians Hit Postmaster Appointment." *News and Observer* 26 May 1974: 1.
Jim McVickers, White, is Pembroke's first non-Indian postmaster. He was selected over two Indian candidates with longer service and, some feel, better qualifications.

813. U.S. Commission on Civil Rights. North Carolina Advisory Committee. *Economic and Political Problems of Indians in Robeson County: A Report.* Washington: The Commission, July 1974. [PSU-MLL]
The N. C. Committee held an open meeting in Robeson County and heard statements from 44 people. Lumbee problems were "nearly all ... attributable in large degree to insensitivity or inaction on the part of county, state or federal government bodies."

814. Smith, W. "Anti-Indian Bias Found." *News and Observer* 18 Sept. 1974: 21.
Summarizes findings and recommendations of entry 813. Gives reactions from Bruce Barton, Brenda Brooks, Gene Warren, and others.

815. Locklear, Linda G. "The LRDA Story." *Carolina Indian Voice* 29 Sept. 1974: 4. [Reviews LRDA's history, purpose, and accomplishments.]

816. Brooks, Dexter. "Memorandum. Subject: A Survey of Federal Voting Law with Applications to Robeson County, North Carolina. To Professor Daniel H. Pollitt, U. of North Carolina School of Law, Chapel Hill." Unpublished typescript. 1 Dec. 1974. 31 p.
Overview of the Voting Rights Act and other topics. The Robeson County section covers county commissioner districts; judicial elections; election of Robeson Technical Institute's Board of Trustees; and annexations by the Lumberton school district.

817. Footlick, Jerrold K., and Eleanor Clift. "Crusading for Death." *Newsweek* 86.3 (21 July 1975): 31. Rpt., with "an alternate view," in *CIV* 7 Aug. 1975: 2.
Britt, after 14 months as district attorney, had asked for the death penalty on 12 people and sent all (4% of the U.S. total) to Death Row. He hopes his capital-punishment campaign will reduce his district's homicide rate.

818. Whittle, Richard. "Small N.C. District Is Giant on Death Penalty." *News and Observer* 22 Dec. 1975: 1, 6.
On Joe Freeman Britt's "blitz" on first-degree murder cases.

819. Sider, Gerald M. "Lumbee Indian Cultural Nationalism and Ethnogenesis." *Dialectical Anthropology* 1.2 (Feb. 1976): 161-72. [PSU-MLL]
Lumbee political history can be considered cultural nationalism, while the Tuscarora Movement is political nationalism. Lumbee cultural nationalism has no future and will not result in ethnogenesis.

820. Clifford, William B., and Patricia L. Tobin. "Labor Force Participation of

Working Mothers and Family Formation." *Demography* 14.3 (Aug. 1977): 273-84.
Examined each race's fertility, expected family size, and female employment after marriage. The longer Indian women were employed after marriage, the more children they desired. Minority women saw no conflict between childbearing and work.

821. Davis, Owen. "Robeson Indian Takes Helm at Lumbee Bank." Raleigh *News and Observer* 18 Sept. 1977: Sec. 4 p. 3.
James A. Hunt, Tar Heel of the Week, is the state's first Indian bank president. The Lumbee Bank is cited as the country's first Indian-owned bank. Note: The Lumbee Bank was renamed Lumbee Guaranty Bank. It celebrated its 20th anniversary on 22 Dec. 1991 (see *Robesonian* 29 Dec. 1991: D1).

822. "Lumbee Regional Development Association, Inc. Perspective." Unpublished typescript. 10 p. Attachment D-6, Pembroke Indian Alcohol Project grant application, 8/1/78 (See entry 484.) [PSU-MLL]
Includes an overview of federal and state relations with Lumbees; a history of LRDA; and a list of programs LRDA has supported, sponsored, or administered.

823. "Deadliest Prosecutor [Joe Freeman Britt]." *Guinness Book of World Records*. New York: Sterling, 1978. P. 394.
Britt, by mid-1976, had secured 23 death verdicts in 28 months, placing 13 persons on Death Row. This entry ran, unaltered, each year through 1986.

824. *Lumbee Business Directory*. Lumbee Regional Development Association, n.d. 26 p. [IERC] [Names and addresses, grouped by classification scheme.]

825. Swofford, Stan. "Are Highway Patrolmen Mistreating Lumbee Indians?" *Greensboro Daily News* 25 June 1978: A1.
On the Terry Lockee case. The N. C. Comm. of Indian Affairs wants an investigation.

826. "Official to Eye Charges of Brutality to Indians." *News and Observer* 29 June 1978: 18.
The North Carolina Secretary of Crime Control will meet with the North Carolina Commission of Indian Affairs to discuss Lumbee charges of brutality by state highway patrol troopers. Lumbees cite five incidents in the past year. Related articles, *News and Observer* 8 Sept. 1978: 31 and 27 Oct. 1979: 13.

827. Schmalleger, Frank, and Joe Freeman Britt. "The Death Penalty: A Case Study of 'Britt's Blitz' in Robeson County." *Carolina Politics* 1.1 (Oct. 1978): [5]-15. [PSU-MLL]
"Britt's Blitz was highly effective in reducing the first-degree murder rate" (p. 10).

828. Evans, W. McKee. "The North Carolina Lumbees: From Assimilation to Revitalization." *Southeastern Indians Since the Removal Era*. Ed. Walter L. Williams. Athens: U of Georgia P, 1979. Pp. 49-71. [PSU-MLL]
After the Lowry Gang era, White historians tried to demonstrate that Lumbees are Indians. Lumbees entered an accommodation period. Evans also discusses later

developments such as locality leaders; the three-tier status system caused by segregation; Lumbee ethnic consciousness; the work pattern of tobacco production; the Klan routing; and the progressive 1970's.

829. Burgess, Harvey. " 'Deadliest Prosecutor' Once Opposed Death Penalty."
         Robesonian 22 Mar. 1979: 4.
Explains Britt's stand on the death penalty and discusses the Velma Barfield trial.

830. Bigelow, Scott. "Violence Seldom Crosses Racial Lines." *Robesonian* 16 April
         1979: 1.
Gives results of a 1978 statistical analysis of over 30,000 Robeson County complaint investigations. In 81.5% of cases, victim and perpetrator were the same race.

831. Burgess, Harvey. "Brooks Named Top Demo." *Robesonian* 20 May 1979: 1.
Mark Brooks is the first Indian chairperson of the county Democratic Party.

832. Vaden, Ted. "Small Businessman of the Year Thought Big." *News and
         Observer* 1 July 1979: Sec. 4 p. 3.
Dennis D. Lowery, Tar Heel of the Week, is president and part owner of Industrial Chemicals Inc. in Charlotte. See also *Robesonian* 30 May 1993: D1.

833. "Lumbee Suit Seeks ... Hiring Goals." *News and Observer* 25 Nov. 1980: 19.
Lumbee River Legal Services filed a motion objecting to a state highway patrol hiring goal that included Blacks and women but not Indians. Michael Chavis, a Lumbee, was turned down for a job even though he met all requirements.

834. N.C. Dept. of Admin. *A Preliminary Review of Arrest and Incarceration Rates
         of Indians vs. Whites in the N.C. Judicial System.* By Darlene Jacobs. Raleigh:
         The Department, 1982. Rpt. in *Anti-Indian Violence* (entry 859), pp. 92-106.
Finds that Robeson County Indians have an arrest rate 11.9% higher than their percentage of the population, a Superior Court indictment rate 25.1% higher, and a District and Superior Court conviction rate over 50% higher.

835. Hall, Bob. "Bucking the System: The Success and Survival of Organized
         Workers in Rural, Anti-Union North Carolina." *Southern Exposure* 10.5
         (Sept.-Oct. 1982): 66-73.
Workers at Mueller Steam Specialty Company, which employs all three races, tried to win and maintain a union contract. Clergy and Laity Concerned (CALC) helped fight company mistreatment of union supporters.

836. Geiger, Maurice D., and Kathryn Fahnestock. "Confidential Memorandum to
         Chief Justice Joseph Branch. Subject: Robeson County Court System." North
         Conway, NH: Fund for Rural Justice, 15 Dec. 1983. 12p.
Cites judicial abuses in six areas: representation by counsel, bail practices, plea taking, court calendar manipulation, misdemeanor appeal policy, and courtroom demeanor.

837. Geiger, Maurice D., and Kathryn Fahnestock. "A Report by the Rural Justice
         Center to the Chief Justice of North Carolina: An Update on Robeson County."

North Conway, NH: Rural Justice Center, [1984?] 8 p.
After 200 days of court monitoring by the county Friend in Court project, concluded
that "in general, all of the problems which existed a year ago are still present."
Discusses each problem.

838. Patterson, Dennis. "Pembroke Editor Fights Odds to Fulfill Dream."
  Robesonian 8 March 1984: 2A.
On Bruce Barton's establishment of the *Carolina Indian Voice*. Reviews changes he
advocated for Robeson County and events he spoke out against. See also "Frustrated
Writer Takes Up Cudgel for Lumbees," *CIV* 7 June 1973: 1, 3; rpt. 20 Jan. 1983: 2A.

839. Remsberg, Bonnie; Donna P. Conley, and Shirley James Longshore. "Fifty
  American Heroines." *Ladies Home Journal* 101 (July 1984): 85, 141.
Brief mention. Includes a thumbnail sketch of Lumbee attorney Arlinda Locklear.

840. N.C. Comm. of Indian Affairs. *American Indians in North Carolina's Criminal
  Justice System.* By Chris Browning. Raleigh: The Commission, Sept. 1984.
Gives percentages of Indians admitted to state prisons, by county; Indian employment
in the county sheriff's department; and data on District Court cases, Superior Court
sentencing, administration of the Bail Bond Act, and court appointment of lawyers.

841. Reid, Dee. " 'Killer DA': In First 28 Months on Job, He Won 23 Death
  Verdicts." *National Law Journal* 7.2 (17 Sept. 1984): 1, 8-9.
On Joe Freeman Britt's "aggressive posture in the courtroom" and alleged abuse of
authority to set the court calendar. Murders in the county numbered the same in 1982
as when he took office.

842. Jacobs, Ben. "The History of Lumbee Regional Development Association, Inc.
  (1968-1985)." Unpublished typescript. 80 p. and appendices.
Documents the formation and accomplishments of LRDA, emphasizing individuals
who played key roles, causes supported, and projects initiated. Covers: LRDA's
administrative structure, Lumbee Homecoming, the N.C. Comm. of Indian Affairs, aid
to Indian-owned businesses, relations with Tuscaroras, ending double-voting, the
"Save Old Main" movement, aid to *Strike at the Wind!*, impact on Indian affairs and
organizations at the local, state, and national levels, and Lumbee River Legal Services.
Includes lists of board members and biographical sketches of LRDA leaders.

843. "Prosecutor Wins Death Sentences: For 37th Time, Lawyer Convinces a Jury
  That Life Isn't Enough." *New York Times* 25 Dec. 1985: 64.
Britt's tactics in winning death penalties have been called theatrical.

844. Jordan, Pat. "The Passions of Joe Freeman Britt." *Southern Magazine* 1.6
  (March 1987): 38-41, 95-99.
Detailed account of Britt's courtroom techniques and rationale for pursuing the death
penalty. See also letters to the editor (May and June, 1987) prompted by this article.

845. N.C. Dept. of Admin. N.C. Comm. of Indian Affairs. Ad Hoc Comm. on
  Indians and the Criminal Justice System. *A Report on the Treatment of Indians*

by the Criminal Justice System. Oct. 1987. Rpt. in entry 859, pp. 31-91. Reviews offenses charged, enforcement of bail bond laws, courtroom procedures, criminal defense services, sentences, and perceptions of Indians by law enforcement officials. Makes ten recommendations.

846. Locklear, Barbara Brayboy-. "King Joe's Court." *Aardvark 88*. Ed. Anne Russell. Pembroke: Journalism Program, Pembroke State University, 1988? Pp. 43-45. [IERC]
Impressions of Joe Freeman Britt's impact on the county's criminal justice system.

847. Bowden, Barry. "Report Says Justice Not Equitable for Indians." *Fayetteville Times* 3 Feb. 1988. [Reviews findings and recommendations of entry 845].

848. Applebome, Peter. "Behind Hostage Case, Issues of Rural Justice." *New York Times* 8 Feb. 1988: 1.
Complaints about the county's criminal justice system may signify neglect by the judicial administration. Cites Rural Justice Center statistics, viewpoints on Joe Freeman Britt, and activism of Concerned Citizens for Better Government.

849. Dew, Joe, and Jane Ruffin. "Drug Money a Powerful Lure in Robeson." *News and Observer* 14 Feb. 1988: 1A.
NC's 13th most populous county had the 6th highest number of drug arrests in 1986.

850. Hitt, Greg. "Reports Allege Racism: Robeson Courts Unfair to Indians, Studies Say." *Winston-Salem Journal* 14 Feb. 1988: A1.
Comments from four reports, local attorneys, and others. Related article, same page.

851. Martin, Terry. "Minorities' Disunity in Robeson County Dilutes Voting Strength." *Winston-Salem Journal* 28 Feb. 1988: A1.
Minorities will not support each others' candidates; Whites dominate elected offices.

852. Oriole, Kim. "Robeson Creates Race Panel." *Fayetteville Observer* 22 March 1988: 1B.
The 21-member Human Relations and Unity Commission was created. County commissioners will choose the first seven members.

853. Flaherty, David T. "Memorandum, March 25, 1988, from ... Secretary, Dept. of Human Resources, to the Governor's Robeson County Task Force, on Billy McKellar's Death." Raleigh: N.C. Dept. of Human Resources, 1988. [17] p.
Investigation of McKellar's death was a condition for release of the *Robesonian* hostages. Notes lapses in jail procedures that may have contributed to the death.

854. Naureckas, Jim. "Drugs, Good Ole Boys and 'Just Another Murder'." *In These Times* 12.20 (13-19 April 1988): 5.
Brief account of Julian Pierce's murder, Sheriff Stone's speedy solution, and other incidents involving the Robeson County Sheriff's Department.

855. Leland, Elizabeth. "Robeson Sorts Out Murders." *Charlotte Observer* 18 April

1988: 4A.
The county has 18 unsolved murders dating from November, 1975. Compares Robeson's rate of unsolved murders to the state average and nearby counties.

856. Menges, Jerri. "LRLS Officials Celebrate Service's 10th Anniversary at Friday Banquet." *Robesonian* 6 Nov. 1988: 1A.
Reviews the purpose and accomplishments of Lumbee River Legal Services.

857. Godfrey, R. L. "Thompson Selected as County's Public Defender." *Robesonian* 29 Dec. 1988: 1A. [Angus B. Thompson fills the newly created position.]

858. Murray, Ottis L., Jr. "An Examination of Low Income Farmworkers' Participation in a CETA Program in Robeson County, North Carolina." Thesis. North Carolina State U, 1989.
Studied client records on participants (mostly Indian) in the Migrant and Seasonal Farmworkers' Program. 66% of workers who participated in a training program later found full-time jobs. On-the-job training was the least successful type of training.

859. U.S. Cong. House. Comm. on the Judiciary. Subcomm. on Civil and Constitutional Rights. *Anti-Indian Violence.* Hearings ... May 4 and 18, 1988. 100th Cong., 2nd Sess. Washington: GPO, 1989. Y4.J89/1: 100/119. *Serial Set*, Serial no. 119. Pp. 20-44, 432-40.
Christine Griffin (Lumbee River Legal Services) explains five forms of discrimination against Lumbees in the county judicial system: (1) law enforcement officers' attitudes; (2) use of force by arresting officers; (3) overuse of secured bail bonds; (4) District Attorney's abuse of power; and (5) inequitable court sentencing. Includes a statement by Bob Warren of Christic Institute South.

860. "New Court Officers Take Up Their Duties." *Robesonian* 5 March 1989: C1.
Angus B. Thompson is public defender. Richard Townsend replaces Joe Freeman Britt as district attorney.

861. Gingrich, Stephanie. "Pembroke Woman Strives to Better the Community." *Robesonian* 27 March 1989: 5A.
Christine Griffin, administrator for Lumbee River Legal Services.

862. Guyton, Nanette. "Official: Report Has Eased Judicial Inequities Against County's Indians." *Robesonian* 26 April 1989: 1A.
Henry E. McKoy cites improvements resulting from entry 845.

863. Rural Advancement Fund Justice Project. "Presentation to Human Relations and Unity Commission." Unpublished typescript. N.d. 7 p.
This report, presented 30 May 1989, examines Robeson County government's employment practices and affirmative action policy. Charts show each department's employment by race. Also discusses PSU, Southeastern General Hospital, the Dept. of Corrections, and Lumberton banks and savings and loans.

864. Godfrey, R. L. "Judicial Officials, Ministers Discuss Problems of County

Justice System." *Robesonian* 28 June 1989: 1A.
Summarizes comments from a judicial forum dinner sponsored by the Robeson County
Human Relations and Unity Commission.

865. Culbreth, John. "County Usurps Power to Appoint Unity Members; Chair
Resigns in Protest." *Robesonian* 25 July 1989: 1A.
Joy Johnson resigned after county commissioners approved bylaws giving themselves
the right to appoint future Human Relations and Unity Commission members.

866. Ruffin, Jane. "He's Moving Up in a System He Helped Open Up." *News and
Observer* 22 Oct. 1989: 3D. Rpt. in *CIV* 2 Nov. 1989: 5.
Dexter Brooks, Tar Heel of the Week, was the first Indian graduate of UNC's law
school. He is the state's first Indian Superior Court judge.

867. "Robeson Crime Rate Drops 35%; State Average Jumps 12%." *Robesonian* 24
Oct. 1989: B1.
In the first six months of 1989, Robeson had the sharpest crime index decline of any
North Carolina county.

868. Wurth-Hough, Sandra J. "The Dialectic of the Lumbee People and Their
Polity." Paper presented at the Western Social Science Annual Convention,
1990? 17 p.
Thorough, wide-ranging, and extensively researched, this paper explains, with many
specific examples, a triad of characteristics (the land, the people, and religion) which
Lumbees exhibit in their orientation toward life and in political or economic concerns.
These characteristics are distinctly Native American. Also illustrates three Lumbee
political techniques (alliance-building, interference, and the role of the individual) that
surface when any of the characteristics are threatened.

869. Orlean, Susan. "Killing: Pembroke, North Carolina." *Saturday Night*. New
York: Alfred A. Knopf, 1990. Pp. 95-111 *passim*.
Brief mention. Discusses Joan Locklear Jacobs' 1986 shooting of Charles Roscoe
Brooks on a Saturday night, and mentions Julian Pierce and Joyce Sinclair. Pembroke
police officer Mickey Strickland describes typical Saturday-night incidents in the town.

870. Rhodes, Barbara. "Horace Locklear's Motions Hearing Scheduled During
Superior Court." *Robesonian* 28 Jan. 1990: 1.
Indictments charge that Locklear promised a client who had pleaded guilty to drug
charges that he would not receive an active prison sentence if he paid Locklear $9,000.
The defense made several requests (listed) regarding the conduct of the trial.

871. Rhodes, Barbara. "Attorney: No Merit to Charges Against Locklear."
Robesonian 27 Feb. 1990: 1A.
Horace Locklear's attorney said Locklear is being tried for something that is common
practice in Robeson County. His request for dismissal due to "selective prosecution"
and "outrageous government misconduct" was denied.

872. Rhodes, B. "Locklear Agrees to Plea Bargain." *Robesonian* 28 Feb. 1990: 1A.

Horace Locklear pleaded guilty to attempted obstruction of justice. He received a
3-year suspended sentence and community service. Related articles, *Robesonian* 22
May 1990: 1A; 10 June 1990: 1A.

873. "Britt Should Be Saluted for ... Sentence." *Robesonian* 11 March 1990: 4A.
Editorial. Superior Court Judge Joe Freeman Britt sentenced drug dealer Alan
Locklear to 72 years in prison and a half-million-dollar fine.

874. Warren, Gene. "Former PSU Professor Elected to N.C. House." *Robesonian* 8
  Nov. 1990: 7A.
On Adolph L. Dial, founder in 1972 and chairperson until 1988 of PSU's American
Indian Studies Department. Dial, the third Indian to be elected to the N.C. General
Assembly, was sworn in by Dexter Brooks (28 Jan. 1991: 1A). See also editorial, 30
Jan. 1991: 4A; Dial's reflections on being the only Indian in the General Assembly, 17
Feb. 1991: 1A; and related article, 15 Dec. 1991: 1A.

875. "Indian-Owned Businesses in N.C. Unite for Support." *Charlotte Observer* 3
  Dec. 1990: 2B.
The North Carolina Indian Business Association was formed by 27 business owners
from seven eastern North Carolina counties. See also *Robesonian* 16 Feb. 1991: 1A,
24 March 1991: 4A.

876. "Lumbee Businessman Could Lose Special Status Under U.S. Tribes' Policy."
  News and Observer 2 April 1991: 4B.
Alex Ray Hunt, part owner of H & M Electrical and Underground Utilities in Apopka,
FL, was dropped from the Florida Dept. of Transportation's list of minority-ownd
firms–because Lumbees are not federally recognized.

877. Bigelow, Scott. "Indian Group Wants House District." *Robesonian* 16 April
  1991: 1A.
The Native American Political Action Committee proposed splitting the county into
two single-member districts, allowing a western Robeson district that is 60% Indian
and splitting off Hoke and Scotland Counties as a separate district. On redistricting,
see also 30 Dec. 1991: 1A; 2 July 1992: 4A (letter); and 1 Dec. 1992: 4A (editorial).

878. Scipio, Sylvester. "County Endorses 8-Member Board." *Robesonian* 26 Sept.
  1991: 1A.
The plan calls for two Black, three Indian, and three White county commissioner
election districts, based on percentages of the three races in the county.

879. "Murder Rate May Be Tied to Culture." *News and Observer* 3 Feb. 1992: 3B.
Gary Willis and Daniel Barbee, PSU faculty, are studying the county's homicides.
Preliminary findings include: (1) from 1982-1987, the homicide rate exceeded rates for
Mecklenburg, Wake, Guilford, Forsyth, and Durham Counties; (2) murders usually
involve people of the same race; and (3) from 1982-1987, 41.2% of those killed were
related to, or romantically involved with, their killers. The state average is 28.8%.

880. Toole, Judith. " 'Revealing Portrait' of County Compiled." *Robesonian* 23

Aug. 1992: 1A.
Members of the Communities in Schools task force are preparing a report (or assessment) including detailed economic, social, and demographic data on the county.

881. Locklear, Barbara Braveboy. "Pembroke Manufacturer Earns Blue Chip
        Award." *Robesonian* 20 June 1993: D1.
Dorothy Locklear, president of 5Gs Manufacturing, was one of four N.C. small business owners to win the award. Article reviews the company's ups and downs since she and husband Gene Eugene Locklear founded it as University Sportswear in 1973. The award helps small businesses benefit from each other's experiences. See also *Nation's Business* 81.3 (Mar. 1993): 40. The plant was renamed DGs Manufacturing. On employee protests, see *Robesonian* 12 July 1993: 1A; 13 July 1993: 3A.

COMMUNITY SERVICE; SPORTS AND ATHLETICS

882. "County Indian Child Welfare Group Formed." *Robesonian* 27 Jan. 1939: 2.
"To locate and help as much as possible the unfortunate Indian children in Robeson County." Lists officers and committee members.

883. "Indian Welfare Group Seeks Information about Orphans." *Robesonian* 5 April
        1939: 5.
The Indian Child Welfare Association is trying to determine the number of Indian orphans in the county.

884. "First Camporee Held by Robeson Indian Scouts." *Robesonian* 6 May 1940: 5.
Troop 27, led by Walter Pinchbeck. Lists candidates for various ranks of scouts.

885. "The Indian Orphanage: An Appeal for Support." *Robesonian* 3 Dec. 1940: 7.
Letter requests donations so that construction can begin on land given 20 years ago.

886. Livermore, Mary. "Odum Home for Indian Orphans." *Robesonian* 15 May
        1941: 3. [History of the home's establishment and its progress thus far.]

887. "Indian Orphanage, Named Odum Home for Founder, Is Operating Nicely.
        History Read at Dedication." *Robesonian* 4 Jan. 1943: 2.
Opened in October, 1942. Mentions the establishment of the Indian Child Welfare Assoc. in 1939, gifts and donations, board members, and child care philosophy.

888. Workman, Bill. "Woman Missionary Carries On Orphanage for Indian
        Children." *Charlotte Observer* 19 June 1949: 20A.
Mrs. P. A. Underwood operates the Odum Home. She and her husband, a minister, came to Pembroke as missionaries for the 26-church Burnt Swamp Baptist Association.

889. "1,000 Indian 4-H Members Now Enrolled in Robeson." [article, 1950?]
        [PSU-MLL-Clippings File.]
On English Jones, the first full-time Indian county agent.

890. Norment, Bill. "Oxendine Sweeps All-Star Honors." [Newspaper article, 1952?]

[PSU-MLL. PSU Clippings File]
Joe "Injun" Oxendine, a Catawba College football player, made the All-North State
Conference post-season team.

891. "PSC Athlete Signed by Bucs." *Robesonian* 5 Nov. 1954: 7.
Forace Oxendine, pitcher, signed with a farm club of the Pittsburgh Pirates.

892. "Indian Home Demonstration Clubs of Robeson Mark First Achievement Day."
Robesonian 22 Nov. 1954: 10.
Nearly 150 women from 12 clubs reported on their activities. Most clubs were
organized in December, 1952.

893. Brown, J. C. "Indian 4-H Boys and Girls Learn Lesson in Living." *Robesonian*
2 Aug. 1955: 7. Rpt. from *Extension Service Review* (USDA), June 1954.
The county's 4-H Club has 182 community leaders working with 1,260 Indian
students. Remarks by English Jones and Helen Sampson.

894. Simkins, Virginia. "Young Foster Mother and 19 Kids Are Transforming an
Institution." *Robesonian* 2 Dec. 1956? [PSU-MLL. PSU Clippings File]
Mrs. Knox Sampson is superintendent of the Odum Home.

895. "Pembroke Scout Troop 328 Marks Its 20th Birthday." *Robesonian* 11 Feb.
1958: [4].
Brief history. Gives names of original scouts, Eagle Scouts, officers, and patrol
members.

896. "Slow, Fascinating Growth of Odum Home." *Charity and Children* 72.33 (3
Mar. 1960): 1, 4. [IERC] Rpt. in *CIV* 27 Oct. 1977: 11.
Detailed history of the Indian orphanage. Includes photographs and mentions many
individuals. See *Robesonian* 25 June 1992: 75 and 12 Oct. 1992: 1A for historical
overviews occasioned by the Odum Home's golden anniversary celebration.

897. "Pembroke Club Gets Charter." *Robesonian* 15 Nov. 1961. [PSU-MLL. PSU
Clippings File] [Kiwanas, the town's first national civic club.]

898. "Lumbee Rec Area Plans Progress, Has 300 [sic] Joiners." *Robesonian* 24 Aug.
1964: 1.
Construction near Red Banks Farm will begin soon. A membership campaign signed
200 members at $300 each to raise the local share of financing. Federal funding
provided $410,000; the state gave $60,000. See also entries 317 and 318.

899. Peebles, Lucy Gray. "Lumbee Recreation Park Exceeds Dreams." *The Lumbee*
11 Nov. 1965: 1.
The complex will include a lake, golf course, pools, picnic shelters, and more. Lester
Bullard was president of the park's board. See *Robesonian* 4 Sept. 1973; rpt. 19 Oct.
1992: 4A for an editorial on Bullard's many contributions as a community leader.

900. "Walter Pinchbeck." [Oral history audiotape.] Appalachian State University.

Oral History Project. Tape no. 133. [1966?] [ASU-APP]
Pinchbeck was 70 when he was interviewed at Pembroke. He discussed buildings in
the Pembroke area; how the town, and its race relations, had changed since his arrival
in 1931; the Ku Klux Klan routing; PSU (including Old Main); and the changing of
Robeson Indians' name to Lumbee. The tape's sound quality is poor.

901. Warren, Gene. "Pinchbeck Dedicates His Life to Working with Boy Scouts."
　　　　Lumberton Post/Scottish Chief 16 March 1969: 11.
On Troop 27, the oldest Indian scout troop east of the Mississippi.

902. "Let's Take a Pilgrimage ... First to Odum Home." *Charity and Children*
　　　　[Thomasville, NC] 87.6 (28 Oct. 1973). [IRM]

903. Eliades, David K. "A Conversation with Walter Pinchbeck." *Pembroke*
　　　　Magazine no. 8 (1977): 206-11. [PSU-MLL]
Pinchbeck, whose parents were Cree, came to Pembroke in 1931 and began organizing
Boy Scout troops in 1938. He was PSU's superintendent of buildings for many years.

904. "At Pembroke, Cottage to Memorialize Indians Dedicated." *Charity and*
　　　　Children [Thomasville, NC] 29 Oct. 1978: 3, 8. [IRM]
A cottage honoring Odum Home founders was paid for by $100,000 in donations,
mainly from Robeson County Indians.

905. Oxendine, Joseph B. *American Indian Sports Heritage.* Champaign, IL:
　　　　Human Kinetics Books, 1987. Pp. 275, 299-303. [IERC] [PSU-MLL]
Discusses Gene Locklear (baseball, Cincinnati Reds and other teams), Dwight Lowry
(baseball, Detroit Tigers), and Victor Elk (cross-country, PSU). Includes photographs.

906. Sloan, Bob. "A Long Mission Completed." *Robesonian* 4 Aug. 1991: 1B.
Powerlifter Harold Collins, who owns the Powerhouse Gym in Pembroke, lifted a
combined total of 2,129 pounds to become the first Native American winner of the
National Powerlifting Championship in the superheavyweight class. Related article,
Robesonian 13 Dec. 1991: 1B.

907. Nye, R. "Collins to Take On World's Best." *Robesonian* 1 Nov. 1992: 7B.
Harold Collins won the National Powerlifting Championship and will represent the
U.S. in the world competition in Birmingham, England, Nov. 18-22. Collins won the
national title last year, also, but was unable to participate in the world competition due
to a knee injury. See letter, 4 Sept. 1992: 4A, on "Iron Bear's" community service.

908. Quillen, Martha. "Pembroke, Home of the Braves, Shies Away from Mascot's
　　　　Image." *News and Observer* 6 Feb. 1992: 1A.
PSU Chancellor Joseph Oxendine banished the mascot, a "hideous" depiction of a
brave which he felt was "not the image we ought to be projecting of American
Indians." He also disallowed the sale of toy tomahawks which were ordered as favors
for the homecoming game. See also editorials on this action, *Robesonian* 10 Feb.
1992: 4A and 17 Feb. 1992: 4A (by Oxendine). Following consultation with faculty,
students, alumni, consultants, and the community, PSU adopted a new logo, showing

an Indian brave and a hawk, drawn by Gloria Tara Lowery (*Robesonian* 22 July 1992: 1B). For Oxendine's official statement on the new mascot (the red-tailed hawk), see *Robesonian* 24 Sept. 1992: 1B. For the unveiling of the mascot, see *Robesonian* 2 Dec. 1992: 1B.

909. Sloan, Bob. "Locklear Fairs (sic) Well at Giants' Spring Training." *Robesonian* 15 April 1992: 1B. [Jeff Locklear, former PSU pitcher.]

910. Peguise, Tiffany. "Coming Home: Martial Arts Expert Buffaloe Returns to Pembroke ..." *Robesonian* 30 June 1993: 1B.
On Kenny Buffaloe, who began studying Kyokushin-kai karate at age 5. He has appeared in several motion pictures, won an N.C. Governor's Award, and conducted anti-drug presentations at schools in the state.

MILITARY SERVICE

911. "The American Indians and the World War." *American Indian Magazine* [Washington: Society of American Indians] 5 (Autumn 1917): 198.
Brief mention of arrival of fourteen Robeson County Cherokees at Camp Jackson, SC.

912. [Untitled.] *Yadkin Ripple* [Yadkinville, NC] 25 Oct. 1917: 2. [ASU-BLK]
Lieutenant J. T. Benbow is training Croatan Indians from Burke County. Indian trainees have separate quarters at Camp Jackson, but in Burke County they were used to "riding in the [train] cars with White people and the same waiting rooms at stations."

913. "Yadkin Boy Now in Camp Writes Letter." *Yadkin Ripple* [Yadkinville, NC] 1 Nov. 1917: 1. [ASU-BLK]
Lieutenant Tom Benbow is drilling 40 Robeson County Indians with 70 Whites from Transylvania County. Indians are "much more intelligent than one might suppose." They enjoy singing hymns and "poring over their hymn books, learning new hymns."

914. "31 Indians Entrained at Red Springs Yesterday." *Robesonian* 30 May 1918: 1.
Lists names and home towns.

915. "Largest Contingent of ... County Boys Who Have Gone to Camp in a Body." *Robesonian* 13 June 1918: 2. [Photo of White and Indian draftees; no names.]

916. "Facts About Registration: Numbers of Different Ages and Races ... in Robeson District No. 1 by Township." *Robesonian* 19 Sept. 1918: 1.

917. "Indians Have Organized Post of American Legion." *Robesonian* 24 Jan. 1921: 4. [Robeson Union Post; officers listed.]

918. "Four Year College Graduates in World War II." "Veterans of World War II in College." Unpublished typescripts. N.d. [5] p. [PSU-MLL]
Lists Robeson County Indian servicemen by region and by country of service.

919. "War Records of Robeson County Indians." N.p., n.d. [PSU-MLL]

PSU's History Dept. conducted a survey on county Indians in World War II. Seventy forms exist, some with letters and photographs attached.

920.   Sharpe, J. A., Jr. "Indian Veterans Parade Before Gov. Cherry and Big Crowd at Pembroke." *Robesonian* 18 March 1946: 1.
The Robeson County Indian Veterans' Day parade of 350 included Indian ex-soldiers and -sailors, veterans of both World Wars, and Indian and White Boy Scouts. Over 5,000 people attended. Photograph reprinted, 20 Nov. 1991: 1C.

921.   "Army Lists 141 Fatalities from County in World War II." *Lumberton Voice* 3 July 1946. [PSU-MLL. PSU Clippings File]
Reprints Robeson County names from the first consolidated list released by the War Department.

922.   "Big Welcome Planned for Returning Pembroke Vets." *Robesonian* 6 Oct. 1953: 6.
Describes a program by the Pembroke VFW Post for returning Korean veterans and discusses two POWs.

923.   "46 Men Listed in Reserve Unit." *Robesonian* 11 July 1956? [PSU-MLL. PSU Clippings File]
First anniversary of the 443rd Ordnance Reserve Co., which included men from Pembroke, Magnolia, and Fairgrove.

SETTLEMENTS OUTSIDE ROBESON COUNTY
Baltimore

924.   Stump, W. "Maryland–Home of the Braves." *Baltimore Evening Sun* 28 May 1950.
Silas Brooks, Lovdie Brooks, and others are farming 300 acres near Mechanicsville.

925.   Stump, William. "Indians Mark a Successful Initial Year on a Farm in St. Marys County." *Baltimore Sun* 24 Dec. 1950. [Two Robeson County Brooks families.]

926.   "Mystery People of Baltimore." *Ebony* 12 (Sept. 1957): 70-73.
Some 2,000 Lumbees live in Baltimore. Describes physical features, disdain for the name "Croatan," aloofness, and "unwritten law against dating or marrying Negroes."

927.   Carroll, John S. "Baltimore's Lumbees: Lost Colonists?" *Baltimore Sun* 27 June 1966.
Lumbees live on East Baltimore Street and work in building trades; some commute to Washington, Pennsylvania, or Virginia.

928.   Batten, James K. "Lumbee Indians Flock to 'Reservation' in Baltimore." *Washington Post* 8 Jan. 1967: B10.
On community size, occupations, adjustment problems, violent image, and politics.

929.   "City Revamps Aid to Lumbees." *Baltimore Sun* 18 June 1967.

An anti-poverty agency finds Lumbees aloof and unwilling to trust outsiders; new approaches are being planned.

930. Murphy, Edith. "On the Trail of the Lumbees." *The VISTA Volunteer* 3.10 (October 1967): 4-8. [PSU-MLL]
Murphy, a Community Action Agency employee who worked in Baltimore's Lumbee neigborhood, visited Lumberton to gain a better understanding of her clients.

931. Parker, Roy, Jr. "Lumbees Leaving Robeson for Baltimore City Life." *News and Observer* 5 Nov. 1967: Sec. 1 p. 6.
Comments from Edith Murphy on her Robeson County visit.

932. Amanullah, Mohammod. "The Lumbee Indians: Patterns of Adjustment." *Toward Economic Development for Native American Communities: A Compendium of Papers.* Vol. 1, Part 1: *Development Prospects and Problems.* U.S. Congress. Subcomm. on Economy in Government. Joint Economic Committee. 1969. Pp. 277-98. [PSU-MLL]
Lumbees left North Carolina to improve their economic conditions but "live in extreme poverty" in Baltimore. Covers housing, employment, education, economic status, occupations, marriage, social life, religion, recreation, and race relations.

933. Peck, John Gregory. *Education of Urban Indians: Lumbee Indians in Baltimore.* (National Study of American Indian Education, Series II, no. 3.) Washington: Office of Education, Bureau of Research, Aug. 1969. ERIC ED 039 977
Reviews the origin and history of the Lumbee settlement in Baltimore. Discusses interaction between Lumbees and their teachers and schools. Includes a map of Lumbee areas of residence.

934. "The American Indian Study Center & Baltimore's Indian Community." Unpub. typescript. Baltimore: American Indian Study Center, N.d. 3 p. [EPFL]
Explains the Center's CETA, Alcoholism and Drug Abuse, Adult Basic Education, cultural, and senior citizens' programs.

935. Pietila, Antero. "Indian Study Center to Open." *Baltimore Sun* 12 June 1970.
Inauguration of the Center. Describes its history and programs.

936. Arnett, Karl. "Indian Center Symbolizes Fells Point Regeneration." *Baltimore Sun* 22 Sept. 1970: B1. [Discusses the Center as well as Lumbee occupations.]

937. Grant, Sandra. "They Work Here But Their Ties Are Elsewhere." *Baltimore Evening Sun* 28 Sept. 1970: C1. Rpt. *Akwesasne Notes* 3.2 (March 1971): 34.
First in a 4-part series, "The Lumbees: What Place is Home?" Migration to Baltimore during World War II, due to job shortages in N.C., led to a colony of 3,500 by 1970. Recounts adjustment problems and the role of churches and the Indian Center.

938. Grant, Sandra. "Indian Study Center Is First Involving City's Lumbees." *Baltimore Evening Sun* 29 Sept. 1970: C1.
Explains the formation of the center, headed by Herbert Locklear. Its success stems

from the fact that it has always been Indian-operated.

939. Grant, Sandra. "Adjusting to Different Pace, Ways of City Life Is Difficult for
    Indian." *Baltimore Evening Sun* 1 Oct. 1970: F1.
Last article in the four-part series. Problems include having to raise children more
restrictively, loosening of family ties, more divorces, and intervention by police.

940. Makofsky, Abraham. "Tradition and Change in the Lumbee Indian Community
    of Baltimore." Diss. Catholic U of America, 1971. [UNC-G]
Uses interviews and personal involvement in Lumbee activities to study Baltimore
Lumbees' employment problems, religion, trouble and violence, Indianness, and
interaction with the community. Explains their determinants of high vs. low status.

941. Jablow, Paul. "Lumbee Indians Gaining in Number but Losing Their Identity."
    Baltimore Sun 9 May 1971.
John Gregory Peck sees Baltimore Lumbees approaching elimination.

942. Gaillard, Frye. "Cities Contradict Lumbees' Values." *Race Relations Reporter*
    2 (21 June 1971): 6-9. [PSU-MLL] Rpt. as "The Lumbees Fight Back" in *News
    and Observer* 11 July 1971: Sec. 4 pp. 1, 7.
On Lumbee adjustment problems in Baltimore. Factors in their Indianness are:
Robeson County as home, closeness to nature, clannishness, and importance of land.
Explains their objections to HEW's desegregation plan for Robeson County schools.

943. Kang, K.. "Mrs. Locklear Seeks New Image for Indians." *Baltimore News
    American* 28 July 1971. [Elizabeth Locklear, American Indian Study Center.]

944. Peck, John Gregory. "Urban Station–Migration of the Lumbee Indians." Diss.
    U of North Carolina at Chapel Hill, 1972. [UNC-G]
Extensive account of Lumbees in Baltimore. Peck tested Lumbee students and parents
in Pembroke and Baltimore. Four cultural themes define Lumbee identity: Home is
Robeson County; Sometimes broke, never poor; A man is a man; and Now for now.

945. Perseghin, G. "Inner City Indians Enrolled." *Catholic Review* 24 March 1972.
Sister Virginia Ann, of St. Michael's School, recruited Lumbee children living nearby.

946. Locklear, H. "American Indian Myths." *Social Work* 17 (May 1972): 72-80.
Herbert H. Locklear, American Indian Study Center director, discusses Baltimore
Indians' problems and the Center's goals.

947. Makofsky, Abraham, and David Makofsky. "Class Consciousness and Culture:
    Class Identifications in the Lumbee Indian Community of Baltimore." *Anthropo-
    logical Quarterly* 46.4 (1973): 261-77. [PSU-MLL]
Found rather high class consciousness among 26 Lumbee manual laborers. Those over
30 were more militant than younger ones. Church members were more militant than
other organizational groups. Union membership was related to class response.

948. Miller, Sue. "City Schools Get Grant to Aid American Indian Students."

Baltimore Sun 4 Sept. 1973.
A coordinator will be hired and teaching materials produced.

949. Henderson, Randi. "Indian Center Wants to Preserve Culture, Help Alcoholics." *Baltimore Sun* 1 May 1974.
American Indian Study Center has a grant to give therapy and education to alcoholics.

950. "American Indian Study Center, Baltimore, MD." Folder. [IERC]
Includes a typescript, "Background and Condition of the Indian Community of Baltimore," and statements against two resolutions affecting Lumbees passed by the NCAI's General Assembly in 1975.

951. Rohzon, T. "Indian Restaurant to Cook Up ... Jobs." *Baltimore Sun* 27 Feb. 1975.
The American Indian Study Center has a grant to open an Indian restaurant in Fells Point as a job training effort.

952. Nawrozki, Joe. "Baltimore's Forgotten Indians." *Baltimore News-American* 19 Oct. 1975.
The Lumbee community faces problems of a high dropout rate, alcoholism, suicide, street fights, and prostitution.

953. Cunningham, Peggy. "Lumbees Feel Problems Have Been Exaggerated." *Baltimore News American* 9 Nov. 1975.
On several Lumbees who enjoy Baltimore, contribute to the community, and dislike their portrayal in a recent federal report.

954. Watson, Patricia. "The Lumbee Indians. Multi-Ethnicity in Maryland–Focus Baltimore–Workshop Project–Ethnic Data Project." Unpublished typescript. 1979. [18] p. [EPFL]
Classroom materials for grades 8 and 9. On the Baltimore Lumbee community, history of North Carolina Lumbees, and education problems of Lumbee children in Baltimore.

955. Robinson, John. "An Eternity of Job-Hunting for Lumbees." *Baltimore News American* 12 May 1979. [On American Indian Study Center's CETA program.]

956. "Red Power Speaks Softly in South Baltimore." *Baltimore News American* 15 Sept. 1979.
The American Indian Study Center offers an Indian education remedial resource program and various social services.

957. Makofsky, Abraham. "Tradition and Change in the Lumbee Indian Community of Baltimore." *Maryland Historical Magazine* 75.1 (1980): 55-71.
Explains Lumbee migration to Baltimore, areas settled, population, occupations, family life, Indianness, and adaptation to city life.

958. *The Baltimore American Indian Community: Issues & Recommendations Prepared for the Baltimore American Indian Center.* [Baltimore, MD]: The

Workshop, May 1980. 104 p.
Since Lumbees "make up the major component of the American Indian community in
Baltimore," they are discussed throughout. Gives an overview of the study area (240
blocks mainly in the Butcher's Hill area, southeast Baltimore), focusing on housing
problems, education issues, health issues, and community issues. Baltimore schools
and housing agencies should coordinate with Robeson County to overcome problems
caused by frequent moves between Baltimore and "home."

959. Makofsky, Abraham. "Struggling to Maintain Identity: Lumbee Indians in
     Baltimore." *Anthropological Quarterly* 55 (April 1982): 74-83. [PSU-MLL]
Considers (1) whether Lumbees are culturally assimilated but still separate from
dominant society; (2) whether their sense of identity is subjective or objective; and (3)
whether they consider themselves oppressed.

960. Makofsky, Abraham. "Demographics and Culture: The 1980 Census Report on
     Lumbee Indians of the Baltimore Metropolitan Area." *Maryland Historical
     Magazine* 79.3 (Fall 1984): 239-46. [PSU-MLL]
In 1980, Lumbees made up only .2% of Baltimore's population but had increased 62%
over the 1970 census. Examines causes of the increase, areas of residence in Baltimore, age categories, occupations, income, education, and housing.

961. Skove, Cynthia. "Persistent Woes Plague Area's Indian Population." *Baltimore
     News American* 3 Nov. 1985: 1A.
Lumbees are "perhaps 90% of Baltimore's 3,000-4,500 Indians." Discusses services of
the Baltimore American Indian Center and problems such as joblessness, low income,
high dropout rate, drug abuse, teen pregnancy, and alcoholism.

962. Skove, Cynthia. "Fighting to Improve Their Lot." *Baltimore News American* 3
     Nov. 1985: 1A.
Discusses efforts of Maryland's Comm. on Indian Affairs and the American Indian
Study Center; attempts at state recognition; and problems faced by Baltimore Indians.

963. Skove, Cynthia. "Squabbling Sets Back Efforts to Help Indians." *Baltimore
     News American* 3 Nov. 1985: 7A.
Explains a dispute between the Commission on Indian Affairs and the American Indian
Center over control of a federal jobs program. The Commission accuses the Center of
"being too exclusive in its services for Lumbees and too tight-knit as an organization."

964. Skove, Cynthia. "Children Drop Out of School at an Alarming Rate." *Balti-
     more News American* 5 Nov. 1985: 1A.
Baltimore's Indian dropout rate is 80-85%. Over 1/3 of Indians over 25 never got
beyond 8th grade. Mentions schools Lumbee children attend.

California-based

The United Lumbee Nation (ULN) considers itself "a brake away [sic] group from
(t)he main body of Lumbees" [Princess Silver Star Reed, *United Lumbee Nation Times*
11.1 (Winter 1988-1989) p. 1]. Reed also explains that ULN members "emigrated to

other parts of the United States over the years from North Carolina. Or was borned after their parents left North Carolina. Who have United together, to regain their Lumbee heritage" [*ULN Times* 12.2 (Summer 1990) p. 6]. The group's belief in its ties to North Carolina Lumbees is evidenced by their adoption of North Carolina Lumbee origin traditions. Examples can be seen in: (1) "Dedication Poem," *Over the Cooking Fires*, p. 31. Ed. Silver Star Reed. Fall River Mills, CA: "On Call" Instant Printing, 1982. (2) *ULN Times* 12.3 (Fall 1990) p. 7. This belief is also shown by the frequent quoting or reprinting, in the *ULN Times* [held by State Historical Society of Wisconsin: 6.3 (July 1989) to present], of published materials on North Carolina Lumbees. Examples are: *ULN Times* 12.2 (Summer 1990) p. 6; *ULN Times* 10.3 (Fall 1988) p. 4. Adolph Dial states that North Carolina Lumbees disclaim the ULN. Some materials cited in this section elaborate on the conflict between the two groups.

965. "Memorandum ... Recommendation and Summary of Evidence for Proposed Finding Against Federal Acknowledgement of the United Lumbee Nation of North Carolina and America, Inc. Pursuant to 25 *CFR* 83." Washington: Bureau of Indian Affairs, U.S. Dept. of Interior, [28 Mar. 1984]. 27 p.
The ULN, founded in 1976, "has no characteristics of an Indian tribe which has maintained tribal relations from historical times." The group "has no relation to the Lumbees of ... Robeson County ... historically, socially, genealogically, politically or organizationally." Gives their background, a bibliography, and a list of federal records.

966. "Bureau of Indian Affairs. Final Determination that the United Lumbee Nation of North Carolina and America, Inc. Does Not Exist as an Indian Tribe. April 19, 1985." *Federal Register* 50.85 (2 May 1985): 18746.
The ULN did not satisfy five of the seven BIA criteria for federal acknowledgement. Their documentation did not prove antecedent Lumbees in California or ties to Lumbees who migrated to California. Membership was too dispersed to be called an Indian community, and there was no tribal authority over members. The ULN granted membership to people who did not meet the their requirement of 1/16 Indian blood.

967. Thompson, Leilani B. "A Proposal for Development and Use of Audio and Video Tape Recordings in the United Lumbee Nation of North Carolina and America." Thesis. San Francisco State U, 1986.
This copiously documented planning study also covers tribal operations; communication; needs and goals. The ULN, a self-declared Indian nation of 2,300 people of varying Indian ancestry, is headquartered in Shasta County, north-central California. It merged from three branches. Few members are North Carolina Lumbees. Explains the roles of Johnnie Reed, Malcolm "Thunderbird" Webber, and Jim Chavis (a N.C. Lumbee). A chart (p. 97) gives the location of clans and bands.

968. United Lumbee Nation of North Carolina and America, Inc. "Clarified and Amended Constitution and By-laws." N.p.: n.p., 1981; rev. 1986. [8] p.
Explains the election and powers of officers, board, and chiefs; membership criteria (proof of at least 1/16 Indian blood, marriage to an Indian member, or majority vote of General Council); organizations within the Nation; and disciplinary actions.

969. Morris, Murl Dale. "Survey and Initiation of a Concept Proposal for the

Implementation of a Community College Educational System Designed
Specifically for the Needs of the Western Band of the United Lumbee Nation."
Diss. U of Mississippi, 1991.
This "informational/planning study" contains background information on the history of
American Indian education and the suitability of the community college philosophy for
Indians. Morris conducted on-site research on the United Lumbee Nation.

Greensboro

970. "Indians Hold Pow-Wow; Discrimination Denied." *News and Observer* 29 Dec.
1959: 16.
Two hundred Lumbees live in Greensboro. Some object to one Lumbee's complaint of
job discrimination.

971. Price, Charles. "City Has 'Tribe' of Croatan Indians." *Greensboro Record* 2
Jan. 1963: B1.
James Locklear, "chief" of Greensboro's Lumbees, estimates the city's Lumbee
population as 3,000-4,000. Discusses employment and other problems.

972. "Greensboro Chapel Has Lumbee Indians As Entire Congregation." *Robesonian*
8 March 1965: 4.
Summarizes a *Charity and Children* story on Fraser Baptist Chapel, a mission of
Immanuel Church. Focuses on George D. Oxendine.

973. Marsh, John. "Church Beckons, and–Lumbees Find a Place to Go." *Greensboro Record* 18 Jan. 1966: B1. [On Immanuel Baptist Church.]

974. "The City–Indians' Limbo Land." *Greensboro Record* 7 Aug. 1968: D1.
Gives observations on prejudice and adjustment problems experienced by several
Greensboro Lumbees.

975. Cheek, L. "Lumbees: A Silent Struggle." *Greensboro Record* 7 Aug. 1968: D1.
2500 Lumbees live in Greensboro; their economic status is improving slowly.

976. Schlosser, J. "Aid Plans: Hit and Miss." *Greensboro Record* 7 Aug. 1968: D1.
Describes efforts of Manpower Improvement Through Community Effort and the
North Carolina Manpower Development Corp.'s Mobility Project.

977. Bledsoe, Jerry. "'The Heart Is –Down Home': Lumbees Return to Robeson
County." *Greensboro Daily News* 20 Jan. 1971: A1.
On Lumbee life in Greensboro; features George Jacobs and Lonnie and Ruth Revels.

978. Tilley, Greta. "Lumbees Aim to End 'Invisible' Status." *Greensboro Record* 2
July 1975: A1.
Lists the aims of the Guilford Native American Association, formed in February.

979. Tilley, Greta. "Indians' Image Barrier in School." *Greensboro Record* 3 July
1975: B1.

Gives statistics on Indian children in Greensboro public schools and results of a statewide survey on the educational level of Indians.

980. Tilley, Greta. "Lumbee Indians Left Farm to Find City Job Bias." *Greensboro Record* 4 July 1975: B2.
Lumbees face problems in getting jobs, adjusting to job pace, and getting promotions. Also discusses the Guilford Native American Association.

981. Schlosser, Jim. "Lumbees Ask School Aide." *Greensboro Record* 20 Feb. 1976: B8.
A Lumbee parent committee will request federal funds to hire a home-school coordinator for Guilford County's Indian students.

982. Alspaugh, Pat. "She Tries to Help Indians Create Pride in Themselves." *Greensboro Daily News* 7 Dec. 1977: B3.
Features Ruth Revels, director of the Guilford Native American Association.

983. Cavin, Winston. "Indians in Guilford in 'Catch-up Game' but GNAA Helping." *Greensboro Daily News* 15 Jan. 1978: B9.
Presents statistics on the county's 3,000 Indians. Highlights the goals of the Guilford Native American Association and the North Carolina Commission of Indian Affairs.

984. "Indians to Plan Recognition Drive Here." *Greensboro Record* 1 Dec. 1978: C1.
Greensboro Native American Association and the North Carolina Commission on Indian Affairs are planning their response to a Congressional proposal to deny federal recognition to tribes lacking a tribal government.

985. Marks, Eddie. "Locklear Honored as Indian of the Year." *Greensboro Daily News* 24 June 1979: B1.
Jimmy Locklear has helped Indians new to Greensboro for 25 years.

986. McIrvin, Ronald. "The Urban Indian: A Profile of the Greensboro Native American Population." *Urban Growth and Urban Life: Proceedings of the 3rd Urban Affairs Conference of N.C.* Charlotte, 1981. Pp. 419-29. [UNC-WL]
Greensboro Native American Association's survey of Greensboro's Indiana revealed that most were from Robeson County. Incomes and home ownership were low, but 77% were employed. Indians disliked public housing and seldom used social services.

987. Taylor, Vincent. "Lonnie Revels Honored for Service to Indians." *Greensboro News and Record* 20 May 1984: D7.
Revels, a City Council member, received the Eagle Feather during Guilford Native American Association's awards banquet.

988. "Guilford Native American Association, Inc." Unpub. typescript. N.p., n.d.
Covers the history of the Association, population served, problems and political status of Guilford County Indians, and problems addressed by the Association.

989. Moser, John J. "Indians Worn Down by Neglect." *Greensboro News & Record*

1 May 1988: 1A.
Indians suffer from high dropout and illiteracy rates, lack of a separate category in government statistics, and poverty. Frequent mention of Lumbees in Greensboro.

Claxton, Georgia

990. Goins, W. W. "High Purpose of Croatan Indians: A Colony in Georgia." *Robesonian* 9 Sept. 1909: 4.
This letter describes the Croatans' "considerable colony" in Bullock County.

991. Avary, James C. "Are There Croatans in Georgia? A Peculiar Race of People There, Said to Have Gone from North Carolina. Correspondence from *New York Sun*." [Newspaper article, 27 Dec. 1909] [UNC-WL, Clippings file through 1975, "Croatan Indians," p. 8.]

992. Harding, A. B. "Sojourning in Georgia–A Prosperous Colony of Indians." *Robesonian* 3 Oct. 1910: 3.
This letter discusses cotton crops, separate schools, and separate churches in Adabelle.

993. "Georgia Indian Settlement: Indian Population Increased from North Carolina." *Robesonian* 25 June 1914: 7.
A new school, taught by C. L. Oxendine, was erected near Claxton.

994. Barton, Bruce. "Robeson County Indian Migration to the Claxton, Georgia Area." Unpublished typescript. Dec. 1985. 300p. [IERC]
Lumbees migrated to Adabelle (eight miles from Claxton) between 1865 and the 1920's to work with turpentine and cotton. Barton discusses the cemetery, schools, churches, and community leaders. Gives text of interviews with surviving residents. Includes reprints of newspaper articles, correspondence during the height of the settlement, excerpts from books, photographs of the cemetery, and genealogical charts.

995. *Letters, Lumbees and Lists.* Statesboro, GA: Auspices, Bulloch County Historical Soc., 1993. Pp. 41-56.
"The Croatan Indians," by Dorothy Durrence Simmons, is a brief note mentioning Washington Manassas Foy and Jasper Locklear. "The Lumbee Indians," by Linda S. Hubbard, is a concise overview of the Claxton settlement. It mentions an incident of racial discrimination and includes Barbara Brayboy-Locklear's poem, "Spirit Words."

Other Locations

996. Adams, H. "Indians Plan Gala Reunion; Red Men in Harnett County Prepare to Greet Brothers from Afar." *Charlotte Observer* 14 Aug. 1938: Sec. 4 p. 8.
Harnett's Indians call themselves Cherokee or Croatan. Their present leader is Joseph Brewington; the first was Enoch Emanuel. Over 500 Indians live in Dunn.

997. Berry, Brewton. "The Mestizos of South Carolina." *American Journal of Sociology* 51 (July 1945): 34-41.
Croatans live in Marlboro, Dillon, Horry and Marion counties. Other mestizos in the

state include Red Bones, Red Legs, Brass Ankles, Turks, and Buckheads. Discusses physical features, probable descent, relations with Blacks and Whites, and education.

998. Bigony, Beatrice. "Migrants to the City: A Study of the Socioeconomic Status of Native Americans in Detroit and Michigan." Diss. U of Michigan, 1974.
Interviewed Indians (several of them Lumbee) in Cass Corridor. Discusses employment, education, family, health, tribal relations, living facilities, and personal outlook.

999. Cumberland County Association for Indian People. "Written Statement for Task Force Ten." Unpublished typescript. 1976. 12 p. [IERC]
The county, in 1970, was less than 1% Indian, including Lumbee, Coharie, Haliwa, and Waccamaw-Siouan. includes history of Indian organizing in the county.

1000. "Demographic Overview of Indians in Metrolina." Presented to the American Indian Policy Review Commission Task Force Hearings, Pembroke, 16-17 April 1976. Unpublished typescript and map. 5p. [IERC]
Tribes in Mecklenburg and nearby counties areaided by the Metrolina Native American Association, chartered 5 Jan. 1976. Discusses their problems and needs.

1001. Chavis-Chitwood, Mary E. "Biography of James M. Chavis." Unpublished typescript. 25 Dec. 1987. 21 p. [IERC]
Interview, with poems and photographs. Chavis, born in Deep Branch, was 72 at the time. Recalls Green Grove School, picking cotton, segregation in Lumberton restaurants, and working at a steel plant in Ecorse, Michigan.

1002. Zucchino, David. "Lumbee Indians: On the Outside Looking In." *Detroit Free Press* 21 Dec. 1979: 1C. Rpt. in *CIV* 8 May 1980: 2.
The Michigan Commission on Indian Affairs refused to grant Lumbees college tuition waivers, causing "an undercurrent of bitterness among the approximately 2,000 Lumbees in the Detroit area." The federal government accepts LRDA certification of 1/4 Indian blood for college scholarships, but the Michigan Commission does not.

1003. Clark, Kenneth D. "Lumbee Indian Migration to Detroit and Their Success in Adjustment." Thesis. Bowling Green State U, 1988. 69 p.
Most migration occurred after World War II, for employment in automobile factories. Examines Lumbee methods of coping with rural-to-urban lifestyle changes, reasons for returning to Robeson County, areas of residence in Detroit, and adjustment problems.

1004. Urban, Rob. "Charlotte Indian Museum at Old Fireman's Hall Is Dream Slow in Coming." *Charlotte Observer* 11 March 1991: 1B.
Metrolina Native American Assoc. is leasing the Hall and raising funds for an Indian museum. About 4,000 Indians (mostly Lumbee) live in the Mecklenburg area.

BIOGRAPHICAL SOURCES

1005. Gridley, Marion E., ed. and comp. *Indians of Today*. 4th ed. Chicago: Indian Council Fire Pubs., 1971.
Includes sketches on Brantley Blue (the first Indian appointed to the Indian Claims

Commission) and Helen Maynor Scheirbeck.

1006. Davidson, Margie. "Indian Women Look to the Future." *News and Observer* 25 March 1973: Sec. 3 p. 1.
Mentions Brenda Brooks, Joyce Locklear, Aileen Holmes, Dr. Norma Jean Thompson, Otha Swett, Peggy Brewington, and Janie Maynor Locklear.

1007. "Biographies of Deceased Lumbee Leaders." Unpublished typescript. Lumberton: Lumbee Indian Education Project, Lumbee Regional Development Association, 1974. 36 p. [IERC]
Brief sketches of eighteen leaders, including O. R. Sampson, Lacy W. Maynor, Lester Bullard, and Herbert G. Oxendine.

1008. Locklear, Janie Maynor, and Drenna J. Oxendine, comps. *Contemporary Lumbee Leaders*. Pembroke: Lumbee Regional Development Association, Dec. 1974. 30 p. [ECU] [Sketches on 19 leaders.]

1009. *Paths Toward Freedom: A Biographical History of Blacks and Indians in North Carolina by Blacks and Indians*. Raleigh: Center for Urban Affairs, North Carolina State U, 1976.
Chapters cover pre-Colonial Indian life, Indian religion, arts and crafts, federal and state relations since 1776, migrations, and economic and professional growth. Many chapters mention Lumbees. Biographical sketches of notable Blacks and Indians.

1010. Robeson County Board of Education. *Historical and Contemporary Indian Leaders of Robeson County*. Lumberton: The Board, 1979. 26p. [IERC]
Sixty-three brief sketches (describing many firsts), grouped by field of achievement: education, religion, law, social, media, community leadership, the arts, medicine, Indian historian, and politics and government. Includes photographs.

1011. *Lumbee Professional Resource Directory*. 2nd ed. Pembroke: Lumbee Regional Development Association [1981?] [IERC]
Lists Lumbees with postsecondary degrees, giving area of expertise, education, address, and position. Includes an index by areas of expertise.

1012. Klein, Barry T. *Reference Encyclopedia of the American Indian*. Vol. 2. New York: Todd Publications, 1986.
Includes sketches on Dean Chavers, Angela Y. Chavis, Thomas Oxendine, Silver Star Reed, Helen Maynor Scheirbeck, and Robert A. Williams, Jr.

GENEALOGICAL MATERIALS; PHOTOGRAPHY

1013. "Robeson Indians Studied by Woman of National Fame." *Robesonian* 30 Sept. 1929: 2.
Photographer Doris Ulmann visited Pembroke and Elrod, "seeking out and getting pictures of Indians representative of the race." Gives names of some individuals photographed. The Ulmann Archives, U. of Oregon Library, has over 100 photographs of Indians, but they are not identified by tribe or location (from correspondence).

1014. Biggs, Kate Britt, comp. *Census of 1850, Robeson County, North Carolina.*
    N.p.: n.p., [1946]. [RCPL]
Gives–for each dwelling–age, sex, color, and profession (for males over 15 only),
value of real estate, place of birth, marital status, and more. Name index to heads of
families.

1015. Biggs, Kate Britt, comp. *Census of 1800, Robeson County, North Carolina.*
    Compiled ... for the Col. Thomas Robeson Chapter of the National Society of
    the Daughters of the American Revolution. N.p.: n.p., [1946]. [RCPL]
Gives head of household; number of residents in household, grouped by age; whether
free or slave; and page number in census.

1016. Lovin, Mable S., comp. *1810 Census for Robeson County, North Carolina.*
    N.p.: n.p., n.d. [RCPL]
Handwritten list of heads of household. Gives number of males and females in various
age categories, and number of people of color and slaves in the county.

1017. Lovin, Mable S., comp. *1820 Census for Robeson County, North Carolina.*
    N.p.: n.p., n.d. [RCPL]
Handwritten list gives name of head of household and number of persons in various
age categories in the household.

1018. Townsend, Peggy T. *Vanishing Ancestors: Cemetery Records of Robeson
    County, North Carolina.* 3 v. N.p.: [Peggy Townsend], 1975-92. [RCPL]
Canvasses 272 cemeteries, including 6,800 inscriptions. Gives directions to cemeteries
and some photographs of churches or tombstones. Surname index.

1019. "The Contemporary Descendants of the '22' Recognized by the Dept. of
    Interior." Unpublished typescript. N.d. 13 p. [IERC]
Lists 22 Siouan Indians certified in 1938 as 1/2 or more Indian blood. Also lists each
family member with (when known) birthdate, birthplace, and parents' names and ages.

1020. Harmon, Elaine Davis, comp. *1850 Federal Census of Robeson County, NC.*
    Copied from Microfilm Roll #642. Raleigh: Elaine Davis Harmon, 1980.
    [RCPL]
Gives name, age, sex, race, and place of birth of each person living in the household.
Includes a name index for heads of households.

1021. [Robeson County Compensatory Indian Education Project.] "U.S. Census
    Abstracts 1784-1900." Unpub. typescript. Compiled 1980-1981? [IERC]
Lists names of Robeson County free persons of color from the North Carolina state
census 1784-1787 and from the U.S. population censuses for North Carolina for 1800,
1810, 1830-1880, and 1900.

1022. Barton, Lew. "Searching the Family Tree." Unpub. typescript. N.D. [IERC]
Barton comments on his own writings and research, and on materials (including Mary
Norment and Hamilton McMillan) researchers interested in Lumbees should read.

1023. Oxendine, Carol Smith, comp. *Twelfth Census of Population, 1900. North Carolina Vol. 56 E. D.s 100-122 (Indian Population)*. Pembroke: LRDA, 1982. [PSU-MLL]
Name index to Robeson County Indian families in the 1900 federal census. Includes people self-identified as Indian and those verified as Indian through research.

1024. "North Carolina State Archives Research. Robeson County Court Minutes, 1797-1843, C. 083.3001." Unpublished typescript. Lumbee Tribal Enrollment Office, 14 June 1984. [ELC]
Transcribes or summarizes entries regarding Robeson County Indians. The court minutes deal with deeds transferred, judgements, bills of sale, and court appearances.

1025. *Where Our People Lie: Inventory of Native American Burial Sites in Robeson County*. Lumberton: Robeson County Compensatory Indian Education Project, Robeson County Board of Education, 1986. [RCPL]
Entries for 102 cemeteries, giving location, a brief history, and a list of burials, grouped by decade. IERC has the original survey forms.

1026. *Robeson County Register* [periodical]. Ed. Morris F. Britt. Quarterly. Charlotte: M. F. Britt, IBS Graphics, 1986- . [RCPL]
Articles describe or reprint "unpublished, primary source documents related to Robeson" which are potentially useful to genealogists or historians. Many contain Lumbee names. Some examples are: "Entry Book of Vacant Lands–Robeson County–Sept. 15, 1854-Sept. 11, 1944" (Feb., 1990 issue) and "Robeson County Poll Tax List, May 2, 1902" (by township; Feb. and May, 1991 issues). Includes annual Ancestral and Contemporary [Name], Place Name, and Subject Indexes. Some articles are ongoing, such as "Abstracts of Robeson County Wills."

1027. Britt, Morris. "Indian Names in Robeson County." *Robeson County Register* 1.3 (Aug. 1986): 113. [RCPL]
Lists 128 surnames self-identified as Indian in the 1900 federal census for Robeson County. Twelve had variant spellings; Locklear had nine, and Lowry had five.

1028. Jordan, Jerry Wright, comp. *Cherokee by Blood: Record of Eastern Cherokee Ancestry in the US Court of Claims 1906-1910*. Bowie, MD: Heritage Books, 1987- . [RCPL] [PSU-MLL]
Reproduces the report of Guion Miller, Special Commissioner to the U.S. Court of Claims, 1906-1910. Gives data on 46,000 applicants who were known as Cherokee, and on White or Black families with strong traditions of Indian ancestry. Includes some Indians from Robeson County; see the personal name index in each volume.

1029. Pate, Albert F. *"... At Your Beginnings ..." Ezekiel, Chapter 36*. Goldsboro, NC: Albert F. Pate, 1988. 181 p. [PSU-MLL]
History of the Pate and Jacobs families; discusses origins of Robeson County Indians.

1030. Barreiro, José, and Steve Wall. "Lumbee Country: Portraits of Elders." *Northeast Indian Quarterly* 5.2 (Summer 1988): 13-33.
Barreiro and *National Geographic* photographer Steve Wall visited the Jesse James

Locklear, William Locklear, and Isaiah Locklear families to capture their customs, memories, and family life. Features the Lumbee River, grannywomen, and hog killing.

1031. West, Sam. "Records of Robeson County in the North Carolina Archives." *Robeson County Register* 3.3 (Aug. 1988): 92-111. [RCPL]
Lists 200 sets of records potentially useful in genealogy or local history research. Gives date and extent (number of volumes, boxes, or folders) for each. Specifies the Robeson County items in the "Miscellaneous Records, 1817-1939" category.

1032. Locklear, Grady. *Genealogy: A Perspective.* Unpublished typescript. Feb. 1989. 394 p. [IERC] [RCPL]
Consists of chapters on 17 Lumbee families or individuals, including the Locklears, the Revels, and Dr. Gerald Dean Maynor. Also covers the history of Lumbee education; religion; muster rolls; cemetery listings; and more. Includes photographs, maps, reprints of newspaper articles, and an index.

1033. "Criminal Papers–Robeson County 1818-18–." *Robeson County Register* 4.2 (May 1989): 60-63. [RCPL]
Transcribes part of the Criminal Records (North Carolina State Archives) dealing with Robeson County. For small debts, only name and amount of money are listed. Includes these Lumbee names: Elizabeth Cumbo, Mary Cumbo, Thomas Lowrie, Celia Lowrie, Noah Locklier, and Clinton Locklier.

1034. Elisha Locklear Collection. PO Box 1180, Pembroke, NC 28372
Locklear, a Tuscarora, did extensive genealogical and local history research for the Tuscarora petition for federal recognition (see entry 755), filed with the BIA in December, 1989. Materials include: documents relating to the 1934 Indian Reorganization Act (primarily personal applications with photographs, genealogical tables and charts, and anthropometric records); maps of the Red Banks project; and over 500 photographs (some identified) of people from the Harper's Ferry/White Hill community. Most of the latter are deceased; some were born as early as the 1820's.

1035. Shoop, Michael I. "Index to Notices of Death Found in the *Robesonian.*" Unpublished typescript. 1989- . [RCPL] [NCS]
The years 1900-1910 have been completed, and two issues each from the years 1872 and 1873. Additional years will be indexed as time and staff permit.

1036. "Robeson County Bastardy Bonds and Records, 1866-1869." *Robeson County Register* 5.1 (Feb. 1990): 34-36. [RCPL]
These records are housed in the North Carolina Archives (C.R. 083.102.1). Seven Locklears (various spellings) are listed.

1037. Mills, Gary B. "Tracing Free People of Color in the Antebellum South: Methods, Sources, and Perspectives." *National Genealogical Society Quarterly* 78.4 (Dec. 1990): 262-78.
Notes problems created by census designations of race for the families of Thomas and Betsy (Going) Nash, Isaac Perkins, and Gilbert Sweat (p. 264). Comments (p. 276, n. 6) that Lumbee surnames also appear among South Carolinas Turks or Free Moors.

1038. Pate, Albert F. *The Search for Johnny Chevin: Being a Poetic Quest Out of the Most Ancient Records and Oldest Traditions for Descendants of Sir Walter Raleigh's Lost Colony.* Pikeville, NC: A. F. Pate, 1991. [UNC] [Not seen.]

1039. Britt, Morris F. "Robeson County Indian Names: An Analysis Based upon the Census of 1910." *Robeson County Register* 6.3 (August 1991): 120-22.
Two lists–one alphabetical by name, the other by township–of all 105 names of families self-identified as Indian in the 1910 federal census for Robeson County. Gives, in the latter, the number of Indian names in the township, then lists the names.

1040. "Church Register for Robeson Circuit, Methodist Episcopal Church, South, 1869-1881." *Robeson County Register* 6.4 (Nov. 1991): 134-41.
Part 2 in a 3-part series of articles. Includes the colored members of Bee Branch, Saddletree, and Union Chapel churches. Surnames include Sampson, Wilkins, Ransom, Lowrie, Chavis, Manor, Hammond, Dial, Oxendine, Revels, Strickland, Locklier, Brooks, Carter, and Brayboy. Note: RCPL has a photocopy of the manuscript of this church register (from correspondence).

1041. Byrd, William L., III, and Sheila Spencer Stover. "In Search of Cultural Identity. Part 2." *North Carolina Genealogical Society Journal* February 1992: 48-54.
Byrd explains obstacles he encountered in tracking Indian ancestors (his paternal grandmother was from Robeson County). Lumbees have been listed, in legal and historical documents, as Negroes, mulattoes, mustees, Whites, or free persons of color. Census enumerators sometimes changed the spelling of Indian surnames. Indians were quiet and cautious during certain periods of history, keeping their Indian identity hidden even within the family and trying to stay off legal documents. Part 1 of this article (May, 1991 issue) provides a more general discussion of problems of genealogical research on North Carolina Indian ancestors.

1042. DeMarce, Virginia Easley. " 'Verry Slitly Mixt': Tri-Racial Isolate Families of the Upper South–A Genealogical Study." *National Genealogical Society Quarterly* 80.1 (March 1992): [5]-35.
Surveys literature on triracial isolates from other fields and indicates how genealogical research can contribute to existing knowledge of their origins and development. Mentions Lumbees throughout the text and footnotes. Detailed discussion of the Chavis and Goins families. Extensively documented. The appendix lists family surnames commonly found in triracial isolate groups. For each surname, gives the groups among which it occurs, and the racial designations (ex. free mulatto, free person of color) used for that group in well-documented studies. Wes Taukchiray responds, in the June, 1992, issue ("Updates" section), to this article's mention of his research.

1043. DeMarce, Virginia Easley. "Looking at Legends: Lumbee and Melungeon: Applied Genealogy and the Origins of Tri-Racial Isolate Settlements." *National Genealogical Society Quarterly* 81.1 (March 1993): 24-45.
Investigates the origin of the Lumbee community by examining land grant records, tax lists, census records, genealogical studies, and other documents. Her analysis yields three conclusions: The earliest documented Lumbee families originated in Tidewater

Virginia and upper N.C.; the records examined use inconsistent ethnic labels; and the nonwhite labels indicate triracial origins. Discusses the proportion of Black, White, and Indian blood in triracial isolates, and possibilities that individuals or families crossed the color line to avoid "Black codes" and "Jim Crow laws." She asserts, "researchers must examine every record in the geographic area of interest, no matter what the racial category listed in the census."

ORAL HISTORY

1044. University of Florida. Southeastern Indian Oral History Project. 126 Florida
State Museum, Gainesville, FL 32611. 904-392-1721. [Not seen.]
This collection is part of the Doris Duke Indian Oral History program. Includes tapes (most done in 1973) and transcriptions on some 190 North Carolina Lumbees. Baltimore Lumbees were also taped (see Ronald Chepesiuk, *American Indian Archival Material: A Guide to Holdings in the Southeast*, 1982, pp. 18-19). Some Whites who were involved in Lumbee affairs or research were interviewed. Topical interviews include: Lumbee Hearings, Indian Protest on Education, Old Main Commission Session, Lure and Lore of the Lumbee, Are They Really Indians?, Prospect School Incident, and Burnt Swamp Baptist Association Readings. A list of Lumbee tapes can be obtained. Materials must be used on-site. [From correspondence.]

1045. "The Origin of 'Scuffletown'." *Lumberton Argus* 15 Nov. 1904: 1.
Wash Lowrie reports that wagoners hauling in whiskey used to camp under a mulberry tree. Men gathered there to drink and scuffle around until their wives took them home. See also Evans (entry 1118), p. 29 note 18.

1046. Pembroke Senior High School. Literary Magazine Class. *Lighter'd Knot*.
1977. [PSU-MLL]
Oral history anthology. Topics include: Tokens, conjuring, home arthritis medicine, medicine tea, stills and moonshine, making sausage, preserves, lye soap, and jelly, hog-killing, Robeson County preaching and churches, and hanging sheetrock.

1047. "The Lighterd Knot." Robeson County Oral History Newsletter. Ed. Kate
Rinzler. Title IVA, Robeson County Indian Education, n.d. [IERC]
Three issues have appeared, containing stories and drawings by Lumbee children. One issue is devoted to hunting and fishing. IERC also has children's drawings of folk dolls and sports, and children's stories of fishing and hunting, collected by Rinzler.

1048. Robeson County Compensatory Indian Education Project. "Oral Histories of
Lumbee Indian Elders." Audiotapes. 1982. [IERC] [Around 70 tapes.]

1049. Robeson County Compensatory Indian Education Project. "Oral History
Videotapes." 1982. [IERC] [Fourteen videotapes of Lumbee elders.]

1050. McMahan, Eva M. "Lumbee Soundings: Voices of the Past." [Script for a
30-minute videotape.] Lumberton: Robeson County Compensatory Indian Education Project, 31 May 1984. 18 p. [IERC]

Features Clement Bullard on farm chores and land ownership, Oscar and Margie Chavis on Hogtown, Ella Baker on Henry Berry Lowry, Rev. Charles Maynor on religion, and Claude Sampson and Mary Locklear on a one-room schoolhouse.

THE LUMBEE RIVER; ENVIRONMENT; ENVIRONMENTALISM

1051. "Lumberton As It Now Is. With a Brief Sketch of Its Early Organization and the Origin of Its Name." *Robesonian* 10 May 1904: 1.
Croatans' ancestors gave the river the name "Lombe," which in their language meant "black." Lumberton, formerly known as Red Bluff, was an Indian trading post.

1052. McNeill, John Charles. "Lumber River." 1905. *Robesonian* Feb. 1951 (Robeson County Historical Edition): Sec. 2 p. 1.
Frequently quoted piece which states that the Indians named the river "Lumbee." Reprinted from *Lumberton Argus* 28 July 1905. See also: McKinnon, Henry A., Jr. "Poets of the Lumbee." *Robesonian* 1 Aug. 1993: C1. [McNeill, Woodberry Lennon, Clare J. Marley, and William Laurie Hill].

1053. Britt, Albert. "Down the Lumbee." *Outing* 80 (Sept. 1922): 262-64.
Britt took a canoe trip from Pine Bluff (which had a canoe club) to Fair Bluff. He rented canoes from the Pine Bluff Inn. Other accounts of canoeing on the Lumbee River include: (1) Haynes, Williams. "Through a Jungle to the Old South." *Outing* 65 (Jan. 1915): 478-86 [PSU-MLL]. (2) Haynes, Williams. "Down the Old Lumbee ... " *Field and Stream* 23.1 (May 1918): 5-7, 48 [PSU-MLL]. (3) "Two Boys in a Boat." *The State* 9.17 (27 Sept. 1941): 10, 26 [PSU-MLL]. Two other early articles are described in Henry A. McKinnon's article, "Fascination with the Lumbee" (*The News of Robeson County* 16 June 1990: 3). See also Colin P. Osborne, "Nature's Sanctuary" (*The State* 58.4 (Sept. 1990): 38-40); it includes John Charles McNeill's poem, "Sunburnt Boys" (originally published in his *Songs Merry and Sad*, 1906, 1932). The river is mentioned in A. R. Ammons' poem, "Alligator Holes down along about Old Dock," *North Carolina Literary Review* 1.2 (Spring 1993): 228.

1054. "Lumbee Young-Old River, Noted Author Gerald Johnson Says." *Pembroke Progress* 27 Nov. 1947: Sec. 2 p. 1.
Reprints a paper by Johnson and mentions John Charles McNeill.

1055. "Name of the River." *Robesonian* 6 May 1971: 22.
This editorial suggests alternatives–including adding "The Lumbee" under "Lumber River" on road signs–to legislatively changing the name of the river.

1056. "Traditional Label." *Robesonian* 7 May 1971: [8].
Editorial. Disagrees with C. F. W. Coker's assertion that the river has "never been called" Lumbee except as a popular corruption. Cites O. M. McPherson, Hamilton McMillan, and A. W. McLean. See Lew Barton's letter, same page.

1057. Moe, Susan Spence. "River Weaves Close-Knit Community." *News and Observer* 19 Sept. 1976: Sec. 3 p. 2.

Describes the Lumbee River's influence on Riverton, first settled in 1807 by Daniel White, a Baptist minister from Scotland. Explains the importance of John Charles McNeill and mentions other notable citizens from Riverton (Gerald Johnson, Lois Johnson, Livingston Johnson, and Archibald Johnson).

1058. Bauer, Ursula. "The River That Wouldn't Die." *Environmental Politics: Lessons from the Grassroots.* Ed. Bob Hall. Durham: Institute for Southern Studies, 1988. Pp. 70-79.
On GSX's efforts to locate a hazardous waste treatment facility in Laurinburg and dump treated discharge into the Lumbee River. Includes Richard Regan's description of Lumbee opposition.

1059. Regan, Richard. "The Lumber River, The Lumbee Indians, and GSX, Inc., Robeson County, North Carolina." *The Egg* [CRESP, Cornell U, Ithaca, NY] Winter 1987-1988: 10-11.
Regan, a Lumbee, works as a community organizer for Robeson County's Center for Community Action. He recounts Lumbee reactions and organized response to the proposed GSX facility.

1060. Regan, Richard. "Building Multi-Racial Environmental Conditions That Work." *The Egg* 9.4 (Winter 1989-90): 14-15.
On Lumbee involvement in a successful grassroots campaign to prevent a GSX facility on the Lumbee River. Lumbees worked with the predominantly White organizations SCAT (Sensible Concerns about Toxics) and LRBC (Lumber River Basin Committee).

1061. Regan, Richard, and Mac Legerton. "Economic Slavery or Hazardous Wastes? Robeson County's Economic Menu." *Communities in Economic Crisis: Appalachia and the South.* Philadelphia: Temple UP, 1990. Pp. 146-57.
Lumbees and Tuscaroras helped thwart the "economic blackmail" that almost located a hazardous waste treatment facility 4,000 feet from the river.

1062. "Judge Rules EPA Can't Interfere with N.C. Waste Facility Sitings." *Robesonian* 13 April 1990: 1.
An administrative law judge ruled that North Carolina can have regulations more stringent than federal ones on dilution of wastewater from hazardous waste treatment facilities. GSX will have time to respond and possibly to appeal.

1063. Ash, Andrew N. *A Preliminary Natural Areas Inventory of the Lumber River Floodplain. A Report Submitted to the North Carolina Natural Heritage Program [and] North Carolina Nature Conservancy.* [Raleigh]: NC Dept. of Environment, Health, and Natural Resources, 14 Nov. 1990.
Surveyed 102 miles of the river– from the South Carolina border to State Road 1412, above Wagram. Survey reports were completed for twelve sites, listing plant communities and species and—on a casual basis—noting animal species. Ranks the sites by importance as natural communities. Ash submitted another report for Year II (1991) on 11 May 1992; it focused on eight sites.

1064. Bridgers, John Bracey. "Groundwater Pollution Potential: A Case Study of

Robeson County, North Carolina." Thesis. Appalachian State U, December 1991. [ASU-BLK]
Uses the National Well Water Association's DRASTIC and Pesticide DRASTIC Indices, related to landcover analysis from satellite imagery, to assess the county's groundwater pollution potential from both water and agricultural sources. Chapter III gives background data on the physiography (including Carolina bays), climate, population, geology and hydrogeology, and land use of the county.

ARCHAEOLOGY OF THE ROBESON COUNTY AREA

1065. Watts, Carroll. "Robeson County 'Dig' Reveals Clues of Former Occupants." *Robesonian* 30 Aug. 1970: 5B.
Dr. David McLean and students investigated the Parham site. It was once a village inhabited by 300 Indians, probably Algonquin. Artifacts will be housed in IMC.

1066. Keel, Bennie C. "Excavations at the Red Springs Mound RB 4, Robeson County 1971." *Southern Indian Studies* 22 (Oct. 1970): 17-22.
Limited investigation of the Buie Mound (see also entry 1069) was done by students Keel supervised. Describes field methods, cultural remains, and skeletal remains.

1067. McLean, David A. "Project BOR 15-500 LWCF: Robeson County Recreation and Parks Commission, Lumberton, NC: Archaeological Reconnaissance." 17 Dec. 1976. 14p. Report no. 5 in: *North Carolina Archaeological Council Publication No. 3*. Raleigh: Archaeological Council and the Archaeology Branch, Div. of Archives and History, N.C. Dept. of Cultural Resources, 1977.
Survey of fifteen areas; all were found "insignificant" except Site One (Meadow Road, 65 acres), which was deemed an "important site." Site One should "be further investigated by salvage mitigation, or ... remain undamaged and designated as an Indian village site." The report summarizes items found at each site.

1068. McLean, David, and Michael Sellon. *Documentary Research of Historic and Pre-historic Sites Located in the Lumber River Basin (d.o. DACW60-78-M-0503)*. 2v. Prepared for the U.S. Army Corps of Engineers, Charleston District, 1978. Ms. on file, St. Andrews Presbyterian College. [IMC]
The basin includes parts 3, South Carolina, and 9, North Carolina (including Robeson County). Provides maps and narrative data on each quad. Final version also at IMC.

1069. Wetmore, Ruth Y. "Report on Excavations at the Buie Mound, Robeson County, North Carolina." *University of South Carolina. Institute of Archaeology and Anthropology. Notebook* 10 (1978): 30-71.
This sand burial mound, two miles south of Red Springs, was excavated several times, mainly 1971-1974. Documents the site's location and history, stratigraphy, cultural remains, and artifacts. Compares it with 13 other North Carolina burial mounds.

1070. Padgett, Thomas J., and J. Chris Baroody. *Final Report. Archaeological Survey and Evaluation. US 74 Maxton Bypass, Robeson and Scotland Counties*. Project no. R-77. N.C. Dept. of Transportation, Jan. 1981. MS. on file, Planning and Research Branch, N.C. Dept. of Transportation. 13 p. [IMC]

Lists artifacts found along the route of the highway; recommends "no further action."

1071. Knick, Stanley. *Robeson Trails Archaeological Survey: Reconnaissance in Robeson County.* Pembroke: Native American Resource Center, Pembroke State U, 1988. [PSU-MLL] NC Docs. Depository: microfiche G85 2: R65
Documents 314 previously unrecorded sites and gives preliminary evaluations of 20 major sites. Shows that Robeson County has been inhabited for at least 14,000 years. Lists, for each site, prehistoric stone materials (Table 1); prehistoric ceramics and historic artifacts (Table 2); time periods (Table 3); and preliminary assessment of significance (Table 4). Lists previous archaeological research (pp. 25-27). NARC received a National Park Service grant for "Robeson Crossroads Archaeological Survey, Phase II," which involved intensive testing of fifteen sites examined in the Robeson Trails reconnaissance. See *CIV* 21 and 28 Oct. 1993: 3.

1072. "Study Reveals Indians Inhabited Robeson County 14,000 Years Ago." *Robesonian* 7 Nov. 1988: B1.
On the Robeson Trails Archaeological Survey (above), which "strongly supports efforts by local Native Americans to gain federal recognition."

1073. Menges, Jerri. "Archaeology Opens Doors for Indian Students." *Robesonian* 7 May 1989: C1.
PSU students helped with Robeson Trails Archaeological Survey (above). Article explains the survey's significance and the course's impact on Indian Studies students.

THE HENRY BERRY LOWRY PERIOD

1074. Wishart, Francis Marion. "Diary of Col. Francis M. Wishart, Commander of Action Against the Lowry Outlaws of Robeson County, North Carolina, 1864-1872, and Comments by an Unknown Author." Typescript. Presented by Mrs. Annabel Wishart Lane. [UNC-WL]
Transcribes some of the diary which, Wishart's son noted, consisted of "personal data jotted down in memorandum books, notes and letters from friends, and [Wishart's] own comments and opinions on current affairs." Includes a description of events leading to the killing of James Barnes, a family history of Henry Berry Lowry, accounts of Wishart's troops' activities on various days, descriptions of the gang, and moving accounts of Wishart's adversity in trying to capture the gang (not enough troops, drunkenness, discipline problems, desertion among troops, and inadequate supplies). The remainder of the Wishart Family Papers (not seen; UNC-WL, Southern Historical Collection, entry 4624) includes Wishart's correspondence and notes on the gang, and a tintype (ca. 1871) showing three men with shotguns and a dead gang member (from OCLC record).

1075. Criminal Action Papers Concerning Henry Berry Lowry. MS. North Carolina State Archives, Raleigh. 1 box. [Not seen]
Contains documents described in Donna Spindel's *Introductory Guide to Indian-Related Records (to 1876) in the North Carolina State Archives* (1977). IERC has photocopies of John Taylor's arrest warrant for gang members (10 Dec. 1870) and testimony from *State v. H. B. Lowry* (14 Dec. 1870), with transcriptions.

1076. "Robin Hood Come Again." *New York Times* 22 July 1871: P. 4 col. 5. Editorial deploring Lowry's recent exploits (see also 12 July 1871: P. 1 col. 7 and 18 July 1871: P. 1 col. 2). Lowry is the "robber baron of the period; his stronghold is an island at the center of an almost inaccessible swamp in Robeson County ..." He is a "chivalric cut-throat" ; his band a "motley crew of Whites and Blacks, runaway slaves ... , deserted soldiers of both armies, and miscellaneous outlaws of every stamp."

1077. "A History of the Capture of the Notorious Outlaw George Applewhite, Alias, Ranse Lowery, of the Lowery Gang of Outlaws, or Robeson County, N.C. ..." Columbus, GA: Thos. Gilbert, 1872. 12 p. [UGa] Rpt. in entry 1125.
Chas. P. Murrah, J. G. Bryant, Geo. N. Murrah, and Albert Sanford captured Applewhite in Harris County, GA despite problems. They reprint and correct a *Columbus Daily Sun* article on the capture. Edwards (entry 1125) analyzes the capture.

1078. Townsend, George Alfred, comp. *The Swamp Outlaws: or, The North Carolina Bandits; Being a Complete History of the Modern Rob Roys and Robin Hoods*. The Red Wolf Series. New York: Robert M. DeWitt, 1872. [PSU-MLL] [UNC] Another edition: *The Swamp Outlaws of North Carolina*. Philadelphia: Old Franklin Publishing House, 1872. [RCPL]
The *New York Herald* sent correspondents to Robeson County to cover the deeds of the Lowry Gang. This book compiles their letters to the *Herald*. The account makes no attempt at journalistic impartiality; its style aims at titillating readers. The Old Franklin edition adds "Miss Patton's account of her experiences among them while a prisoner in their hands." See comments by Evans (entry 1118), p. 272.

1079. U.S. Cong. Joint Select Comm. to Inquire into the Condition of Affairs in the Late Insurrectionary States. *Report ... on the Condition of Affairs in the Late Insurrectionary States*. Made to the Two Houses of Congress, 19 Feb. 1872. 42nd Cong., 2nd Sess. Report No. 41, Part 1. 1872. Rpt. New York: AMS, 1968. See Vol. 2, pp. 283-304.
Giles Leitch of Lumberton, who had served as county registrar and state senator, testified on Croatans, the Lowry Gang's deeds and politics, and Ku Klux Klan activity in the county. His testimony is mentioned in Blu (entry 55) and Sider (entry 59).

1080. "A New Expedition: Proposition to Capture the Lowery Gang of Outlaws–Singular Enterprise of a Fourth Ward Character." *New York Times* 18 March 1872: P. 5 col. 3.
George Abbot says he is "in correspondence with some of the most prominent citizens of North Carolina" and is gathering a small force to capture the Lowry Gang. He is interested in the reward being offered. He was in Robeson County earlier under the name Jack Allen, as a travelling salesman. He "had shooting matches on several occasions with Lowery's outlaws," often talked to Lowery, and even loaned him $10.00. Abbot had run-ins with the Ku Klux Klan and wants to avenge the incidents.

1081. "The North Carolina Bandits." *Harper's Weekly* 16 (30 March 1872): 249, 251-2.
Sympathetic account of Lowry and his gang's exploits. Includes drawings (frequently reprinted) of Thomas Lowry; Calvin Oxendine; Henry Berry Lowry and his gang in the

swamp; Henderson Oxendine; George Applewhite; the rescue of Lowry's wife and children; and "a shrewd maneuver."

1082. "The Lowery Gang." *New York Times* 4 May 1874: P. 2 col. 3.
Quotes two articles from the *Robesonian*. Bryan Oxendine, "brother-in-law of the late Henry B. Lowery," shot and seriously wounded his wife on April 10 during an argument while the couple were dispensing whiskey for a customer. On April 16, James and Marcus Dial were gigging fish at a mill-dam near Scuffletown when they were fired on from ambush. James was seriously injured; the shot was fired from his own gun, which he had left on the bank.

1083. Norment, Mary C. *The Lowrie History, As Acted in Part by Henry Berry Lowrie, the Great North Carolina Bandit. With Biographical Sketches of His Associates. Being a Complete History of the Modern Robber Band in the County of Robeson and State of North Carolina.* Wilmington: Daily Journal Printer, 1875.
–Reprints: Weldon, NC: Harrell's Printing House, 1895; Lumberton: Lumbee Publishing Co., 1900, 1909. [PSU-MLL] [RCPL] The 1875 edition was serialized in the *Charlotte Observer* 1905: 19 Mar. p. 15; 26 Mar. p. 15; 2 Apr. p. 16; 9 Apr. p. 14; 16 Apr. p. 15; 23 Apr. p. 18; 30 Apr. p. 14; 7 May p. 16; 14 May p. 16; 21 May p. 14; 28 May p. 16; 4 June p. 10; 11 June p. 18. The 1909 edition was microfilmed by Yale University Library in 1990.
–A standard, frequently-quoted source. Evans states that, although "strongly partisan," Norment "seems to make few factual errors" (entry 1118, pp. 273-275). Includes a genealogy of gang members, description of Scuffletown's origin and geography, account of "the true condition of affairs in Robeson County," 1864 through late 1870; and sections on people who were robbed or killed by the gang. The appendix of the 1909 edition is a condensation of a series of newspaper articles by Col. F. A. Olds. Weeks (entry 508) asserts that this book was actually written by Joseph B. McCallum. W. McKee Evans was never able to substantiate this claim. He has not seen any mention of Norment being celebrated as an author but speculates that a ghost writer could have used her name for publicity purposes (from correspondence).

1084. "Two of the Lowery Gang." [Charleston, S.C.] *News and Courier* 23 July 1878: 1.
John Locklear (alias John Revels) and Neill Locklear (alias Neill Revels) were tried at Bennettsville, S.C., for the murder of Frank Bryce, an Irish peddler. Detailed description of the shooting incident, the trial, and the two gang members.

1085. Triplett, Frank. *History, Romance and Philosophy of Great American Crimes and Criminals* .... New York: N. D. Thompson and Co., 1884. Pp. 464-92.
Describes the Lowry Band and their deeds with a writing style and bias much like Townsend's (entry 1078). Calls them, for instance, "mongrel outlaws, to whom murder was a pleasant excitement and robbery but a pastime." Numerous engravings.

1086. Gorman, John C. "Henry Berry Lowry Paper." Unpublished manuscript. [1894?] Housed in the North Carolina Division of Archives and History, Raleigh, N.C. 26p. [Photocopy at RCPL]

A radio mention of the Lowry Gang made the author, formerly North Carolina Adjutant General, decide to write a more accurate account. Gorman and his troops, commissioned by the state's governor, tried to capture the gang in 1870-71. The paper is mentioned in Farris (entry 1099) and Evans (entry 1118). Evans dates it at 20 years after the demise of the gang.

1087. "Rhoda Lowrie: Widow of the Noted Outlaw in Jail for Retailing Liquor Without License." *Robesonian* 10 Nov. 1897: [3].

1088. "Through Scuffletown." *The Argus* 14 June 1904: 4.
The editor of *The Argus* and his friends ride to Pates and meet Wash Lowrie. The editor predicts, "The days of the 'Lowrie Gang' will possibly furnish themes for poetry and romance when the Croatans are a cultured people–how long hence?"

1089. "Personal and Local Dept.–[untitled note]." *Robesonian* 3 Feb. 1905: 5.
A Scotland Countian received a letter from Henry Berry Lowry, in Mexico, asking him to persuade the governor to pardon him so he can return to Robeson County.

1090. "Henry Berry Lowry Is Dead." Lumberton *Argus* 3 Nov. 1905: 3.
Quotes an article from the Florence *Times*. An Oxendine, brother-in-law of Lowry who became wealthy through mining in Mexico, recently stated there was no truth to the rumors (see entry 1089) that the outlaw was alive in Mexico. Oxendine himself helped bury the outlaw in a hollow log in the swamp.

1091. Fulton, David Bryant. *"Eagle Clippings" by Jack Thorne [pseud.], Newspaper Correspondent and Storyteller ... a Collection of His Writings [submitted] to Various Newspapers.* Brooklyn: D. B. Fulton, 1907. Pp. 65-71. [UNC-WL]
Fulton was Black; his mother, Lavinia Robinson, was born in Robeson County. Reprints his story on Henry Berry Lowry, an "octoroon outlaw," from *The Citizen*.

1092. Humphrey, J. W. "Henry Berry Lowery: Another Version of How He Became an Outlaw." *Robesonian* 6 July 1908: 2.
Letter on Lowry's resentment of being conscripted to work with Blacks on fortifications. Neighbor James P. Barnes was a member of a board which denied Lowry's request for exemption.

1093. A Scotchman. "The Lowrie Gang: A Portion of Col. Olds' Article False and Misleading." *Robesonian* 13 July 1908: 1.
Disagrees with Olds' rationale (see entry 8, July 6) for Lowry's lawlessness. States that Lowry, accused of stealing James Barnes' hogs, shot Barnes from ambush. Barnes identified him before dying. Related article, *Robesonian* 13 July 1908: 2. H. L. Edens defends Olds (*Robesonian* 27 July 1908: 2) and urges temperance in judgement of Lowry; "that ... [he] has become a historic character none will doubt."

1094. Cy. "The Lowry Outlaws." *The Guilford Collegian* 24.3 (Nov. 1911): 90-94; 24.5 (Jan. 1912): 152-57; 24.8 (Apr. 1912): 285-96. [GPL-NC Biog Clippings File]
Recounting, in a literary magazine, of "the adventures of one of the greatest personages

among the descendants of the 'Lost Colony'."

1095. "Murdock MacDonald: A True Story of the Days of the Outlaws in Robeson
   County, North Carolina." *Charlotte Observer* 3 March 1912: 13.
Earnest story of a man who attempted to track down the Lowry Gang, came too close,
and was ambushed and killed.

1096. Currie, A. D. "A Run from the Lowrie Gang." *Robesonian* 1 Jan. 1917: 3; 29
   Jan. 1917: 2.
Letter. The author and Thomas Fry visited a neighbor and found the Lowry Gang at
her house.

1097. Bibson, J. Press, Sr. "What Became of Henry Berry Lowrey, Notorious
   Robeson Bandit Chief?" *Robesonian* 12 June 1922: 6.
Two Indian friends of the author–Oxendine Lowery and Sam Locklear–told Bibson,
many years ago, that Henry Berry Lowry did not die. Rather, he went to a secret
hiding place, "an island in an impenetrable swamp" with a subterranean passage to
another location. Lowry stayed there for a year, then moved on to South America.
Includes information on mounds from "Dr. Hair, an Indian doctor" in Marlboro
County. H. S. Hair is also mentioned in entry 452.

1098. "Fake Picture Famous Bandit." *Robesonian* 4 Aug. 1924: 5.
Letter to the editor from A. N. Locklear and J. R. Lowry of the I.B.S. (Indian Better-
ment Society of Eastern North Carolina). The *Fayetteville Observer* had recently
reported on a "crayon enlargement" of Henry Berry Lowry, found by C. D. Brewington
and claimed by Brewington to be the only picture of Lowry in existence. Locklear and
Lowry have taken the picture to "H. B. Lowry's brother and to many others who knew
him personally"; all said it was "fake." Locklear and Lowry "do not see anything
ennobling and uplifting in harking back to such."

1099. Farris, James J. "The Lowrie Gang: An Episode in the History of Robeson
   County, N.C.:1864-1874." *Historical Papers Published by the Trinity College
   Historical Society*. Ser. XV. Durham: Duke UP, 1925. Pp. 55-93. [PSU-MLL]
Uses interviews, journals, newspapers, and local traditions to explain political, social,
and economic factors in the gang's deeds. Evans (entry 1118) notes a factual error.

1100. "Museum Gets Henry Berrie Lowrey's Gun." *Robesonian* 31 Oct. 1927: 3.
A rifle was donated to the Duke University Library by Alene McCall.

1101. Martin, L. "Robeson's 10-Year Reign of Terror Recalled." *Charlotte Observer*
   22 April 1934: Sec. 3 p. 2. Rpt. *Robesonian* 26 Apr. 1934: 7; 3 May 1934: 7.

1102. "Last of Lowry Gang [John Dial] Baptised at 83." *Robesonian* 16 May 1935: 1.

1103. "Claims Henry Berry Lowry, Leader of Band of Outlaws, Alive at 92."
   Robesonian 5 April 1937: 1. Rpt. in *News and Observer* 9 May 1937: 1.
Earl C. Lowry says his uncle went from Norfolk to Florida. This lengthy article
explains the outlaw's background and activist beliefs. Note: Lowry conducted research

on "multiple military actions regarding the [Lumbees], especially during the Lowry days, 1860-1872." He is writing a book on Lowry (from correspondence).

1104. "Famed Outlaw's Rifle Returned." *Robesonian* 12 April 1937: 7.
The rifle was found near Reuben King's home and returned to Kermit Lowry (Henry Berry Lowry's great-nephew) by W. N. Harris of Wilmington.

1105. "Hero of Lowry Gang Episode Passes at Age of 89 Years." *Robesonian* 23 Feb. 1938: I-1. [Henry H. Biggs, who shot Zack McLauchlin in Dec. 1870.]

1106. Newsom, Ruby Crockett. "McKay Birthday Celebration." *Robesonian* 16 June 1939: 4.
James Frank McKay, who was part of a posse which pursued the Lowry Gang, celebrated his 90th birthday.

1107. Lawrence, R. C. "Wishart and the Loweries." *The State* 26 Aug. 1939: 6-7. Rpt. in *Robesonian* 28 Aug. 1939: 8.
On Wishart's efforts to end the deeds of the Lowry Gang, and his death. Quotes from several of Wishart's letters, including his fearful Aug. 28, 1871, letter to North Carolina's Adjutant General.

1108. Franklin, John Hope. "The Enslavement of Free Negroes in North Carolina." *Journal of Negro History* 29.4 (Oct. 1944): 401-28.
Background data on N.C.'s laws regarding free persons of color, the intended effect of the laws, the actual consequences, and petitions for private enslavement laws.

1109. McEachern, Stuart. "Eight Years of Terror." *The State* 20.26 (29 Nov. 1952): 6.
Discusses incidents that provoked Lowry's actions, his means of escape, how gang members were killed, and Lowry's presumed death.

1110. "'Rubber' Coffin Check Rattles Outlaw's Bones." *Greensboro Daily News* 7 Sept. 1956. [Included in entry 468.]
James N. Lowery was sentenced for writing a worthless check to Locklear Funeral Home. He bought a copper casket purportedly to display Henry Berry Lowry's bones.

1111. Manning, Charles. "Last of Lowerys Recalls Saga of Death and Terror." *Greensboro Daily News* 19 Jan. 1958: A13.
B. W. Lowry, 97-year-old nephew of Henry Berry Lowry.

1112. Rockwell, Paul A. "Lumbees Rebelled Against Proposed Draft by South." *Asheville Citizen-Times* 2 Feb. 1958. [UNC-WL Clippings File]
Letter on Zebulon Vance's attempts to conscript Croatans; quotes C. M. Pepper and Kate Lilly Blue.

1113. Dunnagan, Claude. "Henry Lowery's Private Six-Year War Against the South." *Male* 11.7 (July 1961): 33-35, 39-45. [PSU-MLL]
Sympathetic, colorfully written account with art by Jim Bama. Emphasizes dog chases, jail breaks, and guns. Notes the "sirens of Scuffletown" who seduced federal

soldiers to gain information for Lowry. Dunnagan was a UNC-Chapel Hill alumnus and Chapel Hill resident. He interviewed Henry Berry Lowry's nephew, Billy Lowrey, for this article's account of the outlaw's escape to New Mexico. See newspaper article, "'Lowery Gang' Chief Is Magazine Subject," PSU-MLL, PSU Clippings File, 1961.

1114. Jenkins, Jay. "Lowry's Daughter Buried by Indians." *Charlotte Observer* 2 April 1962: Sec. B p. 1.
Polly Lowry, 95-year-old daughter of Henry Berry Lowry, was buried at White Hill Freewill Baptist Church.

1115. Woodward, Susan Holly. "A Grandfather's Tales of the Lowery Brothers." *North Carolina Folklore* 10.2 (Dec. 1962): 17-19.
Woodward's grandfather, A. N. Mitchell, describes Henry Berry and Steve Lowry's encounter with the author's great-grandfather (a young boy at the time). Woodward's great-grandmother's trunk was stolen from her loom house by the gang.

1116. Regan, Mary. "Dark Fame Surrounded 'Queen'." *News and Observer* 23 Apr. 1967: Sec. 4 p. 1.
Provides descriptions of Rhoda's physical appearance and differing accounts of her role in the deeds of the Lowry Gang.

1117. Arrowood, Charles F. "The Outlaws of Scuffletown." Unpublished typescript. N.d. 14 p. [PSU-MLL]
Rumors in 1906 that Henry Berry Lowry had been seen in Scuffletown prompted this description of Lowry, Scuffletown, the county, and the gang's activities. Includes A. W. McLean's interview with 80-year-old Wash Lowrie (see also entry 522).

1118. Evans, W. McKee. *To Die Game: The Story of the Lowry Band, Indian Guerillas of Reconstruction.* Baton Rouge: Louisiana State UP, 1971. [PSU-MLL]
Detailed, extensively researched, and engagingly written account of Lowry, his family, all gang members, and others involved in the incidents (including Capt. Owen C. Norment, John Sanders, Andrew Strong, and Col. Frank Wishart). Analyzes the political background of the gang's activities. Reviews various accounts of Lowry's death or disappearance. Copious footnotes and an evaluative "Essay on Sources."

1119. "Lowry: 'He Didn't Kill As Many ... As Moses'." *Greensboro Daily News* 17 Jan. 1971: A15. [Interview with Doctor Fuller Lowry, nephew of the outlaw.]

1120. Arendell, Banks. " 'Shake' Cheats the Hangman." *The State* 39.13 (1 Dec. 1971): 17-18.
Andy "Shake" Winecoff, a Black member of the Lowry Gang, received a facial injury in the gang's robbery of a payroll delivery bound for the Lumbee River Cotton Mill. "Shake" was also employed for a time running errands in the office of Zebulon Vance.

1121. Barton, Lew. "Henry Berry Lowry, Lumbee Guerilla Warrior of Reconstruction Days." *Indian Voice* 1.7 (14 Sept. 1972). [PSU-MLL]
Reviews the gang's activities and Lowry's significance to Lumbee people. Ends with a

plea to "Save Old Main," "one of the main remnants of Lumbee pride."

1122.   Barton, Bruce. "Henry Berry Lowry and the Lumbee Indians." *Lutheran
        Women* 13.5 (May 1975): 3-7.
Reviews the Lumbees' recent problems. Also discusses origin theories, name changes,
the period of disfranchisement, and activities of the Lowry Gang. Ends with a moving
statement of what Henry Berry Lowry symbolizes for Lumbee people.

1123.   Blackburn, Charles. "The Nefarious Adventures of the Lowry Gang." *The
        Near East* 3.4 (Sept.-Oct. 1975): 18-21. Also in *Tar Heel* 8.5 (July 1980):
        24-25, 63. [UNC-WL]
Explains conditions that led to the formation of the gang, outlines their major activities,
and gives stories about Lowry's death or escape to "New Mexico." Includes excerpts
from the *Raleigh Register* and illustrations from *Harper's Weekly.*

1124.   Barton, Garry Lewis. *The Life and Times of Henry Berry Lowry.* Pembroke:
        Lumbee Pub. Co., 1979. [PSU-MLL] New edition. N.p.: Published and
        printed by Garry Lewis Barton, Feb. 1992. [PSU-MLL]
The 1979 edition first appeared as weekly installments in *CIV*, 24 Oct. 1974–8 Dec.
1977. Includes many quotations from other published sources on the Gang, most cited
in this bibliography. Explains the importance of Henry Berry Lowry to Lumbee
Indians. The new edition has many illustrations, including a reproduction of an
authentic photograph of Lowry. Reprints the *Harper's Magazine* illustrations (entry
1081); has photographs of tombstones of several of Lowry's family members.

1125.   Edwards, John Carver. "Harris County Bounty Men and the Ubiquitous Mr.
        Applewhite." *Atlanta Historical Journal* 24.1 (Spring 1980): 53-62.
On the disappearance of Black gang member George Applewhite and his later
"capture" by Hamilton, Georgia, businessmen Charles P. and George Nobles Murrah.
After the Murrahs' pamphlet (entry 1077) was published, Robeson County Sheriff
McMillan met with the prisoner and proclaimed that they had captured the wrong man.

1126.   Brown, Dick. "More Lowry Saga." *Fayetteville Observer* 5 July 1981: E1.
        [PSU-MLL]
A recently discovered broadside gives statements of George Applewhite from the
Whiteville Jail. James Sinclair, a Scotchman, tipped off the gang to hunting parties.

1127.   Jones, Rosalyn Jacobs. "Upward Mobility: A Historical Narrative. The John
        W. Jacobs Story." Diss. Middle Tennessee State U, 1983. [ECU] [UNC-WL]
This folklore research project collects stories on John W. Jacobs (1852-1925), whose
wife, Mary Margaret Lowry, was a niece of Henry Berry Lowry. Mary's father was a
member of the Lowry gang. Chapter 4 discusses the Lowry era's effects on Mary.

1128.   Cooper, Richard. *Henry Berry Lowry: Rebel With a Cause.* Famous Tar
        Heels. Raleigh: Creative Publications, 1985. [IERC]
Brief, illustrated juvenile account of Lowry's exploits and importance to Lumbees.

1129.   Wetmore, Ruth. "Henry Berry Lowrie, The Swamp Outlaw." *News and*

Observer, 400th anniversary edition, July 1985: Sec. 6 p. 16.
Brief overview. Mentions the gang's triracial composition.

1130. Massengill, Stephen E. "The Detectives of William W. Holden, 1869-1870."
North Carolina Historical Review 62.4 (Oct. 1985): 448-87.
Holden used two dozen detectives in an attempt to stop the Ku Klux Klan. See pp.
467-71 on efforts of detectives Lewis H. Mowers, George W. Tillou, and Cyrus S.
Reno to deal with the Lowry Band and with Ku Klux Klansman Ash DeVane.

1131. Henderson, David H. "Face to Face with the Lumbee Ghost?" *The State* 56.5
(Oct. 1988): 10-13.
Henderson and his friend Billy Oxendine went bird hunting in Bear Swamp between
World War II and the Korean War. They encountered the ghost of Henderson
Oxendine and escaped a fire that almost took Allen Lowrie's cabin.

1132. Conley, Manuel A., and Ginger Oxendine-Roberts. "Henry Berry Lowry
House, North Carolina Indian Cultural Center: Preliminary Evaluation of
Interpretive Data." Paper for Public History (HST 370). Pembroke State U,
7 Dec. 1988. [PSU-MLL]
Analyzes data compiled by David E. Wilkins in July, 1988, to verify the authenticity of
the house, which the Cultural Center has acquired and plans to restore. Summarizes
seven property deeds, which "fall short of providing a complete record of ownership"
linking the house to Henry Berry Lowry. Also lists published materials, theses and
dissertations, court records, laws, and archival materials Wilkins gathered on Lowry.

1133. Waldman, Carl. *Who Was Who in Native American History: Indians and
Non-Indians from Early Contacts Through 1900*. New York: Facts on File,
1990. Pp. 211-12. [PSU-MLL]
Brief mention. Explains the formation of the Lowry Band, the routing at Wire Grass
Landing, and Henry Berry Lowry's disappearance.

1134. Evans, W. McKee. "Henry Berry Lowry." *Dictionary of North Carolina
Biography*. Ed. William S. Powell. Vol. 4. Chapel Hill: U of North Carolina
P, 1991. Pp. 104-05. [PSU-MLL]

1135. Knick, Stanley. "Did Henry Berry Lowrie Escape Robeson to Become the
Modoc's Captain Jack?" *Robesonian* 25 Feb. 1993: 4A.
Among many versions of Lowrie's death or disappearance is the dubious idea that he
escaped to Oregon, joined the Modoc Indians, and became Captain Jack (their leader),
known for his role in the Modoc War of 1872-83. This story was reported in the
Robesonian and, later (1873), the Weldon (NC) *Roanoke News*.

RED BANKS MUTUAL ASSOCIATION, AGRICULTURE, AND FARMING

Red Banks Mutual Association, incorporated in June, 1938, was one of about 27 Farm
Security Administration cooperative corporation farms, in which "a number of farm
families ... operate jointly a large farming enterprise and ... share the returns of their

group effort according to the amount of work contributed by each" [Joseph W. Eaton, *Research Guide on Cooperative Group Farming*, H. W. Wilson, 1942, p. 54].

1136.   "Fuller Locklear." *Robesonian* 28 June 1926: 3.
Obituary. Locklear, a farmer, was active in the Burnt Swamp Baptist Association.

1137.   "Settlement for Indian Families Is Investigated." *Robesonian* 4 July 1935: 1.
Interior Department official Fred Baker investigated several areas of the county, including a 3,500-acre tract near Harper's Ferry.

1138.   Baker, Fred A. *Report on Siouan Tribe of Indians in Robeson County, North Carolina.* Washington: Bureau of Indian Affairs, US Dept. of Interior, 9 July 1935. [IERC] [National Archives and Records Admin., Washington, DC. File 37889-1935-310-(?) Cherokee, filed with 36208-1935-310-General Services, Central Classified Files, 1907-1939, RG 75.] [*Lumbee Petition*, Exhibit A58]
Thirteen-page narrative, with 15 exhibits. Baker surveyed available land, the number of Siouan Indians, and the present condition of farming in preparation for a land purchase and work relief project under the Resettlement Administration. Extensive details on agriculture. Baker was very supportive of the project.

1139.   Pearmain, John. *"Reservation": Siouan Tribe of Indians of Robeson County, North Carolina.* Indian Office Handbook of Information. Washington: Bureau of Indian Affairs, U.S. Dept. of Interior, compiled Oct. 1935. [Not seen.]

1140.   Pearmain, John. *Report ... on Conditions of the Indians in Robeson County.* Washington: Resettlement Admin., 11 Nov. 1935. [National Archives and Records Admin., Washington, DC. File 64190-1935-066-General Services.] [IERC] [*Lumbee Petition*, exhibit A1)5]
Pearmain interviewed numerous individuals (listed in the index in front of the report); he describes their housing, occupation, family size, farms, and desires from the resettlement project. Compiles data on housing and land needs. Gives a map of the project as proposed.

1141.   Corbin, A. S. "Preliminary Report/Proposed Settlement 100 Families–Pembroke–Robeson County–N. C." Unpub. typescript. N.d. [PSU-MLL]
Statistics on farms, tenants, crops, and drainage canals near Pembroke. The town's population was 4,000. The county had 9,000 Indians; 1,800 were males over 21.

1142.   "Plan to Place 1,000 Tenants on Small Farms of Their Own." *Robesonian* 2 Dec. 1935: 6.
The chief of the Resettlement Administration explains this plan, which should solve the South's tenant farming problem.

1143.   *By-laws of the Red Banks Mutual Association.* National Archives and Records Administration. Record Group 96. Farmers Home Administration. File no. 100, Correspondence Relative to Resettlement Project. N.d. 11 p.

1144.   "Purchase of 10,000 Acres Farm Land in Robeson by RA [Resettlement

Administration] Given Final Approval." *Robesonian* 29 June 1936: 1.
The settlement, near Pembroke, would be primarily Indian, with 100 one-horse and 100 two-horse farmsteads. The cost of the land, farm equipment, 200 houses, and community facilities would exceed a million dollars.

1145. Sharpe, J. A. "Rural Indian Resettlement Project Is Large-Scale Federal
   Undertaking in Pembroke Section of Robeson County." *Robesonian* 29 June
   1938: 1.
Discounts several rumors about the project. Discusses amount of land purchased,
homesteads being built, and wages paid laborers.

1146. "Official Figures Show Nearly $386,000 Spent on Indian Resettlement
   Project." *Robesonian* 8 July 1938: 4.
Of a total allotment of $461,000. Figures are from a Farm Security Admin. report.

1147. "Before and After." *Robesonian* 3 March 1939: 8.
Photographs of a farmhouse built at Pembroke Farms, and the house it replaced. The
average expenditure for project homes is $1300.

1148. Walker, Charles R. "Homesteaders–New Style." *Survey Graphic: Magazine
   of Social Interpretation* 28.6 (June 1939): 377-81, 408.
Brief mention. Discusses two Farm Security Administration tenant farms: Roanoke
Farms (Halifax, NC) and Pembroke Farms (Red Banks Mutual Association). Notes
that the Pembroke Farms homesteaders, previously illiterate, were learning to read.
Explains the principles of the cooperative farming program, with statistics.

1149. Thompson, Marshall. "Robeson County Indians Make Forward Strides;
   Scuffletown Makes Way for Churches and Homes." *Robesonian* 23 May
   1940: 3. [Also discusses Pembroke Farms.]

1150. U.S. Congress. House. *Hearings before the Subcommittee of the Comm. on
   Appropriations ... on the Agriculture Department Appropriation Bill for 1943*.
   77th Cong. 2nd Sess. Washington: GPO, 1942. Y4.Ap6/1: Ag8/943/pt. 2
Brief mentions in charts. Pp. 228-29 shows Pembroke Farms' operating costs and
income as of June 30, 1941. P. 253 shows the number of farmers and farmstead units
as of Dec. 31, 1941. P. 257 shows the expiration date of Red Banks' lease, as of Jan.
1, 1942. P. 258 shows the number of units sold and acreage sold.

1151. U.S. Congress. Senate. *Hearings before the Subcommittee of the Committee
   on Appropriations ... on H. R. 6709, a Bill Making Appropriations for the
   Dept. of Agriculture for the Fiscal Year Ending June 30, 1943...* 77th Cong.
   2nd Sess. GPO, 1942. Y4.Ap6/2: Ag8/943
Brief mentions. P. 653 shows Pembroke Farms' date of beginning operations, total
acreage, tillable acreage, acreage per member, number of full-time members, and race
of members, as of March, 1942. Table A, p. 657, shows Red Banks' years in existence,
total operating loans, total surplus on Dec. 31, 1941, and average equity per settler.

1152. "Dr. Eaton Makes Report on Red Banks Survey." *Pembroke Progress* 8 July

1948: 1.

Sociologist Joseph W. Eaton, from Wayne State University, interviewed all current and many former Red Banks members. Of the 24 cooperative farms organized by the Resettlement Administration in the 1930's, Red Banks is the only one still operating. Red Banks is mentioned in two tables (pp. 66 and 151) in Eaton's *Exploring Tomorrow's Agriculture* (New York: Harper & Brothers, 1943).

1153. "Reservation Superintendent in Visit to Pembroke Area." *Pembroke Progress*
        1 Dec. 1949. [PSU-MLL. PSU Clippings File]

Dr. Joe Gennings, superintendent of the Cherokee Reservation, visited Red Banks with Clifton Oxendine of PSC. Red Banks was the only remaining cooperative, and Gennings wanted "to learn just why this project still survives while others did not."

1154. Barton, Lew, and Simeon Oxendine. "Amaziah Chavis: The Success Story of
        One Lumbee Farmer." *Scottish Chief* 21 May 1958. [PSU-MLL. PSU
        Clippings File] [Discusses Chavis' land acquisitions and views on farming.]

1155. "'Billy' Lowry, 100 Saturday, Plans to Hunt Deer This Fall." *Robesonian* 29
        Sept. 1960: 7.

Lowry was a businessman and farmer. The land for Pembroke High School and most of the land for PSU was purchased from him.

1156. Brown, D. "'Radical' Farm Venture for Indians Nears End." *News and
        Observer* 15 Jan. 1967: III-12.

1157. Peebles, Lucy Gray. "Co-Op Will Disband After 29 Years." *The Lumbee* 26
        Jan. 1967: 1. [PSU-MLL] [History, with comments from present members.]

1158. Brown, Dick. "U.S. Stakes Lumbees to New Future." *News and Observer* 7
        July 1968: Sec. 3 p. 8.

Reviews Red Banks' history; discusses the government's settlement with the five remaining members. Now dissolved, it was the only remaining project of its type.

1159. Bledsoe, Jerry. "Mr. Winkley Likes the Old." *Greensboro Daily News* 17 Jan.
        1971: A14. Rpt. (with modifications) in Bledsoe's *Just Folks: Visitin' with
        Carolina People* (Charlotte: Fast & McMillan, 1980), pp. 51-54.

Winkley Locklear, at age 78, was interviewed by Bledsoe and Adolph Dial. A long-time farmer owning over 260 acres, Locklear tells of hunting, fishing, his smokehouse, service in World War I, and how times have changed.

THE KU KLUX KLAN ROUTING

1160. "Klan-Indian Violence Is Feared in Rural North Carolina Area" *New York
        Times* 17 Jan. 1958: P. 10 col. 5.

The Klan burned two crosses on Indian property and will hold a rally in Maxton. Evans (entry 991, p. 255) notes an error in accounts of the St. Pauls cross-burning.

1161. Morrison, Julian. "Armed Indians Break Up Klan Meeting." *Greensboro*

Daily News 19 Jan. 1958: 1.
Describes the routing on evening of January 18. Similar article, *New York Times* 19 Jan. 1958: 1.

1162. "Cole Says His Rights Violated." *Greensboro Daily News* 20 Jan. 1958: A1.
Rights to assembly and free speech. James W. Cole also feels he was denied police protection because of his race.

1163. "The Lumbees Ride Again." *Greensboro Daily News* 20 Jan. 1958: 4A.
Editorial condemns the violence of the routing but admits Lumbees had provocation.

1164. "'The Law' Treads Lightly to Avert Maxton Violence." *Robesonian* 20 Jan. 1958: 1.
Only one Klansman was arrested. Two patrol cars were filled with confiscated weapons. Tear gas was dropped into the crowd, and shooting lasted only 20 minutes.

1165. Morrison, Julian. "Sheriff Seeks Klan Leader's Indictment: Cole Accused of Inciting Riot Involving Indians and Ku Klux." *Greensboro Daily News* 20 Jan. 1958: A1-3.

1166. "No Racial Rift." *Robesonian* 21 Jan. 1958: 4.
Editorial. The newspaper office got out-of-state letters and calls asking why Robeson County's Whites and Indians can't get along better. The editor replied that the routing "was an anti-Ku Klux demonstration, recognized as such by members of both races."

1167. "Cole Faces Indictment; Disgusted ... Quits." *Robesonian* 21 Jan. 1958: 1.
A county jury, including two Blacks and two Indians, indicted James Cole and James Garland Martin for inciting a riot. Martin says he has attended his last Klan rally.

1168. Ryan, Ethel. "Indians Who Crushed Rally Were Mature Tribesmen." *Greensboro Record* 21 Jan. 1958: A1.
A correspondent's personal observations on the Lumbees.

1169. "Judge Deplores Klan Entry into Peaceful Indian Land." *Robesonian* 22 Jan. 1958: 1.
Lumbee judge Lacy Maynor sentenced James Garland Martin and chastized, "You have helped to bring about nation-wide advertisement to a people who do not want that kind of advertisement."

1170. Cuthrell, Harold Glenn. "The Charge of the Lumbee Indians." *Scottish Chief* [Maxton, NC] 23 Jan. 1958: 1. [IERC] [PSU-MLL]
Poem on the routing. The typescript is on display at PSU-NARC. Another poem, "Old Time Preacher" by James P. Hunt, is included in entry 1191.

1171. "Redskins Whoop Lumbee Victory." *Robesonian* 23 Jan. 1958: 1.
Mayor J. C. Oxendine and son Simeon have received telegrams, messages, and clippings from Indians across the nation–including offers of money, physical force, and rifles if they need to face the Klan again.

1172. Brown, Dick. "The Indians Who Routed the 'Catfish'." *News and Observer* 26 Jan. 1958: Sec. 3 p. 1. [Describes the incident and reviews Lumbee history.]

1173. Grimsley, Will. "Robeson Area Is Tensed as Ugly Rumors Abound." *Winston-Salem Journal and Sentinel* 26 Jan. 1958: 6A.
Another rally of 50,000 ?) Klansmen is planned for Maxton. See also *Robesonian* 27 Jan. 1958: 1.

1174. "North Carolina: Indian Raid." *Newsweek* 51 (27 Jan. 1958): 27.
Lumbees "gave the U.S. the first war-whooping, gun-shooting Indian raid it had seen in 50 years and more." Many photographs of Lumbees with rifles and KKK flag.

1175. "Bad Medicine for the Klan: North Carolina Indians Break Up Kluxers' Anti-Indian Meeting." *Life* 44 (27 Jan. 1958): 26-28.
Brief text, with photographs of several stages of the rally. Includes a full-page photograph of Charlie Warriax and Simeon Oxendine–the latter wearing his VFW cap–wrapped in a flag torn from a Klan car.

1176. "King Katfish Kole Kries Against Robeson ...." *Robesonian* 28 Jan. 1958: 1.
Cole wants a change of venue; he believes he can't get a fair trial with three Indians and two Blacks on Robeson County's jury.

1177. "Southern Indians Battle the Klan." *Christian Century* 75 (29 Jan. 1958): 124.
Lumbees should not have taken the law into their own hands. They nevertheless should be commended for showing that other races besides Blacks and Whites are concerned about school segregation.

1178. "Hodges Denounces KKK for Maxton Incident." *Robesonian* 30 Jan. 1958: 1.
N.C. Governor Luther Hodges places full responsibility on the Klan. He wants his position understood because of rumors of another Klan rally in Robeson County.

1179. "Within the Framework of Law." *Greensboro Daily News* 31 Jan. 1958: A6.
Editorial. Public reaction sided with the Lumbees, but "the law is intended for Indians and Klansmen alike."

1180. "When Carolina Indians Went on the Warpath–." *U. S. News and World Report* 44 (31 Jan. 1958): 14.
"Relations between the races had been good until Indians were aroused by two cross burnings on Indian property."

1181. "Indians Rout the Klan." *Commonweal* 67 (31 Jan. 1958): 446.
Lumbees "revert[ed] ... to ancient Indian customs in order to protect their rights as Americans."

1182. "Indians Back at Peace and the Klan at Bay." *Life* 44 (3 Feb. 1958): 36-36A.
James G. Martin was upbraided by Lumbee judge Lacy Maynor, and Lumbees benefited from "a bond of friendship between Whites and Indians that never developed before." Photographs include Lacy Maynor and Scoutmaster Walter Pinchbeck.

1183. Ruark, Henry G. "Fear Klan Revival in the Carolinas." *Christian Century* 75 (26 Feb. 1958): 257-58.
Many reacted with "quiet satisfaction" to the Lumbee routing and the indictment of Catfish Cole. Others objected to the Lumbees' "taking the law into their own hands."

1184. "Lumbee Indians Put Klansmen to Rout in 'Uprising'." *The Amerindian* [American Indian Review] 6.3 (Jan.-Feb. 1958): [1]-2.
Quotes Simeon Oxendine on Lumbee intentions to "take the Klan rally apart a little bit at a time" without harming anyone. The incident was covered in the Soviet Union.

1185. "Klan Wizard Cole Gets 2-Year Sentence; Titan Martin Draws 12 Months. Both Free on Bond; Both File Appeal." *Robesonian* 14 March 1958: 1.

1186. "Heap Bad Kluxers Armed with Gun, Indian Angry Paleface Run." *Ebony* 13 (April 1958): 25-26, 28.
Brief description, concluding that "the Indian laughed and the Negro nearly died laughing with him." Numerous photographs.

1187. "Lumbee Indians Form Own News Service." *News and Observer* 10 April 1958: 23.
To disseminate accurate information about the Lumbees in wake of attention generated by Klan routing.

1188. Newman, John U., Jr. "We Ran the Klan Out of Carolina." By a Lumbee Woman as Told to Newman. *Official Detective Stories* 28 (May 1958): 8-13. [IERC]
Discusses the Klan's brutal beating of Christine Rogers in South Carolina; Lumbee preparation for the rally; Lacy Maynor's sentencing of Catfish Cole; and background on Cole from a Kinston, N.C., newspaper. Numerous photographs.

1189. Reynolds, Malvina. "The Battle of Maxton Field." *Sing Out!* 8.1 (Spring 1958): 4-5.
A description of the routing precedes words and music of the song. Rpt. in Reynolds' *Little Boxes and Other Handmade Songs* (Oak Publications, 1964–not seen); performed on *Malvina Reynolds Sings the Blues* (Columbia, 1967; CL2614, R67-437–not seen). Wurth-Hough (entry 868) notes that it was performed by the Limelighters.

1190. Craven, Charles. "The Robeson County Indian Uprising Against the Ku Klux Klan." *South Atlantic Quarterly* 57 (Autumn 1958): 433-42. [PSU-MLL]
Craven, a *News and Observer* reporter who covered the Maxton rally, describes the routing, gives background on Catfish Cole and what drew his interest to Robeson County, and explains the aftermath.

1191. *Klash Kluxer Kaput.* Scrapbook compiled by Lacy Maynor. [IERC]
Magazine articles, correspondence, and newspaper articles from many cities.

1192. Barton, Lew. "Lumbee Indians Honored Seawell with 1959 'First American Award'." *The Lumbee* 13 Jan. 1966: 2.

Welton Lowry, of the Indian Schoolmasters' Club, presented the award to Malcolm B. Seawell on March 20, 1959; signers and attendees listed. Seawell lived in Lumberton for many years. Seawell's appointment by the governor to chair an investigation of Klan activities in the state reminded Barton of the 1959 award.

1193. Clay, Russell. "Injunction Bars Klan from Robeson Rally." *News and Observer* 18 March 1966: 1.
The Klan announced another rally in Maxton. A Superior Court judge issued a temporary restraining order forbidding Klan gatherings within 25 miles of the county.

1194. "Membership in Klan Is Offered to Indians." *New York Times* 22 March 1966: 43.
After reports that the Indians were stockpiling weapons, the Klan's scheduled cross-burning at the site of the 1958 routing was forbidden by a Superior Court injunction. As a new approach, the Grand Dragon of the North Carolina Klan is offering membership to the Lumbees and plans a recruiting trip. The Klan wants to ally with the Indians and help them gain civil rights.

1195. "State of North Carolina ex rel. John B. Regan, etc. v. Invisible Empire, United Klans, Knights Ku Klux Klan, etc., et al. Robeson County, North Carolina, Superior Court, March 17 and April 22, 1966." *Race Relations Law Reporter* 11 (Fall 1966): 1162-65.
Gives the text of a temporary restraining order to prevent the Klan from holding a rally planned for March 27, 1966; also gives the later order which dissolved the restraining order. The judge justified the restraining order by: the results of the 1958 Klan rally; the Klan's previous acts of violence in North Carolina; inflammatory notices of the planned rally mailed to Indians in Robeson County; and the fact that "feelings and effects generated by the 1958 rally still exist ..." so that another rally would result in "a general uprising against the Klan" and "irreparable harm and damage," making it "impossible for local law enforcement to maintain peace."

1196. "Oh, I Remember Them: Lumbees Famous for Routing ... in 1958." *Greensboro Daily News* 17 Jan. 1971: A15. [Interview, Simeon Oxendine.]

1197. Craven, Charles. "The Night the Klan Died in North Carolina." *True Magazine* March 1975. [PSU-MLL] Rpt. in *CIV* 22 Jan. 1976: 1, 4-6.
Detailed account of events prior to and on Jan. 18, 1958. The Klan had burned crosses to protest an Indian woman who dated a White man (incorrectly reported; see Evans [entry 1118] p.255 n. 26), and an Indian family who moved into a White neighborhood.

1198. Fox, Cynthia Gregory. "The Battle of Hayes Pond: The Ku Klux Klan versus the Lumbee Indians, Robeson County, North Carolina, 1958." Thesis. East Carolina U, 1979.
Thorough, well-researched study. Contends that, in convicting two Klan members for inciting the Indians virtually to riot, "North Carolina used vague, anachronistic common law doctrine to effectively silence unpopular political opinions."

1199. Van Dyke, Jeffrey Alan. "Bedsheets and Broadsheets: Covering the Ku Klux

Klan in North Carolina." Thesis. U of North Carolina at Chapel Hill, 1986.
Pp. 41-45, 55-57.
On reactions of state newspapers to the routing. Governor Luther Hodges upbraided
the media for overzealousness. The Klan announced (1966) another rally at Maxton
Field. After much media attention, a judge ruled to allow it; but it never occurred.

1200. Henderson, Bruce. "Robeson Civic Leader Dies at 69: Simeon Oxendine Won
Fame Confronting Klan." *Charlotte Observer* 28 Dec. 1988: 1B.
Oxendine also served in the "Hell's Angels" bomb squad in World War II, was chief of
the Pembroke VFD, a Pembroke Town Council member, and a Robeson County Board
of Education member.

LUMBEE AND TUSCARORA ACTIVISM
SINCE THE LATE 1980'S

1201. Swofford, Stan. "Blacks, Lumbees Want Answers." *Greensboro News and
Record* 14 Dec. 1986: A1.
The killing of Jimmy Earl Cummings united the county's Blacks and Indians. Detailed
account of the incident and its aftermath.

1202. "Justice Dept. Examining Robeson Slaying." *Carolina Indian Voice* 29 Jan.
1987: 1. [On Jimmy Earl Cummings.]

1203. Struck, Doug. "Baltimore Man Leads 3 'Voices' in N.C. Protest." *Baltimore
Sun* 3 May 1987: 1A.
Herbert H. Locklear, uncle of Jimmy Earl Cummings, led a triracial protest.

1204. "Shooting of Lumbee Outrages Robeson Citizens—NCARRV Joins Coalition."
NCARRV Newsletter [North Carolinians Against Racist and Religious Vi-
olence] 5 (Spring 1987): 1-3, 6.
Detailed account of the killing of Jimmy Earl Cummings by Deputy Kevin Stone.

1205. Henderson, Bruce. "Lumbee Indian Strives for Equality for All Races."
Charlotte Observer 29 Nov. 1987: D1.
John Godwin, founder of Concerned Citizens of Robeson County, received the Nancy
Susan Reynolds Award for advocacy.

1206. Henderson, Bruce, and Elizabeth Leland. "Indians Free Hostages at Paper."
Charlotte Observer 2 Feb. 1988: 1A.
Tuscaroras Eddie Hatcher and Timothy Jacobs held *Robesonian* employees hostage for
ten hours to draw attention to unsolved murders, drug trafficking, and jail conditions.

1207. Wilson, Susan Price. "Tension Has Grown Since [19]86 Shooting." *Winston-
Salem Journal* 2 Feb. 1988: 4.
Summary of events since 1979, including Terry Lockee's police-brutality lawsuit (see
entries 825 and 826) and Jimmy Earl Cummings' death.

1208. Harrison, Eric. "Some Hail N.C. Hostage-Takers as Heroes of Oppressed."

Philadelphia Inquirer 7 Feb. 1988: C1.
Background on problems that led to the hostage-taking.

1209. Mangiameli, Mike. "Hatcher, Jacobs Indicted." *Robesonian* 10 Feb. 1988: 1A.
Indian activists were indicted by a federal grand jury for hostage-taking and weapons violations. Maximum sentence would be life in prison.

1210. Stinebaker, Joe. "Eddie Hatcher: Willing to Walk to the Edge for What Is Right." *Winston-Salem Journal* 14 Feb. 1988: A11.
Comments from friends on Hatcher's interests and concerns. See related articles on Timothy Jacobs and Hubert Stone, same page.

1211. Godfrey, R. L. "About 4,500 Petition for Dismissal of Charges Against Hatcher, Jacobs." *Robesonian* 15 Feb. 1988: 1A.
Petitioners demand that federal hostage-taking and firearms charges be dropped.

1212. Moss, Gary. "John Hunt Sums Up His Situation: 'I'm Terrified'." *Fayetteville Times* 28 Feb. 1988: 1A.
Hunt worked for the State Bureau of Investigation as a drug informant. His removal from the Robeson County Jail was one of the hostage-takers' demands.

1213. "Critics Say Robeson Task Force Backing Off Mandate." *Fayetteville Times* 1 March 1988: 1B.
The governor's task force to investigate conditions leading to the hostage-taking should come to the county and observe first-hand.

1214. Ola, Akinshiju C. "Newspaper Office Seized in Protest." *The Guardian: Independent Radical Newsweekly* 2 Mar. 1988: 7.

1215. Rankin, Sam. "Civil Rights Lawyer Takes Hatcher's Case." *Fayetteville Times* 2 March 1988: 1B.
William Kunstler of the Center for Constitutional Rights.

1216. Hitt, Greg. "Robeson's Unsolved Murders Feed Unrest." *Winston-Salem Journal* 13 March 1988: A1.
Lists seventeen unsolved murders since the mid-1970's, including Joyce Sinclair.

1217. Henderson, Bruce. "Robeson Activist John Godwin Dies." *Charlotte Observer* 24 March 1988: 2C.
Godwin founded Concerned Citizens for Better Government. He also won the Indian Elder of the Year, Henry Berry Lowry, and Nancy Susan Reynolds awards in 1987.

1218. Martin, Terry. "Julian Pierce, Lumbee Indian Activist, Is Shot to Death." *Winston-Salem Journal* 27 March 1988: A1.
Pierce, former director of Lumbee River Legal Services, was a Superior Court judgeship candidate.

1219. Ruffin, Jane. "Pierce's Sturdy Determination Recalled." *News and Observer*

27 March 1988. Rpt. in *NewsBank Names in the News* 1988: fiche 101: C11.
Reflects on Pierce's concerns about Robeson County's problems, his accomplishments,
and warnings he received during his Superior Court judgeship campaign.

1220. Rezendes, Michael. "Candidate's Slaying Shocks County: Motive Sought in
   Apparent Assassination of Indian Seeking Judgeship." *Washington Post* 28
   Mar. 1988: A3.
Many Robeson Countians initially suspected Pierce's murder was related to his
promising campaign for a newly created judgeship.

1221. Hitt, Greg, and Terry Martin. "Young Lumbee Killed Pierce, Then Himself,
   Authorities Say." *Winston-Salem Journal* 30 March 1988: 1.
John Anderson Goins killed Julian Pierce over a lovers' quarrel, then killed himself,
according to authorities.

1222. Plott, Monte. "Slain Indian Activist Eulogized as 'Real Hero' at N.C. Funeral
   Service." *Atlanta Constitution* 31 Mar. 1988: 3.
About 1,500 attended Julian Pierce's funeral. Summarizes official and unofficial
explanations for the murder.

1223. Plott, Monte. "Tolerance of Drugs Blamed for N.C. County's Troubles."
   Atlanta Journal and Constitution 3 April 1988: 8A.
A "look the other way" attitude toward drug trafficking is the county's biggest
problem. Other problems are discussed.

1224. "Indians Unsatisfied with Lumbee Murder Victim Probe." *IPN Weekly Report*
   [Highland, MD: Crowflying] 4 April 1988.
Quotes Indian activists Young Bear (Tuscarora), Vernon Bellecourt (AIM), and Bill
Simmons (International Indian Treaty Council).

1225. Smothers, Ronald. "Steps Taken to Ease Tension in Carolina County." *New
   York Times* 10 April 1988: 26.
A second Superior Court judgeship was created. Notes prior events causing tension.

1226. Ola, Akinshiju C. "Anyone Who Doesn't Want to Stand Up Is Crooked or
   Crazy." *The Guardian: Independent Radical Newsweekly* 40.28 (13 April
   1988): 7.
Brief comments on Pierce's assassination and the *Robesonian* hostage-taking. Jimmy
Hunt compares recent activism to the 1958 Ku Klux Klan routing.

1227. Brower, Montgomery, and Bill Shaw. "The Murder of Julian Pierce Provokes
   Grief and Grievances in Troubled Robeson County." *People Weekly* 29.15 (18
   April 1988): 60-62, 65.
On Sheriff Hubert Stone's solution of the crime in less than 48 hours, earlier unsolved
crimes, the shooting of Jimmy Earl Cummings, and the *Robesonian* hostage-taking.

1228. "Background Paper on Robeson County, North Carolina: A Special Report
   Prepared for the Fannie Lou Hamer Convention, July 1988." Lumberton:

Center for Community Action/CALC, 1988. 2 p.
Concise account of efforts to achieve social change since 1980, as well as critical
events since 1985.

1229. "Cocaine, Corruption and Killings in Robeson County." *Akwesasne Notes* 20.1
(Early Spring 1988): 10.
Reviews the *Robesonian* hostage-taking, Julian Pierce's murder, and Billy McKellar's
death in the Robeson County Jail.

1230. Wright, Ed. "Judgement Day in Robeson County: Forcing a Community to
Face Its Past." *Southern Magazine* 2.8 (May 1988): 15-16.
Brief account of the hostage-taking and other events causing tension in the county.

1231. Shapiro, Joseph P., and Ronald A. Taylor. "There's Trouble in Robeson
County." *U.S. News and World Report* 104.17 (2 May 1988): 24, 27.
Summary of Julian Pierce's murder, the *Robesonian* hostage-taking, problems in the
county criminal justice system, drug trafficking, Jimmy Earl Cummings' death, the
school system merger, and the formation of a county human rights commission.

1232. "Motive for Slaying of Lumbee Indian Activist Is Questionable." *IPN Weekly
Report* [Highland, MD: Crowflying] 6 May 1988.
The House Judiciary Committee's Subcommittee on Criminal Justice is investigating
Julian Pierce's slaying and alleged drug trafficking and corruption in the county.

1233. Segrest, Mab. "Robeson County's 'Third World Ills'." *Christian Century* 11
May 1988: 468-69. Rpt. (with modifications) in: *Southern Changes* [Atlanta:
Southern Regional Council] 10.4 (July/Aug. 1988): 14-16.
"Third World ills" came from a local organizer. Julian Pierce's murder symptomized
problems such as poverty, unemployment, low educational levels, drugs, and violence.
Discusses Concerned Citizens for Better Government and the school system merger.

1234. Mangiameli, M. "Hunt Gets 30 Year Sentence." *Robesonian* 29 May 1988: 1A.
Lengthy interview with John D. Hunt, sentenced for robbery and assault. .

1235. "Drug Terror at Lumbee: Prosecutor Becomes Judge Over Murdered Op-
ponent." *Daybreak* 2.3 (Summer 1988): [28].
Summarizes Julian Pierce's campaign, his murder, criticisms of the county criminal
justice system, and threats against those who attempted to expose corruption.

1236. "Assassination of Julian Pierce." *Human Rights Internet Reporter* 12.3
(Spring/Summer 1988): 25.
National Congress of American Indians called the murder a "political assassination."

1237. Tumulty, Karen. "Killing of Indian Brings N.C. Racial Problems to Fore."
Akwesasne Notes 20.1 (Early Spring 1988): 10-11.
On Pierce's murder and prior events; reprinted from *Los Angeles Times* 14 April 1988.

1238. North Carolina. Office of the Governor. Robeson County Task Force. *Interim*

Report. By Phillip J. Kirk, Jr., Chairman. Raleigh, 8 June 1988.
Comments, point by point, on actions taken to meet the conditions on which Hatcher and Jacobs released the *Robesonian* employees they held hostage. Notes additional actions taken to alleviate long-standing problems.

1239. Urban, Rob. "Report on Robeson: Proof of Corruption Sparse." *Charlotte Observer* 15 June 1988: C1.
Discusses the report from the governor's task force to investigate Hatcher and Jacobs' charges. Includes Christic Institute lawyer Alan Gregory's comments.

1240. "Robeson Compromise Reached on Britt Judgeship." *Fayetteville Observer/ Fayetteville Times* 25 June 1988: 1A.
Britt will be senior judge, but the governor's appointee for the new judgeship will choose the staff of the public defender's office.

1241. "Tuscarora Activists Released on Bond." *IPN Weekly Report* [Highland, MD: Crowflying] 15 July 1988.
The pair were released after five months in jail, on $100,000 unsecured bond.

1242. Flesher, John. "Hostage-Trial Defendant Says 13 Witnesses Dead, Others Are Threatened." *Charlotte Observer* 6 Aug. 1988: 3E.
Hatcher says 13 of 50 planned witnesses have died since the hostage-taking.

1243. Marson, Stephen M. "The Murder of Julian Pierce: Can Sandy Jordan Chavis Receive a Fair Trial?" Report submitted to Evander M. Britt et al., attorneys at law. Lumberton: Marson and Associates, 13 Aug. 1988. 18 p.
Survey data on 1,052 persons shows Chavis definitely could not receive a fair trial in Robeson County and probably could not in surrounding counties. Also presents three qualitative factors in favor of moving the trial from the region.

1244. "Judge Allows Necessity Defense for Hatcher." *Greensboro News & Record* 25 Sept. 1988: C5.
The district court will allow evidence that Hatcher and Jacobs acted to save their lives.

1245. Hitt, Greg. "Hatcher Accuses Government: 40 Indictments Put Off to Get Convictions, Attorney Says." *Winston-Salem Journal* 27 Sept. 1988: 15.
Hatcher's attorney feels federal prosecutors are delaying drug indictments of Robeson Countians to ensure his conviction.

1246. Hitt, Greg. "Indians Get Sympathy of Editor." *Winston-Salem Journal* 1 Oct. 1988: 5.
On *Robesonian* editor Bob Horne's testimony in Hatcher and Jacobs' federal trial.

1247. Henderson, Bruce. "No One Was to Be Hurt in Siege, Jacobs Said." *Charlotte Observer* 12 Oct. 1988: 4B.
Hatcher feared for his life because he possessed drug maps.

1248. Rives, Julie Powers. "Jury Finds Indian Pair Not Guilty." *News and Observer*

15 Oct. 1988: 1A.
After 6 1/2 hours' deliberation, the jury found Hatcher and Jacobs not guilty on all federal charges.

1249. Wilkie, Lorrie. "*Robesonian* Staffers Express Disbelief." *Fayetteville Observer/Fayetteville Times* 15 Oct. 1988: 1B.
Reaction to Hatcher and Jacobs' acquittal. Bob Horne felt "the violation of our employees called for them to spend more time in prison than they have."

1250. "Robeson Group Seeks Focus on Old Problems." *Fayetteville Observer* 17 Oct. 1988: 1B.
Fellowship of Reconciliation, National Council of Churches, and Human Relations and Unity Commission are discussing problems which provoked the hostage-taking.

1251. Henderson, Bruce. "Acquittals Draw Protest." *Charlotte Observer* 19 Oct. 1988: C1.
Robesonian reporter Mike Mangiameli filed a complaint with the N.C. Bar Association over the "subversive" tactics of the lawyers who won acquittal for Hatcher and Jacobs.

1252. Menges, Jerri. "Britt Doing Groundwork for Possible State Charges." *Robesonian* 20 Oct. 1988: 1A.
Britt cannot proceed with charges against Hatcher and Jacobs until his successor as district attorney is named.

1253. Ola, Akinshiju C. "It Is the People Who Have Brought Justice, Not the System." *The Guardian: Independent Radical Newsweekly* 26 Oct. 1988: 3.
Announces the not-guilty verdict in Hatcher and Jacobs' trial on federal charges.

1254. "Martin's Task Force Presented Documents 'Proving Drug Trafficking'." *Robesonian* 30 Oct. 1988: 1A.
Attorneys Lewis Pitts and Barry Nakell presented 100 pages of documents.

1255. "The Fire Is Corruption." *Daybreak* 2.2 (Midwinter 1988): 37.
Editorial. The assassination of Julian Pierce is "narco-terrorism." His death is one of 19 "controversial murders" in Robeson County during the last 10 years. Drugs and violence are the smoke, while corruption is the fire.

1256. Barreiro, José. "Drug Terror at Lumbee: Does Justice Mean 'Just-Us' in Robeson County?" *Daybreak* 2.2 (Midwinter 1988): 13, 15-16, 28-29, 35.
On the hostage-taking, Pierce's murder, John Godwin's death, and drug investigations. Gives reactions of Connee Brayboy, Arlinda Locklear, and Mac Legerton.

1257. Barreiro, José. "One Murder Too Many: The Assassination of Julian Pierce." *Daybreak* 2.2 (Midwinter 1988): 14.
Describes the Superior Court judgeship race and quotes from an interview with Pierce one month before his death.

1258. "Reporter Threatens Lawsuit Against Tuscarora Activists." *IPN Weekly Report*

[Highland, MD: Crowflying] 4.44 (1 Nov. 1988): 3-4.
Mike Mangiameli, former *Robesonian* crime reporter, will not file another lawsuit against Hatcher and Jacobs if they promise to give the county schools any profits from the story of their siege.

1259. *A County on the Brink.* Videotape. "Stateline." University of North Carolina Center for Public Television and WTVD, Raleigh. Broadcast: 3 Nov. 1988.
Background data, enhanced by numerous interviews, on incidents since 1987 in Robeson County. Concentrates on the murder of Julian Pierce. Interviewees include Bob Horne, Bob Warren, Lula Mae Cummings, Bobby Griffin, Ruth Locklear, Christine Griffin, Charles Locklear, Curtis Pierce, Mark Locklear, Sandy Chavis, Randy Chavis, Dr. Joe Sandlin, and Jimmy Goins.

1260. "First Words." *Northeast Indian Quarterly* 5.4 (Winter 1988): 2-3, 52.
On Timothy Jacobs' reception by the Onondaga Council of Chiefs when he sought refuge at the reservation. Discusses conditions which prompted the hostage-taking, and reactions to Jacobs in central New York.

1261. *Hold On! Robeson County's Fight for Justice.* Videotape. Written and narrated by Mab Segrest. Durham: North Carolinians Against Racist and Religious Violence, 1988. 35 min.
Covers the *Robesonian* hostage-taking, Julian Pierce's murder, Concerned Citizens for Better Government, the county's drug trade and criminal justice system, and other accidents and murders. Numerous interviews.

1262. "Hatcher Demands Counsel of Choice." *Robesonian* 7 Dec. 1988: 1A.
Hatcher and Jacobs were indicted on state kidnapping charges for the hostage-taking.

1263. "Hatcher Flees, Takes Sanctuary in N.Y." *Robesonian* 18 Dec. 1988: 1A.
Hatcher went to the Onondaga Indian Reservation, in violation of bond posted by the National Council of Churches.

1264. Godfrey, R. L. "Gov. Martin Names New D.A., Judge." *Robesonian* 18 Dec. 1988: 1A.
Dexter Brooks fills the newly created Superior Court judgeship; Richard Townsend is the new district attorney.

1265. Horne, Bob. "Remorseful Jacobs: Hatcher 'Has Just Destroyed Me'." *Robesonian* 21 Dec. 1988: 1A. [Jacobs regrets his role in the hostage-taking.]

1266. Segrest, Mab. *1988 Report: Bigoted Violence and Hate Groups in North Carolina.* Durham: North Carolinians Against Racist and Religious Violence, 1989. Pp. 7-9.
Capsule summaries of Billy McKellar's death, the *Robesonian* hostage-taking, the school system merger, the murder of Julian Pierce, the Superior Court judgeship race, and Hatcher and Jacobs' trial on federal charges. Includes recommendations.

1267. Henderson, Bruce. "A Year Later, Elements Still Linger in Robeson Hostage

Drama." *Charlotte Observer* 1 Feb. 1989: 1B.
Hatcher and Jacobs' lawyers file suit to stop state prosecution on kidnapping charges.

1268. Menges, Jerri. "Feb. 1, 1988: Impact of Hostage Incident Debated." *Robesonian* 1 Feb. 1989: 1A. [Reflections from ten community leaders.]

1269. Menges, Jerri. "Reporter Honored for Bravery in Takeover." *Robesonian* 1
Feb. 1989: 1B.
Raymond L. Godfrey received the Governor's Award for Bravery and Heroism.

1270. "Hatcher Arrested After Soviets Refuse to Grant Asylum Plea." *Asheville
Citizen* 11 March 1989: 1A.
Hatcher fled after his indictment on state kidnapping charges stemming from the
Robesonian hostage-taking.

1271. Godfrey, R. L. "Mrs. Cummings, Son, Each Get 26-Month Terms." *Robeso-
nian* 12 March 1989: 1A.
Lula Mae Cummings, mother of Jimmy Earl Cummings, was tried on drug offenses.
Her lawyers assert the drug raid was retaliation for her civil suit against the Robeson
County Sheriff's Deptartment for the shooting death of her son.

1272. "Hatcher Faces Federal Charges in Extradition Battle." *Charlotte Observer* 14
March 1989: 3D.
Charges of unlawful flight. Hatcher sought refuge at two Indian reservations and at the
Soviet consulate in San Francisco after indictment on state kidnapping charges.

1273. Godfrey, R. L. "Witnesses: No Fair Trial for Chavis in County." *Robesonian*
14 March 1989: 1A.
Article describes a hearing on the defense's motion to have the trial of Sandy Jordan
Chavis moved out of Robeson County, due to the extensive publicity Pierce's murder
has received. See also Marson (entry 1243).

1274. "Judge in N.Y. Rejects Jacobs's Bid for Asylum." *Charlotte Observer* 15
March 1989: 4E.
A Madison County judge rejected Jacobs's claims that his life would be in danger if he
returned to North Carolina.

1275. Godfrey, R. L. "Venue Changed for Chavis Trial." *Robesonian* 24 March 1989:
1A.
The trial was moved to Smithfield, in Johnson County. Defense attorney Byrd
submitted over 100 articles to show the murder's publicity.

1276. "130 Attend Memorial Honoring Godwin, Pierce." *Robesonian* 28 March
1989: 1A.
A service was held at Prospect Methodist Church. The article reviews the accomplishments of John Godwin and Julian Pierce.

1277. "AG's Office: Hatcher's Suit Has No Basis." *Robesonian* 6 April 1989: B1.

Hatcher, Jacobs, and the Robeson Defense Committee filed suit in January, accusing state and county officials of "running a campaign of intimidation and harassment."

1278. Pitts, Lewis. "Available Evidence Warrants an Investigation." *Robesonian* 27 April 1989: 4A.
Hatcher and Jacobs' lawyer objects to print media's stance that only "direct proof" will substantiate the activists' claims. Cites circumstantial evidence already documented.

1279. "Jacobs Gets 6 Years Active After Guilty Plea." *Robesonian* 4 May 1989: 1A.
The sentence was 6 years in prison, followed by a 6-year suspended sentence under probation, for state kidnapping charges.

1280. "County DA, Ex-Hostage Oppose Similar 'Deal' with Hatcher." *Robesonian* 5 May 1989: 1A.
Discussion of the amount of time Jacobs will probably serve and differences between his and Hatcher's cases.

1281. "Witness' No-Show Postpones Trial of Sandy Chavis." *Robesonian* 13 June 1989: 1A.
Kim Locklear Jr., a key witness for the state, failed to appear in Johnston County Superior Court. The trial was postponed indefinitely.

1282. "State Rebukes Hatcher-Jacobs Lawyers." *Robesonian* 15 June 1989: 1.
The Attorney General's Office asked a federal judge to levy a financial penalty against William Kunstler, Barry Nakell, and Lewis Pitts for filing a lawsuit which was "a propaganda and plea-bargaining tool."

1283. Bailey, Sean M. "Lawyers Deny Claim They Filed Frivolous Lawsuit Against State." *News and Observer* 8 Aug. 1989: 1C.
Hatcher and Jacobs' lawyers filed a response in U.S. District Court, denying their lawsuit was "baseless and abusive." They have dropped their suit, but the state has filed a suit for financial sanctions against them.

1284. "Nakell: Morgan Killed ... County Probe." *Robesonian* 22 Aug. 1989: 1A.
Nakell, Hatcher's lawyer, says he was told that State Bureau of Investigation director Robert Morgan squelched an investigation of SBI agents' activities during their probe of the *Robesonian* hostage-taking. The investigation was killed because of politics.

1285. "Hatcher Attorneys Fined." *Charlotte Observer* 30 Sept. 1989: 5B.
The attorneys were charged legal fees and damages for a lawsuit "initiated ... to gain publicity and to influence the state prosecution then under way." A federal appeals court upheld the sanctions. Related articles: *Robesonian* 20 Sept. 1990: 1A; 16 April 1991: 1A; 8 Dec. 1991: 2A; 4 Feb. 1992: 1A; 6 Feb. 1992: 1A; 14 Sept. 1993: 1A. Liz Seymour briefly discusses the sanctions and Rule 11's effect on civil rights attorneys in *Southern Exposure* 19.2 (Summer 1991): 7.

1286. Emerson, Pamela Marie. "A Newspaper Held Hostage: A Case Study of Terrorism and the Media." Honors essay. Chapel Hill: School of Journalism,

U of North Carolina at Chapel Hill, 1989. 71 p. [UNC-WL]
Concludes that Hatcher and Jacobs committed an act of terrorism. Hatcher used the media. Instead of giving him a soapbox, journalists should have delved more deeply into conditions in the county. Opinions vary on whether the incident caused reform.

1287. Huck, Susan. *Legal Terrorism: The Truth about the Christic Institute.* McLean, VA: New World Publishing, 1989. Pp. 122-34.
Claims Christic Institute South and William Kunstler employed manipulation of the media, leftist tactics, and a groundless civil lawsuit in representing Hatcher and Jacobs.

1288. "Former Hostage Suing Hatcher." *Robesonian* 25 Jan. 1990: 1A.
Mike Mangiameli wants $20,000 for damages, to come from funds Hatcher might raise through books, speeches, or screenplays about the hostage-taking, or from funds raised for him by Robeson Defense, Christic Institute South, or other groups.

1289. "Hatcher Gets 18 Years After Guilty Plea." *Robesonian* 14 Feb. 1990: 1A.
Hatcher, represented by Barry Nakell and public defender Angus Thompson, entered into a "plea arrangement." The maximum sentence would have been 420 years.

1290. "Kunstler: Case Was Winnable." *Robesonian* 15 Feb. 1990: 1A.
Kunstler notes disappointment at not having the opportunity to try the case. He feels the state beat Hatcher down, especially through his time in Central Prison.

1291. Dew, Joe, and Julie Powers Rives. "Minorities Seeing Changes in Robeson County." *News and Observer* 19 Feb. 1990: 1B.
Highlights changes since the hostage-taking: a second Superior Court judgeship, a public defender's office, election of one female and three Indian county commissioners, and formation of the Human Relations and Unity Commission.

1292. "Cummings Family Accepts $65,000 Suit Settlement." *Robesonian* 14 March 1990: 1A.
The family of Jimmy Earl Cummings will drop their suit against the county, Sheriff's Deputy Kevin Stone, and Sheriff Hubert Stone.

1293. "Hatcher Sues Hostage, Newspaper Thru Counterclaim." *News of Robeson County* 4 April 1990: 1.
Sues Mike Mangiameli and *The News of Robeson County* for libel for comments made in an editorial article based on a taped interview with Hatcher's family. See also *Robesonian* 22 May 1990: 1A.

1294. Rhodes, Barbara. "Hatcher's Attorney Sued for $1 Million in Damages." *Robesonian* 1 May 1990: 1A.
Mike Mangiameli, representing himself, asks $1 million in punitive damages. He claims Barry Nakell did not "follow basic legal proceedings" in filing a counterclaim of libel against him.

1295. Rhodes, Barbara. "Guilty Plea Gets Chavis Suspended Sentence in Trial." *Robesonian* 5 June 1990: 8A.

Sandy Chavis pled guilty to accessory after the fact in the murder of Julian Pierce. He received a five-year suspended sentence and unsupervised probation.

1296. Rhodes, Barbara, and John Culbreth. "Jacobs Released from Jail, Plans to Stay in Charlotte." *Robesonian* 24 July 1990: 1A.
Jacobs, sentenced in May, 1989 to six years in prison for the *Robesonian* hostage-taking, was released on parole. See editorial, *Robesonian* 25 July 1990: 4A, and related articles, *News and Observer* 2 Dec. 1990: 2C; *Robesonian* 4 Dec. 1990: 1A.

1297. Rhodes, Barbara. "Private Probe Questions Pierce Death." *Robesonian* 26 Aug. 1990: 1A.
Sandy Jordan Chavis's family has allied with Julian Pierce's family, the Rural Advancement Fund Justice Project, and others for a private probe of Pierce's murder. This article raises questions about the state's resolution of the case. Related articles, *Robesonian* 26 Sept. 1990: 1A, 30 Sept. 1990: 1A, and 4 Nov. 1990: 1A.

1298. Seessel, Adam. "Coalition Struggles in Robeson County." *Southern Exposure* 19.2 (Summer 1991): 7.
Since the *Robesonian* hostage-taking, social change has continued. The triracial cooperation which brought about the school system merger, however, has frayed. Now, each race in the county has its own agenda.

1299. Carter, Kevin. "Conspiracy to Kill Native Amerian Activist?" *GreenLine* Nov. 1991: 10-11.
Eddie Hatcher claims his stabbing in a prison at Troy, N.C. was set up by prison officials. Hatcher considers himself a political prisoner. The stabbing is being investigated by the State Bureau of Investigation, and Hatcher's claims of Dept. of Corrections prejudice are being examined by the N.C. Commission of Indian Affairs.

1300. Ruffin, Jane. "UNC-CH Law Teacher Loses Appeal of Contempt Case." Raleigh *News and Observer* 18 Dec. 1991: 2B.
Barry Nakell was charged with contempt of court by Superior Court Judge I. Beverly Lake for his conduct during Hatcher's 1989 pretrial hearing on hostage-taking charges. Nakell appealed to the state Court of Appeals, which affirmed the lower court's ruling. This article quotes from the lengthy opinion (see also 104 N.C. App. 638, 1991). A federal appeals court ruled that Nakell must complete his 10-day jail sentence (*News and Observer* 27 Feb. 1992: 3B).

1301. Hammond, Wendy [screenwriter]. [Independent film on the life of Julian Pierce.] Forthcoming. [Announced in *Charlotte Observer* 14 Feb. 1990: 1D.]

FEDERAL BILLS; STATE AND FEDERAL LAWS; FEDERAL HEARINGS AND REPORTS; COURT CASES

1302. 1809 *Laws of North Carolina* Ch. 32, "An Act to Facilitate and Open the Navigation of Lumber River, from M'Farland's Turnpike to the South Carolina Line."
Changes the name of Drowning Creek between the specified points to Lumber River.

Establishes the Lumber River Navigation Company.

1303.   1831-1832 *Laws of North Carolina* Ch. 13, "An Act to Provide for the
          Collection of Fines Imposed upon Free Negroes or Free Persons of Colour."
A free Negro or free person of color who is convicted of an offense and cannot pay the
fine can be hired out to someone who will pay it in exchange for work. This law led to
"tied mule" incidents (see entry 54, pp. 44-45).

1304.   1870-'71 *North Carolina Session Laws* ch. 68, "An Act Authorizing the
          Governor to Offer a Reward for the Arrest of Henry B. Lowery and Others."
          18 Feb. 1871
Offers $2,000 for the arrest and delivery, dead or alive, of Henry Berry Lowry, and
$1,000 each for Boss Strong, Stephen Lowry, Thomas Lowry, Henderson Oxendine,
and George Applewhite.

1305.   1871-'72 *North Carolina Session Laws* ch. 122, "An Act Concerning the
          Robeson County Outlaws." 8 Feb. 1872
Offers $10,000 for arrest and delivery, dead or alive, of Henry Berry Lowry, and
$5,000 each for Boss Strong, Stephen Lowry, Thomas Lowry, George Applewhite, and
Andrew Strong.

1306.   1885 *Laws of North Carolina* ch. 51, "An Act to Provide for Separate Schools
          for Croatan Indians in Robeson County." 10 Feb. 1885. Rpt. in Dial and
          Eliades (entry 54), Appendix B, and in McPherson (entry 49), Exhibit L 5 1/2.
Designates Robeson County Indians "Croatans." They will have Indian school
committees and select their own teachers. School districts will be formed, a census of
Indian children aged 6-21 taken, and their pro rata share of county funds set aside.

1307.   1887 *North Carolina Public Laws* ch. 254, "An Act to Amend Section One
          Thousand Eight Hundred and Ten of the Code." 7 March 1887. Rpt. in
          McPherson (entry 49), Exhibit L7.
Makes all marriages between an Indian and a Negro, or between an Indian and a person
of Negro descent to the third generation, void. Applies only to Croatan Indians.

1308.   1887 *North Carolina Session Laws* ch. 400, "An Act to Establish a Normal
          School in the County of Robeson." 7 March 1887. Rpt. in McPherson (entry
          49), Exhibit L6; Dial and Eliades (entry 54), Appendix B; and Eliades and
          Oxendine (entry 264), Appendix A.
Names trustees who will acquire property for the school. Allots $500 annually for two
years. Students must be at least 15 and agree to teach Croatan youth after graduation.

1309.   1889 *Laws of North Carolina* ch. 60, "An Act to Amend the Laws of 1885 and
          1887 So As to Provide Additional Educational Facilities for the Croatan
          Indians, Citizens of Robeson County, North Carolina." 2 Feb. 1889. Rpt. in
          McPherson (entry 49), Exhibit L9.
Excludes Negro children to the fourth generation from attending schools for Croatan
children. Extends indefinitely the annual $500 appropriation for the Croatan Normal
School. Lowers the minimum age for Normal School students from fifteen to ten.

1310. 1889 *Laws of North Carolina* ch. 458, "An Act to Amend Chapter Fifty-One, Acts of One Thousand Eight Hundred and Eighty-Five, In Reference to the Schools of Croatan Indians in Richmond County." 11 March 1889. Rpt. in McPherson (entry 49), Exhibit L8.

The provisions of entry 1306, establishing separate schools for Croatans in Robeson County, shall also apply to Croatans in Richmond County.

1311. *McMillan v. School Committee*, 107 N.C. 609, 12 S.E. 330 (8 Dec. 1890)

Nathan McMillan, by reputation a slave whose father was White, married a Croatan and obtained a statement from the county Board of Education that his children could attend a Croatan school. The school committee refused them admittance. The Superior Court and the state Supreme Court upheld this decision, stating that McMillan's children were Negro to the fourth generation.

1312. 1893 *North Carolina Public Laws* ch. 515, "An Act to Amend Ch. 60, Sec. 3, of the Laws of 1889." 6 March 1893.

Croatan children 13 or older may attend the normal school; those 11 or 12 can attend if they pass an examination.

1313. 1895 *North Carolina Private Laws* ch. 171, "An Act to Incorporate the Town of Pembroke, in the County of Robeson." 8 March 1895.

Also establishes corporate limits and provides for annual election of a mayor, three commissioners, and a town marshall.

1314. 1897 *North Carolina Public Laws* ch. 536, "An Act in Relation to the Croatan Normal School in Robeson County." 9 Mar. 1897.

Credits an unexpended $281.25 to the school and pays P. B. Hiden $40.

1315. 56th Cong. 1st Session. H.R. 4009. "A Bill to Provide for the Education of the Children of the Croatan or Hatteras Indians, in the Southeastern Part of North Carolina." Introd. by Bellamy, 13 Dec. 1899.

Would provide for the purchase of land, erect a building, and provide equipment and furnishings. Allocated $50,000.

1316. 1901 *North Carolina Private Laws* ch. 401, "An Act in Relation to the Croatan Normal School in Robeson County." 13 March 1901.

Allots $246.25 from the State Treasury.

1317. 57th Cong. 1st Session. H. R. 186. "A Bill to Provide for the Eduction and Support of the Children of the Croatan or Hatteras Indians, in the Southeastern Part of North Carolina." Introd. by Bellamy; sent to the Committee on Indian Affairs.

Not seen. Cited in *Congressional Record*, 57th Cong., 1st Sess., 2 Dec. 1901, p. 54.

1318. 1905 *North Carolina Private Laws* ch. 49, "An Act to Extend and Amend Ch. 171, Private Laws of 1895 ..." 8 Feb. 1905.

Amends the act incorporating the Town of Pembroke to allow for biennial, rather than annual, election of a mayor and three commissioners. The town clerk, treasurer, marshal, attorney, and policeman will be elected by the town council.

1319.   1909 *North Carolina Public Laws* ch. 720, "An Act to Provide Separate
            Schools for the Indian Race in Scotland County." 6 March 1909.
No child of Negro blood or of Indian blood to the eighth degree shall attend a public
school for the White race. Croatan children cannot attend Scotland County's Indian
schools but will be taught in public schools for them exclusively. Indian children other
than Croatans may attend White schools if patrons of that school do not object.

1320.   61st Cong. 2nd Session. H.R. 19036. "A Bill to Change the Name of the
            Croatan Indians of the State of N.C. to their Original Name, Cherokee."
            Introd. by Godwin, 24 Jan. 1910. Rpt. in McPherson (entry 49), Exhibit M.
States that Croatans are a branch of the Cherokees. Provides only for a name change.

1321.   1911 *North Carolina Public Laws* ch. 168, "An Act to Empower the Trustees
            of the Indian Normal School of Robeson County to Transfer Title to Property
            of Said School by Deed to State Board of Education, and to Provide for the
            Appointment of Trustees for Said School." 8 March 1911. Rpt. in McPherson
            (entry 49), Exhibit L11 and Dial and Eliades (entry 54), Appendix B.
The N.C. Board of Education will appoint seven Croatans to a Board of Trustees,
authorized to employ or fire teachers and to prevent Negroes from attending the school.

1322.   1911 *Public Laws of North Carolina* ch. 215, "An Act the Change the Name of
            the Indians in Robeson County and to Provide for Said Indians Separate
            Apartments in the State Hospital." 8 March 1911. Rpt. in McPherson (entry
            49), Exhibit L12 and Dial and Eliades (entry 54), Appendix B.
Croatans are renamed Indians of Robeson County. The Normal School is renamed
Indian Normal School of Robeson County. Gives Indians separate rooms in the State
Hospital for the Insane, County Jail, and County Home for the Aged and Infirm.

1323.   62nd Cong. 1st Session. S. 3258. "A Bill to Acquire a Site and Erect
            Buildings for a School for the Indians of Robeson County ... and for Other
            Purposes." Introd. by Simmons, 16 Aug. 1911. Rpt. in entry 1326.
Would appropriate $50,000 for the site and for construction of the school, then allow
another $10,000 for maintenance in the ensuing fiscal year.

1324.   Pierce, Charles F. [Visit Among the Croatan Indians, Living in the Vicinity of
            Pembroke, North Carolina.] Report, in the Field at Pipestone, Minn., to the
            Commissioner of Indian Affairs, U.S. Indian Service, Dept. of the Interior, 2
            Mar. 1912. [National Archives and Records Admin., Washington, D.C. File
            23202-1912-123 General Services.] [IERC] [*Lumbee Petition*, Exhibit A30]
            Summarized in entry 62.
Pierce's report was ordered because Croatans would soon request federal funds for a
government boarding school. Discusses population, origins, language, school
enrollment, wages, property value, and land ownership. Concludes that Croatans
would benefit from a boarding school, but federal funding "would be taking a backward step in our Indian School policy" and would create a precedent for other tribes
"that are now cared for by the various states."

1325. 62nd Cong. 2nd Session. *Indians in Robeson County, N.C. Hearing Before the Committee on Indian Affairs, U.S. Senate, ... on S. 3258, a Bill to Acquire a Site and Erect Buildings for a School for the Indians of Robeson County, N.C., and for Other Purposes.* Dated 4 April 1912. 7 p. [Not seen.] Microfilmed by the Library of Congress.

1326. 62nd Cong. 2nd Session. *School for Indians of Robeson County: Hearings Before the [House] Committee on Indian Affairs on S. 3258 to Acquire a Site and Erect Buildings for a School for the Indians of Robeson County, N.C. and for Other Purposes.* Dated 14 Feb. 1913. 27 p. [PSU-MLL]
Includes a letter from the Commission on Indian Affairs listing nonreservation Indian schools and stating that they are open to all children 1/4 or more Indian. States that Croatans are descendents of the Cherokees. Includes muster rolls for Robeson County for the War of 1812, and reprints A. W. McLean's "Historical Sketch of the Indians of Robeson County, North Carolina." Microfilmed by the Library of Congress.

1327. 1913 *Public Laws of North Carolina* ch. 123, "An Act to Restore to the Indians Residing in Robeson and Adjoining Counties Their Rightful and Ancient Name." 11 March 1913. Rpt. in McPherson (entry 49), Exhibit L13 and Dial and Eliades (entry 54), Appendix B.
Indians of Robeson County are renamed Cherokee Indians of Robeson County. The Indian Normal School of Robeson County is renamed Cherokee Normal School of Robeson County. The act does not impose on powers, privileges, or rights of the Eastern Band of the Cherokees.

1328. 1913 *Public Laws of North Carolina* ch. 199, "An Act to Provide for the Maintenance and Support of the Indian Normal School of Robeson County." 12 March 1913. Rpt. in McPherson (entry 49), Exhibit L14.
Adds $500 to the appropriation for the Normal School for 1913 and 1914.

1329. 63rd Cong. 1st Session. S. 2717. "A Bill to Change the Name of the Indians Residing in Robeson and Adjoining Counties, in the State of North Carolina, Who Have Heretofore Been Known as 'Croatan Indians' or 'Indians of North Carolina,' to the Name 'Cherokee Indians of Robeson County'." Introd. by Simmons; sent to the Committee on Indian Affairs. [Not seen.]
Cited in *Congressional Record*, 63rd Cong., 1st Sess., 10 July 1913, p. 2365.

1330. 63rd Cong. 1st Session. S. 3217. "A Bill to Acquire a Site and Erect Buildings for a School for the Indians of Robeson County, N.C., and for Other Purposes." Introd. by Simmons; sent to the Committee on Indian Affairs. [Not seen.]
Cited in *Congressional Record*, 63rd Cong., 1st Sess., 13 Oct. 1913, p. 5611.

1331. 63rd Cong. 2nd Session. S.Res. 410. "Resolution Directing the Secretary of the Interior to Cause an Investigation to be Made as to the Condition and Tribal Rights of Certain Indians in North Carolina, and to Make a Report Thereon to Congress." Introd. by Simmons, 30 June 1914.

The investigation should determine whether the Indians are due any money, land, or educational support from the federal government. Resulted in the *McPherson Report* .

1332.   *Goins et al. v. Board of Trustees of Indian Normal Training School at Pembroke*, 169 NC 736, 86 SE 629 (27 Oct. 1915).
The lower court had ruled that Croatans from an adjacent county who became residents of Robeson County were eligible to attend the Normal School. The Board of Trustees appealed, arguing that the plaintiff's children had Negro blood and were not designated as Croatans. The lower court's decision was upheld. The *Lumbee Petition* (83.7 (a) (2) p. 46) identifies this as the Smiling School suit, which eventually led to a school system for a fourth race in the county. Discussed in Sider (entry 59).

1333.   64th Cong. 1st Session. H. R. 11332. "A Bill to Acquire a Site and Erect Buildings for a School for the Indians of Robeson County, N.C., and for Other Purposes." Introd. by Godwin. [Not seen.]
Cited in *Congressional Record*, 64th Cong., 1st Session, 11 Feb. 1916, p. 2438.

1334.   1917 *North Carolina Private Laws* ch. 63, "An Act to Provide for the Appointment of a Mayor and Four Commissioners for the Town of Pembroke in Robeson County." 9 Jan. 1917.
Repeals the law providing for an elected mayor and town commissioners. Authorizes their appointment by the North Carolina governor.

1335.   1917 *North Carolina Public-Local Laws* ch. 509, "An Act to Provide for Separate Schools for the Croatan Indians of Sampson County." 2 March 1917.
Croatans in Sampson County must attend either of two Indian schools, which will receive a pro rata share of school funds.

1336.   1917 *North Carolina Session Laws* ch. 163, "An Act to Control ... Distribution of Funds to the Cherokee Normal School of Robeson County." 5 March 1917.
Allots $1,000 of the Cherokee Normal School's funds to establish an Indian training school at Union Chapel.

1337.   1919 *North Carolina Public Laws* ch. 211, "An Act to Amend Section 4545, Revisal of 1905, Relative to the Treatment of Croatan Indians in the Insane Hospital." 10 March 1919.
Any insane or inebriate Cherokees of Robeson County, or Croatans of other counties, will have separate wards in the Raleigh Hospital for the Insane and will receive equitable treatment.

1338.   1921 *North Carolina Public-Local Laws* ch. 426, "An Act for the Protection of the Public Schools of Robeson County." 5 March 1921. Partial reprint in Eliades and Oxendine (entry 264), Appendix D.
Forms a committee of Robeson County Indians to have exclusive jurisdiction in questions concerning the race of applicants to county Indian schools. Their decisions can be appealed to the Superior Court.

1339.   68th Cong. 1st Session. H.R. 8083. "A Bill to Designate the Croatan

Indians of Robeson and Adjoining Counties in North Carolina as Cherokee Indians." Introd. by Lyon, 20 March 1924.
Croatans would be renamed Cherokees–without changing their political status or property rights, giving them rights to land or money of other Cherokees, or prohibiting their children's attendance at federal Indian schools (see *Robesonian* 17 March 1924: 1). A one-page report, consisting of letters of approval from the House Committee on Indian Affairs and the Dept. of Interior, was printed on 22 May 1924 (H.Rept. no. 826). See debate, *Congressional Record*, 68th Cong., 1st Session, 5 June 1924, p. 10745.

1340. 1927 *North Carolina Public-Local Laws* ch. 213, "An Act to Provide Separate Schools for the Cherokee Indians in Columbus County." 26 Feb. 1927.
Columbus County Indians–who claim descent from Cherokee Indians of Robeson County–are designated Cherokee Indians of Columbus County. Columbus County will form separate schools for them and exclude children with Negro blood.

1341. 1929 *North Carolina Public Laws* ch. 195, "An Act to Amend Ch. 126, Public-Local Laws 1921 ... and Prescribe the Racial Qualifications of Those Seeking Admission into Cherokee Indian Normal School ... and in the Common Schools of Robeson County for the Indian Race." 16 March 1929.
Also refers all questions on race of applicants to a committee of Indian residents, with right of appeal to the Superior Court.

1342. 1931 *North Carolina Public Laws* ch. 141, "An Act to Amend Sec. 5,445 of the Consolidated Statutes so as to Provide Keeping Separate Records for the Public Schools for the Cherokee Indians of Robeson County." 20 Mar. 1931.
The county school superintendent will keep separate records on operations of the Cherokee Indian schools.

1343. 1931 *North Carolina Public Laws* ch. 276, "An Act to Amend Ch. 61, Public Laws 1921, ... Relating to the Supervision of the Cherokee Indian State Normal School, by the State Board of Education." 9 April 1931.
The Board will supervise funds, hiring, and any changes in organization for the school.

1344. 1931 *North Carolina Public Laws* ch. 275, "An Act to Amend Ch. 238, Public Laws of 1929, Relating to Appointment of Trustees for Cherokee Indian Normal School ...." 9 April 1931. [Board will have eleven members.]

1345. 72nd Cong. 1st Session. S. 4595. "A Bill Providing for the Recognition and Enrollment as Cherokee Indians of Certain Indians in the State of North Carolina." Introd. by Bailey, 9 May 1932. [Similar to the 1924 bill.]

1346. 73rd Cong. 1st Session. H.R. 5365. "A Bill Providing for the Recognition and Enrollment as Cheraw Indians of Certain Indians in the State of North Carolina." Introd. by Clark, 1 May 1933.
Croatans would be renamed Cheraws. The bill includes the same provisions as H.R. 8083 (entry 1339). A parallel bill, S. 1632, was introduced the same day (not seen).

1347. 73rd Cong. 2nd Session. *Siouan Indians of Lumber River*. S.Rept. no. 204

(to accompany S. 1632). Dated 23 Jan. 1934. *Serial Set*, serial no. 9769, v. 1. Recommends amending S. 1632 to read "Siouan Indians," rather than "Cheraw," and disavows federal wardship or government benefits.

1348. 73rd Cong. 2nd Session. *Siouan Indians of Lumber River*. H.Rept. no. 1752 (to accompany H.R. 5365). Dated 23 May 1934. *Serial Set*. Serial no. 22245. Similar to S.Rept. no. 204, above. The Secretary of the Interior opposes the bill unless it forbids federal wardship or other government rights or benefits.

1349. 1933 *North Carolina Public Laws* ch. 490, "An Act to Provide for Admission into the Stonewall Jackson Training School and Samarcand Manor of Delinquent Boys and Girls of the Cherokee Indian Race, of Robeson County." 13 May 1933. [Indian children will be separated from White children.]

1350. 1935 *North Carolina Public Laws* ch. 316, "An Act to Amend Ch. 490, Public Laws of 1933, Relating to Delinquent Children of the Indian Race." 7 May 1935.
Provides $20,000 to erect a separate building for Cherokee Indian children at Stonewall Jackson Training School.

1351. 1939 *North Carolina Public-Local Laws* ch. 256, "An Act to Create and Establish the Fairmont Administrative Unit and Providing for the Administration and Control Thereof." 20 March 1939.
Indians are excluded from all provisions of the act. Indian schools within the Unit's boundaries will operate as before.

1352. 1941 *North Carolina Public-Local Laws* ch. 422, "An Act to Provide Separate Schools for Indians in Averasboro and Duke Townships, Harnett County." 15 March 1941.
These Indians, claiming descent from Robeson County Croatans, will be designated "Cherokee Indians of Averasboro and Duke Townships, Harnett County" and will have separate schools, from which Negro children are excluded.

1353. 1941 *North Carolina Public Laws* ch. 323, "An Act to Change the Name of the Cherokee Indian Normal School of Robeson County, and for Other Purposes." 15 March 1941.
The school's name is changed to "Pembroke State College for Indians." The "principal" is now called "president."

1354. 1941 *North Carolina Public Laws* ch. 370, "An Act to Provide Better Educational Advantages for Members of the Indian Race in Eastern North Carolina Not Otherwise Provided For." 15 March 1941.
The North Carolina Board of Education may establish a vocational and normal school for Indians of Sampson, Hoke, Scotland, Cumberland, Bladen, Person, and Harnett counties and may allocate up to $15,000.

1355. 1945 *North Carolina Session Laws* ch. 410, "An Act to Amend the Charter of the Town of Pembroke." 7 March 1945.

The mayor and four town commissioners will be elected, rather than appointed by the North Carolina governor.

1356. 1945 *North Carolina Session Laws* ch. 817, "An Act Relating to the Cherokee Indians of Robeson County and Pembroke State College for Indians Located at Pembroke, North Carolina." 19 March 1945.
Trustees can elect their own chairperson. The act forms a committee of county Indians to handle questions of race regarding applicants to the college and also allows Indians from BIA-recognized tribes to attend.

1357. 1949 *North Carolina Session Laws* ch. 58, "An Act to Change the Name of the Pembroke State College for Indians." 11 Feb. 1949.
To "Pembroke State College."

1358. 1953 *North Carolina Session Laws* ch. 487, "An Act to Amend Article 5 of ch. 116 of the General Statutes Relating to the Admission of Students to Pembroke State College." 26 March 1953.
Allows other Indian, or White, students to attend if approved by the Board of Trustees.

1359. 1953 *North Carolina Session Laws* ch. 874, "An Act Relating to the Lumbee Indians of North Carolina." 20 April 1953.
The Indians living in Robeson County are renamed "Lumbee Indians of North Carolina." Repeals all laws in conflict with this law.

1360. 84th Cong. 1st Session. H.R. 4656. "A Bill Relating to the Lumbee Indians of North Carolina." Introd. by Carlyle, 7 March 1955.
States the Indians' origin from colonists and coastal Indian tribes and designates them "Lumbee Indians of North Carolina."

1361. 84th Cong. 2nd Session. *Relating to the Lumbee Indians of North Carolina.* H.Rpt. no. 1654. 2 p. Dated 18 Jan. 1956. *Serial Set*, Serial no. 11897, *House Reports*, vol. 1. [Reports favorably on H.R. 4656.]

1362. 84th Cong. 2nd Session. *Relating to the Lumbee Indians of North Carolina.* S.Rept. no. 2012. Dated 16 May 1956. *Serial Set*, Serial no. 11888, vol. 3, *Senate Reports*. Rpt. in *U.S. Code Congressional and Administrative News*, 84th Cong., 2nd Session, vol. 2, pp. 2715-16.
Recommends passage of H.R. 4656, with an amendment making Lumbees ineligible for federal services normally accorded Indians (i.e., BIA services) and unaffected by statutes affecting Indians.

1363. 84th Cong. 2nd Session. P.L. 84-570. "An Act Relating to the Lumbee Indians of North Carolina." 70 Stat. 254. Dated 7 June 1956. Rpt. in *U. S. Code Congressional and Administrative News*, 84th Cong., 2nd Session (1956), vol. 1, *Laws*; Dial and Eliades (entry 54), Appendix B.
Same as H.R. 4656 but includes the "termination language" added by S.Rept. no. 2012.

1364. *State of North Carolina v. James Cole, James Garland Martin and Others to*

the State Unknown. 249 N.C. 733, 107 S.E.2d 732 (25 March 1959).
Cole and Martin appealed their Superior Court conviction for inciting a riot. The case
report gives detailed information on circumstances prior to and during the Ku Klux
Klan routing at Maxton. The Supreme Court ruled "no error" regarding Cole and "new
trial" regarding Martin.

1365. 1961 *North Carolina Session Laws* ch. 97, "An Act Relating to Elections in the
          Town of Pembroke in Robeson County." 24 March 1961.
Abolishes primaries for nominating town officers. A mayor and two commissioners
will be elected biennially.

1366. 1969 *North Carolina Session Laws* ch. 388, "An Act to Establish Pembroke
          College as a Regional University with the Designation of 'Pembroke State
          University'." 1 July 1969.

1367. 92nd Cong. 2nd Session. S. 2763. "A Bill to Prohibit Discrimination Against
          the Lumbee Indians of N.C." Introd. by Jordan, 28 Oct. 1971. [Not seen.]
Jordan stated (*Congressional Record*, vol. 117, 28 Oct. 1971, p. 37902) that the bill
would give Lumbees "the same rights, privileges and benefits accorded other Indians
not living on reservations" by repealing one sentence of the Lumbee Act.

1368. 93rd Cong. 2nd Session. H.R. 12216. "A Bill to Amend the Act Relating to
          the Lumbee Indians of North Carolina." Introd. by Rose, 22 Jan. 1974.
Strikes out the "Nothing in this Act ..." sentence. A more explicit bill to achieve the
same purpose (S. 4045) was introduced by Helms on 25 Sept. 1974.

1369. 93rd Cong. 2nd Session. *Amending the Act Relating to the Lumbee Indians of
          North Carolina*. H.Rpt. no. 1394. 10 p. Dated 1 Oct. 1974. *Serial Set*, Serial
          no. 13061-9. Rpt. in S.Hrg. 100-881 (entry 1380).
Reports favorably on H.R. 12216 and recommends passage with amendments, making
Lumbees eligible only for federal services "for which other non-federally recognized
Indian tribes are or may hereafter become eligible." A bill containing these recom-
mendations (S. 159) was introduced by Helms on 16 Jan. 1975.

1370. *Janie Maynor Locklear v. N.C. State Board of Elections*, 379 F.Supp. 2 (20
          June 1974). Reversed, 514 F.2d 1152 (23 April 1975). Affirmed, 529 F.2d
          515 (26 Sept. 1975).
The "double-voting" case. The U.S. District Court ruled for the defendants, finding
that the North Carolina statute was not unconstitutional, since "residents of city
administrative units were substantially affected by decisions of the county board." The
U.S. Circuit Court of Appeals reversed and remanded the district court's decision,
saying voters in the city units did not have sufficient interest in functions performed by
the county board to justify their voting in elections for county school board members.

1371. *Janie Maynor Locklear et al. v. N.C. State Board of Elections, et al., on Appeal
          from the U.S. District Court for Eastern District of North Carolina,
          Fayetteville Division. Brief for Appellants*. By Barry Nakell and Adam Stein,
          attorneys for appellants. [1975?] 40p. [IERC]

Includes a statement of issues, statement of the case, argument, conclusion, an opinion letter from the North Carolina Attorney General, and a table of authorities cited.

1372. *Lawrence Maynor, Appellant, v. Rogers C. B. Morton, Secretary, Dept. of the Interior*, 510 F.2d 1254 (4 April 1975). Rpt. in S.Hrg. 100-881 (entry 1380).
Held that Maynor, one of the "Original 22," remained eligible for benefits under the 1934 Indian Reorganization Act, in spite of the "Nothing in this act" clause of the 1956 Lumbee Act. "Background Facts" gives thorough documentation on the Original 22's attempts to gain federal assistance.

1373. 1975 *Session Laws of North Carolina* ch. 381, "An Act to Provide for the Nomination and Election of the Board of Education of Robeson County." 26 May 1975.
Outlaws double-voting. Persons living in a city or town administrative unit are not eligible for election to the county board of education and cannot vote in these elections.

1374. "In the Matter of the Lumbee Indians of North Carolina." 58 Comp. Gen. 699. (Decisions of the U.S. Comptroller General, no. B-185659) 1 Aug. 1979. 10 p. GA1.5:58
The final paragraph of the Lumbee Act intends "to leave the rights of the Lumbee Indians unchanged," not to bar their access to all benefits they might receive by virtue of their status as Indians. Each program from which the Lumbees seek aid must be examined separately.

1375. *State v. Chavis*, 45 N.C.App 438, 263 S.E.2d 356 (4 March 1980). Petition for writ of certiorari denied, 449 U.S. 1035, 66 L.Ed.2d 496, 101 *S.Ct.* 610 (8 Dec. 1980).
Defendants had received suspended sentences of imprisonment for violating the compulsory school attendance law during the 1978-79 school year. When the county desegregation plan assigned their children to Oxendine School rather than Prospect School, they sent their children to Prospect School; the children remained on the premises but received no instruction. Defendants said the Civil Rights Act of 1964 did not apply to them. The lower court's decision was upheld. See also entry 1376.

1376. "Compulsory Attendance: No Exemption for American Indians/Misunderstand- ing of Law No Defense. State v. Chavis, 45 N.C.App. 438, 263 S.E.2d 356 (1980)." *School Law Bulletin* [U of North Carolina at Chapel Hill, Inst. of Government] 12.3 (July 1981): 20.
The court ruled that, in terms of public school desegregation, Indians are subject to the Civil Rights Act.

1377. 1981 *North Carolina Session Laws* ch. 1294, "An Act to Appropriate Funds to the Board of Governors of the University of North Carolina to Provide Non-Service Scholarships for Resident N.C. Indians." 23 June 1982.

1378. 1987 *North Carolina Session Laws* ch. 605, "An Act to Merge All of the School Administrative Units in Robeson County, Subject to a Referendum." 13 July 1987.

1379. 100th Cong. 1st Session. S. 2672. "A Bill to Provide Federal Recognition for
          the Lumbee Tribe of North Carolina." Introd. by Sanford, 29 July 1988.
Cites Lumbee descent from coastal North Carolina tribes, mainly Cheraw. Sets aside
the first section of the Lumbee Act, and makes Lumbees eligible–once the tribal roll is
verified and funds solely for Lumbees appropriated–for federal benefits and services
generally applicable to Indians and Indian tribes. Similar bill (H.R. 5042) introd. by
Rose, 14 July 1988.

1380. 100th Cong. 2nd Session. *Federal Recognition of the Lumbee Indian Tribe of
          North Carolina.* Hearing, Senate Select Comm. on Indian Affairs. S.Hrg.
          100-881. Dated 12 Aug. 1988. 160p. Y4.In2/11: S.hrg.100-881.
Hearing on S. 2672. Reprints testimony from Ross O. Swimmer, Jack Campisi,
Adolph Dial, Suzan Harjo, Raymond Fogelson, Daniel K. Inouye, Arlinda Locklear,
Lonnie Revels, William Sturtevant, Jonathan L. Taylor (Eastern Band of Cherokee
Indians), and others. Includes letters and resolutions from several tribes.

1381. 100th Cong. 2nd Session. *Providing for Federal Recognition for the Lumbee
          Tribe of North Carolina.* Report, Senate Select Comm. on Indian Affairs.
          S.Rept. 100-579. 37 p. Dated 30 Sept. 1988. Y1.1/5: 100-579.
Recommends passage of S. 2672, with an amendment in the nature of a substitute. See
pp. 1-4 for a useful overview of Lumbee history and attempts at federal recognition.

1382. 101st Cong. 1st Session. H.R. 2335. "A Bill to Provide Federal Recognition
          for the Lumbee Tribe of North Carolina." Introd. by Rose, 11 May 1989.
Would amend the Lumbee Act to make the "Lumbee Tribe of Cheraw Indians of N.C."
eligible for "all laws and regulations of the U.S. of general application to Indians and
Indian tribes." No services would be provided until funds were appropriated. Similar
bill (S. 901) introduced by Sanford, 3 May 1989.

1383. 101st Cong. 1st Session. *To Provide Federal Recognition for the Lumbee
          Tribe of North Carolina.* Hearing, House Comm. on Interior and Insular
          Affairs [on H.R. 2335]. Serial no. 101-57. 235 p. Dated 26 Sept. 1989.
          Y4.In8/14: 101-57. Washington: GPO, 1992.
Includes a letter of support from James H. Merrell, who spent ten years researching a
book on the Catawbas and their neighbors. He asserts that 18th-century documentation
"does indeed suggest that the Lumbees are descended from one or more towns of
Cheraws, with the probable addition of remnants of other Eastern Siouan peoples ..."
(p. 222). His other letter (pp. 229-234) summarizes this documentation, while touching
on other tribal origin theories. Jack Campisi discusses the 18th-century documentation
the *Petition* presents. Patrick Hayes, of the BIA, feels the documentation does not
support Cheraw origins. Ruth Locklear explains tribal membership criteria. Arlinda
Locklear, tribal attorney, gives a legal history of the tribe's attempts at federal
recognition and discusses Congressional action on other tribes.

1384. 101st Cong. 2nd Session. *Providing Federal Recognition for the Lumbee
          Tribe of North Carolina.* Report, House Comm. on Interior and Insular
          Affairs. Report no. 101-685. 12 p. Dated 10 Sept. 1990. Y1.1/8: 101-685.
Amends H.R. 2335 to state that the 1956 Lumbee Act does not bar processing of the

Lumbee Petition. The BIA must publish proposed findings on the *Petition* no later than 18 months after LRDA's response to any notice of obvious deficiencies in the *Petition*. The BIA cannot consider size of the Lumbee tribe in its decision.

1385. 102nd Cong. 1st Session. H.R. 1426. "To Provide for the Recognition of the Lumbee Tribe of Cheraw Indians of North Carolina, and for Other Purposes." Introd. by Rose, 13 March 1991.

The tribe shall be subject to all U.S. laws and regulations of general application to Indians and Indian tribes. Services and benefits shall not be available until separatefunds are appropriated. Other Robeson County Indians not on the Lumbee tribal roll can petition for federal acknowledgement. *See also entry 692.

1386. 102nd Cong. 1st Session. *Provide for the Recognition of the Lumbee Tribe of Cheraw Indians of North Carolina*. Joint Hearing, House Comm. on Interior and Insular Affairs and Senate Select Comm. on Indian Affairs, on H.R. 1426 and S. 1036. Dated 1 Aug. 1991. Serial no. 102-JH 1. 274 p. Y4.In8/14: 102-JH 1. Washington: GPO, 1993.

Includes statements from Ron Eden (BIA), F. H. Faleomavaega (American Samoa), Adolph Blue, Ruth Locklear, Jack Campisi, Welton Lowry, Johnnie P. Bullard, Claude Lowry, Arlinda Locklear, Leola Locklear, George Waters and Jonathan Taylor (Eastern Band of Cherokees), Glenn Miller (Menominee), and Lloyd Powless (Oneida). Jack Campisi believes the Lumbee meet every criteria for federal recognition, with the possible exception of never having been subject to Congressional termination. He addresses the problem of the BIA's requirement that the tribe document descent from an historic tribe. Siouan groups were almost totally decimated by the 18th century, but the BIA wants additional 18th-century documentation.

1387. 102nd Cong. 1st Session. *Providing for the Recognition of the Lumbee Tribe of Cheraw Indians of North Carolina, and for Other Purposes*. Report, House Comm. on Interior and Insular Affairs. Report no. 102-215. 29 p. Dated 24 Sept. 1991. Y1.1/8: 102/215

Reports favorably on H.R. 1426; recommends passage. Detailed "Background" section shows Lumbee efforts for federal recognition since 1899. The Congressional Budget Office estimates that when funds are appropriated, the bill will cost $80-$90 million annually. Minority views oppose circumventing the federal acknowledgement process.

1388. 102nd Cong. 1st Session. *Providing for the Recognition of the Lumbee Tribe of Cheraw Indians of North Carolina, and for Other Purposes*. Report, Senate Select Comm. on Indian Affairs. Report no. 102-251. 26 p. Dated 26 Nov. 1991. Y1.1/5: 102-251

Recommends passage of H.R. 1426 without amendment. Includes text of the bill, a useful background statement, and a section-by-section analysis. The BIA's Office of Tribal Services strongly opposes enactment of the bill, believing that the Lumbees should go through the petition process. The major deficiency found in the *Petition* is that "the Lumbees have not documented their descent from a historic tribe" (p. 16).

1389. 103rd Cong. 1st Session. H.R. 334. "To Provide for the Recognition of the Lumbee Tribe of Cheraw Indians of North Carolina, and for Other Purposes."

Introd. by Rose, 5 Jan. 1993. [Identical to H.R. 1426; see entry 1385, above.]

See also items 5, 11, 49, 188, 195, 535, 606, 607, 608, 685, 687, 813, 834, 840, 845, 965, 966, 1079, 1138, 1139, 1140, and 1238.

NEWSPAPERS

1390a. *The Argus*. Microfilm. [RCPL] 20 Aug. 1902--29 Dec. 1905.

1390b. *The Carolina Indian Voice*. 18 Jan. 1973- . Weekly.
Microfilm and current subscription: PSU-MLL, RCPL. Also at State Historical Soc. of Wisconsin (24 May 1979–June, 1989 on microfilm, and paper copies to present) and at Navajo Community College Library (Oct. 20, 1977 to present, paper copies only).

1391. *The Indian Observer*. 1911- ?.
Edited by C. D. Brewington and A. S. Locklear. Short-lived. See announcement of the paper's beginning: *Robesonian* 18 Sept. 1911: 4. PSU-MLL has a photocopy of vol. 1, no. 1 (13 Sept. 1911).

1392. *The Lumbee*. Microfilm. 28 Oct. 1965–24 Feb. 1966; 5 Jan. 1967–5 Sept. 1968, p. 1. [PSU-MLL] [RCPL]

1393. "Copy of *Odago* Given Library ... ." *Pembroke Progress* 8 Dec. 1949: 1.
The first copy of *Odago* (Indian word meaning "friendship") was given to PSC Library, to be placed in the college museum. The paper's editor was Dr. John B. May; others on the staff were G. Gordon Hunt, Ira Pate Lowry, and Venus Brooks.

1394. *Pembroke Progress*. Microfilm. 1 Jan. 1948–29 Dec. 1949. [PSU-MLL] [RCPL]

1395. *Robesonian*. Microfilm and current subscription. RCPL has: 20 June 1892–20 Aug. 1893 (scattered); 1897; 19 June 1900- . PSU-MLL has: Feb., 1951 Historical Edition and 1958- .

CURRICULUM MATERIALS

1396. *The Indians of Robeson County: A People Proud and Free*. Videotape series. Lumberton: Robeson County Compensatory Indian Education Project, 1979? [IERC]
These videotapes, made from earlier filmstrips, are loaned by IERC to county schools. Parts 1 and 2: "A People Proud and Free"; Part 3: "Education: Key to Past and Future"; Part 4: "Indian Folkways Yesterday and Today"; Part 5: "Indians and Government."

1397. *Ethnic Studies Guide and Resources Manual for the Carolinas*. By Rachel A. Bonney. Washington: Office of Education (DHEW), Ethnic Heritage Studies Branch, 1979. ERIC ED 183 494 [Brief mention, pp. 47-52.]

1398. *Study Prints*. Billy E. Barnes, designer. Lumberton: Title IV, Part A Indian

Education Project, Robeson County Board of Education, 1979. [IERC]
Twenty-eight large-format prints, each on a different theme, with attractive
photographs and brief text. Topics include: farming, Henry Berry Lowry, *Strike at the
Wind!*, Lumbee Homecoming, PSU, the Lumbee River, Lumbee artists, craftspersons,
and businessmen, Old Main, LRDA, and Lumbees in town, county, state, and national
government.

1399. *United Native Instruction to Youth: An Indian Studies Curriculum for Grades
K-5 and 8-9.* Developed by Title IV Part A, Robeson County Compensatory
Indian Eduction Project and Robeson County Board of Education. 1979.
[IERC] [PSU-MLL] Also ERIC ED 219 214.
Pp. 20-23 gives a capsule history of Lumbee education. Includes songs and poems to
reinforce Lumbee identity. *Indians of North Carolina* (also at MLL) is a series of six
Indian Studies Skillstexts for use with the guide; each touches on Lumbees.

1400. *Indian Historical Sites in Southeast North Carolina.* Pembroke: Lumbee
Regional Development Association, 1981. [IERC]
Teacher's guide for field trips in and near Robeson County. Covers Old Main, a
one-room schoolhouse, the Native American Library, Henry Berry Lowry, and the
Indian Museum of the Carolinas.

1401. Duensing, Ed, and Helen M. Scheirbeck, comps. *Campfires: Legends and
Tales of the Eastern Indians.* Lumberton: Div. of Compensatory Education,
Title IV, Part A, Indian Education Project, Robeson County Board of Ed-
ucation, 1985. [PSU-MLL]
Four tales, illustrated by Robert Locklear, involving Robeson County Indians.
Epilogue explains Robeson County's Title IV, Part A Indian Education Project.

1402. Knick, Stanley. *Along the Trail: A Reader About Native Americans.* Pembroke: Native American Resource Center, Pembroke State U, 1992.
Forty-eight readings for public school students on a variety of topics, each accompanied by a glossary and discussion questions. The readings grew out of Knick's
weekly newspaper column, "Along the Robeson Trail." Lumbees are mentioned in
many of the readings, but see especially "Where Did the Lumbees Come From?" (pp.
29-30) and "The Land of the Lumbee Was a Cultural Crossroads" (pp. 31-32).

RESOURCE CENTERS

1403. Indian Religion Museum [IRM]. Located behind the Burnt Swamp Baptist
Association Building, across from Pembroke State University's Performing
Arts Center. (919)-521-9850
Contains record books, photographs, albums, annual session programs, songbooks,
newsletters, and clippings related to the Odum Home and the 53 churches in the Burnt
Swamp Baptist Association. Each church has a separate display panel. Has a copy of
the Indian Child Welfare Assoc.'s constitution. See *Robesonian* 17 Sept. 1993: 9A.

1404. North Carolina State Archives. Division of Archives and History. N.C. Dept.
of Cultural Resources. 109 E. Jones St. Raleigh, NC 27611 [Not seen.]

Houses genealogical and local history resources (see West, entry 1031) and criminal action papers on the Lowry Band (entry 1075). Other materials are listed in Donna Spindel's *Introductory Guide to Indian-related Records (to 1876) in the North Carolina State Archives (Div. of Archives and History, 1977)*, pp. 23-24.

1405. Pembroke State University. Mary Livermore Library [PSU-MLL]. Pembroke, NC 28372. (919)-521-6000
Materials relevant to Lumbee research include: (1) the PSU Archives [catalogs, papers, reports, pamphlets, yearbooks, brochures, minutes, and memorabilia concerning the history of PSU and its faculty, from its founding in 1887 to the present.] (2) the PSU Clippings File [newspaper articles from 1943-1980, mainly from the *Robesonian*. News about Pembroke and Robeson County is included but is secondary to PSU news.] (3) the Special Collection [the standard monographs, some dissertations, literary works, historical works mentioning Lumbees, government publications, and a separately catalogued series of articles from periodicals.] All materials in the Special Collection are non-circulating but may be photocopied.

1406. Pembroke State University. Native American Resource Center [PSU-NARC]. Old Main. Pembroke, NC 28684. (919)-521-6000
The Center's displays and exhibits emphasize Lumbee artifacts, artwork, and historical events, but some include other Native American nations. Since Nov. 1987 it has produced a quarterly newsletter, *Spirit! of the Center* (North Carolina Documents Depository microfiche, G85 7:S75). The display on the Ku Klux Klan routing is permanent. Has a Reading Room (materials are non-circulating) and a collection of videotapes and audiotapes.

1407. Pembroke State University. Telecommunications Department. Film Library. Pembroke, NC 28372 (919)-521-6000 [Not seen.]
Houses videotapes produced for WPSU programs and other events. Topics include: Native American Protestantism; the *Robesonian* hostage-taking; *Strike at the Wind!*; Lumbee Homecoming parade and race, 1989; the PSU Centennial; shape-note singing; and interviews with Joseph Oxendine and Adolph Dial. To view the tapes, set up an appointment with the Telecommunications Department two weeks in advance. Copies can be ordered for $10.00 per tape. [From correspondence.]

1408. Public Schools of Robeson County. Indian Education Resource Center [IERC]. PO Box 847. Pembroke, NC 28372. (910)-521-1881 or 521-2054.
This collection emphasizes Robeson County Indians but also has information on other North Carolina tribes. Holdings include books, genealogical resources, oral history tapes, reports, scrapbooks, newspaper clippings, curriculum materials, and materials collected by prominent Lumbees. The Center houses many unique and valuable items and has a strong service orientation.

1409. Wilkins, David E., comp. "A Bibliography of Historical Documents, Materials, and Resources." Lumberton: Robeson County Compensatory Indian Education Project, n.d. 16p. [IERC] [Partially annotated; arranged by format.]

1410. Robeson County Public Library [RCPL]. 101 N. Chestnut St. Lumberton, NC

28359. (919)-738-4859

Noted for its extensive collection on Robeson County genealogy and local history. Reference service is strong in these areas. Owns the standard materials on Lumbees and on North Carolina Indians. The Genealogy Room contains: Robeson County court minutes; a cross-index to guardian returns, wills, settlements, and real estate conveyances; indexes to marriage bonds; records of estates, land grants, marriages and cohabitations, pensions, settlements, and wills; cemetery records; family and individual histories and genealogies; church histories; name indexes for the federal population census (Robeson County townships); and more. An obituary index to the *Robesonian* is in progress (see entry 1035).

1411. University of North Carolina at Chapel Hill. North Carolina Collection. Louis Round Wilson Library [UNC-WL]. Chapel Hill, NC. (919-962-1175)

Lumbee materials in many formats are listed in the card catalog. Materials added in recent years appear in UNC's online catalog. An extensive collection of newspaper clippings, *Indians of North Carolina* (3 vols.; also on microfilm), ranges from 1907 to 1975. Look under "Croatan Indians," "Lumbee Indians," and other relevant headings. Ask for later clippings at the Reference Counter. Materials do not circulate, but most can be photocopied.

1412. Ericson, Timothy L. "Establishing a Tribal Archives: An Archival Program Consultant Report for the Lumbee Regional Development Association." Unpublished manuscript. April 1985. [RCPL]

LRDA uncovered extensive historical materials on Lumbees during its federal recognition project and asked Ericson to help determine the most suitable location for a repository. Three potential sites completed a self-study and were visited by Ericson.

CHRONOLOGY OF SIGNIFICANT EVENTS
IN THE HISTORY OF ROBESON COUNTY INDIANS

DATE(S)   EVENT / SOURCE of DATE

12,000 B.C. – 1700   **1413**. Paleo-Indian, Archaic, and Woodland
                                 Periods. Projectile points discovered in the
                                 Robeson Trails Archaeological Survey prove
                                 Robeson County was occupied by Indians
                                 during these periods. [entry 1071, p. 15]

c. 1700 – 1708   **1414**. John Lawson encountered the Hatteras
                                 Indians, many of whom had gray eyes. They
                                 reported several White ancestors.
                                 [entry 505, p. (69)]

1835 (June 4 – July 11)   **1415**. A North Carolina constitution was
                                 enacted which disfranchised free Negroes,
                                 free mulattoes, and free persons of mixed
                                 blood. The constitution also forbade them to
                                 bear arms. [*N.C. Constitution, Amendments
                                 of 1835*, article 1, sec. 3, clause 3. Rpt. in
                                 North Carolina Government, 1585–1979
                                 (Raleigh, 1981), p. 820.]

1865 (March 3)   **1416**. Execution of Allen and William
                                 Lowry by the Home Guard. Beginning of
                                 Lowry Band period. [entry 1118, pp. 3, 15]

1865 – 1920's   **1417**. Period of Lumbee migration to the
                                 Claxton, Georgia area. [entry 994]

1874 (c. Feb. 23)   **1418**. Steve Lowry was killed by bounty
                                 hunters, marking the end of the Lowry Band
                                 period. [entry 1118, p. 241]

179

1875

1419. Publication of Mary C. Norment's *The Lowrie History*, the earliest detailed account of the Lowry Band. [entry 1083]

1875 (Sept. 6 – Oct. 11)

1420. The revised N.C. constitution restored the vote to free persons of color (males, 21 or older). [*N.C. Constitution, Amendments of 1875*, article 6 section 1]

1877

1421. The Burnt Swamp Baptist Association was organized during a meeting at Old Burnt Swamp Church. It was sponsored by the Rev. F. Prevatte, with the Rev. Cary Wilkins as the first moderator. [entry 396]

1885 (Feb. 10)

1422. Passage of a N.C. law naming county Indians "Croatan Indians" and providing for separate schools. [entry 1306]

1887 (March 7)

1423. Passage of a North Carolina law establishing a Croatan normal school (the predecessor of Pembroke State University). [entry 1308]

1887 (Fall)

1424. Beginning of classes at the Croatan Normal School. [entry 264, p. 19]

1888

1425. Publication of *Sir Walter Raleigh's Lost Colony* by Hamilton McMillan, proposing Lumbee descent from the Lost Colonists and Manteo's tribe. [entry 506]

1888 (Dec. 4)

1426. A petition with 54 signatures, asserting Croatan Indian identity and requesting funds for the Croatan Normal School, was recorded as received by the U.S. Congress [*Congressional Record*, 50th Cong., 2nd Sess., 4 Dec. 1888, p. 25]. This petition has been cited as Robeson County Indians' first attempt at federal recognition and their first request for assistance from the federal government (see entry 1380, pp. 1, 100). Rpt. in entry 49, exhibit B1. See entry 57, Table 11, for a list of names on this petition and on the 1887 petition to the North Carolina legislature.

1911 (Mar. 8)

1427. A North Carolina law changed the tribal name from "Croatan Indians" to

"Indians of Robeson County." [entry 1322]

1912 (March 2)

1428. Charles F. Pierce, U.S. Indian Service, reported on a visit to Pembroke and recommended against federal funding of a boarding school for county Indians. [entry 1324]

1913 (March 11)

1429. Passage of a North Carolina law changing the tribal name from "Indians of Robeson County" to "Cherokee Indians of Robeson County." [entry 1327]

1914 (Sept. 19)

1430. Completion of the *McPherson Report*, the most detailed study of the origins and conditions of Robeson County's Indians that had ever been undertaken. It was transmitted to the Senate on Jan. 4, 1915 ["Letter of Transmittal," entry 49, p. 5].

c. 1930's–1945

1431. Period of heaviest Lumbee migration to Baltimore. [entry 944, pp. 43-44]

1933

1432. Appearance of John R. Swanton's paper, "Probable Identity of the 'Croatan' Indians," which began a movement for federal recognition as Siouans. [entry 535]

1935 (April 8)

1433. Felix Cohen's memorandum states that Robeson County Indians with 1/2 or more Indian blood can organize and receive federal benefits under the Wheeler-Howard Indian Reorganization Act of 1934. [entry 606]

1938 (June 25)

1434. A certificate of incorporation for Red Banks Mutual Association was filed in the North Carolina Secretary of State's office. [*Robesonian* 27 June 1938: 2]

1938 (Dec. 12)

1435. William Zimmerman (federal Office of Indian Affairs) notified Joseph Brooks that 22 of 209 Siouan Indians tested by Carl Seltzer were eligible for federal recognition under the Wheeler-Howard Act. [entry 610]

1940 (May 31)

1436. Cherokee Indian Normal School graduated its first four-year-degree students (four men and one woman). [*Robesonian* 3 June 1940: 3]

1940 (Dec. 5)	**1437.** First performance of Ella Deloria's pageant, "The Life Story of a People," in the Cherokee Indian Normal School gymnasium. [*Robesonian* 6 Dec. 1940: 1]
1942 (October)	**1438.** Opening of the Odum Home Indian Orphanage. [entry 887]
1945 (April 24)	**1439.** Town of Pembroke held its first popular election for town officials. They had been appointed by the governor. [entry 781]
1953 (April 20)	**1440.** Passage of a North Carolina law changing the tribal name to "Lumbee Indians of North Carolina." [entry 1359]
1954 (Dec. 5)	**1441.** Early Bullard was sworn into office as judge of the Maxton Recorder's Court. He was the county's first Indian judge and was said to be the first Indian to hold a county-level elected office. [*Robesonian* 7 Dec. 1954: 9; entry 790]
1956 (June 7)	**1442.** Passage of the federal Lumbee Act (PL 84-570), designating the Indians living in Robeson County "Lumbee Indians of North Carolina." [entry 1363]
1958 (Jan. 18)	**1443.** Lumbee routing of the Ku Klux Klan, near Maxton. [entry 1161]
1958 (May 31)	**1444.** Tracy Sampson was elected as Robeson County's first Indian county commissioner. [*Robesonian* 2 June 1958: 1]
1963 (April 1)	**1445.** Harry West Locklear began his term as the first Indian member of the Robeson County Board of Education. [entry 99]
1963 (June)	**1446.** English E. Jones became the first Lumbee president of Pembroke State College. He had served as interim president since Sept., 1962. [entry 54, pp. 60, 84]
1967	**1447.** Appearance of Lew Barton's *The Most Ironic Story in American History*, the first detailed, commercially published history of Lumbee Indians. [entry 53]

1968 (Jan. 31)	**1448**. The Regional Development Association was chartered. It was later renamed Lumbee Regional Development Association. [entry 57, p. 209]
1968 (c. April 23)	**1449**. For the first time, nonwhite voter registration in Robeson County exceeded White registration. [entry 796]
1968 (c. July)	**1450**. Red Banks Mutual Association, the last surviving Farm Security Administration cooperative farming project, was dissolved [entry 1158]. The corporation was suspended by the North Carolina Secretary of State on 9-21-70. The charter expired on 9-21-75. [From correspondence]
1969	**1451**. Brantley Blue was the only Indian appointed to the 4-member Indian Claims Commission. [entry 1010]
1969 (July 1)	**1452**. Pembroke State College gained regional university status and was renamed Pembroke State University. [entry 1366]
1970 (May 25)	**1453**. First formal meeting of Independent Americans for Progress–called the first Lumbee political organization. [entry 798]
1970 (June 19)	**1454**. Formal inauguration of Baltimore's American Indian Study Center, which had operated informally for two years. [entry 935]
1970 (July 4)	**1455**. First Lumbee Homecoming was held at Pembroke. [*Robesonian* 5 July 1970: 8A]
1970 (Sept. 10)	**1456**. End of Indian students' sit-ins over the county's desegregation plan. [entry 113]
1971	**1457.** Appearance of W. McKee Evans' *To Die Game*, the most comprehensive published history of the Lowry Band. [entry 1118]
1971 (July 20)	**1458**. Passage of a North Carolina law creating the North Carolina State Commission of Indian Affairs. Bruce Jones, Lumbee, has served as Director. [1971 *Session Laws of North Carolina* ch. 1013]

1971 (Dec. 22)

1459. Opening ceremonies were held for the Lumbee Bank of Pembroke. [*Robesonian* 23 Dec. 1971: 2]

1971 (December 30)

1460. Formation of the Eastern Carolina Indian Organization. [entry 724]

1972 (August)

1461. Pembroke State University's American Indian Studies Department began offering courses. [*Robesonian* 3 Aug. 1972: 16]

1972 (September)

1462. Horace Locklear became the first Indian to practice law in N.C. [entry 804]

1972 (October)

1463. 150 Tuscaroras (Eastern Carolina Indian Organization) went to Washington to support the Trail of Broken Treaties. They helped occupy the BIA Building and stole 7,200 pounds of records. [entry 751, p. 7]

1972 (Dec. 15)

1464. Tuscarora Indians in Robeson and surrounding counties organized and elected Howard Brooks as their chief. [entry 727]

1973 (Jan. 18)

1465. The first weekly issue of the *Carolina Indian Voice* was published. [entry 56 p. (3)]

1973 (March 15)

1466. Henry Ward Oxendine became the first Indian to serve in the N.C. House of Representatives. [*Robesonian* 18 March 1973: 1A]

1973 (March 18)

1467. Burning of Old Main (PSU's first brick building, constructed in 1923). [entry 229]

1974 (Sept. 30)

1468. Indian Education Act funds were granted to county schools and LRDA, due to Lumbees' status as Indians. Beginning of the county's Title IV, Part A Compensatory Indian Education Act program. [entry 140, p. 434]

1975

1469. Publication of Dial and Eliades' *The Only Land I Know*. [entry 54]

1975 (early March)

1470. Adolph Dial was one of five Indians appointed to the American Indian Policy Review Commission. [entry 644]

1975 (April 4)

1471. In *Maynor v. Morton*, the federal court

held that the "Original 22" remained eligible for benefits under the Wheeler-Howard Indian Reorganization Act of 1934, despite the Lumbee Act. [entry 1372]

1975 (April 23)

1472. The U.S. Court of Appeals, in *Janie Maynor Locklear vs. North Carolina Board of Elections*, ruled that double-voting was unconstitutional. [entry 1370]

1975 (Sept. 5)

1473. Guilford Native American Association was incorporated. [entry 988, p. (1)]

1976 (Jan. 5)

1474. Metrolina Native American Association was incorporated. [entry 1000]

1976 (July 1)

1475. First performance of "Strike at the Wind!" [*Robesonian* 2 July 1976: 1]

1978 (Nov. 22)

1476. Lumbee River Legal Services was incorporated by Julian T. Pierce. [Articles of Incorporation, Lumbee River Legal Services]

1980

1477. Appearance of Karen Blu's *The Lumbee Problem*. [entry 55]

1980 (Feb. 16)

1478. Rededication of Old Main, seven years after it was gutted by arsonists. [entry 255]

1980 (c. June 18–20)

1479. Lumbees were voted into membership of the National Congress of American Indians at the NCAI's mid-year conference in Reno, Nevada. [*CIV* 31 July 1980: 1]

1984 (Jan. 26)

1480. The Tuscarora Tribe of North Carolina was chartered by the state of North Carolina. It encompasses the Hatteras Tuscaroras, Drowning Creek Tuscaroras, and Eastern Carolina Tuscaroras. [entry 755, p. 68]

1985 (December)

1481. Establishment of a corporation to manage planning for the North Carolina Indian Cultural Center, marking the beginning of that project. [*CIV* 21 March 1991: 5]

1986 (Nov. 1)

1482. Jimmy Earl Cummings was killed by Deputy Kevin Stone. The event prompted the formation of Concerned Citizens for Better

Government and a new era of Indian activism in Robeson County. [entry 1201 p. A5]

1987 (March 5)   **1483**. Pembroke State University celebrated its centennial with many activities. [entry 268]

1987 (Dec. 17)   **1484**. Submission of *Lumbee Petition* to the Branch of Acknowledgement and Research, Bureau of Indian Affairs. [entry 1380, p. 58]

1988   **1485**. Completion of the Robeson Trails Archaeological Survey, documenting 314 previously unrecorded sites. [entry 1071]

1988 (Feb. 1)   **1486**. Eddie Hatcher and Timothy Jacobs, Tuscaroras, held *Robesonian* employees hostage for 10 hours, protesting inequities toward Robeson County Indians. [entry 1206]

1988 (March 8)   **1487**. Robeson County residents voted to merge their five school systems into one system. [*CIV* 10 March 1988: 1]

1988 (March 26)   **1488**. Murder of Julian Pierce, Lumbee lawyer and judgeship candidate. [entry 1218]

1988 (July 14)   **1489**. Introduction of first of a series of bills seeking true federal recognition for Lumbee Indians. [entries 1379, 1382, 1385, 1389]

1989 (Jan. 3)   **1490**. Dexter Brooks became North Carolina's first Indian Superior Court judge. [*CIV* 5 Jan. 1989: 1; entry 866]

1989 (Oct. 27)   **1491**. Joseph B. Oxendine was installed as the second Lumbee president (now called chancellor) of Pembroke State University. [entry 277]

1989 (Dec. 5)   **1492**. Tuscarora Tribe of N.C. submitted a petition for federal recognition to the BIA. [entry 756]

1992 (Nov. 3)   **1493**. Ronnie Sutton was elected the first state representative from N.C.'s new, largely Indian District 85. [*CIV* 5 Nov. 1992: 1]

1993   **1494**. Appearance of Gerald Sider's *Lumbee Indian Histories*. [entry 59]

A DECADE OF SERVICE; PROGRESS
By Lew Barton

[From: *Carolina Indian Voice*, 10th Anniversary Edition, January 20, 1980, p. 1.]

Since January 1, 1973, my eldest son Bruce Barton has been articulating the affairs and concerns of the North Carolina Indians ... and of all Indians generally. Aided and abetted by a younger brother (Garry Lewis Barton) and a younger sister (Connee Brayboy), he has made journalistic and publishing history. For one thing, although a number of former attempts were made, theirs has been the only Indian periodical in the state to survive, all the others sooner or later falling by the wayside. *The Indian Observer*, the *Pembroke Progress*, the *Lumbee* ... these and other "voices" saw the light of day for a brief span, then lapsed into silence. Yet for a full decade, come Hades or high water, the *Carolina Indian Voice* has prevailed, issue after issue appearing as regularly as clockwork.

In a tri-racial setting such as ours in Robeson County, North Carolina, that is no small accomplishment. I salute these younger people, armed only with Indian determination and their brighter dreams of a more glorious tomorrow for all our people. They have truly made Robeson a better county in which to live. They have, in fact, enhanced Indian life throughout the state.

Interestingly enough, the life of the *Carolina Indian Voice* has coincided with the Indian renaissance, experienced not only in this but also in other states of the nation. We saw our Robeson Indians become national models for Indian education and Indian economic advancement generally. We saw individuals from our own group take high and great places of natural Indian leadership, and come away with honor after honor. And so it is that the *Carolina Indian Voice* has much to celebrate, much for which to be justly proud.

The news covered during those ten years has not been all good, but neither has it been all bad. And there have been more success stories, I believe, than stories of violence and mayhem. The paper has observed, reported, formulated and expressed opinion. But it has not only observed and reported upon life in unique Robeson. It has also become an integral part of that life.

One of the most important functions of the *Carolina Indian Voice* is that it has helped one Indian in one location keep in touch with another Indian in another. And it has helped to keep the Indian community at large functioning as a single unit, in a very real sense. We have no longer been totally isolated from each other, striving to continue without communication.

God bless the *Carolina Indian Voice* and those who strive so faithfully to keep it afloat, in good times and bad. It has touched all our lives, and mostly for good. May it continue to publish and flourish in all the decades ahead for the blessing and edification of us all!

The paper has helped to right wrongs, air grievances, improve bad situations and make our very lives more liveable. Any community without a voice is a sad community, indeed. And no matter what anyone may contend to the contrary, the *Carolina Indian Voice*, in fact, has been just that ... a community voice.

Some ten years ago, I had fears that the Indian community might eventually disappear altogether. We no longer had our community schools and their related activities, per se. What was going to happen to us? Now, a decade later, I am more confident than ever that the Indian community will go on forever.

We are experts at survival. I still grow misty-eyed when I recall from Indian tradition how that little band of colonists and Indians set out from "Roanoke in Virginia" (now Roanoke Island, North Carolina) to brave the perils of a vast, untamed wilderness in 1587. We have faced up to all the rigors and dangers between that point in time and now and have been victorious.

Yes, Brandi, my sweet little granddaughter, and Dennis, my equally sweet little grandson, in case you ever ask, as I am sure you will, there will always be Robeson Indians. Bruce, Connee and Garry, like their father, have printer's ink in their veins. Moreover, they have the love of their community in their hearts, and thus I am reassured.

EDITOR'S NOTE:

Since the original article was written in 1983 as part of the *Carolina Indian Voice*'s 10th year anniversary, some changes have occurred. The most obvious and traumatic one is that Bruce Barton resigned as editor of the *Carolina Indian Voice* in 1986; he was ably replaced by Connee Barton Brayboy, who continues to carry the Bartons' journalistic tradition forward. Bruce Barton, whose only explanation for stepping down is that "... I was spiritually depleted ...," is now a social studies teacher in the Robeson County Schools. Lew Barton, the progenitor of the Barton clan, now lives sublimely in retirement in Pembroke resting on his 73 years of laurels. Garry Lewis Barton continues as a typesetter and darkroom mechanic for a newspaper chain in nearby South Carolina.

Bruce Barton
Pembroke, North Carolina
May 1, 1991

Index to the *Carolina Indian Voice*
January 18, 1973 - February 4, 1993*

A

A & A Insurance
Agency
-Opening:
Ag 3 78: 1.
AIDS
Dc 19 91: 3.
Accountants
Ag 26 82: 6.
Achievement Test
Scores:
Ag 3 78: 9.
Achievements
*Ap 26 73: 1.
L Ag 30 73: 2.
L Se 20 73: 2.
•See also Firsts.
Akwesasne Notes
Nv 22 73: 4.
Alcohol Abuse
-Counseling:
Ja 12 78: 6.
•See also
Pembroke
Center.
Alcohol Abuse
-Robeson
County
--Statistics:
Ap 6 78: 6.
Alcoholic
Beverages
-Referendum:

Nv 6 75: 1.
Alcoholic
Beverages
-Sale:
Dc 11 75: 1.
Dc 18 75: 1.
Allen, Young H.
L Ap 18 74: 2.
Ap 10 75: 1.
E Ju 5 75: 1, 2.
"Along the
Robeson Trail."
•By Stan Knick.
Weekly column,
beginning
5/24/90.
Alpha Cellulose
E Jl 19 90: 2.
American Indian
Movement:
E Ap 5 73: 2.
Ja 31 74: 2.
American Indian
Policy Review
Commission:
Ja 2 75: 5.
E Mr 13 75: 1.
Ap 17 75: 7.
Jl 24 75: 1.
Ag 7 75: 1.
Fe 12 76: 2.
E Fe 19 76: 2.
L Fe 26 76: 2.
Ap 1 76: 2.

Ap 15 76: 1.
My 5 77: 8.
My 19 77: 1.
•See also Dial,
Adolph.
American Indian
Studies:
My 15 75: 5.
Nv 6 75: 8.
Ammons, Kirby
BP Fe 23 84: 1.
P My 23 85: 1.
Ancipio, Forenzio
Nv 11 76: 6.
Oc 19 78: 6.
Anderson, Wallace
Mr 12 87: 8.
Andrade, Adrian:
Fe 25 93: 1.
P Jl 15 93: 1.
Annexations, see
Education and
Schools--School
Districts--
Annexations.
Applewhite,
George:
Dc 5 91: 2.
Archaeology
-Buie Mound:
P Fe 6 75: 1-2.
-Excavations:
E Fe 6 75: 1, 2.
Jl 21 83: 1.

AP Jl 2 87: 1.
Chavis, Perry
   Oc 15 87: 1.
Chavis, Randall
   BP My 26 83: 1.
Chavis, Reedie L.
   BP Ja 7 93: 1.
Chavis, Sandy J.:
   Mr 16 89: 1.
   E Ju 15 89: 2.
   Ju 7 90: 1.
Chavis, Spencer
   BP My 19 83: 1.
   Jl 19 84: 10.
Chavis, Ted
   P Se 24 87: 1.
Chavis, Walter S.
   OP Jl 31 75: 1.
Chavis, William E.:
   Mr 24 77: 1.
Chavis, Z. R.
   (Zimmie):
   AP Se 9 76: 4.
   B Oc 27 77: 7.
Chavis Alarm and
   Lock Co.:
   Se 24 87: 1.
Cherokee Chapel
   Baptist Church
-History:
   Ja 13 77: 4.
Cherokee Indians
   Oc 24 74: 1.
   E Nv 7 74: 2.
   L Ja 27 77: 2.
Cherokee Indians of
   Hoke County:
   Mr 24 83: 2.
   L Dc 15 83: 2.
   L Dc 27 84: 2.
   L Ja 10 85: 2.
   My 5 88: 1.
   E Dc 14 89: 2.
   L Ju 21 90: 6.
   L Jl 19 90: 4.
-Christian Mission
   School:
   Se 8 83: 7.

-Lawsuits:
   L Ap 12 90: 2.
-Recognition
   (State):
   O 19 89: 2.
Cherokee Indians of
   Robeson County:
   E Ag 10 78: 2.
   L Ag 17 78: 2.
   L Ju 28 79: 2.
   Oc 29 92: 2.
•See also United
   Cherokee Nation
   of North
   Carolina, Inc.;
   Tribal Name
Cherokee Indians of
   Western North
   Carolina:
   Ju 19 86: 1.
   L Mr 1 90: 5.
   L Ju 11 '92: 2.
-Bingo:
   Jl 7 83: 6.
-Festivals:
   Se 29 88: 1.
Cherokee-Powhatan
   Indian Associ-
   ation (Person
   County):
   Mr 1 84: 5.
Children
-Health:
   L Fe 7 85: 2.
   E Fe 14 85: 2.
   My 28 92: 2.
Church of God
-Removal of local
   ministers:
   Fe 8 79: 1, 9.
   Mr 1 79: 1.
   Mr 8 79: 1.
Churches
-Overview:
   *Oc 27 77: 4.
•See also names
   of specific
   churches; names

of denominations
   or ministers.
Citizens' Groups
   Ja 8 81: 1.
•See also names
   of groups.
Clark, Celeste
   P Se 9 92: 4.
Clark, Pete
   BP Ja 26 84: 1.
Clark, Raymond L.
   BP Mr 21 91: 1.
Clark, Telford
   BP Ja 28 88: 1.
Clark, Tony
   P Ja 24 91: 1.
Clark, Vinita
   AP Dc 5 91: 1.
Clark's Body Shop
   P Ja 28 88: 1.
Claxton (GA)
   Se 4 75: 3.
   E Se 19 85: 2.
   E Se 26 85: 2.
   E Oc 3 85: 2.
   Oc 10 85: 2.
   Dc 5 85: 2.
   Dc 12 85: 2.
   Dc 19 85: 2.
   Ja 2 86: 2.
   Ja 9 86: 2.
   Ja 30 86: 2.
   Fe 27 86: 2.
   P Ju 22 89: 4.
   Nv 29 90: 1.
   Ja 31 91: 1.
   Ja 14 93: 2.
   Ja 21 93: 2.
Clyburn Pines, see
   Lumberton (City)
   -School Dis-
   trict-An-
   nexations.
Coalition of Eastern
   Native
   Americans:
   Ja 18 73: 1.
   EP Ja 24 74: 1,

Nv 20 75: 8.
Crime, see
  Pembroke
  (Town)–Crime.
Criminal Justice
  System (Lumbees
  and), see
  Robeson
  County–Criminal
  Justice System.
Cruising
  E Mr 15 90: 2.
Crusade, Interde-
  nominational, see
  Robeson County
  Area-Wide
  Crusade.
Culture, see Identity
  /Indianness/Cul-
  ture
Cumberland County
  Association of
  Indian People:
  Se 4 75: 1.
  Dc 11 75: 3.
  Fe 12 76: 8.
  Oc 6 77: 6.
  Ap 9 81: 6.
  Dc 30 82: 6.
Cumberland County
  Indians
  -Les Maxwell
  School:
  Dc 13 79: 1.
Cummings, C. H.
  Ja 29 87: 4.
Cummings, C. M.
  (Rev. Coolidge
  Mack):
  BP Ag 20 92: 1.
Cummings, DeLora
  P Oc 1 87: 3.
  BP Ju 21 90: 1.
  Ju 28 90: 1.
Cummings, Earl
  BP Nv 15 84: 9.
  BP Dc 20 84: 4.
Cummings, Evelyn

BP Mr 17 88: 1.
Cummings, Evelyn
  L.:
  B Jl 15 76: 1.
Cummings, Foy
  BP My 26 88: 1.
Cummings, Frances
  M.:
  P Fe 20 75: 3.
Cummings, Frances
  McArthur:
  A Ag 13 87:1.
Cummings, Grady
  O Se 12 85: 2.
Cummings, Greg
  P Ap 18 85: 1.
Cummings, Hilda
  "Bloss":
  BP My 26 88: 1.
Cummings, Jimmy
  Earl:
  E Nv 20 86: 1, 2.
  Nv 27 86: 1.
  L Dc 4 86: 1, 2.
  Ja 1 87: 2.
  EL Ja 8 87: 1, 2.
  Ja 15 87: 2.
  L Ja 22 87: 2.
  Ja 29 87: 1.
  Fe 5 87: 1.
  L Fe 12 87: 2.
  L Mr 12 87: 2.
  Ap 16 87: 1.
  Ap 23 87: 1, 3.
  Ju 18 87: 1.
  Nv 3 88: 1.
  E Nv 10 88: 2.
  E Mr 23 89: 2.
  L Ju 15 89: 2.
  E Ja 18 90: 2.
  EP Mr 8 90: 1-2.
  *Mr 15 90: 1.
  -Coroner's Inquest:
  *Nv 5'87: 5-8.
Cummings, Lula
  Mae:
  E Mr 16 89: 2.
  E Ag 31 89: 2.

Cummings,
  McDuffie:
  P Ja 30 75: 5.
  E Mr 6 80: 1, 2.
  Mr 13 80: 1.
  E Mr 17 88: 1, 2.
Cummings, Oscar
  BP Ap 5 84: 1.
Cummings, Robin
  Ja 30 75: 3.
Cummings, Robin
  G. (Dr.):
  BP Ag 20 92: 1.
Cummings, Robin
  Gary:
  P Ju 2 83: 1.
Cummings, Samuel
  M. (Dr.):
  BP Dc 19 91: 1.
Cummings,
  Simeon:
  Ju 7 73: 1.
  Ju 9 83: 1.
  Ju 23 83: 9.
  Ju 14 84: 2.
Cummings, Simeon
  Dufrene:
  P Ju 2 83: 1.
  A Ju 7 84: 1.
Cummings, Simeon
  F.:
  Ju 14 79: 1.
Cummings, Stacy,
  Jr.:
  P Fe 24 83: 8.
Cummings, Susan
  BP Jl 14 83: 7.
Cummings Family
  (Singing Group):
  E Ja 3 91: 2.
  P Ap 16 92: 1.
Cut and Sew
  Fabrics:
  Nv 5 87: 1.

D

D & L Gospel

Fe 27 75: 4.
Nv 30 78: 1.
Dial, Danford
  E Jl 19 73: 1, 2,
  3.
  Jl 26 73: 2.
  Nv 29 84: 2.
  B P Ap 25 91: 1.
Dial, Elizabeth
-Family Reunion:
  P Ag 2 73: 1.
Dial, Faye Oxend-
ine:
  P Mr 27 80: 1.
Dial, Harold G.
  Ja 3 91: 3.
Dial, Harriet
  P Oc 17 91: 3.
Dial, Herman
  E Ag 3 78: 2.
  P *Se 23 82: 1.
  *Se 30 82: 1.
Dial, James (Rev.)
  Fe 21 85: 1.
Dial, James H.
  B Oc 8 81: 1.
Dial, James M.
  B Se 16 82: 7.
  Se 23 82: 6.
  Se 30 82: 6.
  OP Fe 3 83: 9.
Dial, Johnny
  Fe 7 85: 1.
  P Fe 14 85: 1.
Dial, Marcus
-Family Reunion:
  P Ag 2 73: 1.
  Dc 28 78: 3.
Dial, Marcus
-Genealogy:
  Se 16 82: 2.
  P Se 23 82: 1.
Dial, Mary Ellen
  Moore:
  O Ju 14 73: 1.
Dial, Nora
  AP Fe 21 85: 1.
Dial, Ruby

-Poem about:
  Jl 21 77: 8.
Dial, Ruby C.
  BP Oc 14 76: 1.
Dial, Sam
  Fe 10 77: 1.
  AP Fe 24 77: 1.
  E Ja 10 80: 2.
  AP Mr 26 87: 1.
  BP Fe 2 89: 1.
  P Oc 31 91: 1.
Dial, Tommie
  Fe 16 84: 2.
Dial, Tommy
  A Dc 25 75: 1.
Dial, William
  Ap 11 85: 1.
Diane's Cosmetic
  Outlet
-Opening:
  P Dc 15 83: 1.
Directories
  Mr 20 75: 7.
  Jl 9 92: 3.
Discrimination, see
  Robeson
  County–Race
  Relations.
Dogwood Baptist
  Church
-History:
  P Fe 17 77: 6.
DOUBLE-VOTING
  E *Ja 18 73: 2
  [Incl. text of
  Attorney
  General's
  opinion].
  *Fe 1 73: 1
  [Incl. text of bill
  to abolish].
  E Fe 8 73: 1, 2.
  Fe 22 73: 2.
  Mr 1 73: 1.
  E *Mr 8 73: 1, 2.
  Mr 15 73: 1, 2.
  Ad. Mr 22 73: 4.
  E Ap 12 73: 2.

L Ap 19 73: 1, 2.
My 3 73: 1.
My 31 73: 1, 3.
L Jl 12 73: 2.
L Jl 26 73: 1.
E Nv 1 73: 2.
L Nv 22 73: 2.
EL Dc 6 73: 1, 2.
L Dc 20 73: 2.
L Dc 27 73: 2.
EL Ja 3 74: 1, 2.
E Ja 10 74: 2, 3.
Ja 17 74: 1.
Ja 24 74: 1.
Fe 7 74: 1, 5.
E *Fe 14 74: 1, 2,
  5.
L *Fe 21 74: 1, 2.
L Mr 7 74: 2.
L Mr 14 74: 2.
Ap 4 74: 1.
*Ju 6 74: 1.
EL *Ju 27 74: 1.
*Jl 4 74: 2.
L Jl 11 74: 2.
L Jl 25 74: 2.
L *Se 26 74: 2.
Nv 14 74: 1.
Dc 24 74: 1.
E Ja 2 75: 2.
E Ja 9 75: 2.
Ja 16 75: 1, 2.
Ja 23 75: 1, 8.
E Mr 27 75: 2.
E Ap 24 75: 2.
E *My 1 75: 1, 2,
  7.
EL My 8 75: 1, 2.
E My 22 75: 2.
My 29 75: 1.
E *Ju 5 75: 1, 2.
*Ju 19 75: 1.
*Jl 10 75: 1.
E Jl 17 75: 2.
E Jl 24 75: 2.
E Oc 2 75: 2.
Nv 20 75: 1.
Fe 5 76: 1.

My 24 79: 1.
Ju 14 79: 12.
Jl 12 79: 1, 8.
Ag 2 79: 1.
Se 13 79: 1.
Oc 11 79: 1.
L Dc 6 79: 2.
Ja 3 80: 1.
Ag 14 80: 1.
E Oc 16 80: 2.
E Ja 22 81: 2.
EL Ja 29 81: 2.
Ap 2 81: 10.
My 7 81: 1.
E My 14 81: 2.
Ju 4 81: 1.
Ju 11 81: 1.
Dc 10 81: 1.
Se 23 82: 1.
L Fe 16 84: 2.
L Mr 1 84: 2.
L Mr 29 84: 2.
L Ap 5 84: 2.
*Nv 29 84: 1.
Fe 14 85: 1.
E My 29 86: 1.
Ju 5 86: 1.
Ju 12 86: 1.
Ju 19 86: 1.
Ju 26 86: 1.
Jl 3 86: 1.
Jl 10 86: 1.
Jl 17 86: 1.
Jl 24 86: 1.
Jl 31 86: 1.
Ag 7 86: 1.
Ag 14 86: 1.
Ja 8 87: 7.
Ja 29 87: 3.
L Fe 12 87: 2.
Fe 19 87: 1.
E Jl 9 86: 1, 2.
E Jl 16 87: 1.
L Jl 23 87: 2.
EL Ag 6 87: 2.
L Ag 13 87: 2.
Dc 17 87: 1.
E Ja 21 88: 2.

L Ja 28 88: 2.
L Fe 4 88: 2.
EL Fe 11 88: 2.
L Fe 18 88: 2.
L 21 78: 2.
Fe 25 88: 1, 2.
EL Mr 3 88: 1, 2.
*Mr 10 88: 1.
*Mr 17 88: 1.
Ag 31 89: 1.
E Ja 17 91: 2.
E Mr 7 91: 2.
E Ap 4 91: 2.
--Redistricting:
    Se 8 83: 2.
    E Se 15 83: 2.
    E Se 22 83: 2, 8.
    E Oc 6 83: 2.
Education, Higher
    L My 7 81: 1.
-1920's-1930's:
    *Jl 12 84: 1, 5.
-Minorities:
    Oc 16 80: 1.
Elders
    L Ju 7 84: 2.
    P Jl 1 93: 6-11.
    P Jl 29 93: 6.
ELECTIONS
    Ag 2 73: 2.
    Oc 11 73: 7.
    Oc 18 73: 1.
    Nv 1 73: 1.
    Ja 17 74: 1, 5.
    P Fe 21 74: 1.
    PE Fe 28 74: 1, 2.
    L Mr 14 74: 2.
    L Mr 21'74: 2.
    L Ap 4 74: 2.
    P My 2 74: 1, 5.
    PL My 9 74: 1, 2.
    PE My 16 74: 1,
      2.
    My 23 74: 2.
    E My 30 74: 1, 2.
    Ju 6 74: 1.
    EL Ju 13 74: 2.
    L Ju 20 74: 2.

Ju 27 74: 1, 4.
Ag 15 74: 1.
P Se 12 74: 1, 7.
Oc 24 74: 1.
Se 25 75: 1.
Oc 2 75: 1.
P Oc 9 75: 1.
P Oc 16 75: 1.
Oc 23 75: 1.
Dc 18 75: 1.
P Mr 11 76: 1.
Ap 8 76: 1.
Oc 31 74: 1.
L Nv 7 74: 1, 2.
P Se 11 75: 1, 6.
Se 18 75: 1.
Ap 15 76: 1.
P My 13 76: 1.
My 20 76: 9.
Ag 5 76: 1.
Ag 19 76: 1.
Oc 21 76: 1.
E Oc 28 76: 1, 2.
Nv 4 76: 1.
Ja 12 78: 1.
Ja 19 78: 1.
Ja 26 78: 1, 2.
Fe 2 78: 1.
Fe 9 78: 1.
Fe 16 78: 1.
Ap 27 78: 1.
My 4 78: 1.
My 11 78: 1.
My 25 78: 1.
Ju 1 78: 1.
Oc 4 79: 1.
Nv 1 79: 1.
Nv 8 79: 1.
Ja 17 80: 1.
Ja 24 80: 1.
Fe 7 80: 1.
Ap 10 80: 1.
Ap 17 80: 2.
Ap 24 80: 1.
My 1 80: 1, 17.
My 8 80: 1.
Ju 5 80: 1.
Nv 6 80: 2.

Hazardous
Waste Disposal.
Epps, Grace Smith
A Se 16 76: 1.
BP Oc 7 76: 4.
O *Ju 4 81: 2, 5.

Fairgrove High
School
-Class of 1959
--Reunion:
P Jl 11 74: 4.
Fairmont (Town)
-Board of Education
--Elections:
Ju 24 76: 1.
Faith Baptist
Church:
Ag 13 87: 3.
Family Dollar Store
-Opening:
Fe 2 84: 1.
P Fe 16 84: 1.
Farming
Se 24 81: 8.
Ap 17 86: 1.
Ap 24 86: 10.
Ap 25 91: 1.
•See also
Tobacco
Farming; Okra
Cutter.
Federal Recog-
nition, see
Recognition
(Federal).
Fertility, see
Vital Statistics.
Festivals, Indian,
see Conferences
and Festivals.
Films
Se 25 80: 10.
Oc 23 80: 9.
Se 11 86: 1.
•See also

Pembroke State
University--
Videotapes.
First American
Civil Rights
Organization:
Ja 8 81: 1.
First American
Cooperative
Warehouse:
L Ja 13 77: 2.
Mr 17 77: 1, 5.
P Mr 24 77: 1.
P Jl 7 77: 8.
P Jl 21 77: 1.
Ju 11 81: 2.
First Baptist Church
(Lumberton):
Se 30 76: 1.
First Union
National Bank
(Pembroke):
P My 15 75: 1.
First United
Methodist Church
(Pembroke):
*Ja 17 91: 1.
Firsts
My 31 73: 3.
Ju 7 73: 1.
Ju 21 73: 1, 4.
*Jl 19 73: 7.
Ag 15 74: 1.
L Ag 22 74: 2.
Ag 11 77: 1.
Se 6 79: 1.
Ag 26 82: 6.
Mr 15 84: 1.
Ju 11 87: 1.
Se 24 87: 1.
Dc 22 88: 1.
Ap 27 89: 1.
5-G's Antique and
Classic Car
Museum:
-Opening:
Ag 28 80: 1.
Se 4 80: 8.

5-G's Day Care
Center
-Opening:
Dc 18 80: 1.
5-G's Man-
ufacturing:
A Ju 17 93: 1.
Fleetwood Mobile
Homes (Pem-
broke Plant):
Se 2 82: 1.
E Se 9 82: 2.
P My 2 85: 1.
P Ap 23 87: 1.
P My 21 87: 1.
P Ap 25 91: 5.
-Strike:
E Ag 22 85: 1.
Folk Medicine
Ap 21 83: 7.
Folklore
Ap 21 77: 3.
Oc 18 90: 2.
Football
Ja 25 73: 3.
P Dc 11 75: 5.
•See also Sports.
4-H, see Robeson
County Agricul-
tural Extension
Service 4-H.
Freda's Kwik Stop
-Opening:
P Ag 26 82: 1.
P Se 2 82: 1.
Freeman, Ursula
Sampson:
AP Se 19 91: 1.
Freeman's Sporting
Goods and
Appliances:
Nv 21 74: 8.
Frinks, Golden
Ap 12 73: 1.
E Ap 19 73: 2.
Fuller's Restaurant
Oc 8 87: 1.

Haliwa-Saponi
  Indians:
  Ju 26 80: 1.
  Nv 13 80: 1.
Hall, Doris H.:
  BP Ju 14 90: 3.
Hammonds, Albert
  BP Se 21 78: 7.
Hammonds, Clara
  P Ja 27 83: 11.
Hammonds, James
  Allen (Shorty):
  BP Ag 10 78: 6.
Hammonds, Ronald
  P Se 9 92: 3.
Happy Echoes
  (Singing Group):
  P Ap 16 92: 1.
Hardee's
  P Ap 24 75: 1.
Hardin, Ben
  Ag 7 80: 1.
Hardin, James
  AP Fe 12 76: 8.
  A Ag 11 83: 8.
  AP Jl 12 90: 1.
  Ap 25 91: 5.
Hardin, James B.
  P My 19 77: 1.
Hardin, James D.
  E Se 20 79: 2.
Hardin, Jim
  Jl 31 86: 1.
Harding, Barry
  BP Fe 26 81: 1.
Harper's Ferry
  Baptist Church:
  P Oc 12 78: 2.
  P Nv 12 81: 9.
-History:
  P Se 15 77: 8.
Harpertones
  (Singing Group):
  Se 6 73: 5.
Harris, Brantley
  Ag 21 86: 1.
  Ag 28 86: 2.
Harris, Janet

AP Nv 28 91: 1.
Harris, Jonathan G.:
  P Mr 20 75: 1.
  P Ap 10 75: 1.
  P My 8 75: 1, 4.
  P Ap 1 76: 1.
  Ap 8 76: 6.
Harris, R. J.
  P Ju 27 85: 6.
Harris, Willie R.
  OP Fe 2 89: 5.
  Se 14 89: 1.
  Jl 19 90: 1.
Hatcher, Eddie, see
  Robesonian
  Hostage-
  Taking.
Hatcher, Lonnie
  O Ag 21 75: 1.
Hattadare Indians
  Se 27 73: 2.
  P Nv 15 73: 6.
  P Ja 10 74: 5.
  Ap 11 74: 5.
  L Oc 24 74: 2.
  Ag 6 81: 1.
  Oc 14 82: 8.
Hatteras Tuscarora
  Indians:
  L Ja 18 90: 2, 9.
-Recognition
  (Federal):
  Mr 22 90: 1.
-Tribal Roll:
  My 2 91: 2.
Hazardous Waste
  Disposal:
  L Ju 13 85: 2.
  Ju 20 85: 2, 7, 9.
  L Jl 4 85: 2.
  Jl 25 85: 1.
  Ag 1 85: 9.
  Ag 15 85: 3.
  Ag 22 85: 1.
  Ag 29 85: 6.
  Mr 20 86: 1.
  Mr 27 86: 1.
  L Ap 3 86: 2.

Ag 7 86: 1.
Ag 28 86: 1.
L Mr 26 87: 2.
L Ap 30 87: 1, 2.
My 21 87: 1.
E My 28 87: 1.
E Ju 4 87: 1, 2.
Healers, see
  Cooper, Vernon;
  Jacobs, Alice;
  Barton, Katie
  Lee; Oxendine,
  Randolph (Jay).
Health and Medical
  Care:
  Ap 24 80: 1.
  My 1 80: 12.
  Oc 18 90: 2.
  Nv 5 92: 1.
  Ja 21 93: 1.
  Fe 25 93: 1.
  Ap 29 93: 1.
  My 6 93: 1.
  My 20 93: 1.
  Ju 10 93: 1.
  •See also
  Children--Health;
  Folk Medicine.
Hersch, Robert
  P Oc 26 89: 3.
  Nv 16 89: 3.
Highway Patrol
  (North Carolina)
-Police Brutality,
  etc.:
  L Ju 24 76: 2.
  My 26 77: 1.
  E Ju 2 77: 1, 2.
  E L Ju 9 77: 2.
  Ju 16 77: 1.
  E Ju 23 77: 2.
  Jl 7 77: 10.
  *Jl 28 77: 1.
  E My 25 78: 2.
  E Ju 8 78: 1, 2.
  Ju 15 78: 3.
  Ju 29 78: 8.
  Jl 13 78: 7.

O Jl 16 87: 2.
OB Jl 23 87: 1-2.
O Ag 6 87: 5.
Hunt, Eula
　BP Fe 21 91: 1.
Hunt, Fearby
　Thomas:
　BP Nv 19 87: 1.
Hunt, Galloway
　BP Oc 22 87: 1.
Hunt, Grady Lee
　Ju 1 89: 1.
Hunt, Hal
　P Mr 11 82: 6.
Hunt, J. R.
　BP Dc 1 83: 1.
Hunt, James
　Fe 8 73: 3.
Hunt, James A.
　P Ag 11 77: 1.
Hunt, James Albert
　(Rev.):
　L Ap 25 91: 2.
Hunt, Jimmy
　BP Mr 5 92: 3.
Hunt, Jimmy Lynn
　(Rev.):
　BP Ju 15 89: 5.
Hunt, John David
　E Ju 2 88: 2.
Hunt, Lora Mae
　BP Dc 16 76: 1.
Hunt, Lorraine
　BP Fe 21 90: 1.
Hunt, Mable
　BP Fe 21 91: 1.
Hunt, Mac
　P Dc 10 87: 8.
Hunt, Mary B.
　AP Nv 10 83: 1.
　BP Ju 7 90: 3.
Hunt, Milton
　AP Ap 2 81: 1.
　P Ju 10 82: 8.
　*BP Jl 23 92: 1.
Hunt, Ralph
　E Se 4 80: 1, 2.
　E Mr 25 82: 2.

Hunt, Robert
　Fe 15 73: 1.
Hunt, Ronnie
　BP Ja 22 81: 7.
　BP Nv 19 81: 1.
Hunt, Ronnie Lee
　BP Oc 22 87: 1.
Hunt, Rozell
　Oxendine:
　Jl 20 78: 1.
　Jl 27 78: 1.
　L Se 7 78: 2, 4.
　Oc 5 78: 1.
Hunt, Tessie
　BP Oc 8 87: 1.
Hunt, Vardell
　P Jl 26 84: 7.
Hunt, Willie
　P Fe 10 83: 7.

I

Identity/Indian-
　ness/Culture:
　My 17 73: 2.
　My 24 73: 1.
　L Ju 21 73: 2.
　E Jl 12 73: 2.
　Jl 26 73: 4.
　Ag 23 73: 4.
　Fe 7 74: 1, 7.
　L Mr 21 74: 7.
　L Mr 28 74: 2.
　Nv 7 74: 2.
　E Fe 6 75: 2.
　L Fe 20 75: 2.
　Fe 27 75: 1, 4.
　Mr 6 75: 1.
　Mr 20 75: 4.
　Mr 27 75: 5.
　Ap 10 75: 7.
　Ju 19 75: 7.
　L Oc 30 75: 2.
　E Ap 15 76: 2.
　Se 16 76: 6.
　L Jl 14 77: 2.
　L Jl 21 77: 2.
　L Oc 6 77: 2.

Nv 9 78: 7.
Nv 16 78: 7.
Ja 15 81: 7.
My 14 81: 2.
Ag 6 81: 2.
Se 10 81: 2.
L Nv 5 81: 2.
E Ag 11 83: 2.
Fe 27 92: 1.
-Poems about:
　Mr 3 77: 7.
　Ap 7 77: 2.
In the Pines Cafe
-Opening:
　P Jl 21 77: 1.
"Indian" (Def-
　inition):
　Mr 20 80: 3.
-Hearing:
　*Ag 24 78: 1.
"Indian" (Use of the
　Term):
　Ap 4 91: 2.
Indian Affairs
　(National):
　E Mr 1 73: 2.
Indian Business and
　Professional
　League:
　Nv 12 81: 4.
Indian Conferences,
　see Names of
　specific confer-
　ences, ex. North
　Carolina Indian
　Unity Confer-
　ence; North
　Carolina Indian
　Unity Youth
　Conference;
　Spirit and
　Substance
　Conference.
Indian Culture, see
　Identity/Indian-
　ness/Culture
INDIAN EDUCATION
　Fe 15 73: 2.

Ag 30 73: 7.
-History:
P Oc 6 77: 4.

Jackson, Jesse
Mr 3 88: 6.
Jacobs, Alice
P My 30 74: 5.
Jacobs, Arlie
P Se 8 77: 4.
Jacobs, Ben
My 4 89: 1.
Jacobs, Brenda
P My 22 75: 3.
P Jl 25 85: 1.
Jacobs, Ed "Boots"
AP My 6 82: 1.
A My 20 82: 5.
Jacobs, George
(Sonny):
P Se 2 82: 7.
Jacobs, Harold D.
AP Fe 19 76: 1.
Jacobs, Josephus D.
BP My 5 88: 1.
Jacobs, L. W.
(Rev.):
AP Jl 5 73: 1.
B Oc 27 77: 7.
Jacobs, Leon
AP Nv 20 75: 3.
Jacobs, Paul
Dc 27 79: 3.
Jacobs, Roscoe
Ag 31 78: 2.
Jacobs, Timothy
Bryan:
BP *Se 15 88: 6.
•See also
Robesonian
Hostage-Taking.
Jacobs Sisters
(Singing Group):
P Jl 19 73: 6.
P Fe 14 74: 1.
Jamestown

Foodstore #2
-Opening:
P Se 15 83: 1.
Jennings, Hoyland
Ju 14 84: 2.
Jo Ann's
-Opening:
Ju 28 84: 1.
Joe's Hoagie and
Rib Shop
-Opening:
Fe 28 85: 1.
Johnson, Gretchen
P Nv 16 78: 4.
Johnson, Joy J.
Fe 1 73: 1.
B Fe 6 75: 7.
L Oc 12 89: 2.
L Jl 23 92: 2.
Johnson, Linda
Faye:
P Oc 19 78: 1.
Jones, A. Bruce
A Dc 25 75: 1.
P Ja 29 76: 3.
Se 14 78: 3.
B Ag 2 79: 9.
E Ag 7 80: 2.
A Oc 27 83: 1.
A Oc 31 91: 1.
Jones, Brenda
A My 22 75: 5.
Jones, Diane
P Ap 7 83: 1.
Jones, Elizabeth
(Betsy):
P Ju 14 90: 1.
Jones, English E.
Ja 18 73: 1.
B Ja 25 73: 1.
BP Dc 5 74: 1.
PJa 30 75: 1.
BP *Se 28 78: 4.
Mr 1 79: 1.
BP *Ap 19 79: 1.
Ap 26 79: 1.
AP Ap 2 81: 8.
O *My 21 81:

1-2, 8; Rpt. Ja
20 83: 13A.
L Ju 25 81: 2.
•See also
Pembroke State
University.
Jones, Etta B.
P Ap 20 89: 3.
Jones, Evalina
Chavis:
BP Ap 18 91: 1.
Jones, Faye
P My 19 83: 4.
Jones, James A.
My 15 75: 1.
BP Ju 9 83: 9.
Jones, James Arthur
BP Ag 16 84: 12.
Jones, James G.
BP Fe 2 89: 1.
AP Fe 16 89: 1.
A Jl 29 93: 1.
Jones, John Robert
AP Oc 16 75: 1.
O Oc 27 83: 2.
Jones, Sonny
Ap 26 73: 2.
Jones, Sterling
E Se 25 75: 2.
P My 8 80: 1.
Ja 24 85: 1.
Jones, Wiley
BP Ja 28 88: 1.
Jones' Appliances
and Hardware:
P My 29 75: 1.
P Ag 7 75: 6.
Journalism
P Mr 14 74: 1.
Mr 21 74: 1, 7.
-Associations:
Ja 10 80: 1.
•See also Media;
Names of
newspapers.
Judges
-Indian:
Dc 11 80: 1.

Locklear, Anderson
-Memorial
  Scholarship:
  P My 16 91: 3.
Locklear, Anna
  Mae
  OP Fe 26 76: 1.
  B Oc 27 77: 7.
Locklear, Annie B.:
  Oc 11 79: 6.
Locklear, Anthony
  P Fe 12 87: 1.
  BP Dc 6 90: 3.
Locklear, Arlinda
  Oc 28 76: 1.
  BP Ap 30 81: 2.
  *Ja 20 83: 1.
  Mr 15 84: 1.
  BP Jl 26 84: 7.
  BP Dc 22 88: 1.
Locklear, Arnold
  P Ag 30 73: 1, 2.
  My 9 85: 1.
  Ag 17 89: 1.
  AP Se 14 89: 1.
Locklear, Barbara
  Brayboy:
  P Oc 3 74: 1.
  P My 3 90: 1.
Locklear, Bemis
  AP Se 2 76: 4.
Locklear, Ben B.
  BP My 12 88: 1.
Locklear, Bertha
  BP Ja 21 88: 1.
Locklear, Bertie L.
  BP Fe 11 88: 1.
Locklear, Bill
  James:
  Ju 14 84: 2.
Locklear, Billy
  P Ja 14 93: 3.
Locklear, Bobby
  Dean:
  AP *Dc 5 91: 1.
Locklear, Brenda
  P Ag 20 92: 1.
Locklear, C. E.

AP Se 9 76: 4.
BA Jl 20 78: 1.
PE Ju 14 79: 2.
P Dc 6 79: 1.
O Ap 17 80: 1, 2.
Locklear, Callie
  P Oc 1 87: 1.
Locklear, Carnell
  Oc 4 73: 8.
  Ag 8 74: 1.
  Ag 15 74: 1.
  Ag 22 74: 1, 8.
  Ag 29 74: 1.
  P Ag 28 75: 2.
  A Se 23 76: 1.
  E Se 30 76: 2.
  E Se 11 80: 2.
  Se 18 80: 1.
  E Se 25 80: 2.
  E Oc 2 80: 2.
  Oc 16 80: 1.
  Oc 23 80: 1.
  Oc 30 80: 1.
  Nv 6 80: 1, 2.
  Dc 25 80: 1.
  Fe 12 81: 1.
Locklear, Cecil
  P Ju 30 77: 1.
Locklear, Cheryl
  Ransom:
  P Se 6 79: 1.
  BP Fe 12 81: 6.
  BP Fe 4 93: 1.
Locklear,
  Christopher L.:
  A Ja 22 87: 1.
  AP Fe 26 87: 2.
Locklear, Clarence
  Eden:
  B Se 22 83: 1.
  P Oc 31 91: 1.
Locklear, Colonel
  P Nv 26 87: 1.
Locklear, Curt
  Dc 23 76: 4.
  Mr 16 78: 1.
Locklear, Curt, Jr.
  P A Se 25 75: 2.

Locklear, Curtis
  A Ap 24 75: 2.
Locklear, Cynthia
  Rene:
  P Ap 27 89: 1.
Locklear, Dalsedia
  -Genealogy:
  Nv 5 92: 2.
Locklear, Danelle
  BP Ag 3 89: 1.
Locklear, David G.
  AP Se 3 81: 8.
Locklear, Dayle
  P Mr 17 88: 1.
Locklear, Delton
  Ray:
  BP My 16 91: 3.
Locklear, Dorothy
  AP Ju 17 93: 1.
Locklear, Dovie
  McMillian:
  BP Mr 7 91: 1.
Locklear, Earl
  Maurice:
  BP Oc 29 87: 1.
Locklear, Elizabeth
  Berry:
  AP Ap 29 82: 8.
  A Nv 22 84: 1.
  A Se 19 85: 12.
Locklear, Elvera
  P Nv 1 79: 10.
Locklear, Emma
  Lee:
  P Jl 19 79: 1.
Locklear, Eugene
  P Ag 28 75: 1.
Locklear, Frank
  Eartle:
  P Mr 17 88: 4.
Locklear, Fuller
  P Oc 8 87: 1.
Locklear, Gail
  Ag 20 92: 1.
Locklear, Garth
  BP Nv 26 87: 1.
Locklear, Gary
  Lynn:

Se 16 82: 1.
Lumbee Pow-Wow
and Cultural
Festival:
P Se 5 91: 1.
Se 3 92: 1.
Lumbee Pride
(Singing Group):
P Mr 3 83: 7.
Lumbee Recreation
Center
-History:
L Se 13 84: 2.
-Purchase (by
Riverside
Country Club):
P Oc 11 73: 1.
LUMBEE REGIONAL
DEVELOPMENT
ASSOCIATION:
Fe 15 73: 1.
Fe 22 73: 1.
Ag 16 73: 3.
Ju 20 74: 1.
Mr 27 75: 5.
Ap 10 75: 7.
Ja 8 76: 3.
Fe 3 77: 7.
Oc 6 77: 1.
E Se 6 79: 1.
L Fe 21 80: 1-2
[issue follows
2/15/79 on
microfilm].
My 22 80: 6.
My 29 80: 6.
Jl 3 80: 2.
Jl 24 80: 5.
My 29 80: 6.
Nv 4 82: 1.
E Ju 7 84: 2.
Jl 31 86: 1.
Ap 25 91: 1.
E Ja 16 92: 2.
E Fe 20 92: 2.
•See also Lumbee
Industries.
Note: A regular

column,
"LRDA in
Action," began
in early 1973
and continued
for some time.
It is not
included in this
index. In the
1970's, LRDA
provided
frequent articles
on its projects
and services,
especially its
CETA
program; these
also are not
included.
-Awards:
E Ju 23 88: 2.
-Board of Directors:
Ag 8 74: 1, 7.
Ag 15 74: 1.
Ag 22 74: 1, 8.
Ag 29 74: 1.
Jl 27 78: 2.
Jl 19 79: 1.
E My 2 85: 2.
--Elections:
E Ag 7 80: 1, 2.
Ag 18 83: 1.
Nv 29 84: 1.
Dc 12 84: 4.
Nv 28 85: 1.
Dc 12 85: 1.
Nv 27 86: 1.
Nv 17 88: 1.
Nv 24 88: 1.
Dc 8 88: 1.
Nv 16 89: 1.
Nv 30 89: 1.
Dc 14 89: 1.
Nv 29 90: 1.
-CETA Program:
Nv 7 74: 6.
Jl 31 75: 1.
Se 7 78: 1.

My 5 83: 1.
E My 12 83: 1.
EL Jl 28 83: 1, 2.
L Ag 4 83: 2.
EL Ag 11 83: 2.
Ag 18 83: 1.
Oc 27 83: 1.
Nv 3 83: 1.
Nv 10 83: 1.
E *Nv 17 83: 1-2.
E Nv 24 83: 2.
-Community Pool:
Ag 13 87: 1.
-Founders:
P Se 9 82: 6.
-Funding:
My 30 74: 1.
-Head Start
Program:
Ap 12 90: 1.
-History:
Nv 4 82: 9.
-Indian Information
Project:
Ag 5 82: 1.
Ag 12 82: 8.
-Library:
P Ag 15 74: 8.
Dc 13 79: 4.
-and Miss N.C.
Pageant:
Mr 23 89: 1.
-and National
Indian Day:
Se 20 79: 1.
-Overview:
*Mr 15 73: 2.
-Programs and
Services:
Mr 1 73: 1.
My 24 73: 6.
Oc 4 73: 4.
Fe 7 74: 3.
Fe 14 74: 1, 8.
Ag 1 74: 3, 6.
Ag 8 74: 5.
Dc 11 75: 7.
*Se 29 77: 4.

-Poems about:
  Mr 3 77: 7.
  Jl 3 80: 2.
  Mr 19 81: 4.
  Ja 20 83: 12A.
-Recollections:
  Se 13 84: 7.
Lumbee River
  Legal Services:
  *Ag 17 78: 1.
  *Se 14 78: 1.
  *Ap 12 79: 1. 4.
  Jl 31 80: 10.
  Ag 28 80: 1.
-Anniversary:
  P *Nv 10 88: 1.
Lumbee River
  Native American
  Center for the
  Arts:
  My 14 81: 1.
  Ag 13'81: 8, 9.
  Se 13 84: 9.
Lumbee River
  Singers:
  Ap 30 81.
Lumbee Warehouse
  EP Fe 27 75: 1, 2.
  E Mr 20 75: 2.
Lumbees & Friends
  (Singing Group):
  Ju 16 77: 7.
Lumber River
  Council of
  Governments:
  Mr 11 76: 1.
  Mr 18 76: 1.
Lumber River
  Quartet
  (Singing Group):
  P Ap 9 92: 1.
Lumberton (City)
-Chamber of
  Commerce
--Sale of maps:
  E Mr 21 91: 2.
-Elections:
  Se 27 79: 1.

-Housing Authority:
  P Ju 21 73: 1.
  Ju 2 77: 1.
  Ju 8 78: 3.
-School District
--Annexations:
  Dc 25 80: 1.
  E Ja 15 81: 2.
  Oc 1 81: 1.
  Oc 22 81: 1.
  Nv 5 81: 1.
  Nv 12 81: 1.
  *Dc 3 81: 5.
  Fe 4 82: 1.
  E Fe 11 82: 1, 2.
  Fe 18 82: 1.
  E Mr 4 82: 2.
  E Mr 11 82: 2.
  Ap 8 82: 8.
  Ju 17 82: 1.
  Se 23 82: 1.
  Ja 20 83: 13A.
  Mr 10 83: 1.
  E Ag 25 83: 2.
  Se 1 83: 1.
  E *Dc 20 84: 2.

M

McDonald, Arthur
  AP Fe 26 76: 1.
McDougald Funeral
  Home (Laurin-
  burg, NC):
  Nv 11 76: 6.
  Oc 19 78: 6.
McEachern, Anita
  Ja 30 75: 3.
McKellar, Billy
  Ap 28 88: 1, 2.
  My 12 88: 1.
  E My 26 88: 2.
  E Ja 26 89: 2.
  E Ap 11 91: 2.
McKendree College
  (IL)
-Lumbee At-
  tendance

--1920's-1930's:
  Jl 12 84: 1, 7.
McLean, Angus
  Wilton:
  Dc 27 79: 6.
McMillan,
  Hamilton:
  L My 17 73: 2.
  Se 22 77: 5.
  Fe 11 82: 1.
  Mr 25 82: 1.
  Ap 1 82: 2.
  Ap 8 82: 2.
  Ap 15 82: 1.
  My 13 82: 1.
  Ju 24 82: 10.
  Jl 1 82: 2.
  Ag 26 82: 4.
  Se 16 82: 1.
  *Se 23 82: 4.
  Ja 20 83: 18A.
  Ja 27 83: 11.
  Fe 16 84: 10.
  Jl 12 84: 8.
  Ja 24 85: 1.
  Nv 21 85: 1.
  Fe 26 87: 3.
  Mr 12 87: 3.
McNeil, Charles
  David:
  BP Mr 24 88: 1.
McNeill Trio
  (Singing Group):
  P Ag 9 73: 6.
McNeill's Bridge
  P Jl 5 90: 1.
McPherson Report
  Nv 30 78: 10.
Mac's Vacuum
  World
-Opening:
  Ag 2 84: 1.
MacLeod, Norman
  O Ju 13 85: 3.
Magnolia High
  School
-Class of 1955
--Reunion:

P Mr 28 85: 1.
Maynor, W. R.
(Rev.):
P Ap 10 75: 5.
Maynor Manor
-Dedication
P Ag 1 74: 1.
P Ag 8 74: 1, 7.
Maynor v. Morton
*Ap 17 75: 1, 6.
Media
P Mr 14 74: 1.
Mr 21'74: 1, 7.
•See also Names
of newspapers;
Journalism.
Methodist Church
Ju 14 79: 1.
Ju 9 83: 1.
Mr 27 86: 1.
-Creative Health
Ministry
(Pembroke):
My 31 90: 1.
-District Lay Rally:
P Mr 1 90: 1.
Mr 15 90: 5.
-Holiness
--Lumber River Conference:
Dc 02 82 [special
issue].
Dc 9 82: 3.
Dc 16 82: 3.
Dc 30 82: 4.
Ja 6 83: 7.
Fe 3 83: 6.
Fe 17 83: 12.
Mr 3 83: 9.
Mr 10 83: 6.
Mr 24 83: 6.
-and Native
Americans:
L Se 22 83: 2.
*Ja 17 91: 1.
*Ju 13 91: 1.
-Robeson County
--History:
C My 3 84: 14.

C My 10 84: 5.
*Ja 17 91: 1.
*Ju 13 91: 1.
Michigan
L My 1 80: 2.
*My 8 80: 2.
L Jl 10 80: 2.
Nv 6 80: 3.
Nv 13 80: 2.
Nv 20 80: 1.
Nv 19 81: 3.
Fe 25 82: 9.
Jl 1 82: 3.
Se 2 82: 2.
-College Tuition
Grants for
Indians:
Ju 3 82: 1, 2.
Jl 4 85: 1.
Mickay, Angela
Chavis:
BP Ju 11 81: 4.
Military Service
Nv 26 87: 1.
Dc 17 87: 6.
Dc 24 87: 1.
Ja 7 88: 1.
Ap 6 89: 4.
*Mr 8 90: 1.
Ju 14 90: 1.
Nv 8 90: 2.
Ju 27 91: 4.
P Dc 5 91: 1.
Se 9 92: 1.
Ja 21 93: 1.
Miller, Karla
P Ja 24 91: 1.
Miss Lumbee
Pageant:
L Jl 16 87: 2.
L Jl 23 92: 2.
•See also Lumbee
Homecoming.
Moody, Albert
My 16 91: 2.
Moore, Claude S.
AP Ju 5 80: 1.
Moore, Luther

Harbert:
A Oc 21 76: 1.
AP Jl 6 78: 1.
Ju 14 79: 1.
Moore, Nora S.
BP Ap 13 78: 4.
Mormons
My 24 79: 4.
Morton, Elizabeth
Nv 16 78: 1.
Mt. Airy Baptist
Church
-History:
P Se 8 77: 4.
Mt. Elim Baptist
Church
-History:
P My 26 77: 8.
Mt. Moriah Baptist
Church
-History:
P Ju 23 77: 6.
Mt. Olive Baptist
Church
-Centennial:
Se 1 83: 4.
Se 8 83: 4.
Mt. Olive Baptist
Church
-History:
P Ju 23 77: 4.
Mt. Olive Pentecos-
tal Holiness
Church (Pem-
broke):
P Ap 18 91: 1.
Mules
Se 24 81: 8.
Murders, Unsolved
-Robeson County:
L Fe 8 90: 2.
Museums and
Resource Centers
*Dc 12 74: 1.
•See also Indian
Education
Resource Center;
Indian Museum

Ja 3 85: 8.
Nicholson, Dierdre
A.:
A Mr 12 87: 1.
Norma Jean (Pig)
L Fe 27 86: 2.
L Mr 6 86: 2.
L Mr 13 86: 2.
North Carolina Arts
Council:
Se 14 78: 8.
Se 21 78: 2.
North Carolina
Board of
Education:
Ap 5 73: 1.
NORTH CAROLINA
COMMISSION OF
INDIAN AFFAIRS:
P Jl 10 75: 7.
Nv 27 75: 1.
Dc 25 75: 1.
Ap 8 76: 3.
Ap 21 77: 1.
L Ju 2 77: 2.
EL Jl 21 77: 1, 2,
6.
Dc 22 77: 1.
Ap 6 78: 2.
Ju 22 78: 10.
Ag 31 78: 2.
Mr 8 79: 1.
Ju 21 79: 1.
Se 13 79: 6.
Oc 25 79: 1.
Se 25 80: 1.
Ap 11 85: 1.
Ju 19 86: 1.
Ag 17 89: 1.
E *Ag 9 90: 1, 2.
-Board of Directors:
Nv 26 87: 4.
--Elections:
Ja 20 83: 2, 5, 7.
L Ja 27 83: 1.
Fe 3 83: 1.
Fe 10 83: 1.
Oc 13 83: 8.

Jl 25 85: 1, 2.
Ag 1 85: 1.
Ag 15 85: 1.
Ag 29 85: 1.
Jl 30 87: 1.
Ag 20 87: 1.
Jl 28 88: 1.
Ag 18 88: 1.
Ag 25 88: 1.
Se 8 88: 1.
Se 5 90: 1.
-High School
Equivalency:
Se 22 83: 7.
-Overview:
Ju 8 78: 8.
-Purpose:
Mr 25 82: 9.
-Talent Search:
Jl 27 78: 6.
North Carolina Fed.
of American
Indians:
Ja 17 91: 1.
*Dc 5 91: 1.
North Carolina
Indian Adventure,
see
Hattadare
Indians.
North Carolina
Indian Business
Assoc.:
Fe 7 91: 1.
North Carolina
Indian Cultural
Center:
Jl 12 84: 1.
Ag 9 84: 1.
L Se 13 84: 2.
Ja 17 85: 5.
Jl 25 85: 1.
MP Ja 30 86: 1.
Jl 24 86: 1.
Ja 15 87: 1.
Ag 27 87: 1.
Se 3 87: 1.
Ja 7 88: 1.

Mr 9 89: 1.
My 4 89: 1.
Ju 8 89: 1.
Se 7 89: 1.
Se 14 89: 2.
L Nv 30 89: 2.
Mr 29 90: 1.
E My 24 90: 1-2,
5.
L My 31 90: 1, 2.
Ju 21 90: 1.
L Ju 28 90: 2.
L Jl 19 90: 4.
E Ag 9 90: 1, 2.
C Ag 23 90: 5.
Mr 21 91: 5.
E My 16 91: 2.
L My 28 92: 4.
L Ju 11 92: 5.
L Ju 18 92: 2.
L Se 24 92: 2.
Oc 1 92: 1.
E My 13 93: 1.
-History:
*Mr 14 91: 1, 4.
-Plan:
*Ag 16 84: 1.
-Pow wow:
Se 13 90: 1, 2.
North Carolina
Indian Heritage
Month:
Se 13 90: 1, 2, 3.
North Carolina
Indian Heritage
Week:
Se 18 80: 1.
Oc 2 80: 1.
Se 3 81: 1.
Se 17 81: 1.
Se 24 81: 6.
Oc 1 81: 1.
Oc 8 81: 5.
Ag 26 82: 6.
Se 16 82: 6.
Se 11 86: 1.
Se 25 86: 1.
Se 10 87: 1.

-History:
E Se 13 73: 2.
-Name:
Fe 18 82: 4.
Jl 23 87: 3.
-Poems about:
My 31 73: 4.
Ja 6 77: 2.
Ag 3 78: 5.
Se 14 78: 2.
-Rededication:
Fe 21 80: 1
[issue follows
2/15/79 on
microfilm].
Ja 20 83: 11A.
Oral History
My 3 73: 2.
Ag 16 73: 7.
Ag 30 73: 1.
Ja 3 74: 1.
Ja 17 74: 6.
Ag 25 77: 3.
Fe 9 84: 12.
My 17 84: 1.
*My 16 91: 1.
Origin (of Lumbee
Indians), see
Tribal Origin.
Original 22, see
Twenty-Two,
Original.
Owl Feather,
LaVita:
P Mr 8 84: 7.
Oxendine, Anthony
L Dc 4 80: 2.
Oxendine, Arber
BP Ju 9 88: 1.
Oxendine, Birtir
P Ap 14 88: 1.
Oxendine, Brenda
Mae:
P Ag 21 80: 2.
Oxendine, Carol
AP Mr 24 77: 6.
Oxendine, Carol
Smith:

P Jl 29 76: 1.
BP Ap 8 82: 7.
Oxendine, Carolene
P My 22 75: 3.
Oxendine, Charity
BP Nv 4 76: 4.
Oxendine, Clifton
O Fe 15 79: 3.
AP Ju 28 84: 1.
A My 15 86: 1, 7.
Ju 18 87: 1.
BO Jl 23 87: 1-3.
Se 24 87: 3.
P Dc 1 88: 1.
B *Dc 15 88: 1.
Oxendine, David
BP My 24 84: 1.
P Ja 22 87: 1.
AP My 28 87: 1.
P Ju 16 88: 1.
AP Mr 8 90: 1.
Oxendine, Dobbs
H.:
AP Fe 23 89: 1.
Oxendine, Docia
BP Fe 20 75: 4.
Oxendine, Dorothy
F.:
P Ja 17 80: 8.
Oxendine, Drenna
J.
P Fe 27 75: 5.
O Jl 14 77: 6.
-Poem about:
Jl 21 77: 8.
Oxendine, Earl
Hughes:
Ap 5 73: 1.
A *Oc 7 76: 1.
AP Ju 13 85: 9.
BP Jl 14 88: 1.
Oxendine, Earl
Hughes, Jr.:
AP Mr 4 82: 1.
Oxendine, Forace
P Ja 8 81: 1.
AP My 6 82: 1.
AP Ju 3 82: 1.

Oxendine, Forn
Ap 26 79: 2.
Oxendine, Gaynor
P Oc 15 87: 5.
Oxendine, Gervais
(Gary):
BP Ju 14 90: 3.
Oxendine, H.
Dobbs:
A Jl 2 87: 1.
Oxendine, Henry
Ward:
P Mr 15 73: 1.
*Mr 22 73: 1, 3.
P Ap 12 73: 1.
P Ag 30 73: 1, 2.
P Ja 24 74: 1.
L Nv 14 74: 2.
AP My 15 75: 1.
AP Mr 17 77: 1.
Oxendine, Herbert
G.:
Ja 18 73: 1.
B Ja 25 73: 1.
Oxendine, Herbert
G., Jr.
AP Ap 11 91: 1.
Oxendine, Hilton
P Ag 14 75: 1.
O Ap 15 76: 1.
Oxendine, Howard
Se 4 80: 1.
P Fe 21 91: 1.
Oxendine, James
Brantly:
Mr 6 80: 10.
L Nv 20 80: 3.
Oxendine, James C.
P Ju 14 90: 1.
Oxendine, James H.
BP Mr 8 90: 1.
Oxendine, James
W.:
PB My 22 75: 1.
AP My 26 77: 1.
BP Ap 18 91: 3.
Oxendine, Jane C.
BP Dc 24 87: 1.

L.:
EL Dc 1 77: 1, 2.
Oxendine, William
Russell:
P Jl 5 73: 1, 3.
Oxendine, Willie
P Mr 27 80: 1.
Oxendine, Winnie
Bell:
BP Fe 7 91: 1.
Oxendine, Wyvis
P Ju 30 77: 4.
BP Fe 24 83: 1.
L Ap 17 86: 2.
Oxendine's Tire
Center:
Ap 14 88: 1.

P

Parnell, David
L Ap 30 92: 2, 8.
Pates Supply
Se 20 79: 6.
Paul, William F.
BP Nv 11 76: 4.
Pee Dee Lumbee
Indian Associa-
ation:
Fe 3 77: 7.
Pemberton Place
Nursing Home:
Nv 7 91: 1.
-Opening:
P Ja 2 92: 1.
Pembroke, see
Pembroke
(Town).
Pembroke Alcohol
Counseling
Center:
Fe 15 79: 1.
Pembroke Bonding
Company:
Fe 28 80: 1.
6 80: 1.
Mr 13 80: 1.
Pembroke Business

and Professional
Women's Club:
Mr 27 75: 1.
Ag 19 76.
Pembroke Carpet
Service
-Opening:
Ju 28 79: 6.
Pembroke Com-
munity Work-
shop:
P Ag 2 79: 1.
Pembroke Depot
Jl 26 84: 1.
PL Ag 9 84: 1, 2.
EL Ag 30 84: 2.
L Se 6 84: 2.
Se 13 84: 1.
P Se 20 84: 1.
EP Oc 4 84: 2.
P Nv 15 84: 8.
Mr 7 85: 1.
E Mr 14 85: 2.
P *Mr 21 85: 1.
E Ap 4 85: 2.
E Ju 27 85: 2.
Jl 18 85: 1.
*Dc 19 85: 2.
Ap 10 86: 1.
Ju 5 86: 1.
*Ju 26 86: 1.
Ju 11 87: 2.
P Ju 18 87: 1.
E Jl 2 87: 2.
Ja 21 88: 1.
Dc 8 88: 1.
Pembroke Elementa-
ry School:
L Oc 17 74: 2.
Ag 24 78: 1.
Pembroke Eye
Clinic
-Opening:
Ju 26 80: 2.
Pembroke Fabric
Care Center
-Opening:
Se 23 76: 2.

P Se 30 76: 1.
Pembroke Farm,
Home and
Garden Supply:
Ja 5 89: 1.
Pembroke Graded
School
-Sixth Grade
Class–1941:
P Ap 12 90: 3.
Pembroke High
School:
E Dc 24 74: 2.
My 8 75: 4.
•See also
Pembroke Middle
School--Building
Renovation.
-Class of 1940
--Reunion:
P Nv 26 81: 9.
P Jl 8 82: 8.
-Class of 1942
--Reunion:
P Jl 15 82: 8.
-Class of 1943
--Reunion:
L Oc 10 91: 1.
---Poem about
Oc 17 91: 5.
-Class of 1945
--Reunion:
P Jl 18 85: 5.
-Class of 1952
--Reunion:
P Ag 20 92: 5.
-Class of 1957
--Reunion:
P Ja 7 88: 2.
-Class of 1960
--Reunion:
P Se 4 80: 8.
P Se 19 85: 1, 4.
-Class of 1961
--Reunion:
P Jl 15 76: 8.
-Class of 1966
--Reunion:

L My 24 79: 1, 2.
My 31 79: 1.
EL Ju 7 79: 2.
L Ju 14 79: 1, 2.
Ju 21 79: 1.
Ju 28 79: 1.
Jl 5 79: 1.
E Jl 12 79: 2.
E Jl 26 79: 2.
My 8 80: 8.
My 15 80: 1.
Ja 20 83: 11A.
Oc 27 88: 4.
Nv 10 88: 4.
E Nv 17 88: 1, 2.
Dc 29 88: 1.
E Ja 5 89: 2.
Mr 23 89: 1.
*Ap 20 89: 1.
My 11 89: 3.
My 18 89: 1.
Ju 29 89: 3.
Ag 10 89: 3.
Oc 19 89: 1, 3.
Oc 26 89: 1, 3.
P Nv 2 89: 1.
Nv 9 89: 1.
E Nv 23 89: 2.
Ja 18 90: 1.
Fe 1 90: 1.
Ap 5 90: 5.
-Chancellor's Club:
Ag 14 75: 1.
Ag 28 75: 1.
•See also names
of members.
-Class of 1926
--Reunion:
P Se 15 77: 3.
-Class of 1927
P Fe 12 87: 1.
-Class of 1932
--Reunion:
P Fe 3 83: 4.
-Class of 1933
--Reunion:
Ju 23 83: 1.
Ju 30 83: 1.

P Nv 2 89: 1.
-Class of 1934
--Reunion:
P Jl 29 76: 6.
-Class of 1936
--Reunion:
Jl 13 89: 4.
Jl 12 90: 1.
-Class of 1937
--Reunion:
P Ap 25 74: 2.
-Class of 1940
--Reunion:
P Jl 12 90: 5.
-Class of 1943
--Reunion:
P Fe 18 93: 4.
-Class of 1945
--Reunion:
P Nv 5 92: 3.
-Class of 1952
--Reunion:
Nv 21 91: 1.
P Fe 20 92: 1.
-Class of 1953
--Reunion:
P Dc 27 73: 3.
-Community
Relations:
Fe 22 73: 1.
Mr 1 73: 1.
E Nv 12 81: *1-2.
E Nv 19 81: 2.
E Fe 24 83: 2.
Mr 3 83: 2.
E Oc 20 83: 2.
E Dc 8 83: 2.
L Dc 15 83: 2.
Dc 11 86: 1.
E Se 8 88: 2.
E Se 22 88: 2.
Ja 26 89: 1.
Ju 1 89: 3.
My 10 90: 1.
Jl 5 90: 4.
*Jl 12 90: 4.
EL Jl 26 90: 2, 4.
-De-Indianization:

L *Mr 13 75: 2.
L *Mr 20 75: 2.
-Desegregation:
Ag 6 81: 2.
-Economic
Development
Office:
Se 28 89: 1.
-Endowment:
P Oc 25 73: 1.
-Enrollment:
Se 10 87: 3.
Se 24 87: 3.
Ag 30 90: 1.
Se 13 90: 3.
-Faculty:
E Oc 4 79: 2.
E Oc 11 79: 2.
E Oc 18 79: 2.
E Oc 25 79: 2.
E Nv 1 79: 2.
-Gospel Choir:
P Ap 11 91: 1.
-Graduates (Oldest
Living):
Ag 3 89: 3.
-Health Careers
Ju 17 93: 5.
-Historical Marker:
P Mr 26 87: 1.
-History:
Ag 12 76: 8.
E Dc 6 79: 2.
Ja 17 80: 2.
E Ja 24 80: 2.
My 9 85: 1.
P Ja 2 86: 2.
Ja 22 87: 1.
Ap 9 87: 1.
Ag 2 90: 1.
Se 27 90: 3.
-Indian Heritage
Week:
Se 14 89: 1-3.
Se 21 89: 1, 3.
-Mary Livermore
Library:
Ap 23 87: 7.

Nv 11 82: 1.
Ag 9 84: 1.
-Crime:
Ap 13 78: 6.
-District Court:
Mr 31 77: 1.
Ap 7 77: 1.
P Jl 21 77: 4.
-Economic Aspects:
Dc 14 78: 5.
-Elections:
P Nv 8 73: 1.
P Oc 30 75: 1.
P Nv 6 75: 1.
Mr 24 76: 1.
Se 15 77: 1.
Se 22 77: 1.
Se 29 77: 1.
Oc 6 77: 1.
Oc 13 77: 1.
Oc 27 77: 1.
Nv 3 77: 1.
Nv 10 77: 1.
Se 13 79: 1.
Se 20 79: 1.
Se 27 79: 1.
Oc 11 79: 1.
Nv 1 79: 1.
Dc 6 79: 1.
Oc 10 85: 1.
Nv 7 85: 1.
E Ag 13 87: 2.
Oc 29 87: 1.
Nv 7 91: 1.
•See also
Elections.
-as Home to
Lumbees:
*Se 6 73: 2.
My 1 75: 1.
-Housing:
Ja 25 73: 3.
Nv 5 87: 1.
-Housing Authority:
P *Se 13 73: 1.
L Dc 13 73: 3.
P Ja 3 74: 3.
Ju 20 74: 1.

Fe 27 75: 1.
Ap 17 75: 1, 8.
Fe 5 76: 1.
Fe 10 77: 1.
Mr 3 77: 1.
Jl 20 78: 1.
Oc 12 78: 7.
Nv 23 78: 4.
Dc 14 78: 1.
*Ja 20 83: 3A.
Mr 9 89: 1.
Ap 6 89: 1.
Mr 15 90: 1.
L Oc 4 90: 1.
E Ja 9 92: 2.
-Magistrate:
Oc 6 77: 6.
-Name:
Ag 11 88: 7.
--Pronunciation of:
Fe 4 82: 1.
Ja 20 83: 21A.
-Planning Board:
M Se 7 78: 1.
-Police Dept.:
Fe 7 80: 2.
-Post Office:
P Dc 8 77: 1.
Ap 12 84: 1.
-Postmaster:
EL My 23 74: 2.
My 30 74: 1.
L Ju 13 74: 2.
Jl 11 74: 1, 6.
My 12 77: 1.
L My 26 77: 2.
My 18 78: 1.
My 25 78: 1.
EL My 16 74: 2,
7.
Ju 15 78: 1.
Jl 17 80: 1.
Jl 31 80: 1.
Se 25 80: 1.
-PSU Students'
Perceptions:
*Jl 12 90: 4.
-Redevelopment

Commission:
Dc 13 90: 1.
E Ja 9 92: 2.
-School District
(Proposed):
Se 1 83: 1.
EL Se 8 83: 2.
Ju 22 89: 6.
-Sidewalk Ordi-
nance:
My 9 78: 1.
-Town Clerk:
Ap 21 77: 1.
Mr 2 78: 1.
-Town Council:
Mr 14 74: 7.
My 23 74: 1.
Nv 7 74: 2.
Dc 5 74: 7.
Mr 13 75: 1.
Ap 3 75: 3.
Fe 5 76: 1.
My 5 77: 1.
M Mr 2 78: 1.
Ap 6 78: 1.
Fe 14 80: 1.
M Ag 7 80: 1.
E Ja 9 92: 2.
--Elections
*Oc 21 76: 1.
Se 19 85: 1.
Se 21 89: 1.
Oc 5 89: 1.
Nv 9 89: 1.
P Ag 14 86: 1.
•See also
Pembroke
Town)--
Elections;
Elections.
--Meetings:
Fe 8 73: 1.
Fe 21 74: 3.
Mr 14 74: 1.
Ap 4 74: 1.
My 9 74: 1.
Ag 8 74: 1.
Ja 8 76: 3.

Highway Patrol
(N.C.)
Politics
  My 31 73: 1.
  EL Fe 7 74: 2.
  L Mr 7 74: 2.
  Mr 28 74: 1.
  Ap 11 74: 8.
  E My 2 74: 2.
  My 30 74: 1.
  L Nv 14 74: 2.
  E Oc 30 75: 10.
  E Ag 19 76: 2.
  E Ag 26 76: 2.
  E Oc 14 76: 2.
  My 24 84: 2.
  E Se 27 84: 2.
  Jl 13 89: 1.
  L Ag 3 89: 2.
  L Mr 8 90: 4.
  E *Ap 26 90: 1,
    2.
  E My 3 90: 1.
  E Ju 7 90: 2.
  E Jl 5 90: 2.
  E Jl 12 90: 2.
  •See also
  Coalitions;
  Democratic
  Party; Elections;
  Indian Solidarity;
  Native American
  Political Action
  Committee;
  North Carolina
  Federation of
  American
  Indians; Redis-
  tricting; Republi-
  can Party;
  Robeson County
  Indian Caucus;
  Voter Registra-
  tion; Voting
  (Minority)--
  Robeson County;
  Voting Machines.
Pollitzer, William

-Genetic Study of
  Lumbees:
  EL My 24 73:
  1-2.
  L My 31 73: 2.
Poverty
-Robeson County:
  P Fe 24 77: 1.
Prine, Berteen
  Nv 10 83: 8.
  P Ja 10 91: 3.
Prisons (North
  Carolina):
  L Nv 11 82: 2.
Proctorville
  Elementary
  School:
  My 21 87: 5.
Prospect High
  School:
  My 15 75: 1.
-Class of 1941
--Reunion:
  P Jl 25 74: 7.
-Class of 1950
--Reunion:
  P Ag 1 74: 5.
-Class of 1962
--Reunion:
  Ja 23 75: 8.
-Class of 1964
--Reunion:
  P Ja 2 75: 4.
  P Ag 30 79: 5.
-Class of 1972
--Reunion:
  P Jl 29 82: 2.
Prospect Jaycees
-Special Sup-
  plement:
  follows Jl 19 73.
Prospect School
-History:
  *Ag 16 84: 12.
-Tuscarora
  Confrontations at:
  *Mr 29 73: 1.
"Prospect Suit"

*Se 28 78: 1.
Mr 1 79: 5.
Ja 20 83: 10A.
  •See also
  Desegregation (of
  Schools).
Prospect United
  Methodist
  Church:
  *P Dc 5 74: 1, 6.
  E Ag 17 78: 2.
  Dc 27 79: 1.
  P Nv 5 81: 13.
  P Ju 22 89: 3.
Purnell Swett High
  School
-Name:
  E Jl 13 89: 2.
  Jl 20 89: 1.
  L Jl 27 89: 2.
  E Oc 19 89: 2.
  E Oc 26 89: 2.
  L Nv 2 89: 2.
  E Ja 11 90: 2.
  E Fe 1 90: 2.
  E Fe 8 90: 2.
  EL Fe 15 90: 2, 5.
Quilts and Quilting
  P Ap 3 75: 7.
  Fe 27 86: 2.
  Mr 6 86: 5.
  Fe 21 91: 1.

R

R & R Grill &
  Paco's:
  P Fe 23 89: 4.
Race Relations
-History
--Race riot of 1913:
  Ja 22 81: 4.
  •See also
  Robeson
  County--Race
  Relations.
Racial Stereotypes
  L Mr 31 88: 2, 7.

P Fe 24 77: 9.
Regan, Richard
   A My 15 86: 1.
Register, Tanya
   B My 28 87: 5.
Reising, Robert
   Dc 1 88: 1.
Religion
   Fe 21 74: 4.
   Fe 28 74: 1.
   •See also Names
   of churches;
   denominations;
   Indian Religion
   Museum;
   Robeson County
   Area-Wide
   Crusade.
Republican Party
   Nv 8 73: 1.
   Fe 14 74: 1.
   E Oc 24 74: 2.
   E Ap 25 91: 2.
Research and
   Scholarship:
   *Mr 1 73: 3.
   Mr 8 73: 1.
   Jl 19 73: 1, 2.
   Se 23 82: 8.
   Ju 10 93: 1.
   Ju 17 93: 3.
-Encyclopedia:
   Fe 28 80: 1.
   Mr 6 80: 2.
   Mr 13 80: 3.
   Mr 20 80: 2.
   Mr 27 80: 2.
   •See also History;
   Dial, Adolph L;
   Eliades, David;
   Blu, Karen I.
Reunions (Family),
   see [Name of
   person]--Family
   Reunion.
Reunions (School
   Graduating
   Classes), see

[Name of
School]--Class of
[Year]--Reunion.
Revels, Juddie
   P Nv 8 73: 1.
   P Dc 6 73: 1.
Revels, Lonnie
   Se 26 74: 1.
   Nv 14 74: 1.
   AP Oc 16 75: 1.
   AP Jl 14 83: 8.
   A Nv 10 83: 1.
   A My 31 84: 1.
   Ap 11 85: 1.
   P Jl 4 85: 1.
   BP Mr 31 88: 1.
   AP Mr 9 89: 1.
   E Ag 9 90: 1, 2.
Revels, Maudie
   Chavis:
   BP Ja 14 88: 1.
Revels, Nancy
   P Nv 23 78: 3.
Revels, Robert
   P Oc 25 90: 1.
Revels, Ronald
   Se 25 80: 1.
Revels, Ruth
   A Se 22 77: 1.
Revels, William P.
   P Dc 5 91: 1.
Revels Family
-Genealogy:
   L Ap 12 79: 2.
Rhyne, Ken
   BP Nv 15 90: 2.
Richardson, Barry
   P Mr 25 82: 8.
Richardson, Joseph
   Oliver:
   Se 24 81: 1.
Richardson, W. R.
   AP Ap 22 82: 1.
Rinzler, Kate
   My 17 84: 1.
Ritchie, Sheila Ann
   P Ag 26 82: 6.
Riverside Country

Club
-Formation:
   Se 13 73: 1.
   P Jl 24 75: 7.
   Nv 27 75: 1.
   Jl 12 84: 1.
   E Ja 10 85: 2.
   •See also Lumbee
   Recreation
   Center.
Road Signs
   Ja 18 73: 3.
"Roanoak"
   (Television
   Program):
   Nv 14 85: 1.
   Nv 28 85: 1.
   My 8 86: 9.
   My 22 86: 1.
   Ju 5 86: 1.
Roberts, Carolyn
   AP Ap 30 87: 1.
Robeson Area
   Minority
   Contractors'
   Association:
   P Jl 25 74: 1.
   Nv 28 74: 6.
Robeson County
   Area-Wide
   Crusade:
   P Mr 10 88: 1.
   Ap 25 91: 1.
ROBESON COUNTY
-Affirmative
   Action:
   E Dc 23 76: 2.
   Ja 6 77: 1.
   Se 21 78: 2.
-Agricultural
   Extension Service
   4-H:
   Mr 12 87: 1.
-Bicentennial:
   Mr 6 86: 1.
   Dc 25 86: 1.
   Ja 1 87: 1.
   Ja 15 87: 1.

Oc 11 79: 1.
Ja 10 80: 10.
Mr 13 80: 1.
Ag 28 80: 1.
Nv 19 81: 2.
Dc 10 81: 1.
Ap 15 82: 1.
My 13 82: 1.
Ju 10 82: 1.
Ag 12 82: 1.
Dc 16 82: 1.
Fe 10 83: 1.
Mr 17 83: 6.
Ap 14 83: 1.
My 12 83: 1.
Ag 16 84: 1.
--Voting Districts:
  Ag 25 83: 1.
-Board of Elections:
  Mr 29 73: 4.
  Ja 3 74: 2.
  E Mr 21'74: 1, 2.
  E Jl 3 75: 2.
  Ju 9 77: 1.
  Ag 18 77: 3.
  Nv 16 78: 1.
  M My 14 81: 1.
  E Mr 31 83: 1, 2.
  M Jl 21 83: 7.
  Oc 20 83: 1.
  •See also Voter
  Registration.
--Personnel Matters:
  Ju 27 74: 1, 4.
-Community
  Penalties
  Program:
  Ap 25 91: 5.
-Conflicts:
  E Ap 21 88: 2.
-Corruption:
  E Mr 31 88: 2.
-Crime:
  E Oc 5 78: 2.
  Ap 12 79: 3.
  Ap 19 79: 18.
  Mr 18 82: 1.
  Oc 17 85: 1.

-Criminal Justice
  System:
  E Nv 28 74: 2.
  L Se 18 75: 2.
  L Oc 16 75: 2.
  Ja 8 76: 3.
  L Oc 21 76: 2.
  E Oc 28 76: 2.
  L Nv 25 76: 2.
  L Fe 3 77: 2.
  L Jl 7 77: 2.
  Ap 20 78: 8.
  L Ja 9 86: 2.
  Ja 16 86: 2.
  Ja 22 87: 1.
  Fe 19 87: 1.
  Mr 19 87: 1.
  Ap 16 87: 1.
  Ap 23 87: 1.
  Se 15 88: 1.
  Oc 13 88: 2.
  Oc 27 88: 1.
  *Dc 15 88: 1.
  Nv 30 89: 1.
  E Mr 8 90: 2.
  Mr 15 90: 1.
  My 31 90: 2.
  •See also
  Robeson
  County--Public
  Defender;
  Robeson
  County--Sheriff's
  Dept.; Robeson
  County--Superior
  Court Judgeship;
  Robeson
  County--
  Community
  Penalties
  Program.
--Treatment of
  Indians
---Hearing:
  Dc 9 82: 1.
---Report:
  EL Dc 16 82: 2.
  L Dc 23 82: 2, 9.

-Dept. of Social
  Services:
  EL Jl 5 84: 2.
  E Jl 19 84: 2.
  L Jl 26 84: 2.
  E Ag 9 84: 2.
  Ag 23 84: 1.
--Lawsuits:
  *Oc 11 84: 1.
-Economic
  Conditions:
  Fe 22 73: 1.
  Mr 8 73: 2.
  Mr 15 73: 2.
  Mr 22 73: 2.
  Mr 29 73: 2.
  Ap 5 73: 2.
  L Fe 13 86: 2.
-History:
  Ap 14 88: 7.
  Ap 21 88: 7.
  Ap 28 88: 7.
  My 5 88: 7.
-Home Life
--History:
  Fe 25 82: 1.
-Human Relations
  and Unity
  Commission:
  M Ag 25 88: 1.
  Oc 6 88: 5.
  Dc 1 88: 1.
  My 4 89: 1.
  E Jl 27 89: 2.
-Jail:
  ˙ L Ap 13 78: 2.
  E Ja 17 91: 2.
-Media Coverage:
  Dc 7 89: 1.
-Newspapers:
  Ja 20 83: 15A.
-Police Dept.:
  Ap 5 73: 1.
-Prison Unit:
  P Se 27 73: 1.
  Ju 19 75: 1.
  L Nv 6 75: 2.
  L My 3 90: 9.

P Dc 11 75: 2.
P Dc 18 75: 1, 5.
P Fe 24 77: 7.
Fe 2 78: 9.
L Ap 12 79: 1.
Nv 22 79: 10.
-Films:
Ja 29 81: 1.
Robeson County
Clergy and Laity
Concerned:
L Ju 21 84: 2.
Ag 23 84: 1.
L Ja 3 85: 2.
Robeson County
Indian Caucus:
My 21 81: 1, 9.
Jl 9 81: 1.
Robeson County
Indian Youth
Unity Festival:
Ap 16 81: 1.
My 7 81: 1.
Ju 11 81: 1.
Robeson Defense
Ja 17 91: 1.
Robeson Family
Practice Associ-
ates (Red
Springs):
Jl 15 82: 1.
P Jl 22 82: 1.
Robeson Farm
Services
-Opening:
P Oc 20 77: 1.
Robeson Health
Care Corp.:
Se 12 85: 2.
Robeson Historical
Drama, Inc.:
Jl 31 75: 1.
A Ju 8 89: 1.
•See also Strike at
the Wind!
Robeson Printing
Co.:
Ju 11 87: 1.

Robeson Record
(Newspaper):
E Ja 19 84: 2.
E Ju 7 84: 2.
Robeson Rentals
-Opening:
P Oc 25 84: 1.
Robeson Savings
and Loan:
E Nv 24 77: 1, 2.
Dc 1 77: 1.
Dc 8 77: 1.
L Ja 5 78: 1, 2.
Fe 9 78: 1.
Robeson Technical
College:
L My 29 75: 2.
L Oc 6 83: 2.
-Board of Directors:
Jl 14 77: 1.
-Buildings:
Ap 25 74: 5.
-Minority Students:
L Ja 5 84: 2.
Robesonian
(Newspaper):
Oc 1 81: 2.
ROBESONIAN
HOSTAGE-
TAKING:
E Fe 4 88: 1, 2.
EL Fe 11 88: 1, 2.
E Fe 25 88: 2, 6.
L Mr 3 88: 2, 10.
Ap 21 88: 1.
Ap 28 88: 7.
E Ju 23 88: 2.
EL Ju 30 88: 1, 2.
Jl 7 88: 1.
E Jl 21 88: 2.
E Jl 28 88: 2.
E Ag 4 88: 1, 2.
E Ag 18 88: 2.
E Ag 25 88: 2.
Se 8 88: 1.
E Se 15 88: 1, 2.
*Se 22 88: 1.
Se 29 88: 1, 2.

E *Oc 6 88: 1, 2.
E *Oc 20 88: 1-2.
E Nv 3 88: 2.
E Nv 17 88: 1, 2.
Dc 8 88: 1.
E Dc 15 88: 1, 2.
*Dc 22 88: 1.
E Ja 5 89: 2.
E Ja 12 89: 2.
Ja 19 89: 1.
E Fe 16 89: 2.
L Fe 23 89: 2.
Mr 16 89: 1.
E Mr 30 89: 2.
My 4 89: 1.
E Mr 11 89: 1, 2.
Jl 13 89: 1, 2.
E Ag 3 89: 2.
E Ag 10 89: 2.
E Ag 17 89: 1, 2.
E Se 7 89: 2.
E Se 14 89: 2.
Oc 12 89: 1.
E Nv 9 89: 2.
Nv 16 89: 1.
Dc 21 89: 1.
Fe 15 90: 1.
E Fe 22 90: 2.
Mr 15 90: 4.
Jl 26 90: 1.
E Ja 10 91: 1, 2.
L Se 5 91: 2.
Jl 9 92: 5.
-Poem about:
Mr 10 88: 2.
-Task Force Report:
Ju 16 88: 6.
Rock of Bethlehem
Church:
P Ag 3 78: 10.
Rogers, Burlin
BP Fe 25 88: 1.
Rogers, Elias
A Oc 20 77: 1.
E Fe 23 78: 2.
Oc 30 80: 1.
AP Jl 7 83: 1.
AP Mr 24 83: 1.

Ag 28 80: 3.
My 22 80: 9.
Dc 25 80: 1.
Mr 26 81: 1.
Ap 9 81: 5.
Ju 11 81: 1.
Ju 18 81: 1, 2.
Ju 25 81: 1.
Jl 2 81: 1.
Jl 16 85: 1.
Jl 23 81: 7.
Jl 30 81: 2.
Ag 13'81: 1.
Ag 20 81: 2.
E Dc 3 81: 1.
Ap 1 82: 1.
Jl 1 82: 2.
Jl 8 82: 1.
Jl 15 82: 1.
Jl 22 82: 1.
Ag 26 82: 9.
E Se 9 82: 2.
Mr 3 83: 1.
Ap 21 83: 2.
My 26 83: 6.
Jl 14 83: 2.
Jl 21 83: 1.
Jl 28 83: 2, 4.
Ag 4 83: 1.
Ag 11 83: 1.
Oc 6 83: 7.
Ap 12 84: 1.
My 24 84: 1.
Ju 28 84: 9.
Jl 5 84: 1, 8.
E Ag 2 84: 1, 2.
Ag 9 84: 9.
Ag 23 84: 3.
Ag 30 84: 6.
Mr 14 85: 1.
Ju 13 85: 1, 2.
Ju 20 85: 2.
Ju 27 85: 1.
Jl 4 85: 1.
Jl 11 85: 1.
E Jl 18 85: 2.
Jl 25 85: 1.
Ag 1 85: 3.

Mr 27 86: 2.
Ju 19 86: 1.
Jl 3 86: 1.
P Jl 31 86: 1.
P Ag 7 86: 1.
P Ag 14 86: 1.
Ag 21 86: 1.
E Ag 28 86: 1, 2.
Oc 9 86: 1.
Fe 26 87: 1.
E Mr 19 87: 2.
L Ap 23 87: 2, 4.
L My 28 87: 2.
E Ju 4 87: 2.
E Ju 11 87: 1, 2.
Ju 18 87: 2.
Ju 25 87: 1.
E Jl 2 87: 2.
Jl 9 87: 1, 2.
L Jl 16 87: 2.
Jl 30 87: 1.
Se 3 87: 1.
Se 10 87: 1.
Mr 24 88: 1.
My 12 88: 1.
Ju 16 88: 1.
Ju 30 88: 1.
Rev. Ag 4 88: 1.
Mr 23 89: 1.
Ju 15 89: 1.
Ju 22 89: 1.
Jl 13 89: 1.
Jl 27 89: 1.
Ag 10 89: 1.
Ag 17 89: 1.
Mr 29 90: 1.
Ju 28 90: 1.
Jl 5 90: 4.
E My 16 91: 2.
Ju 27 91: 1.
Ag 20 92: 3.
L Se 9 93: 3.
Strong, Andrew
    B My 31 84: 7.
    -Cabin:
    P Jl 19 90: 1.
Strong, Gerald
    P Ag 16 84: 10.

Sturtevant, William
-on Lumbee Tribe:
    Mr 21 91: 5.
Surnames
    Fe 10 77: 5.
    Ag 19 82: 10.
Sutton, Ronnie N.
    BP Jl 29 82: 1.
    BP Fe 21 91: 3.
    Ap 18 91: 1.
    BP Ja 2 92: 1.
    Ap 2 92: 1.
    L Ap 23 92: 2.
    *P Nv 5 92: 1.
Swanton, John
Reed:
    Dc 8 88: 1.
Swett, Otha
    P Ag 7 75: 1.
    AP Nv 13 75: 3.
    Mr 18 76: 1.
Swett, Purnell
    P Oc 10 74: 1.
    Nv 21 74: 1, 2.
    EL Dc 5 74: 2.
    BP My 19 77: 1.
    P Jl 7 77: 1.
    *Nv 22 79: 1, 4.
    AP Jl 22 82: 1.
    BP Ja 20 83: 4A.
    BP Mr 14 85: 1.
    A Ju 15 89: 1, 5.
    L Dc 10 92: 2.
Swett, Thomas M.
    BP Se 23 76: 4.
    B P Ju 30 83: 1.
    BP Se 27 84: 1.
    OP Ja 31 85: 1-2.
Swett, Tommy D.
    P Ju 5 75: 6.
    AP Ag 26 76: 4.
    BP Oc 28 76: 1.
Syrup, Cane
    P Nv 21 74: 7.

T

Tabernacle Baptist

Turner, Felicia W.
  P Ju 22 89: 6.
  AP Ja 18 90: 1.
TUSCARORA INDIANS
  OF ROBESON
  COUNTY:
  *Ja 18 73: 1.
  L Mr 8 73: 1, 2.
  Mr 15 73: 1;
    cartoon: 2.
  *Mr 29 73: 1, 2.
  Ap 5 73: 1, 3.
  P Ap 12 73: 1.
  Ap 19 73: 1.
  Ju 14 73: 1, 3.
  L Ag 2 73: 2.
  Ag 23 73: 4.
  P *Se 20 73: 1.
  Ja 10 74: 1.
  L Fe 14 74: 2.
  Ap 11 74: 1.
  Ap 18 74: 7.
  *Jl 18 74: 4.
  Nv 7 74: 2.
  E Ja 30 75: 1, 2.
  L Fe 6 75: 2.
  *Ap 17 75: 1, 6.
  Nv 11 76: 6.
  Oc 6 77: 3.
  Ag 17 78: 1.
  L Ag 28 80: 2.
  L Nv 13 80: 2.
  Jl 15 82: 1.
  Nv 22 84: 1.
  Oc 30 86: 1.
  Ja 1 87: 1.
  Ja 15 87: 1.
  L Ja 22 87: 2.
  Ja 29 87: 6.
  Fe 5 87: 1.
  Mr 12 87: 8.
  Ja 12 89: 1, 4.
  Ju 8 89: 1.
  Nv 23 89: 1.
  Dc 7 89: 1.
  Oc 18 90: 1.
  L Nv 15 90: 4.
  Nv 29 90: 1*

  Ja 31 91: 1.
  Ju 13 91: 1.
  Se 19 91: 1.
  L Oc 10 91: 5.
  Oc 24 91: 1.
  *Dc 22 91: 1.
  E Ju 11 92: 2.
  Ja 14 93: 1.
  Ja 21 93: 1.
  •See also Brooks,
    Howard; Hatteras
    Tuscarora
    Indians; Twenty-
    two, Original.
  -and AIM:
    Ja 31 74: 2.
  -BIA documents
    theft:
    Ap 12 73: 1.
    *P Ap 19 73: 1.
    My 3 73: 1, 2.
    My 17 73: 1.
    Ag 23 73: 1.
    Se 13 73: 1.
    P Dc 13 73: 1, 8.
    *Dc 20 73: 1.
  -Cultural Survival
    School:
    Nv 7 91: 1.
    Nv 14 91: 1.
    Dc 12 91: 1.
    Ja 21 93: 1.
  -Federal Recogni-
    tion and Benefits:
    Mr 22 73: 3, 4.
    P Mr 29 73: 1.
    Jl 31 75: 1.
    Ag 28 75: 1.
    P Se 4 75: 1.
    Se 25 75: 7.
    Jl 14 77: 8.
    Se 22 77: 2.
    Jl 5 79: 3.
    Jl 6 89: 1.
  -History:
    *My 16 91: 1.
  -Houses Built for,
    by BIA:

  *Oc 6 77: 6.
  -Lawsuits:
    Nv 24 83: 2.
  -Political Activities:
    Ju 14 73: 2.
  -Pow-wows:
    My 22 80: 1.
  -Six Nations
    Enrollment:
    My 2 91: 1.
  -Trials:
    Se 27 73: 1.
    Ju 6 74: 4.
    Oc 2 75: 1.
    E Ju 11 92: 2.
  -Tribal Council:
    L Ag 20 92: 2.
  -Tribal Roll:
    Ju 20 85: 1.
    Ja 24 91: 1.
  -Voter Registration
    Drive:
    Ap 26 73: 1.
  Twenty-Two,
    Original:
    Mr 22 73: 3, 4.
    *Ap 17 75: 1, 6.
    Jl 3 75: 1.
    *Oc 6 77: 6.
  Twice as Nice
    Thrift Shop:
    Ap 27 89: 2.
  Ty's Mini Mart
    Se 23 76: 2.
    P Se 30 76: 1.
  Union Baptist
    Church:
    P Ap 28 77: 8.
  Union Chapel
    School
  -Class of 1954:
  --Reunion:
    P Ja 8 81: 1.
  United Cherokee
    Nation of N.C.,
    Inc.:
    Nv 18 76: 2.
    E Nv 25 76: 2.

*The Index is
complete through
May 16, 1991;
with selected
articles through
October 28, 1993.
See "Introduc-
tion."

Author Index

Subject Index

Attorney General's Objections and
Rulings 82, 147
Audiotapes, see Recordings and
Audiotapes.
Bailey, Josiah William 1236
Baker, Ella 1050
Baker, Fred 57 1137
Baltimore (MD)–Lumbee
Settlement in 123, 471, 477,
480, 482, 486, 487, 490, 958,
1431. •See also "Settlements
Outside Robeson County"
section of bibliography.
Baltimore American Indian Center
490, 934, 958, 1454. •See also
"Settlements Outside Robeson
County" section of bibliography.
Banks, Dennis 737
Baptist Church 57. •See also
"Religion" section of bibliogra-
phy; names of churches.
Barfield, Velma Bullard 829, 843
Barnes, James P. 1092, 1093
Barns, Elwell 1044
Barton, Bruce 838, 1010, 1044
Barton, Earl 1044
Barton, Herman 1044
Barton, Lew 52, 118, 226, 330,
558, 1010, 1022, 1044, 1398,
1447
Barton, Ricky 1044
Bastardy Bonds (Robeson County)
1036. •See also "Genealogical
Materials" section of bibliogra-
phy.
Baxley, Jim 778
Bell (Surname/Genealogy) 1032
Bell, Albert (Mr. & Mrs.) 1044
Bell, Jones E. 1048
Bellamy, John D. 57
Bellecourt, Vernon 732
Biggs, Henry H. 1105
Biographical Sketches 53, 415,
422, 842, 994. •See also
"Biographical Sources" section
of bibliography; names of
individuals.

Blacks (Lumbee Relations with),
see Race Relations.
Bledsole, Henry 589
Bledsole, William J. 589
Blood and Genetic Studies 57,
444, 448, 719. •See also
"Literature on Tri-racial
Isolates" section of bibliography.
Blood Quantum 57, 666, 700, 742.
•See also Seltzer, Carl; "Tribal
Name and Identity" section of
bibliography.
Blu, Karen 57, 1044
Blue, Brantley 842, 1005, 1010,
1044, 1398, 1451
Blue, Brantley (Mrs.) 1044
Blue, Elsie Mae 1044
Blue, Kate Lilly 1112
Blue, Patricia 1044
Bonnin, Gertrude Simmons 604
Bonnin, Raymond T. 57
Braboy, James K. 422
Branch Street United Methodist
Church (Lumberton) 411, 422
Braveboy (Surname/Genealogy)
575. •See also "Genealogical
Materials" section of bibliogra-
phy; Surnames.
Brayboy, James K. 1044
Brayboy, John 1044
Brayboy, Nepsie 58
Brewer, Ollis Bell 1048
Brewington, Bill 589, 798
Brewington, Bob 1044
Brewington, C. D. 1097
Brewington, Hardy A. 589
Brewington, James Dofphus 1044
Brewington, Joseph 996
Brewington, Peggy 1006
"Brick House" Indian 55, 59
Bridgeman, John 160
Britt, Joe Freeman 56, 817, 818,
823, 827, 829, 841, 843, 844,
846, 848, 873, 1235, 1240, 1257
Brooks, Aaron 581
Brooks, Andrew 1044
Brooks, Brenda 1006, 1010, 1044